EXAM✓CRAM

CompTIA®
Network+

N10-007

Sixth Edition

Emmett Dulaney

PEARSON IT
CERTIFICATION

800 East 96th Street
Indianapolis, Indiana 46240 USA

Trademarks

All terms mentioned in this book that are known to be trademarks or service marks have been appropriately capitalized. Pearson IT Certification cannot attest to the accuracy of this information. Use of a term in this book should not be regarded as affecting the validity of any trademark or service mark.

CompTIA is a registered trademark of CompTIA, Inc.

Warning and Disclaimer

Every effort has been made to make this book as complete and as accurate as possible, but no warranty or fitness is implied. The information provided is on an "as is" basis. The author and the publisher shall have neither liability nor responsibility to any person or entity with respect to any loss or damages arising from the information contained in this book.

Special Sales

For information about buying this title in bulk quantities, or for special sales opportunities (which may include electronic versions; custom cover designs; and content particular to your business, training goals, marketing focus, or branding interests), please contact our corporate sales department at corpsales@pearsoned.com or (800) 382-3419.

For government sales inquiries, please contact governmentsales@pearsoned.com.

For questions about sales outside the U.S., please contact intlcs@pearson.com.

Editor-in-Chief
Mark Taub

Product Line Manager
Brett Bartow

Acquisitions Editor
Michelle Newcomb

Development Editor
Ellie Bru

Managing Editor
Sandra Schroeder

Senior Project Editor
Tonya Simpson

Copy Editor
Barbara Hacha

Indexer
Erika Millen

Proofreader
Abigail Manheim

Technical Editor
Chris Crayton

Publishing Coordinator
Vanessa Evans

Cover Designer
Chuti Prasertsith

Compositor
codeMantra

Contents at a Glance

Table of Contents

About the Author

Emmett Dulaney (CompTIA Network+, Cloud+, Security+, A+, and others) is the author of numerous books on certifications and operating systems. He is a columnist for *Certification Magazine* and a professor at a small university. He is also the author of *CompTIA A+ Complete Study Guide* and *CompTIA Security+ Study Guide*.

Dedication

For Wolfgang
—Emmett Dulaney

Acknowledgments

An enormous amount of credit for this book goes to Christopher A. Crayton, without whom this edition would be only a shadow of what it is. It was an honor to work with him again, and I owe him enormous gratitude. Thanks are also due to Mike Harwood, who wrote the first few editions, and to the team of talented individuals at Pearson who work behind the scenes and make each title the best it can be.

—Emmett Dulaney

About the Technical Editor

Chris Crayton (MCSE) is an author, technical consultant, and trainer. Formerly, he worked as a computer technology and networking instructor, information security director, network administrator, network engineer, and PC specialist. Chris has authored several print and online books on PC repair, CompTIA A+, CompTIA Security+, and Microsoft Windows. He has also served as technical editor and content contributor on numerous technical titles for several of the leading publishing companies. Chris holds numerous industry certifications, has been recognized with many professional teaching awards, and has served as a state-level SkillsUSA competition judge.

We Want to Hear from You!

As the reader of this book, *you* are our most important critic and commentator. We value your opinion and want to know what we're doing right, what we could do better, what areas you'd like to see us publish in, and any other words of wisdom you're willing to pass our way.

We welcome your comments. You can email or write to let us know what you did or didn't like about this book—as well as what we can do to make our books better.

Please note that we cannot help you with technical problems related to the topic of this book.

When you write, please be sure to include this book's title and author as well as your name and email address. We will carefully review your comments and share them with the author and editors who worked on the book.

Email: feedback@pearsonitcertification.com

Mail: Pearson IT Certification

ATTN: Reader Feedback
      800 East 96th Street
      Indianapolis, IN 46240 USA

Reader Services

Register your copy of *CompTIA Network+ N10-007 Exam Cram* at www.pearsonitcertification.com for convenient access to downloads, updates, and corrections as they become available. To start the registration process, go to www.pearsonitcertification.com/register and log in or create an account*. Enter the product ISBN 9780789758750 and click Submit. When the process is complete, you will find any available bonus content under Registered Products.

*Be sure to check the box that you would like to hear from us to receive exclusive discounts on future editions of this product.

CompTIA.

Becoming a CompTIA Certified IT Professional is Easy

It's also the best way to reach greater professional opportunities and rewards.

Why Get CompTIA Certified?

Growing Demand

Labor estimates predict some technology fields will experience growth of over 20% by the year 2020.* CompTIA certification qualifies the skills required to join this workforce.

Higher Salaries

IT professionals with certifications on their resume command better jobs, earn higher salaries and have more doors open to new multi-industry opportunities.

Verified Strengths

91% of hiring managers indicate CompTIA certifications are valuable in validating IT expertise, making certification the best way to demonstrate your competency and knowledge to employers.**

Universal Skills

CompTIA certifications are vendor neutral—which means that certified professionals can proficiently work with an extensive variety of hardware and software found in most organizations.

Learn   Certify   Work

Learn more about what the exam covers by reviewing the following:

- Exam objectives for key study points.

- Sample questions for a general overview of what to expect on the exam and examples of question format.

- Visit online forums, like LinkedIn, to see what other IT professionals say about CompTIA exams.

Purchase a voucher at a Pearson VUE testing center or at CompTIAstore.com.

- Register for your exam at a Pearson VUE testing center:

- Visit pearsonvue.com/CompTIA to find the closest testing center to you.

- Schedule the exam online. You will be required to enter your voucher number or provide payment information at registration.

- Take your certification exam.

Congratulations on your CompTIA certification!

- Make sure to add your certification to your resume.

- Check out the CompTIA Certification Roadmap to plan your next career move.

Learn more: **Certification.CompTIA.org/networkplus**

* Source: CompTIA 9th Annual Information Security Trends study: 500 U.S. IT and Business Executives Responsible for Security
** Source: CompTIA Employer Perceptions of IT Training and Certification

Introduction

Welcome to *CompTIA Network+ N10-007 Exam Cram*. This book is designed to prepare you to take—and pass—the CompTIA Network+ exam. The Network+ exam has become the leading introductory-level network certification available today. It is recognized by both employers and industry giants as providing candidates with a solid foundation of networking concepts, terminology, and skills. The Network+ exam covers a broad range of networking concepts to prepare candidates for the technologies they are likely to work with in today's network environments.

About Network+ Exam Cram

Exam Crams are designed to give you the information you need to know to prepare for a certification exam. They cut through the extra information, focusing on the areas you need to get through the exam. With this in mind, the elements within the Exam Cram titles are aimed at providing the exam information you need in the most succinct and accessible manner.

In this light, this book is organized to closely follow the actual CompTIA objectives for exam N10-007. As such, it is easy to find the information required for each of the specified CompTIA Network+ objectives. The objective focus design used by this Exam Cram is an important feature because the information you need to know is easily identifiable and accessible. To see what we mean, compare the CompTIA objectives to the book's layout, and you can see that the facts are right where you would expect them to be.

Within the chapters, potential exam hot spots are clearly highlighted with Exam Alerts. They have been carefully placed to let you know that the surrounding discussion is an important area for the exam. To further help you prepare for the exam, a Cram Sheet is included that you can use in the final stages of test preparation. Be sure to pay close attention to the bulleted points on the Cram Sheet because they pinpoint the technologies and facts you probably will encounter on the test.

Finally, great effort has gone into the questions that appear throughout the chapter and the practice tests to ensure that they accurately represent the look and feel of the ones you will see on the real Network+ exam. Be sure, before taking the exam, that you are comfortable with both the format and content of the questions provided in this book.

About the Network+ Exam

The Network+ (N10-007 Edition) exam is the newest iteration of several versions of the exam. The new Network+ objectives are aimed toward those who have at least 9 months of experience in network support or administration. CompTIA believes that new Network+ candidates should have A+ certification (or its equivalent), but it is not required, and this should not discourage those who do not.

You will have a maximum of 90 minutes to answer the 90 questions on the exam. The allotted time is quite generous, so when you finish, you probably will have time to double-check a few of the answers you were unsure of.

By the time the dust settles, you need a minimum score of 720 to pass the Network+ exam. This is on a scale of 100 to 900. For more information on the specifics of the Network+ exam, refer to CompTIA's main website at http://certification.comptia.org/.

CompTIA Network+ Exam Topics

Table I-1 lists general exam topics (that is, objectives) and specific topics under each general topic (that is, subobjectives) for the CompTIA Network+ N10-007 exam. This table also lists the chapter in which each exam topic is covered.

TABLE I-1 **CompTIA Network+ Exam Topics**

Chapter	N10-007 Exam Objective	N10-007 Exam Subobjective
1 (Introduction to Networking Technologies)	1.0 Networking Concepts	1.5 Compare and contrast the characteristics of network topologies, types and technologies.
2 (Models, Ports, Protocols and Networking Services)	1.0 Networking Concepts	1.1 Explain the purposes and uses of ports and protocols.
		1.2 Explain devices, applications, protocols, and services at their appropriate OSI layers.
		1.8 Explain the functions of network services.
3 (Addressing, Routing, and Switching)	1.0 Networking Concepts	1.3 Explain the concepts and characteristics of routing and switching.
		1.4 Given a scenario, configure the appropriate IP addressing components.
4 (Network Components and Devices)	2.0 Infrastructure	2.2 Given a scenario, determine the appropriate placement of networking devices on a network and install/configure them.
		2.3 Explain the purposes and use cases for advanced network devices.

Chapter	N10-007 Exam Objective	N10-007 Exam Subobjective
5 (WAN Technologies)	2.0 Infrastructure	2.5 Compare and contrast WAN technologies.
6 (Cabling Solutions)	2.0 Infrastructure 5.0 Network Troubleshooting and Tools	2.1 Given a scenario, deploy the appropriate cabling solution. 5.3 Given a scenario, troubleshoot common wired connectivity and performance issues.
7 (Wireless Solutions)	1.0 Networking Concepts 5.0 Network Troubleshooting and Tools	1.6 Given a scenario, implement the appropriate wireless technologies and configurations. 5.4 Given a scenario, troubleshoot common wireless connectivity and performance issues.
8 (Cloud Computing and Virtualization)	1.0 Networking Concepts 2.0 Infrastructure	1.7 Summarize cloud concepts and their purposes. 2.4 Explain the purposes of virtualization and network storage technologies.
9 (Network Operations)	3.0 Network Operations	3.1 Given a scenario, use appropriate documentation and diagrams to manage the network. 3.2 Compare and contrast business continuity and disaster recovery concepts. 3.3 Explain common scanning, monitoring and patching processes and summarize their expected outputs. 3.4 Given a scenario, use remote access methods. 3.5 Identify policies and best practices.
10 (Network Security)	4.0 Network Security	4.1 Summarize the purposes of physical security devices. 4.2 Explain authentication and access controls. 4.3 Given a scenario, secure a basic wireless network. 4.4 Summarize common networking attacks. 4.5 Given a scenario, implement network device hardening. 4.6 Explain common mitigation techniques and their purposes.
11 (Network Troubleshooting)	5.0 Network Troubleshooting and Tools	5.1 Explain the network troubleshooting methodology. 5.2 Given a scenario, use the appropriate tool. 5.5 Given a scenario, troubleshoot common network service issues.

Booking and Taking the Network+ Certification Exam

Unfortunately, testing is not free. You're charged $320 for each test you take, whether you pass or fail. In the United States and Canada, tests are administered by Pearson VUE testing services. To access the VUE contact information and book an exam, refer to the website at http://www.pearsonvue.com or call 1-877-551-7587. When booking an exam, you need to provide the following information:

▶ Your name as you would like it to appear on your certificate.

▶ Your Social Security or Social Insurance number.

▶ Contact phone numbers (to be called in case of a problem).

▶ Mailing address, which identifies the address to which you want your certificate mailed.

▶ Exam number and title.

▶ Email address for contact purposes. This often is the fastest and most effective means to contact you. Many clients require it for registration.

▶ Credit card information so that you can pay online. You can redeem vouchers by calling the respective testing center.

What to Expect from the Exam

If you haven't taken a certification test, the process can be a little unnerving. Even if you've taken numerous tests, it is not much better. Mastering the inner mental game often can be as much of a battle as knowing the material. Knowing what to expect before heading in can make the process a little more comfortable.

Certification tests are administered on a computer system at a VUE authorized testing center. The format of the exams is straightforward: Each question has several possible answers to choose from. The questions in this book provide a good example of the types of questions you can expect on the exam. If you are comfortable with them, the test should hold few surprises. Many of the questions vary in length. Some of them are longer scenario questions, whereas others are short and to the point. Carefully read the questions; the longer questions often have a key point that will lead you to the correct answer.

Most of the questions on the Network+ exam require you to choose a single correct answer, but a few require multiple answers. When there are multiple correct answers, a message at the bottom of the screen prompts you to "Choose all that apply." Be sure to read these messages.

A Few Exam-Day Details

It is recommended that you arrive at the examination room at least 15 minutes early, although a few minutes earlier certainly would not hurt. This will give you time to prepare and will give the test administrator time to answer any questions you might have before the test begins. Many people suggest that you review the most critical information about the test you're taking just before the test. (Exam Cram books provide a reference—the Cram Sheet, located inside the front of this book—that lists the essential information from the book in distilled form.) Arriving a few minutes early will give you some time to compose yourself and mentally review this critical information.

You will be asked to provide two forms of ID, one of which must be a photo ID. Both of the identifications you choose should have a signature. You also might need to sign in when you arrive and sign out when you leave.

Be warned: The rules are clear about what you can and cannot take into the examination room. Books, laptops, note sheets, and so on are not allowed in the examination room. The test administrator will hold these items, to be returned after you complete the exam. You might receive either a wipe board or a pen and a single piece of paper for making notes during the exam. The test administrator will ensure that no paper is removed from the examination room.

After the Test

Whether you want it or not, as soon as you finish your test, your score displays on the computer screen. In addition to the results appearing on the computer screen, a hard copy of the report prints for you. Like the onscreen report, the hard copy displays the results of your exam and provides a summary of how you did on each section and on each technology. If you were unsuccessful, this summary can help you determine the areas you need to brush up on.

When you pass the Network+ exam, you will have earned the Network+ certification, and your certificate will be mailed to you within a few weeks. Should you not receive your certificate and information packet within 5 weeks of passing your exam, contact CompTIA at fulfillment@comptia.org, or call 1-630-268-1818 and ask for the fulfillment department.

Last-Minute Exam Tips

Studying for a certification exam is no different than studying for any other exam, but a few hints and tips can give you the edge on exam day:

▶ **Read all the material:** CompTIA has been known to include material not expressly specified in the objectives. This book has included additional information not reflected in the objectives to give you the best possible preparation for the examination.

▶ **Watch for the Exam Tips and Notes:** The Network+ objectives include a wide range of technologies. Exam Tips and Notes found throughout each chapter are designed to pull out exam-related hot spots. These can be your best friends when preparing for the exam.

▶ **Use the questions to assess your knowledge:** Don't just read the chapter content; use the exam questions to find out what you know and what you don't. If you struggle, study some more, review, and then assess your knowledge again.

▶ **Review the exam objectives:** Develop your own questions and examples for each topic listed. If you can develop and answer several questions for each topic, you should not find it difficult to pass the exam.

Good luck!

Companion Website

Register this book to get access to the Pearson Test Prep practice test software and other study materials plus additional bonus content. Check this site regularly for new and updated postings written by the author that provide further insight into the more troublesome topics on the exams. Be sure to check the box that you would like to hear from us to receive updates and exclusive discounts on future editions of this product or related products.

To access this companion website, follow these steps:

1. Go to www.pearsonITcertification.com/register and log in or create a new account.

2. Enter the ISBN: 9780789758750.

3. Answer the challenge question as proof of purchase.

4. Click the **Access Bonus Content** link in the Registered Products section of your account page, to be taken to the page where your downloadable content is available.

Please note that many of our companion content files can be very large, especially image and video files.

If you are unable to locate the files for this title by following the steps at left, please visit www.pearsonITcertification.com/contact and select the Site Problems/Comments option. Our customer service representatives will assist you.

Pearson Test Prep Practice Test Software

As noted previously, this book comes complete with the Pearson Test Prep practice test software containing two full exams. These practice tests are available to you either online or as an offline Windows application. To access the practice exams that were developed with this book, please see the instructions in the card inserted in the sleeve in the back of the book. This card includes a unique access code that enables you to activate your exams in the Pearson Test Prep practice test software.

> **Note**
>
> The cardboard sleeve in the back of this book includes a piece of paper. The paper lists the activation code for the practice exams associated with this book. Do not lose the activation code. On the opposite side of the paper from the activation code is a unique, one-time-use coupon code for the purchase of the Premium Edition eBook and Practice Test.

Accessing the Pearson Test Prep Software Online

The online version of this software can be used on any device with a browser and connectivity to the Internet, including desktop machines, tablets, and smartphones. To start using your practice exams online, follow these steps:

1. Go to www.PearsonTestPrep.com.

2. Select **Pearson IT Certification** as your product group.

3. Enter your email/password for your account. If you don't have an account on PearsonITCertification.com, you will need to establish one by going to PearsonITCertification.com/join.

4. In the My Products tab, click the **Activate New Product** button.

5. Enter the access code printed on the insert card in the back of your book to activate your product.

6. The product will now be listed in your My Products page. Click the **Exams** button to launch the exam settings screen and start your exam.

Accessing the Pearson Test Prep Software Offline

If you want to study offline, you can download and install the Windows version of the Pearson Test Prep software. There is a download link for this software on the book's companion website, or you can enter the following link in your browser:

www.pearsonitcertification.com/content/downloads/pcpt/engine.zip.

To access the book's companion website and the software, follow these steps:

1. Register your book by going to PearsonITCertification.com/register and entering the ISBN: 9780789758750.

2. Respond to the challenge questions.

3. Go to your account page and select the **Registered Products** tab.

4. Click the **Access Bonus Content** link under the product listing.

5. Click the **Install Pearson Test Prep Desktop Version** link under the Practice Exams section of the page to download the software.

6. After the software downloads, unzip all the files on your computer.

7. Double-click the application file to start the installation, and follow the onscreen instructions to complete the registration.

8. When the installation is complete, launch the application and select the **Activate Exam** button on the My Products tab.

9. Click the **Activate a Product** button in the Activate Product Wizard.

10. Enter the unique access code found on the card in the sleeve in the back of your book, and click the **Activate** button.

11. Click **Next** and then **Finish** to download the exam data to your application.

12. You can now start using the practice exams by selecting the product and clicking the **Open Exam** button to open the exam settings screen.

Note that the offline and online versions will synch together, so saved exams and grade results recorded on one version will be available to you on the other as well.

Customizing Your Exams

After you are in the exam settings screen, you can choose to take exams in one of three modes:

▶ Study Mode

▶ Practice Exam Mode

▶ Flash Card Mode

Study Mode enables you to fully customize your exams and review answers as you are taking the exam. This is typically the mode you would use first to assess your knowledge and identify information gaps. Practice Exam Mode locks certain customization options, because it is presenting a realistic exam experience. Use this mode when you are preparing to test your exam readiness. Flash Card Mode strips out the answers and presents you with only the question stem. This mode is great for late-stage preparation when you really want to challenge yourself to provide answers without the benefit of seeing multiple choice options. This mode will not provide the detailed score reports that the other two modes will, so it should not be used if you are trying to identify knowledge gaps.

In addition to these three modes, you will be able to select the source of your questions. You can choose to take exams that cover all the chapters, or you can narrow your selection to a single chapter or the chapters that make up specific parts in the book. All chapters are selected by default. If you want to narrow your focus to individual chapters, first deselect all the chapters, then select only those on which you want to focus in the Objectives area.

You can also select the exam banks on which to focus. Each exam bank comes complete with a full exam of questions that cover topics in every chapter. The two exams printed in the book are available to you as well as two additional exams of unique questions. You can have the test engine serve up exams from all four banks or just from one individual bank by selecting the desired banks in the exam bank area.

You can make several other customizations to your exam from the exam settings screen, such as the time of the exam, the number of questions, whether to randomize questions and answers, whether to show the number of correct answers for multiple answer questions, or whether to serve up only specific types of questions. You can also create custom test banks by selecting only questions that you have marked or questions on which you have added notes.

Updating Your Exams

If you are using the online version of the Pearson Test Prep software, you should always have access to the latest version of the software as well as the exam data. If you are using the Windows desktop version, every time you launch the software, it will check to see if there are any updates to your exam data and automatically download any changes that were made since the last time you used the software. This requires that you are connected to the Internet at the time you launch the software.

Sometimes, due to many factors, the exam data may not fully download when you activate your exam. If you find that figures or exhibits are missing, you may need to manually update your exams.

To update a particular exam you have already activated and downloaded, select the **Tools** tab and then click the **Update Products** button. Again, this is an issue only with the desktop Windows application.

If you want to check for updates to the Pearson Test Prep exam engine software, Windows desktop version, select the **Tools** tab and click the **Update Application** button. This will ensure that you are running the latest version of the software engine.

Assessing Exam Readiness

Exam candidates never really know whether they are adequately prepared for the exam until they have completed about 30 percent of the questions. At that point, if you are not prepared, it is too late. The best way to determine your readiness is to work through the "Do I Know This Already?" quizzes at the beginning of each chapter and review the foundation and key topics presented in each chapter. It is best to work your way through the entire book unless you can complete each subject without having to do any research or look up any answers.

Premium Edition eBook and Practice Tests

This book also includes an exclusive offer for 70% off the Premium Edition eBook and Practice Tests edition of this title. Please see the coupon code included with the cardboard sleeve for information on how to purchase the Premium Edition.

CHAPTER 1

Introduction to Networking Technologies

This chapter covers the following official Network+ objective:

▶ Compare and contrast the characteristics of network topologies, types and technologies.

This chapter covers CompTIA Network+ objective 1.5. For more information on the official Network+ exam topics, see the "About the Network+ Exam" section in the Introduction.

A variety of physical and logical network layouts are in use today. As a network administrator, you might find yourself working on these different network layouts or topologies. Therefore, you must understand how they are designed to function.

This chapter reviews general network considerations, such as the various topologies used on today's networks, *local-area networks* (LANs), *wide-area networks* (WANs), and some of the *Institute of Electrical and Electronics Engineers* (IEEE) standards.

Wired and Wireless Network Topologies

▶ **Compare and contrast the characteristics of common network topologies, types, and technologies.**

CramSaver

If you can correctly answer these questions before going through this section, save time by skimming the Exam Alerts in this section and then completing the Cram Quiz at the end of the section.

1. Which topology (star, bus, or ring) would utilize a switch?

2. With which topology does every node have a direct connection to every other node?

Answers

1. Of the choices given, only a star topology would utilize a switch.

2. With a mesh topology, every node has a direct connection to every other node.

A *topology* refers to a network's physical and logical layout. A network's *physical* topology refers to the actual layout of the computer cables and other network devices. A network's *logical* topology refers to the way in which the network appears to the devices that use it.

Several topologies are in use on networks today. Some of the more common topologies are the bus, ring, star, mesh, and wireless. The following sections provide an overview of each.

Bus Topology

A *bus topology* uses a trunk or backbone to connect all the computers on the network, as shown in Figure 1.1. Systems connect to this backbone using *T connectors* or taps (known as a vampire tap, if you must pierce the wire). To avoid signal reflection, a physical bus topology requires that each end of the physical bus be terminated, with one end also being grounded. Note that a hub or switch is not needed in this installation.

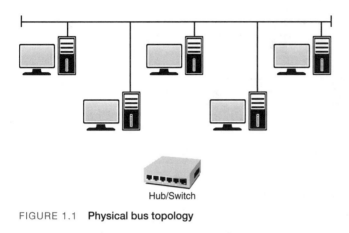

Hub/Switch

FIGURE 1.1   **Physical bus topology**

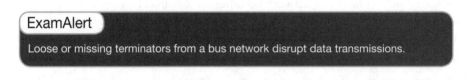

ExamAlert

Loose or missing terminators from a bus network disrupt data transmissions.

The most common implementation of a linear bus is the IEEE 802.3 Ethernet standard. Table 1.1 summarizes the advantages and disadvantages of the bus topology.

TABLE 1.1   **Advantages and Disadvantages of the Bus Topology**

Advantages	Disadvantages
Compared to other topologies, a bus is cheap and easy to implement.	Network disruption might occur when computers are added or removed.
Requires less cable than other topologies.	Because all systems on the network connect to a single backbone, a break in the cable prevents all systems from accessing the network.
Does not use any specialized network equipment.	Difficult to troubleshoot.

Ring Topology

The *ring topology* is a logical ring, meaning that the data travels in a circular fashion from one computer to another on the network. It is not a physical ring topology. Figure 1.2 shows the logical layout of a ring topology. Note that a hub or switch is not needed in this installation either.

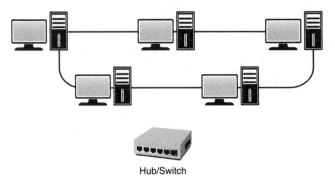

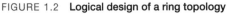

Hub/Switch

FIGURE 1.2   **Logical design of a ring topology**

In a true ring topology, if a single computer or section of cable fails, the signal is interrupted. The entire network becomes inaccessible. Network disruption can also occur when computers are added to or removed from the network, making it an impractical network design in environments where the network changes often.

As just mentioned, if a single system on the ring fails, the whole network fails. This is why ring networks can be set up in a fault-tolerant design, meaning that they have a primary and secondary ring. If one ring fails, data can use the second ring to reach its destination. Naturally, the addition of the second ring adds to the cost of the network as well as the complexity.

Ring networks are most commonly wired in a star configuration. In a token ring network, a *multistation access unit (MSAU)* is equivalent to a hub or switch on an Ethernet network. The MSAU performs the token circulation internally. To create the complete ring, the *ring-in (RI)* port on each MSAU is connected to the *ring-out (RO)* port on another MSAU. The last MSAU in the ring is then connected to the first to complete the ring. Table 1.2 summarizes the advantages and disadvantages of the ring topology.

TABLE 1.2   **Advantages and Disadvantages of the Ring Topology**

Advantages	Disadvantages
Cable faults are easily located, making troubleshooting easier.	Expansion to the network can cause network disruption.
Ring networks are moderately easy to install.	A single break in the cable can disrupt the entire network.

Star Topology

In the *star topology*, all computers and other network devices connect to a central device called a *hub* or *switch*. Each connected device requires a single cable to be connected to the hub or switch, creating a point-to-point connection between the device and the hub or switch.

Using a separate cable to connect to the hub or switch allows the network to be expanded without disruption. A break in any single cable does not cause the entire network to fail. Figure 1.3 shows a star topology.

> ## ExamAlert
>
> Among the network topologies discussed in this chapter, the star topology is the easiest to expand in terms of the number of devices connected to the network.

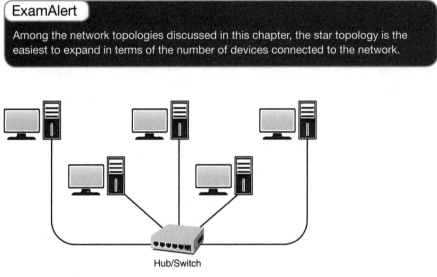

FIGURE 1.3   **Star topology**

The star topology is the most widely implemented network design in use today, but it is not without shortcomings. Because all devices connect to a centralized hub or switch, this creates a single point of failure for the network. If the hub or switch fails, any device connected to it cannot access the network. Because of the number of cables required and the need for network devices, the cost of a star network is often higher than other topologies. Table 1.3 summarizes the advantages and disadvantages of the star topology.

TABLE 1.3   **Advantages and Disadvantages of the Star Topology**

Advantages	Disadvantages
Star networks are easily expanded without disruption to the network.	Requires more cable than most of the other topologies.
Cable failure affects only a single user.	A central connecting device allows for a single point of failure.
Easy to troubleshoot and implement.	Requires additional networking equipment to create the network layout.

Wired Mesh Topology

The *wired mesh topology* incorporates a unique network design in which each computer on the network connects to every other, creating a point-to-point connection between every device on the network. The purpose of the mesh design is to provide a high level of *redundancy*. If one network cable fails, the data always has an alternative path to get to its destination; each node can act as a relay.

The wiring for a mesh network can be complicated, as illustrated by Figure 1.4. Furthermore, the cabling costs associated with the mesh topology can be high, and troubleshooting a failed cable can be tricky. Because of this, the mesh topology is not the first choice for many wired networks but is more popular with servers/routers.

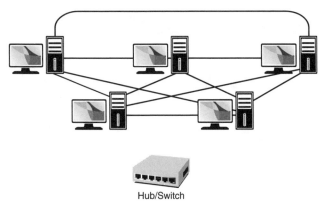

Hub/Switch

FIGURE 1.4 **Mesh topology**

A variation on a true mesh topology is the hybrid mesh. It creates a redundant point-to-point network connection between only specific network devices (such as the servers). The hybrid mesh is most often seen in WAN implementations but can be used in any network.

Another way of describing the degree of mesh implementation is by labeling it as either *partial* or *full*. If it is a true mesh network with connections between each device, it can be labeled full mesh, and if it is less than that—a hybrid of any sort—it is called a *partial mesh network*.

Table 1.4 summarizes the advantages and disadvantages of the mesh topology.

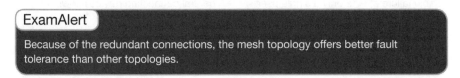

ExamAlert

Because of the redundant connections, the mesh topology offers better fault tolerance than other topologies.

TABLE 1.4 **Advantages and Disadvantages of the Mesh Topology**

Advantages	Disadvantages
Provides redundant paths between LAN topologies.	Requires more cable than the other topologies.
The network can be expanded without disruption to current users.	Complicated implementation.

Wireless Topologies

Wireless networks typically are implemented using one of three wireless topologies:

▶ The *infrastructure*, or managed, wireless topology

▶ The *ad hoc*, or unmanaged, wireless topology

▶ The *mesh* wireless topology

The following sections describe these three wireless topologies in greater detail.

Infrastructure Wireless Topology

The infrastructure wireless topology is commonly used to extend a wired LAN to include wireless devices. Wireless devices communicate with the wired LAN through a base station known as an *access point (AP)* or *wireless access point.* The AP forms a bridge between a wireless and wired LAN, and all transmissions between wireless stations, or between a system and a wired network client, go through the AP. APs are not mobile and have to stay connected to the wired network; therefore, they become part of the wired network infrastructure (thus the name). In infrastructure wireless networks, there might be several access points providing wireless coverage for a large area or only a single access point for a small area, such as a single home or small building.

> **Note**
>
> **WAP or AP?**   Notice that although we call it a wireless access point, it is commonly referred to as an AP. As you study for the exam, know that it can be called either an AP or a WAP, and—just to make matters confusing—WAP is also the acronym for the Wireless Application Protocol.

Ad Hoc Wireless Topology

In a wireless ad hoc topology, devices communicate directly among themselves without using an access point. This peer-to-peer network design is commonly used to connect a small number of computers or wireless devices. For example, an ad hoc wireless network may be set up temporarily between laptops in a boardroom or to connect systems in a home instead of using a wired solution. The ad hoc wireless design provides a quick method to share files and resources among a small number of systems. Connecting mobile devices together or to a printer using Bluetooth is an example of an ad hoc network.

Figure 1.5 shows an ad hoc wireless network, and Figure 1.6 shows the infrastructure network using the AP.

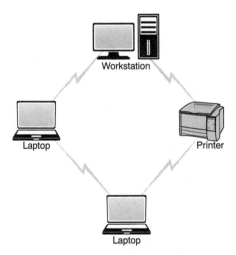

FIGURE 1.5 **Ad hoc wireless topology**

> **Note**
>
> In an infrastructure wireless network, devices use a wireless AP to connect to the network.

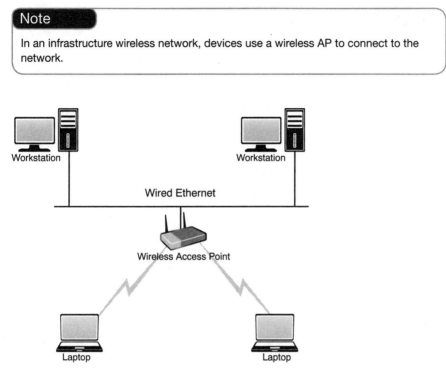

FIGURE 1.6   **Infrastructure wireless topology**

Wireless Mesh Topology

As discussed earlier, wired mesh networks are costly because of the cabling required to interconnect all computer systems. Wireless mesh networks obviously do not need cables running between systems, making wireless mesh networks fairly common in the networking world. In the wireless mesh network, as with the wired mesh, each network node is interconnected to other nodes on the network. With a wired mesh, the wireless signal starts at a wireless base station (access point) attached to a wired network. A wireless mesh network extends the transmission distance by relaying the signal from one computer to another. Unlike the wired mesh, in which a complex and expensive collection of physical cables is required to create the mesh, the wireless mesh is inexpensive to implement. Figure 1.7 shows a wireless mesh topology.

> **Note**
>
> **Wireless Mesh** A wireless mesh network is created through the connection of wireless access points installed at each network user's locale. Data signals in a wireless mesh rely on all nodes to propagate signals. Wireless mesh networks can be identified by the interconnecting signals between each node.

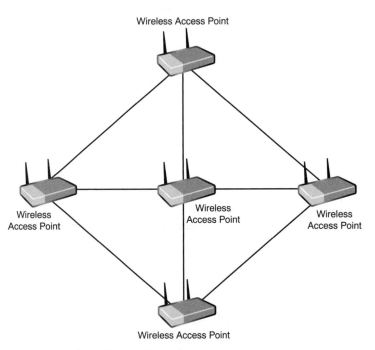

FIGURE 1.7 **A wireless mesh topology**

The wireless mesh network has several key advantages. Because a wireless mesh network is interconnected with one or more nodes on the network, the data can travel multiple paths to reach its destination. When a new node is added, it provides new paths for other nodes, which in turn improves network performance and decreases congestion. Advantages of the wireless mesh include the following:

▶ **Self-healing:** Wireless mesh networks are known as self-healing, which refers to the network's ability to adapt to network failure and even function should a node be moved from one location to another. Self-healing in a wireless mesh environment is possible because of the interconnected connections and because of the wireless media.

▶ **Scalable:** Wireless mesh networks are highly scalable. Using wireless, it is possible to add new systems to the network without the need for expensive cables.

▶ **Reliability:** Of all network topologies, the mesh network provides the greatest reliability. The redundant number of paths for the data to travel ensures that data can reach its destination.

▶ **Cost:** One disadvantage of the wired mesh is the cost associated with running the cabling and the support costs of such a complex network. Wireless mesh networks are essentially self-configuring and do not have cabling requirements. Therefore, systems can be added, removed, and relocated with little cost or disruption to the network.

Hybrid Topologies

As you might expect, topology designs are not black and white. Many of the topologies found in large networking environments are a hybrid of physical topologies. An example of a hybrid topology is the star bus—a combination of the star topology and the bus topology. Figure 1.8 shows how this might look in a network implementation.

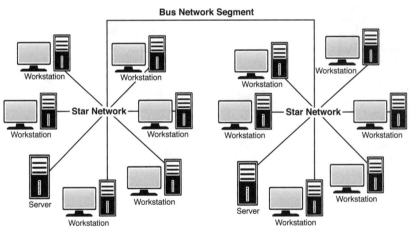

FIGURE 1.8 **A star bus topology**

ExamAlert

Another meaning: The term *hybrid topology* also can refer to the combination of wireless and wired networks. For the Network+ exam, however, the term *hybrid* most likely refers to the combination of physical networks.

Cram Quiz

1. You have been asked to install a network that will give the network users the greatest amount of fault tolerance. Which of the following network topologies would you choose?

   ○ **A.** Star

   ○ **B.** Ring

   ○ **C.** Mesh

   ○ **D.** Bus

2. Which of the following topologies allows for network expansion with the least amount of disruption for the current network users?

   ○ **A.** Bus

   ○ **B.** Ring

   ○ **C.** LAN

   ○ **D.** Star

3. What topology is represented in the following figure?

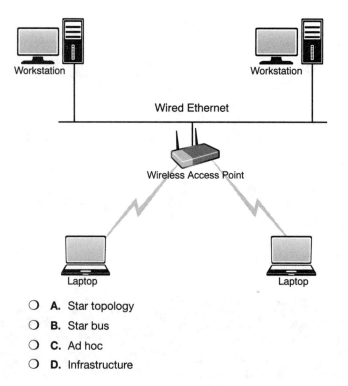

   ○ **A.** Star topology

   ○ **B.** Star bus

   ○ **C.** Ad hoc

   ○ **D.** Infrastructure

4. Which network topology offers the greatest level of redundancy but has the highest implementation cost?

- ○ **A.** Wireless mesh
- ○ **B.** Wired mesh
- ○ **C.** Hybrid star
- ○ **D.** Bus network

5. Which of the following statements are associated with a bus LAN network? (Choose all correct answers.)

- ○ **A.** A single cable break can cause complete network disruption.
- ○ **B.** All devices connect to a central device.
- ○ **C.** It uses a single backbone to connect all network devices.
- ○ **D.** It uses a dual-ring configuration.

6. As a network administrator, you are called in to troubleshoot a problem on a token ring network. The network uses two MSAUs connected using the ring-in ports on both devices. All network cards are set at the same speed. What is the likely cause of the problem?

- ○ **A.** Bad network card
- ○ **B.** Faulty cabling
- ○ **C.** MSAU configuration
- ○ **D.** Network card configuration

Cram Quiz Answers

1. **C.** A mesh network uses a point-to-point connection to every device on the network. This creates multiple points for the data to be transmitted around the network and therefore creates a high degree of redundancy. The star, ring, and bus topologies do not offer the greatest amount of fault tolerance.

2. **D.** On a star network, each network device uses a separate cable to make a point-to-point connection to a centralized device, such as a hub or a switch. With such a configuration, a new device can be added to the network by attaching the new device to the hub or switch with its own cable. This process does not disrupt the users who are currently on the network. Answers A and B are incorrect because the addition of new network devices on a ring or bus network can cause a disruption in the network and cause network services to be unavailable during the installation of a new device.

3. **D.** The infrastructure wireless topology is commonly used to extend a wired LAN to include wireless devices. Wireless devices communicate with the wired LAN through a base station known as an access point (AP) or wireless access point. The AP forms a bridge between a wireless and wired LAN, and all transmissions between wireless stations or between a system and a wired network client go through the AP.

4. **B.** The wired mesh topology requires each computer on the network to be individually connected to every other device. This configuration provides maximum reliability and redundancy for the network. However, it is very costly to implement because of the multiple wiring requirements.

5. **A, C.** In a bus network, a single break in the network cable can disrupt all the devices on that segment of the network, a significant shortcoming. A bus network also uses a single cable as a backbone to which all networking devices attach. A star network requires networked devices to connect to a centralized device such as a hub, switch, or MSAU. Therefore, answer B is incorrect. Answer D is also incorrect because it uses a dual-ring configuration.

6. **C.** To create the complete ring, the ring-in (RI) port on each MSAU is connected to the ring-out (RO) port on another MSAU. The last MSAU in the ring is then connected to the first to complete the ring.

WANs

A *wide-area network (WAN)* is a network that spans more than one geographic location, often connecting separated LANs. WANs are slower than LANs and often require additional and costly hardware, such as routers, dedicated leased lines, and complicated implementation procedures. Figure 1.10 shows an example of a WAN.

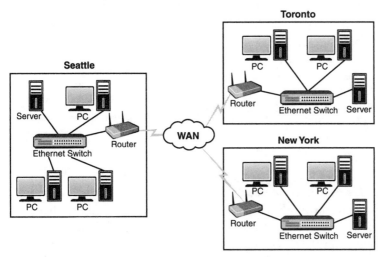

FIGURE 1.10   **A wide-area network**

MANs

Occasionally, a WAN will be called a *metropolitan-area network (MAN)* when it is confined to a certain geographic area, such as a university campus or city. No formal guidelines dictate the differences between a MAN and a WAN; technically, a MAN *is* a WAN. Perhaps for this reason, the term *MAN* is used less often than *WAN*. If any distinction exists, it is that a MAN is smaller than a WAN. A MAN is almost always bigger than a LAN and usually is smaller than or equal to a WAN. MANs utilize an Internet service provider (ISP) or tele-communications (telco) provider.

CANs

When it comes to terminology and definitions, a computer network in a defined area that links buildings and consists of multiple LANs within that limited geographical area is usually called a *Campus-Area Network (CAN)*. The CAN may encompass the whole college campus, or a portion of it. It may also have nothing to do with a college but consists of office buildings in an enterprise "campus," industrial complex, military base, or anywhere else. In reality, a CAN is a WAN, but what makes it distinct is the confined geographic area it includes.

SANs

A *storage-area network (SAN)* consists of just what the name implies: networked/shared storage devices. With clustered storage, you can use multiple devices to increase performance. SANs are subsets of LANs and offer block-level data storage that appears within the operating systems of the connected devices as locally attached devices.

File systems built on top of SANs can provide file-level access, but the SAN itself does not provide file abstraction, only block-level operations.

PANs

A *personal-area network (PAN)* is essentially a LAN created to share data among devices associated with you. Wireless technologies have taken PAN further and introduced a new term—*wireless personal-area network (WPAN)*. WPAN refers to the technologies involved in connecting devices in very close proximity to exchange data or resources, usually through the use of Bluetooth, infrared, or *near-field communication (NFC)*. An example is connecting a laptop with a smartphone to synchronize an address book. Because of their small size and the nature of the data exchange, WPAN devices lend themselves well to ad hoc wireless networking. Ad hoc wireless networks are those that have devices connect to each other directly, not through a wireless access point.

Cram Quiz

1. When a WAN is confined to a certain geographic area, such as a city, it is known as a:

   ○ **A.** LAN

   ○ **B.** MAN

   ○ **C.** VAN

   ○ **D.** VPN

2. Which of the following is a computer network in a defined area that links buildings and consists of multiple LANs within that limited geographical area?

- ○ **A.** SAN
- ○ **B.** PAN
- ○ **C.** DAN
- ○ **D.** CAN

3. Which of the following provides a flexible and secure data communications system that augments an Ethernet LAN or, in some cases, replaces it altogether?

- ○ **A.** PHLAN
- ○ **B.** MAN
- ○ **C.** WLAN
- ○ **D.** CRAN

Cram Quiz Answers

1. B. A WAN can be referred to as a metropolitan-area network (MAN) when it is confined to a certain geographic area, such as a city.

2. D. A campus-area network (CAN) is a computer network in a defined area that links buildings and consists of multiple LANs within that limited geographical area.

3. C. A wireless LAN (WLAN) augments an Ethernet LAN or, in some cases, replaces it altogether.

IoT Technologies

▶ **Compare and contrast the characteristics of network topologies, types and technologies.**

CramSaver

If you can correctly answer these questions before going through this section, save time by skimming the Exam Alerts in this section and then completing the Cram Quiz at the end of the section.

1. What is the access method employed by the 802.11 wireless standards?

2. What technologies are considered the biggest developments for 802.11n/802.11ac and the keys to the newer speeds?

Answers

1. All the 802.11 wireless standards employ the CSMA/CA access method.

2. Multiple input, multiple output (MIMO) and multiuser MIMO (MU-MIMO) antenna technologies are the biggest developments for 802.11n/802.11ac and the key to the new speeds.

In the IT world of today, one of the fastest growing areas is that of embedded devices such as thermostats, water softeners, and other appliances. This interconnection via the Internet of computing devices embedded in everyday objects is known as the *Internet of Things (IoT)*. The goal is to enable them to send and receive data. To do this, technologies are needed that facilitate such interaction. Those are discussed in the sections that follow.

ExamAlert

The seven items listed here constitute those associated with IoT beneath the Network+ objective 1.5. You should make certain that you know them as you study for the exam.

Z-Wave

When it comes to HVAC, automated window coverings, home cinema, and some security system/home access controls, *Z-Wave* is a popular communications protocol. Focused on the office/residential/automation market, it requires a Z-Wave gateway (central control device), which acts as both the hub controller and the portal (typically to the Internet). Up to 232 devices can be on a Z-Wave network, and each new device has to be paired (or "included") for it to be recognized by the controller.

An estimated 50 million devices that are Z-Wave compliant have been shipped since the standard was developed by the Danish company Zen-Sys. The standard is now governed by the members of the Z-Wave Alliance. The frequency it uses varies by country, but in the United States, the two frequencies are 908.4 and 916.

Each Z-Wave network is identified by a 32-bit Network ID (known as the Home ID), and each device is identified by an 8-bit Node ID that must be unique within the network.

Ant+

Although not open per se, the Z-Wave protocol is associated with many companies. ANT+, on the other hand, is governed by Garmin through its ANT+ Alliance. Similar to Z-Wave, it is a wireless protocol but is often used to control lighting systems, television sets, and other indoor entities, such as a line of fitness monitoring equipment licensed by Garmin.

ANT+ operates in the 2.4 GHz range, and a typical ANT-enabled device includes an application host MCU interfaced with an ANT module, chipset, or chip. Communication utilizes bidirectional, serial messages across a channel. Each channel has a master and at last one slave participant.

Bluetooth

When it comes to wireless standards for short distances, Bluetooth is the industry leader. Using the 2.4 to 2.485 GHz band, the technology is popular for personal-area networks (PANs) and is based on the IEEE 802.15.1 standard. The IEEE no longer maintains the standard, and it is now managed by the Bluetooth Special Interest Group (SIG).

There are 79 Bluetooth channels available, and each channel has a bandwidth of 1 MHz. Bluetooth is a packet-based protocol with a master-slave structure; one master can communicate with up to seven slaves. A number of Bluetooth "versions" or standards have been released since 1.0 first appeared. Some of the main versions of Bluetooth evolution include v1.2, v2.0, v2.1, v3.0, v4.0, and v4.1. As of this writing, the most recently announced was 5, and it is focused on the Internet of Things (IoT). It provides double the speed (2 Mbps), fourfold the range, and eightfold the data broadcasting capacity of transmissions compared to Bluetooth 4.x.

ExamAlert

Up until the most recent version, the numbers have always included a point and a decimal: 1.0, 1.2, and so on. With the latest, there is no point or decimal. After much discussion, it was decided it was less confusing to go with a whole number: Bluetooth 5.

NFC

Near field communication (NFC) is a technology that requires a user to bring the client close to a wireless access point (AP) in order to verify—often through Radio Frequency Identification (RFID) or Wi-Fi—that the device is present. The popularity of this has grown with phones being used as a part of payment systems, and it can also be used between two phones to "bump" and send data from one to another. Although there is no hardcoded standard defining "near," the industry tends to use 4cm (1.6 inches) as the distance.

IR

Infrared (IR) has been around for a long time; perhaps your first experience with it was the TV remote. The commands entered into the remote-control travel over an infrared light wave to the receiver on the TV. Infrared technology has progressed, and today infrared development in networking is managed by the *Infrared Data Association (IrDA)*. However, its use in mobile devices and peripherals has been displaced by more modern Wi-Fi and Bluetooth wireless technologies that do not require a direct line-of-sight and offer less-restrictive distance limitations.

Infrared wireless networking uses infrared beams to send data transmissions between devices. Infrared wireless networking offers higher transmission rates, reaching 10 Mbps to 16 Mbps.

As expected, infrared light beams cannot penetrate objects; therefore, the signal is disrupted when something blocks the light. Infrared can be either a directed (line-of-sight) or diffuse technology. A directed infrared system provides a limited range of approximately 3 feet and typically is used for personal-area networks. Diffused infrared can travel farther and is more difficult to block with a signal object. Diffused infrared wireless LAN systems do not require line-of-sight, but usable distance is limited to room distances.

Infrared provides a secure, low-cost, convenient cable-replacement technology. It is well suited for many specific applications and environments. Some key infrared points follow:

- ▶ It provides adequate speeds—up to 16 Mbps.

- ▶ Infrared devices use less power and therefore do not drain batteries as much.

- ▶ Infrared is a secure medium. Infrared signals typically are a direct-line implementation in a short range and therefore do not travel far outside the immediate connection. This eliminates the problem of eavesdropping or signal tampering.

- ▶ Infrared is a proven technology. Infrared devices have been available for some time and as such are a proven, nonproprietary technology with an established user and support base.

- ▶ It has no RFI issues or signal conflicts.

- ▶ It replaces cables for many devices, such as keyboards, mice, and other peripherals.

- ▶ It uses a dispersed mode or a direct line-of-sight transmission.

- ▶ Transmissions travel over short distances.

RFID

Although NFC is a newer standard, it is built on the older standards created for RFID, which allows compatible hardware both to supply power to and communicate with an otherwise unpowered and passive electronic tag using radio waves. RFID is widely used for identification, authentication, and tracking applications.

"Proximity reader" is a catchall term for any ID or card reader capable of reading proximity cards. Proximity cards go by a number of different titles, but they are just RFID cards that can be read when close to a reader and truly never need to touch anything. The readers work with 13.56 MHz smart cards and 125 kHz proximity cards, and they can open turnstiles, gates, and any other physical security safeguards after the signal is read.

802.11

802.11 represents the IEEE designation for wireless networking. Several wireless networking specifications exist under the 802.11 banner. The Network+

objectives focus on 802.11a, 802.11b, 802.11g, 802.11n, and 802.11ac. All these standards use the Ethernet protocol and the Carrier Sense Multiple Access/ Collision Detection (CSMA/CA) access method.

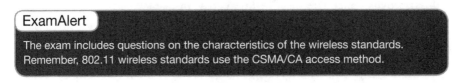
ExamAlert

The exam includes questions on the characteristics of the wireless standards. Remember, 802.11 wireless standards use the CSMA/CA access method.

The 802.11 wireless standards can differ in terms of speed, transmission ranges, and frequency used, but in terms of actual implementation, they are similar. All standards can use either an infrastructure or ad hoc network design, and each can use the same security protocols:

▶ **IEEE 802.11:** There were two variations on the initial 802.11 wireless standard. Both offered 1 or 2 Mbps transmission speeds and the same RF of 2.4 GHz. The difference between the two was in how data traveled through the RF media. One used Frequency Hopping Spread Spectrum (FHSS), and the other used Direct Sequence Spread Spectrum (DSSS). The original 802.11 standards are far too slow for modern networking needs and are now no longer deployed.

ExamAlert

With this iteration of the exam, CompTIA wants you to know the acronyms FHSS and DSSS, but no longer tests on the intricacies of either technology. In the interest of completeness, these technologies are discussed in more detail at the end of this chapter to round out your knowledge.

▶ **IEEE 802.11a:** In terms of speed, the 802.11a standard was far ahead of the original 802.11 standards. 802.11a specified speeds of up to 54 Mbps in the 5 GHz band, but most commonly, communication takes place at 6 Mbps, 12 Mbps, or 24 Mbps. 802.11a is incompatible with the 802.11b and 802.11g wireless standards.

▶ **IEEE 802.11b:** The 802.11b standard provides for a maximum transmission speed of 11 Mbps. However, devices are designed to be backward compatible with previous 802.11 standards that provided for speeds of 1, 2, and 5.5 Mbps. 802.11b uses a 2.4 GHz RF range and is compatible with 802.11g.

▶ **IEEE 802.11g:** 802.11g offers wireless transmission over distances of 150 feet and speeds up to 54 Mbps compared with the 11 Mbps of the 802.11b standard. Like 802.11b, 802.11g operates in the 2.4 GHz range and therefore is compatible with it.

▶ **IEEE 802.11n:** One of the more common wireless standards today is 802.11n. The goal of the 802.11n standard was to significantly increase throughput in both the 2.4 GHz and the 5 GHz frequency ranges. The baseline goal of the standard was to reach speeds of 100 Mbps, but given the right conditions, it is stated that the 802.11n speeds can reach a theoretical 600 Mbps. In practical operation, 802.11n speeds are much slower. Multiple Input, Multiple Output (MIMO) was introduced with 802.11n.

▶ **IEEE 802.11ac:** The newest of the wireless standards listed in the Network+ objectives is 802.11ac, which became an approved standard in January of 2014 and can be thought of as an extension of 802.11n. Any device using this standard must support all the mandatory modes of both 802.11n and 802.11a. The goal of the standard is 500 Mbps with one link and 1.3 Gbps with multiple links. It has support for up to eight MIMO streams and increased channel bonding, as well as support for up to four *multiuser MIMO (MU-MIMO)* clients. 802.11ac is a 5 GHz-only technology and is available with most wireless routers sold today.

ExamAlert

Be prepared to answer questions on the specific characteristics of wireless standards. Performance-based questions might ask you to select or place the appropriate standard or wireless configuration setting for a particular scenario.

The Magic Behind 802.11n and 802.11ac

802.11n took the best from the 802.11 standards and mixed in some new features to take wireless to the next level. First among these new technologies was *multiple input, multiple output (MIMO)* antenna technology.

MIMO was unquestionably the biggest development for 802.11n and the key to the new speeds. Essentially, MIMO uses multiplexing to increase the range and speed of wireless networking. Multiplexing is a technique that combines multiple signals for transmission over a single line or medium. MIMO enables the transmission of multiple data streams traveling on different antennas in the same channel at the same time. A receiver reconstructs the streams, which have multiple antennas as well. By using multiple paths, MIMO provides a significant capacity gain over conventional single-antenna systems, along with more reliable communication.

While 802.11n can transmit more than one spatial stream at the same time, the streams are directed to a single address (MIMO). 802.11ac allows for MU-MIMO to let an AP send multiple frames to multiple clients at the exact same time (thus allowing the AP to act like a switch instead of just a hub).

In addition to MIMO, 802.11n enabled *channel bonding* that essentially doubled the data rate. What is channel bonding? The 802.11b and 802.11g wireless standards use a single channel to send and receive information. With channel bonding, you can use two channels at the same time. As you might guess, the capability to use two channels at once increases performance. Bonding can help increase wireless transmission rates from the 54 Mbps offered with the 802.11g standards to a theoretical maximum of 600 Mbps with 802.11n. 802.11n uses the Orthogonal Frequency Division Multiplexing (OFDM) transmission strategy—a scheme used as a digital multicarrier modulation method in which a large number of closely spaced orthogonal subcarrier signals are used to carry data on several parallel data streams or channels. It is discussed in more detail shortly.

802.11ac extends this by increasing the maximum from 40 MHz to 80 MHz (with hypothetical of 160 MHz). By doubling the channel bandwidth, twice as much data can be carried in the same time.

> **Note**
>
> In wireless networking, a single channel is 20 MHz in width. When two channels are bonded, they are a total of 40 MHz. 802.11n systems can use either the 20 MHz channels or the 40 MHz channel. 802.11ac supports the 20 MHz, 40 MHz, 80 MHz, and 160 MHz channels.

Aggregation is the other big difference, allowing data to be packaged together to increase speeds. 802.11n brought the technology to the mainstream, and 802.11ac simply builds on it.

A Summary of 802.11 Wireless Standards

Table 1.5 highlights the characteristics of the various 802.11 wireless standards.

TABLE 1.5 **802.11 Wireless Standards**

IEEE Standard	Frequency/ Medium	Speed	Topology	Transmission Range	Access Method
802.11	2.4 GHz	1 to 2 Mbps	Ad hoc/ infrastructure	20 feet indoors	CSMA/CA
802.11a	5 GHz	Up to 54 Mbps	Ad hoc/ infrastructure	25 to 75 feet indoors; range can be affected by building materials	CSMA/CA
802.11b	2.4 GHz	Up to 11 Mbps	Ad hoc/ infrastructure	Up to 150 feet indoors; range can be affected by building materials	CSMA/CA
802.11g	2.4 GHz	Up to 54 Mbps	Ad hoc/ infrastructure	Up to 150 feet indoors; range can be affected by building materials	CSMA/CA
802.11n	2.4 GHz/ 5 GHz	Up to 600 Mbps	Ad hoc/ infrastructure	175+ feet indoors; range can be affected by building materials	CSMA/CA
802.11ac	5 GHz	Up to 1.3 Gbps	Ad hoc/ infrastructure	115+ feet indoors; range can be affected by building materials	CSMA/CA

ExamAlert

For the exam, you should know the values in Table 1.5.

Spread spectrum refers to the manner in which data signals travel through a radio frequency. With spread spectrum, data does not travel straight through a single RF band; this type of transmission is known as *narrowband transmission*. Spread spectrum, however, requires that data signals either alternate between carrier frequencies or constantly change their data pattern. Although the shortest distance between two points is a straight line (narrowband), spread spectrum is designed to trade bandwidth efficiency for reliability, integrity, and security. Spread-spectrum signal strategies use more bandwidth than in the case of narrowband transmission, but the trade-off is a data signal that is clearer and easier to detect. The two types of spread-spectrum radio are *frequency hopping* and *direct sequence*.

Table 1.6 compares wireless standards and the spread spectrum used.

TABLE 1.6   **Comparison of IEEE 802.11 Standards**

IEEE Standard	RF Used	Spread Spectrum	Data Rate (in Mbps)
802.11	2.4 GHz	DSSS	1 or 2
802.11	2.4 GHz	FHSS	1 or 2
802.11a	5 GHz	OFDM	54
802.11b	2.4 GHz	DSSS	11
802.11g	2.4 GHz	DSSS	54
802.11n	2.4/5 GHz	OFDM	600 (theoretical)
802.11ac	5 GHz	OFDM	1300 (theoretical)

Frequency-Hopping Spread-Spectrum Technology

Frequency-hopping spread-spectrum (FHSS) requires the use of narrowband signals that change frequencies in a predictable pattern. The term *frequency hopping* refers to data signals hopping between narrow channels. For example, consider the 2.4 GHz frequency band used by 802.11b/g. This range is divided into 70 narrow channels of 1 MHz each. Somewhere between 20 and several hundred milliseconds, the signal hops to a new channel following a predetermined cyclical pattern.

Because data signals using FHSS switch between RF bands, they have a strong resistance to interference and environmental factors. The FHSS signal strategy makes it well suited for installations designed to cover a large geographic area and where using directional antennas to minimize the influence of environmental factors is not possible.

FHSS is not the preferred spread-spectrum technology for today's wireless standards. However, FHSS is used for some lesser-used standards and for cellular deployments for fixed *broadband wireless access (BWA)*, where the use of DSSS (discussed next) is virtually impossible because of its limitations.

Direct-Sequence Spread-Spectrum (DSSS) Technology

With DSSS transmissions, the signal is spread over a full transmission frequency spectrum. For every bit of data sent, a redundant bit pattern is also sent. This 32-bit pattern is called a *chip*. These redundant bits of data provide both security and delivery assurance. The reason transmissions are so safe and reliable is because the system sends so many redundant copies of the data, and only a single copy is required to have complete transmission of the data or information. DSSS can minimize the effects of interference and background noise.

As for a comparison between the two, DSSS has the advantage of providing better security and signal delivery than FHSS, but it is a sensitive technology, affected by many environmental factors.

Orthogonal Frequency-Division Multiplexing

Orthogonal frequency-division multiplexing (OFDM) is a transmission technique that transfers large amounts of data over 52 separate, evenly spaced frequencies. OFDM splits the radio signal into these separate frequencies and simultaneously transmits them to the receiver. Splitting the signal and transferring over different frequencies reduces the amount of crosstalk interference. OFDM is associated with IEEE 802.11a, 802.11g, 802.11n, and 802.11ac wireless standards as well as 4G mobile phone standards.

A multiuser version of OFDM is orthogonal frequency-division multiple access (OFDMA). It assigns subsets of subcarriers to individual users to allow for simultaneous data transmission from multiples users, and it is considered scalable.

Cram Quiz

1. You are installing a wireless network solution, and you require a standard that can operate using either 2.4 GHz or 5 GHz frequencies. Which of the following standards would you choose?

   ○ **A.** 802.11a

   ○ **B.** 802.11b

   ○ **C.** 802.11g

   ○ **D.** 802.11n

   ○ **E.** 802.11ac

2. You are installing a wireless network solution that uses a feature known as MU-MIMO. Which wireless networking standard are you using?

   ○ **A.** 802.11a

   ○ **B.** 802.11b

   ○ **C.** 802.11n

   ○ **D.** 802.11ac

Cram Quiz Answers

1. **D.** The IEEE standard 802.11n can use either the 2.4 GHz or 5 GHz radio frequencies. 802.11a uses 5 GHz, and 802.11b and 802.11g use 2.4 GHz. 802.11ac operates at 5 GHz.

2. **D.** MU-MIMO is used by the 802.11ac standard and makes multiuser MIMO possible (increasing the range and speed of wireless networking). MIMO itself enables the transmission of multiple data streams traveling on different antennas in the same channel at the same time.

What's Next?

This chapter created a foundation upon which Chapter 2, "Models, Ports, Protocols, and Networking Services," builds. It examines the Open Systems Interconnect (OSI) reference model—a conceptual model describing how network architecture allows data to be passed between computer systems. It also examines how common network devices relate to the model.

CHAPTER 2

Models, Ports, Protocols, and Networking Services

This chapter covers the following official Network+ objectives:

▶ Explain the purposes and uses of ports and protocols.

▶ Explain devices, applications, protocols, and services at their appropriate OSI layers.

▶ Explain the functions of network services.

This chapter covers CompTIA Network+ objectives 1.1, 1.2, and 1.8. For more information on the official Network+ exam topics, see the "About the Network+ Exam" section in the Introduction.

One of the most important networking concepts to understand is the *Open Systems Interconnect (OSI)* reference model. This conceptual model, created by the *International Organization for Standardization (ISO)* in 1978 and revised in 1984, describes a network architecture that enables data to be passed between computer systems.

This chapter looks at the OSI and describes how it relates to real-world networking. It also examines how common network devices relate to the OSI model. Even though the OSI model is conceptual, an appreciation of its purpose and function can help you better understand how protocol suites and network architectures work in practical applications.

Note

The TCP/IP model, which performs the same functions as the OSI model, except in four layers instead of seven, is no longer a Network+ objective. Because this is the protocol suite predominantly in use today, it is still important to know it to understand the underlying principles of networking.

The OSI Networking Model

▶ **Explain devices, applications, protocols and services at their appropriate OSI layers.**

CramSaver

If you can correctly answer these questions before going through this section, save time by skimming the Exam Alerts in this section and then completing the Cram Quiz at the end of the section.

1. Which layer of the OSI model converts data from the application layer into a format that can be sent over the network?

2. True or false: Transport protocols, such as UDP, map to the transport layer of the OSI model and are responsible for transporting data across the network.

3. At what layer of the OSI model do FTP and TFTP map?

Answers

1. The presentation layer converts data from the application layer into a format that can be sent over the network. It also converts data from the session layer into a format the application layer can understand.

2. True. Transport protocols map to the transport layer of the OSI model and are responsible for transporting data across the network. UDP is a transport protocol.

3. FTP and TFTP map to the application layer of the OSI model.

For networking, two models commonly are referenced: the OSI model and the TCP/IP model. Both offer a framework, theoretical and actual, for how networking is implemented. Objective 1.2 of the Network+ exam focuses only on the OSI model. A thorough discussion of it follows with a brief discussion of the TCP/IP model tossed in for further understanding.

The OSI Seven-Layer Model

As shown in Figure 2.1, the OSI reference model is built, bottom to top, in the following order: physical, data link, network, transport, session, presentation, and application. The physical layer is classified as Layer 1, and the top layer of the model, the application layer, is Layer 7.

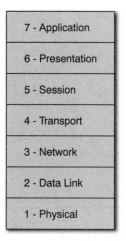

FIGURE 2.1   **The OSI seven-layer model**

ExamAlert

On the Network+ exam, you might see an OSI layer referenced either by its name, such as network layer, or by its layer number. For instance, you might find that a router is referred to as a Layer 3 device. An easy mnemonic that you can use to remember the layers from top to bottom is: All People Seem To Need Data Processing.

Each layer of the OSI model has a specific function. The following sections describe the function of each layer, starting with the physical layer and working up the model.

Physical Layer (Layer 1)

The physical layer of the OSI model identifies the network's physical characteristics, including the following specifications:

▶ **Hardware:** The type of media used on the network, such as type of cable, type of connector, and pinout format for cables.

▶ **Topology:** The physical layer identifies the topology to be used in the network. Common topologies include ring, mesh, star, bus, and hybrid.

Protocols and technologies such as USB, Ethernet, DSL, ISDN, T-carrier links (T1 and T3), GSM, and SONET operate at the physical layer.

In addition to these characteristics, the physical layer defines the voltage used on a given medium and the frequency at which the signals that carry the data operate. These characteristics dictate the speed and bandwidth of a given medium, as well as the maximum distance over which a certain media type can be used.

Data Link Layer (Layer 2)

The data link layer is responsible for getting data to the physical layer so that it can transmit over the network. The data link layer is also responsible for error detection, error correction, and hardware addressing. The term *frame* describes the logical grouping of data at the data link layer.

The data link layer has two distinct sublayers:

▶ **Media Access Control (MAC) layer:** The MAC address is defined at this layer. The MAC address is the physical or hardware address burned into each network interface card (NIC). The MAC sublayer also controls access to network media. The MAC layer specification is included in the IEEE 802.1 standard.

▶ **Logical Link Control (LLC) layer:** The LLC layer is responsible for the error and flow-control mechanisms of the data link layer. The LLC layer is specified in the IEEE 802.2 standard.

Protocols and technologies such as *High-Level Data Link Control (HDLC)*, *Layer 2 Tunneling Protocol (L2TP)*, *Point-to-Point Protocol (PPP)*, *Point-to-Point Tunneling Protocol (PPTP)*, *Spanning Tree Protocol (STP)*, and *virtual LANs (VLANs)* operate at the data link layer.

Network Layer (Layer 3)

The primary responsibility of the network layer is *routing*—providing mechanisms by which data can be passed from one network system to another. The network layer does not specify how the data is passed, but rather provides the mechanisms to do so. Functionality at the network layer is provided through routing protocols, which are software components.

Protocols at the network layer are also responsible for *route selection*, which refers to determining the best path for the data to take throughout the network. In contrast to the data link layer, which uses MAC addresses to communicate on the LAN, network layer protocols use software configured addresses and special routing protocols to communicate on the network. The term *packet* describes the logical grouping of data at the network layer.

When working with networks, routes can be configured in two ways: *statically* or *dynamically*. In a static routing environment, routes are manually added to the routing tables. In a dynamic routing environment, routing protocols such as *Routing Information Protocol (RIP)* and *Open Shortest Path First (OSPF)* are used. These protocols communicate routing information between networked devices on the network. Other important network layer protocols include *Internet Protocol (IP)*, *Address Resolution Protocol (ARP)*, *Reverse Address Resolution Protocol (RARP)*, *Asynchronous Transfer Mode (ATM)*, *Intermediate System-to-Intermediate System (IS-IS)*, *IP Security (IPsec)*, *Internet Control Message Protocol (ICMP)*, and *Multiprotocol Label Switching (MPLS)*.

Transport Layer (Layer 4)

The basic function of the transport layer is to provide mechanisms to transport data between network devices. Primarily it does this in three ways:

▶ **Error checking:** Protocols at the transport layer ensure that data is correctly sent or received.

▶ **Service addressing:** A number of protocols support many network services. The transport layer ensures that data is passed to the right service at the upper layers of the OSI model.

▶ **Segmentation:** To traverse the network, blocks of data need to be broken into packets of a manageable size for the lower layers to handle. This process, called *segmentation*, is the responsibility of the transport layer.

Protocols that operate at the transport layer can either be connectionless, such as *User Datagram Protocol (UDP)*, or connection oriented, such as *Transmission Control Protocol (TCP)*.

The transport layer is also responsible for *data flow control*, which refers to how the receiving device can accept data transmissions. Two common methods of flow control are used:

▶ **Buffering:** When buffering flow control is used, data is temporarily stored and waits for the destination device to become available. Buffering can cause a problem if the sending device transmits data much faster than the receiving device can manage.

▶ **Windowing:** In a windowing environment, data is sent in groups of segments that require only one acknowledgment. The size of the window (that is, how many segments fit into one acknowledgment) is defined when the session between the two devices is established. As you can imagine, the need to have only one acknowledgment for every five segments, for instance, can greatly reduce overhead.

Session Layer (Layer 5)

The session layer is responsible for managing and controlling the synchronization of data between applications on two devices. It does this by establishing, maintaining, and breaking sessions. Whereas the transport layer is responsible for setting up and maintaining the connection between the two nodes, the session layer performs the same function on behalf of the application. Protocols that operate at the session layer include NetBIOS, *Network File System (NFS)*, and *Server Message Block (SMB)*.

Presentation Layer (Layer 6)

The presentation layer's basic function is to convert the data intended for or received from the application layer into another format. Such conversion is necessary because of how data is formatted so that it can be transported across the network. Applications cannot necessarily read this conversion. Some common data formats handled by the presentation layer include the following:

▶ **Graphics files:** JPEG, TIFF, GIF, and so on are graphics file formats that require the data to be formatted in a certain way.

▶ **Text and data:** The presentation layer can translate data into different formats, such as *American Standard Code for Information Interchange (ASCII)* and *Extended Binary Coded Decimal Interchange Code (EBCDIC)*.

▶ **Sound/video:** MPEG, MP3, and MIDI files all have their own data formats to and from which data must be converted.

Another important function of the presentation layer is *encryption*, which is the scrambling of data so that it can't be read by anyone other than the intended recipient. Given the basic role of the presentation layer—that of data-format translator—it is the obvious place for encryption and decryption to take place. For example, the cryptographic protocol *Transport Layer Security (TLS)* operates at the presentation layer.

Application Layer (Layer 7)

In simple terms, the function of the application layer is to take requests and data from the users and pass them to the lower layers of the OSI model. Incoming information is passed to the application layer, which then displays the information to the users. Some of the most basic application layer services include file and print capabilities.

The most common misconception about the application layer is that it represents applications used on a system, such as a web browser, word processor, or spreadsheet. Instead, the application layer defines the processes that enable applications to use network services. For example, if an application needs to open a file from a network drive, the functionality is provided by components that reside at the application layer. Protocols defined at the application layer include *Secure Shell (SSH)*, *Border Gateway Protocol (BGP)*, *Dynamic Host Configuration Protocol (DHCP)*, *Domain Name System (DNS)*, *Network Time Protocol (NTP)*, *Real-time Transport Protocol (RTP)*, *Session Initiation Protocol (SIP)*, *Simple Mail Transfer Protocol (SMTP)*, *Server Message Block (SMB)*, *File Transfer Protocol (FTP)*, *Hypertext Transfer Protocol (HTTP)*, *Hypertext Transfer Protocol Secure (HTTPS)*, *Internet Message Access Protocol (IMAP)*, and *Post Office Protocol version 3 (POP3)*.

ExamAlert

Be sure you understand the OSI model and its purpose. You will almost certainly be asked questions on it during the exam.

OSI Model Summary

Table 2.1 summarizes the seven layers of the OSI model and describes some of the most significant points of each layer.

TABLE 2.1 **OSI Model Summary**

OSI Layer	Major Function
Physical (Layer 1)	Defines the physical structure of the network and the topology.
Data link (Layer 2)	Provides error detection and correction. Uses two distinct sublayers: the Media Access Control (MAC) and Logical Link Control (LLC) layers. Identifies the method by which media are accessed. Defines hardware addressing through the MAC sublayer.
Network (Layer 3)	Handles the discovery of destination systems and addressing. Provides the mechanism by which data can be passed and routed from one network system to another.
Transport (Layer 4)	Provides connection services between the sending and receiving devices and ensures reliable data delivery. Manages flow control through buffering or windowing. Provides segmentation, error checking, and service identification.
Session (Layer 5)	Synchronizes the data exchange between applications on separate devices.
Presentation (Layer 6)	Translates data from the format used by applications into one that can be transmitted across the network. Handles encryption and decryption of data. Provides compression and decompression functionality. Formats data from the application layer into a format that can be sent over the network.
Application (Layer 7)	Provides access to the network for applications.

Comparing OSI to the Four-Layer TCP/IP Model

The OSI model does a fantastic job outlining how networking should occur and the responsibility of each layer. However, TCP/IP has also has a reference model and has to perform the same functionality with only four layers. Figure 2.2 shows how these four layers line up with the seven layers of the OSI model.

TCP/IP Model	OSI Model
Application Layer	Application Layer Presentation Layer Session Layer
Transport Layer	Transport Layer
Internet Layer	Network Layer
Network Interface Layer	Data Link Layer Physical Layer

FIGURE 2.2   The TCP/IP model compared to the OSI model

The network interface layer in the TCP/IP model is sometimes referred to as the network access or link layer, and this is where Ethernet, FDDI, or any other physical technology can run. The Internet layer is where IP runs (along with ICMP and others). The transport layer is where TCP and its counterpart UDP operate. The application layer enables any number of protocols to be plugged in, such as HTTP, SMTP, *Simple Network Management Protocol (SNMP)*, DNS, and many others.

Identifying the OSI Layers at Which Various Network Components Operate

When you understand the OSI model, you can relate network connectivity devices to the appropriate layer of the OSI model. Knowing at which OSI layer a device operates enables you to better understand how it functions on the network. Table 2.2 identifies various network devices and maps them to the OSI model.

ExamAlert

For the Network+ exam, you are expected to identify at which layer of the OSI model certain network devices operate.

TABLE 2.2 **Mapping Network Devices to the OSI Model**

Device	OSI Layer
Hub	Physical (Layer 1)
Wireless bridge	Data link (Layer 2)
Switch	Data link (Layer 2) or network (Layer 3)
Router	Network (Layer 3)
NIC	Data link (Layer 2)
Access point (AP)	Data link (Layer 2)

Cram Quiz

1. At which OSI layer does an AP operate?

   ○ **A.** Network

   ○ **B.** Physical

   ○ **C.** Data link

   ○ **D.** Session

2. Which of the following are sublayers of the data link layer? (Choose two.)

   ○ **A.** MAC

   ○ **B.** LCL

   ○ **C.** Session

   ○ **D.** LLC

3. At which two OSI layers can a switch operate? (Choose two.)

   ○ **A.** Layer 1

   ○ **B.** Layer 2

   ○ **C.** Layer 3

   ○ **D.** Layer 4

4. Which of the following OSI layers is responsible for establishing connections between two devices?

   ○ **A.** Network

   ○ **B.** Transport

   ○ **C.** Session

   ○ **D.** Data link

Cram Quiz Answers

1. **C.** A wireless access point (AP) operates at the data link layer of the OSI model. An example of a network layer device is a router. An example of a physical layer device is a hub. Session layer components normally are software, not hardware.

2. **A, D.** The data link layer is broken into two distinct sublayers: Media Access Control (MAC) and Logical Link Control (LLC). LCL is not a valid term. Session is another of the OSI model layers.

3. **B, C.** A switch uses the MAC addresses of connected devices to make its forwarding decisions. Therefore, it is called a data link, or Layer 2, network device. It can also operate at Layer 3 or be a multilayer switch. Devices or components that operate at Layer 1 typically are media based, such as cables or connectors. Layer 4 components typically are software based, not hardware based.

4. **B.** The transport layer is responsible for establishing a connection between networked devices. The network layer is most commonly associated with route discovery and datagram delivery. Protocols at the session layer synchronize the data exchange between applications on separate devices. Protocols at the data link layer perform error detection and handling for the transmitted signals and define the method by which the medium is accessed.

Ports and Protocols

▶ **Explain the purposes and uses of ports and protocols.**

CramSaver

If you can correctly answer these questions before going through this section, save time by skimming the Exam Alerts in this section and then completing the Cram Quiz at the end of the section.

1. With TCP, a data session is established through a three-step process. This is known as a three-way _____.

2. What FTP command uploads multiple files to the remote host?

3. The SSH protocol is a more secure alternative to what protocol?

4. What ports do the HTTPS, RDP, and DHCP protocols use?

Answers

1. This is known as a three-way handshake.

2. The `mput` command uploads multiple files to the remote host in FTP.

3. SSH is a more secure alternative to Telnet.

4. HTTPS uses port 443, RDP uses port 3389, and DHCP uses ports 67 and 68.

When computers were restricted to standalone systems, there was little need for mechanisms to communicate between them. However, it wasn't long before the need to connect computers for the purpose of sharing files and printers became a necessity. Establishing communication between network devices required more than a length of cabling; a method or a set of rules was needed to establish how systems would communicate. Protocols provide that method.

It would be nice if a single protocol facilitated communication between all devices, but this is not the case. You can use a number of protocols on a network, each of which has its own features, advantages, and disadvantages. What protocol you choose can have a significant impact on the network's functioning and performance. This section explores some of the more common protocols you can expect to work with as a network administrator.

Connection-Oriented Protocols Versus Connectionless Protocols

Before getting into the characteristics of the various network protocols and protocol suites, you must first identify the difference between connection-oriented and connectionless protocols.

In a *connection-oriented* communication, data delivery is guaranteed. The sending device resends any packet that the destination system does not receive. Communication between the sending and receiving devices continues until the transmission has been verified. Because of this, connection-oriented protocols have a higher overhead and place greater demands on bandwidth.

ExamAlert

Connection-oriented protocols such as TCP can accommodate lost or dropped packets by asking the sending device to retransmit them. They can do this because they wait for all the packets in a message to be received before considering the transmission complete. On the sending end, connection-oriented protocols also assume that a lack of acknowledgment is sufficient reason to retransmit.

In contrast to connection-oriented communication, *connectionless* protocols such as User Datagram Protocol (UDP) offer only a best-effort delivery mechanism. Basically, the information is just sent; there is no confirmation that the data has been received. If an error occurs in the transmission, there is no mechanism to resend the data, so transmissions made with connectionless protocols are not guaranteed. Connectionless communication requires far less overhead than connection-oriented communication, so it is popular in applications such as streaming audio and video, where a small number of dropped packets might not represent a significant problem.

ExamAlert

As you work through the various protocols, keep an eye out for those that are connectionless and those that are connection oriented. Also, look for protocols such as TCP that guarantee delivery of data and those such as UDP that are a fire-and-forget or best-delivery method.

Internet Protocol

Internet Protocol (IP), which is defined in RFC 791, is the protocol used to transport data from one node on a network to another. IP is connectionless, which means that it doesn't guarantee the delivery of data; it simply makes its best effort to do so. To ensure that transmissions sent via IP are completed, a higher-level protocol such as TCP is required.

> **Note**
>
> In this chapter and throughout the book, the term *Request For Comments (RFC)* is used. RFCs are standards published by the *Internet Engineering Task Force (IETF)* and describe methods, behaviors, research, or innovations applicable to the operation of the Internet and Internet-connected systems. Each new RFC has an associated reference number. Looking up this number gives you information on the specific technology. For more information on RFCs, look for the Internet Engineering Task Force online.

> **ExamAlert**
>
> IP operates at the network layer of the OSI model.

In addition to providing best-effort delivery, IP also performs fragmentation and reassembly tasks for network transmissions. Fragmentation is necessary because the *maximum transmission unit (MTU)* size is limited in IP. In other words, network transmissions that are too big to traverse the network in a single packet must be broken into smaller chunks and reassembled at the other end. Another function of IP is addressing. IP addressing is a complex subject. Refer to Chapter 3, "Addressing, Routing, and Switching," for a complete discussion of IP addressing.

Transmission Control Protocol

Transmission Control Protocol (TCP), which is defined in RFC 793, is a connection-oriented transport layer protocol. Being connection oriented means that TCP establishes a mutually acknowledged session between two hosts before communication takes place. TCP provides reliability to IP communications. Specifically, TCP adds features such as flow control, sequencing, and error detection and correction. For this reason, higher-level applications that need guaranteed delivery use TCP rather than its lightweight and connectionless brother, UDP.

How TCP Works

When TCP wants to open a connection with another host, it follows this procedure:

1. It sends a message called a SYN to the target host.

2. The target host opens a connection for the request and sends back an acknowledgment message called an ACK (or SYN ACK).

3. The host that originated the request sends back another acknowledgment, saying that it has received the ACK message and that the session is ready to be used to transfer data.

When the data session is completed, a similar process is used to close the session. This three-step session establishment and acknowledgment process is called the *TCP three-way handshake*.

> ### ExamAlert
> TCP operates at the transport layer of the OSI model.

TCP is a reliable protocol because it has mechanisms that can accommodate and handle errors. These mechanisms include timeouts, which cause the sending host to automatically retransmit data if its receipt is not acknowledged within a given time period.

User Datagram Protocol

User Datagram Protocol (UDP), which is defined in RFC 768, is the brother of TCP. Like TCP, UDP is a transport protocol, but the big difference is that UDP does not guarantee delivery like TCP does. In a sense, UDP is a "fire-and-forget" protocol; it assumes that the data sent will reach its destination intact. The checking of whether data is delivered is left to upper-layer protocols. UDP operates at the transport layer of the OSI model.

Unlike TCP, with UDP no session is established between the sending and receiving hosts, which is why UDP is called a connectionless protocol. The upshot of this is that UDP has much lower overhead than TCP. A TCP packet header has 14 fields, whereas a UDP packet header has only four fields. Therefore, UDP is much more efficient than TCP. In applications that don't need the added features of TCP, UDP is much more economical in terms of bandwidth and processing effort.

> **ExamAlert**
>
> Remember that TCP is a connection-oriented protocol and UDP is a connectionless protocol.

File Transfer Protocol

As its name suggests, *File Transfer Protocol (FTP)* provides for the uploading and downloading of files from a remote host running FTP server software. As well as uploading and downloading files, FTP enables you to view the contents of folders on an FTP server and rename and delete files and directories if you have the necessary permissions. FTP, which is defined in RFC 959, uses TCP as a transport protocol to guarantee delivery of packets.

FTP has security mechanisms used to authenticate users. However, rather than create a user account for every user, you can configure FTP server software to accept anonymous logons. When you do this, the username is anonymous, and the password normally is the user's email address. Most FTP servers that offer files to the general public operate in this way.

In addition to being popular as a mechanism for distributing files to the general public over networks such as the Internet, FTP is also popular with organizations that need to frequently exchange large files with other people or organizations. For example, the chapters in this book were sent between the author and Pearson using FTP. Such a system is necessary because the files exchanged were sometimes larger than can be easily accommodated using email. A number of apps/programs are available that simplify the process. For example, FileZilla is a cross-platform graphical FTP, SFTP, and FTPS file management tool for Windows, Linux, Mac OS X, and more (more information on FileZilla can be found at https://sourceforge.net/projects/filezilla/)

> **ExamAlert**
>
> Remember that FTP is an application layer protocol. FTP uses ports 20 and 21 and sends information unencrypted, making it unsecure.

All the common network operating systems offer FTP server capabilities; however, whether you use them depends on whether you need FTP services. All popular workstation operating systems offer FTP client functionality, although it is common to use third-party utilities such as FileZilla (mentioned earlier), CuteFTP, or SmartFTP instead. By default, FTP operates on ports 20 and 21.

FTP assumes that files uploaded or downloaded are straight text (that is, ASCII) files. If the files are not text, which is likely, the transfer mode must be changed to binary. With sophisticated FTP clients, such as CuteFTP, the transition between transfer modes is automatic. With more basic utilities, you must manually perform the mode switch.

Unlike some of the other protocols discussed in this chapter that perform tasks transparent to the user, FTP is an application layer service frequently called upon. Therefore, it can be useful to know some of the commands supported by FTP. If you use a client such as CuteFTP, you might never need to use these commands, but they are useful to know in case you use a command-line FTP client. Table 2.3 lists some of the most commonly used FTP commands.

ExamAlert

You might be asked to identify the appropriate FTP command to use in a given situation.

TABLE 2.3 **Commonly Used FTP Commands**

Command	Description
ls	Lists the files in the current directory on the remote system
cd	Changes the working directory on the remote host
lcd	Changes the working directory on the local host
put	Uploads a single file to the remote host
get	Downloads a single file from the remote host
mput	Uploads multiple files to the remote host
mget	Downloads multiple files from the remote host
binary	Switches transfers into binary mode
ascii	Switches transfers into ASCII mode (the default)

Secure File Transfer Protocol

One of the big problems associated with FTP is that it is considered unsecure. Even though simple authentication methods are associated with FTP, it is still susceptible to relatively simple hacking approaches. In addition, FTP transmits data between sender and receiver in an unencrypted format. By using a packet sniffer, a hacker could easily copy packets from the network and read the contents. In today's high-security computing environments, you need a more robust solution.

That solution is the *Secure File Transfer Protocol (SFTP)*, which, based on *Secure Shell (SSH)* technology, provides robust authentication between sender and receiver. It also provides encryption capabilities, which means that even if packets are copied from the network, their contents remain hidden from prying eyes.

SFTP is implemented through client and server software available for all commonly used computing platforms. SFTP uses port 22 (the same port SSH uses) for secure file transfers.

Trivial File Transfer Protocol

A variation on FTP is *Trivial File Transfer Protocol (TFTP)*, which is also a file transfer mechanism. However, TFTP does not have the security capability or the level of functionality that FTP has. TFTP, which is defined in RFC 1350, is most often associated with simple downloads, such as those associated with transferring firmware to a device such as a router and booting diskless workstations.

Another feature that TFTP does not offer is directory navigation. Whereas in FTP, commands can be executed to navigate and manage the file system, TFTP offers no such capability. TFTP requires that you request not only exactly what you want but also the particular location. Unlike FTP, which uses TCP as its transport protocol to guarantee delivery, TFTP uses UDP. By default, TFTP operates on port 69.

> **ExamAlert**
>
> TFTP is an application layer protocol that uses UDP, which is a connectionless transport layer protocol. For this reason, TFTP is called a *connectionless file transfer method*.

Simple Mail Transfer Protocol

Simple Mail Transfer Protocol (SMTP), which is defined in RFC 821, is a protocol that defines how mail messages are sent between hosts. SMTP uses TCP connections to guarantee error-free delivery of messages. SMTP is not overly sophisticated and requires that the destination host always be available. For this reason, mail systems spool incoming mail so that users can read it later. How the user then reads the mail depends on how the client accesses the SMTP server. The default port used by SMTP is 25.

> **Note**
>
> SMTP can be used to both send and receive mail. Post Office Protocol version 3 (POP3) and Internet Message Access Protocol version 4 (IMAP4) can be used only to receive mail.

Hypertext Transfer Protocol

Hypertext Transfer Protocol (HTTP), which is defined in RFC 2068, is the protocol that enables text, graphics, multimedia, and other material to be downloaded from an HTTP server. HTTP defines what actions can be requested by clients and how servers should answer those requests.

In a practical implementation, HTTP clients (that is, web browsers) make requests on port 80 in an HTTP format to servers running HTTP server applications (that is, web servers). Files created in a special language such as *Hypertext Markup Language (HTML)* are returned to the client, and the connection is closed.

> **ExamAlert**
>
> Make sure that you understand that HTTP is a connection-oriented protocol that uses TCP as a transport protocol. By default, it operates at port 80.

HTTP uses a *uniform resource locator (URL)* to determine what page should be downloaded from the remote server. The URL contains the type of request (for example, http://), the name of the server contacted (for example, www.microsoft.com), and optionally the page requested (for example, /support). The result is the syntax that Internet-savvy people are familiar with: http://www.microsoft.com/support.

Hypertext Transfer Protocol Secure

One of the downsides of using HTTP is that HTTP requests are sent in clear text. For some applications, such as e-commerce, this method to exchange information is unsuitable—a more secure method is needed. The solution is *Hypertext Transfer Protocol Secure (HTTPS)*, which uses a system known as *Secure Sockets Layer (SSL)*, which encrypts the information sent between the client and host. The port changes from 80 (HTTP's default) to 443.

For HTTPS to be used, both the client and server must support it. All popular browsers now support HTTPS, as do web server products, such as Microsoft

Internet Information Services (IIS), Apache, and almost all other web server applications that provide sensitive applications. When you access an application that uses HTTPS, the URL starts with https rather than http—for example, https://www.mybankonline.com.

Post Office Protocol Version 3/Internet Message Access Protocol Version 4

Both *Post Office Protocol Version 3 (POP3)*, which is defined in RFC 1939, and *Internet Message Access Protocol Version 4 (IMAP4)*, the latest version which is defined in RFC 1731, are mechanisms for downloading, or pulling, email from a server. They are necessary because although the mail is transported around the network via SMTP, users cannot always immediately read it, so it must be stored in a central location. From this location, it needs to be downloaded or retrieved, which is what POP3 and IMAP4 enable you to do.

POP3 and IMAP4 are popular, and many people access email through applications that are POP3 and IMAP4 clients. The default port for POP3 is 110 and for IMAP4, the default port is 143.

One of the problems with POP3 is that the password used to access a mailbox is transmitted across the network in clear text. This means that if people want to, they could determine your POP3 password with relative ease. This is an area in which IMAP4 offers an advantage over POP3. It uses a more sophisticated authentication system, which makes it more difficult for people to determine a password.

ExamAlert

POP3 and IMAP4 can be used to download, or pull, email from a server, but they cannot be used to send mail. That function is left to SMTP, which can both send and receive. Also remember, POP3 uses port 110 and IMAP4 uses port 143.

Note

Although accessing email by using POP3 and IMAP4 has many advantages, such systems rely on servers to hold the mail until it is downloaded to the client system. In today's world, a more sophisticated solution to anytime/anywhere email access is needed. For many people, that solution is web-based mail. Having an Internet-based email account enables you to access your mail from anywhere and from any device that supports a web browser. Recognizing the obvious advantages of such a system, all the major email systems have, for some time, included web access gateway products.

Telnet

Telnet, which is defined in RFC 854, is a virtual terminal protocol. It enables sessions to be opened on a remote host, and then commands can be executed on that remote host. For many years, Telnet was the method by which clients accessed multiuser systems such as mainframes and minicomputers. It also was the connection method of choice for UNIX systems. Today, Telnet is still used to access routers and other managed network devices. By default, Telnet operates on port 23.

One of the problems with Telnet is that it is not secure. As a result, remote session functionality is now almost always achieved by using alternatives such as SSH.

> **ExamAlert**
>
> Telnet is used to access UNIX and Linux systems. Telnet uses port 23 and is insecure. SSH is considered the secure replacement for Telnet.

Secure Shell

Created by students at the Helsinki University of Technology, *Secure Shell (SSH)* is a secure alternative to Telnet. SSH provides security by encrypting data as it travels between systems. This makes it difficult for hackers using packet sniffers and other traffic-detection systems. It also provides more robust authentication systems than Telnet.

Two versions of SSH are available: SSH1 and SSH2. Of the two, SSH2 is considered more secure. The two versions are incompatible. If you use an SSH client program, the server implementation of SSH that you connect to must be the same version. By default, SSH operates on port 22.

Although SSH, like Telnet, is associated primarily with UNIX and Linux systems, implementations of SSH are available for all commonly used computing platforms, including Windows and Mac OS. As discussed earlier, SSH is the foundational technology for *Secure File Transfer Protocol (SFTP)*.

> **ExamAlert**
>
> Remember that SSH uses port 22 and is a more secure alternative to Telnet.

Internet Control Message Protocol

Internet Control Message Protocol (ICMP), which is defined in RFC 792, is a protocol that works with the IP layer to provide error checking and reporting functionality. In effect, ICMP is a tool that IP uses in its quest to provide best-effort delivery.

ICMP can be used for a number of functions. Its most common function is probably the widely used and incredibly useful ping utility, which can send a stream of ICMP echo requests to a remote host. If the host can respond, it does so by sending echo reply messages back to the sending host. In that one simple process, ICMP enables the verification of the protocol suite configuration of both the sending and receiving nodes and any intermediate networking devices.

However, ICMP's functionality is not limited to the use of the ping utility. ICMP also can return error messages such as "Destination unreachable" and "Time exceeded." (The former message is reported when a destination cannot be contacted and the latter when the *Time To Live [TTL]* of a datagram has been exceeded.)

In addition to these and other functions, ICMP performs source quench. In a source quench scenario, the receiving host cannot handle the influx of data at the same rate as the data is sent. To slow down the sending host, the receiving host sends ICMP source quench messages, telling the sender to slow down. This action prevents packets from dropping and having to be re-sent.

ICMP is a useful protocol. Although ICMP operates largely in the background, the ping utility makes it one of the most valuable of the protocols discussed in this chapter.

Network Time Protocol

Network Time Protocol (NTP), which is defined in RFC 958, is the part of the TCP/IP protocol suite that facilitates the communication of time between systems. NTP operates over UDP port 123. The idea is that one system configured as a time provider transmits time information to other systems that can be both time receivers and time providers for other systems.

Time synchronization is important in today's IT environment because of the distributed nature of applications. Two good examples of situations in which time synchronization is important are email and directory services systems. In each of these cases, having time synchronized between devices is important because without it there would be no way to keep track of changes to data and applications.

In many environments, external time sources such as radio clocks, *Global Positioning System (GPS)* devices, and Internet-based time servers are used as sources of NTP time. In others, the system's BIOS clock is used. Regardless of what source is used, the time information is communicated between devices by using NTP.

> **Note**
>
> Specific guidelines dictate how NTP should be used. You can find these "rules of engagement" at http://support.ntp.org/bin/view/Servers/RulesOfEngagement.

> **ExamAlert**
>
> Remember that NTP is used for time synchronization and is implemented over UDP port 123.

NTP server and client software is available for a variety of platforms and devices. If you want a way to ensure time synchronization between devices, look to NTP as a solution.

Lightweight Directory Access Protocol

Lightweight Directory Access Protocol (LDAP) is a protocol that provides a mechanism to access and query directory services systems. LDAP uses port 389. In the context of the Network+ exam, these directory services systems are most likely to be UNIX/Linux based or Microsoft Active Directory based. Although LDAP supports command-line queries executed directly against the directory database, most LDAP interactions are via utilities such as an authentication program (network logon) or locating a resource in the directory through a search utility.

Lightweight Directory Access Protocol over SSL (LDAPS), also known as Secure LDAP adds an additional layer of security. It operates at port 636 and differs from LDAP in two ways: 1) upon connection, the client and server establish

TLS session before any LDAP messages are transferred (without a start operation) and 2) the LDAPS connection must be closed if TLS closes.

> **ExamAlert**
>
> Remember that LDAP uses port 389, and LDAPS (secure LDAP) uses port 636.

H.323

H.323 is a widely accepted ITU-T standard that addresses call, multimedia, and bandwidth control for voice and videoconferencing. It operates at port 1720 and the standard addresses call signaling and control, multimedia transport and control, and bandwidth control for point-to-point and multi-point conferences.

Simple Network Management Protocol

The *Simple Network Management Protocol (SNMP)* uses port 161. It enables network devices to communicate information about their state to a central system. It also enables the central system to pass configuration parameters to the devices.

> **ExamAlert**
>
> SNMP uses port 161. It is a protocol that facilitates network management functionality. It is not, in itself, a *network management system (NMS)*, simply the protocol that makes NMS possible.

Components of SNMP

In an SNMP configuration, a central system known as a *manager* acts as the central communication point for all the SNMP-enabled devices on the network. On each device to be managed and monitored via SNMP, software called an SNMP agent is set up and configured with the manager's IP address. Depending on the configuration, the SNMP manager then communicates with and retrieves information from the devices running the SNMP agent software. In addition, the agent can communicate the occurrence of certain events to the

SNMP manager as they happen. These messages are known as *traps*. Figure 2.3 shows how an SNMP system works.

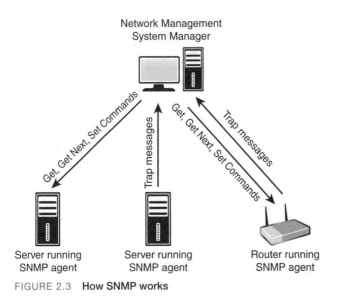

FIGURE 2.3   **How SNMP works**

As Figure 2.3 illustrates, there are a number of components to SNMP. The following discussion looks at the management system, the agents, the management information base, and communities.

SNMP Management Systems

An SNMP management system is a computer running a special piece of software called a *network management system (NMS)*. These software applications can be free, or they can cost thousands of dollars. The difference between the free applications and those that cost a great deal of money normally boils down to functionality and support. All NMS applications, regardless of cost, offer the same basic functionality. Today, most NMS applications use graphical maps of the network to locate a device and then query it. The queries are built in to the application and are triggered by pointing and clicking. You can issue SNMP requests from a command-line utility, but with so many tools available, this is unnecessary.

> **Note**
>
> Some people call SNMP managers or NMSs *trap managers*. This reference is mis-leading, however, because an NMS can do more than just accept trap messages from agents.

Using SNMP and an NMS, you can monitor all the devices on a network, including switches, hubs, routers, servers, and printers, as well as any device that supports SNMP, from a single location. Using SNMP, you can see the amount of free disk space on a server in Jakarta or reset the interface on a router in Helsinki—all from the comfort of your desk in San Jose. Such power, though, brings with it some considerations. For example, because an NMS enables you to reconfigure network devices, or at least get information from them, it is common practice to implement an NMS on a secure workstation platform such as a Linux or Windows server and to place the NMS PC in a secure location.

SNMP Agents

Although the SNMP manager resides on a PC or server, each device that is part of the SNMP structure also needs to have SNMP functionality enabled. This is performed through a software component called an *agent*.

An SNMP agent can be any device that can run a small software component that facilitates communication with an SNMP manager. SNMP agent functionality is supported by almost any device designed to be connected to a network.

In addition to providing a mechanism for managers to communicate with them, agents can tell SNMP managers when a threshold is surpassed. When this happens, on a device running an SNMP agent, a trap is sent to the NMS, and the NMS then performs an action, depending on the configuration. Basic NMS systems might sound an alarm or flash a message on the screen. Other more advanced products might dial a cell phone or send an email message.

Management Information Bases

Although the SNMP trap system might be the most commonly used aspect of SNMP, manager-to-agent communication is not a one-way street. In addition to reading information from a device using the SNMP commands Get and Get Next, SNMP managers can issue the Set command. If you have a large sequence of Get Next commands to perform, you can use the Walk command to automatically move through them. The purpose of this command is to save a manager's time: you issue one command on the root node of a subtree, and the command "walks" through, getting the value of every node in the subtree.

To demonstrate how SNMP commands work, imagine that you and a friend each have a list on which the following four words are written: four, book, sky, and table. If you, as the manager, ask your friend for the first value, she, acting as the agent, can reply "four." This is analogous to an SNMP Get command. Now, if you ask for the next value, she would reply "book." This is analogous to an SNMP Get Next command. If you then say "set green," and your friend changes the word *book* to *green*, you have performed the equivalent of an SNMP Set command. Sound simplistic? If you can imagine expanding the list to include 100 values, you can see how you could navigate and set any parameter in the list, using just those commands. The key, though, is to make sure that you and your friend have exactly the same list—which is where *Management Information Bases (MIBs)* come in.

SNMP uses databases of information called MIBs to define what parameters are accessible, which of the parameters are read-only, and which can be set. MIBs are available for thousands of devices and services, covering every imaginable need.

To ensure that SNMP systems offer cross-platform compatibility, MIB creation is controlled by the *International Organization for Standardization (ISO)*. An organization that wants to create a MIB can apply to the ISO. The ISO then assigns the organization an ID under which it can create MIBs as it sees fit. The assignment of numbers is structured within a conceptual model called the *hierarchical name tree*.

SNMP Communities

Another feature of SNMP that enables manageability is communities. *SNMP communities* are logical groupings of systems. When a system is configured as part of a community, it communicates only with other devices that have the same community name. In addition, it accepts Get, Get Next, or Set commands only from an SNMP manager with a community name it recognizes. Typically, two communities are defined by default: a public community, intended for read-only use, and a private community, intended for read-and-write operations.

ExamAlert

For the exam, you should understand the SNMP concepts of Get, Trap, Walk, and MIBS.

Whether you use SNMP depends on how many devices you have and how distributed your network infrastructure is. Even in environments that have just a few devices, SNMP can be useful because it can act as your eyes and ears, notifying you if a problem on the network occurs.

SNMPv3

SNMP, which runs by default on port 161, is now on its third version, and this version has some significant differences. One of the most noticeable changes is that, unlike SNMPv1 and SNMPv2, SNMPv3 supports authentication and encryption:

▶ **Authentication:** Authentication protocols ensure that the message is from a valid source.

▶ **Encryption:** Encryption protocols ensure that data cannot be read by unintended sources.

> **ExamAlert**
>
> You might be asked to know the differences between SNMPv2 and SNMPv3. Remember, SNMPv3 supports authentication and encryption.

Session Initiation Protocol

Long-distance calls are expensive, in part because it is costly to maintain phone lines and employ technicians to keep those phones ringing. *Voice over IP (VoIP)* provides a cheaper alternative for phone service. VoIP technology enables regular voice conversations to occur by traveling through IP packets and via the Internet. VoIP avoids the high cost of regular phone calls by using the existing infrastructure of the Internet. No monthly bills or expensive long-distance charges are required. But how does it work?

Like every other type of network communication, VoIP requires protocols to make the magic happen. For VoIP, one such protocol is *Session Initiation Protocol (SIP)*, which is an application layer protocol designed to establish and maintain multimedia sessions, such as Internet telephony calls. This means that SIP can create communication sessions for such features as audio/videoconferencing, online gaming, and person-to-person conversations over the Internet. SIP does not operate alone; it uses TCP or UDP as a transport protocol. Remember, TCP enables guaranteed delivery of data packets, whereas UDP is a fire-and-forget transfer protocol. The default ports for SIP are 5060 and 5061.

> **ExamAlert**
>
> SIP operates at the application layer of the OSI model and is used to maintain a multimedia session. SIP uses ports 5060 and 5061.

> **Tip**
>
> SIP also includes a suite of security services, which include denial-of-service pre-vention, authentication (both user-to-user and proxy-to-user), integrity protection, and encryption and privacy services.

Remote Desktop Protocol

Remote Desktop Protocol (RDP) is used in a Windows environment for remote connections. It operates, by default, on port 3389. *Remote Desktop Services (RDS,* formally known as Terminal Services) provides a way for a client system to connect to a server, such as Windows Server, and, by using RDP, operate on the server as if it were a local client application. Such a configuration is known as *thin client computing*, whereby client systems use the resources of the server instead of their local processing power.

Windows Server products and recent Windows client systems have built-in support for remote connections using the Windows program Remote Desktop Connection. The underlying protocol used to manage the connection is RDP. RDP is a low-bandwidth protocol used to send mouse movements, keystrokes, and bitmap images of the screen on the server to the client computer. RDP does not actually send data over the connection—only screenshots and client keystrokes.

Server Message Block

Server Message Block (SMB) is used on a network for providing access to resources such as files, printers, ports, and so on that are running on Windows. If you were wanting to connect Linux-based hosts to Windows-shared print-ers, for example, you would need to implement support for SMB; it runs, by default, on port 445.

One of the most common ways of implementing SMB support is by running Samba.

Understanding Port Functions

As protocols were mentioned in this chapter, the default ports were also given. Each TCP/IP or application has at least one default port associated with it. When a communication is received, the target port number is checked to determine which protocol or service it is destined for. The request is then forwarded to that protocol or service. For example, consider HTTP, whose assigned port number is 80. When a web browser forms a request for a web page, that request is sent to port 80 on the target system. When the target system receives the request, it examines the port number. When it sees that the port is 80, it forwards the request to the web server application.

TCP/IP has 65,535 ports available, with 0 to 1023 labeled as the well-known ports. Although a detailed understanding of the 65,535 ports is not necessary for the Network+ exam, you need to understand the numbers of some well-known ports. Network administration often requires you to specify port assignments when you work with applications and configure services. Table 2.4 shows some of the most common port assignments.

> **Note**
>
> Both DNS and DHCP appear in the table but were not discussed in this section. To avoid overlap with the discussion of the objectives, they are discussed in depth later in this chapter.

> **ExamAlert**
>
> You should concentrate on the information provided in Table 2.4 and apply it to any port-related questions you might receive on the exam. For example, the exam may present you with a situation in which you can't access a particular service; you may have to determine whether a port is open or closed on a firewall.

TABLE 2.4 **TCP/UDP Port Assignments for Commonly Used Protocols**

Protocol	Port Assignment
TCP Ports	
FTP	20
FTP	21
SSH/SFTP	22
Telnet	23
SMTP	25
DNS	53
HTTP	80
POP3	110
NTP	123

Protocol	Port Assignment
IMAP4	143
LDAP	389
HTTPS	443
SMB	445
LDAPS	636
H.323	1720
RDP	3389
SIP	5060
SIP	5061
UDP Ports	
DNS	53
DHCP (and BOOTP server)	67
DHCP (and BOOTP client)	68
TFTP	69
SNMP	161
RDP	3389
SIP	5060

ExamAlert

The term *well-known ports* identifies the ports ranging from 0 to 1023. When CompTIA says to "identify the well-known ports," this is what it refers to.

Note

You might have noticed in Table 2.4 that two ports are associated with FTP (and some other protocols, as well). With FTP, port 20 is considered the data port, and port 21 is considered the control port. In practical use, FTP connections use port 21. Port 20 is rarely used in modern implementations.

ARP and RARP

Address Resolution Protocol (ARP), which is defined in RFC 826, is responsible for resolving IP addresses to *Media Access Control (MAC)* addresses. When a system attempts to contact another host, IP first determines whether the other host is on the same network it is on by looking at the IP address. If IP determines that the destination is on the local network, it consults the ARP cache to see whether it has a corresponding entry. The ARP cache is a table on the local system that stores mappings between data link layer addresses (the MAC address or physical address) and network layer addresses (IP addresses). Following is a sample of the ARP cache:

```
Interface: 192.168.1.66 --- 0x8
Internet Address      Physical Address      Type
192.168.1.65          00-1c-c0-17-41-c8     dynamic
192.168.1.67          00-22-68-cb-e2-f9     dynamic
192.168.1.254         00-18-d1-95-f6-02     dynamic
224.0.0.2             01-00-5e-00-00-02     static
239.255.255.250       01-00-5e-7f-ff-fa     static
```

If the ARP cache does not have an entry for the host, a broadcast on the local network asks the host with the target IP address to send back its MAC address. The communication is sent as a broadcast because without the target system's MAC address, the source system cannot communicate directly with the target system.

Because the communication is a broadcast, every system on the network picks it up. However, only the target system replies because it is the only device whose IP address matches the request. The target system, recognizing that the ARP request is targeted at it, replies directly to the source system. It can do this because the ARP request contains the MAC address of the system that sent it. If the destination host is determined to be on a different subnet than the sending host, the ARP process is performed against the default gateway and then repeated for each step of the journey between the sending and receiving host. Table 2.5 lists the common switches used with the `arp` command.

ExamAlert

ARP links IP addressing to Ethernet addressing (MAC addressing).

TABLE 2.5 **Commonly Used ARP Command Switches**

Switch	Description
-a	Displays the entries in the ARP cache
-s	Manually adds a permanent entry to the ARP cache
-d	Deletes an entry from the ARP cache

When you work with the ARP cache, you can dynamically or statically make entries. With dynamic entries, the ARP cache is automatically updated. The ARP cache is maintained with no intervention from the user. Dynamic entries are the ones most used. Static entries are configured manually using the arp -s command. The static entry becomes a permanent addition to the ARP cache until it is removed using the arp -d command.

Reverse Address Resolution Protocol (RARP) performs the same function as ARP, but in reverse. In other words, it resolves MAC addresses to IP addresses. RARP makes it possible for applications or systems to learn their own IP address from a router or *Domain Name Service (DNS)* server. Such a resolution is useful for tasks such as performing reverse lookups in DNS. RARP is defined in RFC 903.

> **Tip**
>
> The function of ARP is to resolve a system's IP address to the interface's MAC address on that system. Do not confuse ARP with DNS or WINS, which also perform resolution functions, but for different things.

Cram Quiz

1. TCP is an example of what kind of transport protocol?

   ○ **A.** Connection oriented

   ○ **B.** Connection reliant

   ○ **C.** Connection dependent

   ○ **D.** Connectionless

2. Which of the following are considered transport protocols? (Choose the two best answers.)

   ○ **A.** TCP

   ○ **B.** IP

   ○ **C.** UDP

   ○ **D.** THC

3. What is the function of ARP?

   ○ **A.** It resolves MAC addresses to IP addresses.

   ○ **B.** It resolves NetBIOS names to IP addresses.

   ○ **C.** It resolves IP addresses to MAC addresses.

   ○ **D.** It resolves hostnames to IP addresses.

4. What is the function of NTP?

   ○ **A.** It provides a mechanism for the sharing of authentication information.

   ○ **B.** It is used to access shared folders on a Linux system.

   ○ **C.** It is used to communicate utilization information to a central manager.

   ○ **D.** It is used to communicate time synchronization information between systems.

5. Which of the following protocols offers guaranteed delivery?

   ○ **A.** FTP

   ○ **B.** POP

   ○ **C.** IP

   ○ **D.** TCP

6. Which of the following ports are associated with H.323?

   ○ **A.** 443

   ○ **B.** 1720

   ○ **C.** 636

   ○ **D.** 3389

7. By default, which protocol uses port 68?

   ○ **A.** DHCP

   ○ **B.** DNS

   ○ **C.** SMB

   ○ **D.** SMTP

8. What are SNMP databases called?

   ○ **A.** HOSTS

   ○ **B.** MIBs

   ○ **C.** WINS

   ○ **D.** Agents

9. What are logical groupings of SNMP systems known as?

   ○ **A.** Communities

   ○ **B.** Pairs

   ○ **C.** Mirrors

   ○ **D.** Nodes

10. What are two features supported in SNMPv3 and not previous versions?

   ○ **A.** Authentication

   ○ **B.** Dynamic mapping

   ○ **C.** Platform independence

   ○ **D.** Encryption

Cram Quiz Answers

1. **A.** TCP is an example of a connection-oriented transport protocol. UDP is an example of a connectionless protocol. *Connection reliant* and *connection dependent* are not terms commonly associated with protocols.

2. **A, C.** Both TCP and UDP are transport protocols. IP is a network protocol, and THC is not a valid protocol.

3. **C.** ARP resolves IP addresses to MAC addresses. Answer A describes the function of RARP, answer B describes an unrelated process, and answer D describes the process of DNS resolution.

4. **D.** NTP is used to communicate time-synchronization information between devices. Network File System (NFS) is a protocol typically associated with accessing shared folders on a Linux system. Utilization information is communicated to a central management system most commonly by using SNMP.

5. **D.** TCP is a connection-oriented protocol that guarantees delivery of data. FTP is a protocol used to transfer large blocks of data. POP stands for Post Office Protocol and is not the correct choice. IP is a network layer protocol responsible for tasks such as addressing and route discovery.

6. **B.** The default port for H.323 is 1720. HTTPS uses port 443 by default, whereas LDAPS uses 636, and RDP uses port 3389.

7. **A.** DHCP uses port 68 by default (along with 67). DNS uses port 53, SMB uses 445, and SMTP uses port 25.

8. **B.** SNMP uses databases of information called MIBs to define what parameters are accessible, which of the parameters are read-only, and which can be set.

9. **A.** SNMP communities are logical groupings of systems. When a system is configured as part of a community, it communicates only with other devices that have the same community name.

10. **A, D.** SNMPv3 supports authentication and encryption.

Network Services

▶ **Explain the functions of network services.**

CramSaver

If you can correctly answer these questions before going through this section, save time by skimming the Exam Alerts in this section and then completing the Cram Quiz at the end of the section.

1. What is the name used for ranges of IP addresses available within DHCP?

2. What is the name of the packet on a system configured to use DHCP broadcasts when it comes onto the network?

3. What is dynamic DNS?

4. Within DNS, what is the domain name, along with any subdomains, called?

Answers

1. Within DHCP, ranges of IP addresses are known as *scopes*.

2. When a system configured to use DHCP comes onto the network, it broadcasts a special packet that looks for a DHCP server. This packet is known as the DHCPDISCOVER packet.

3. Dynamic DNS is a newer system that enables hosts to be dynamically registered with the DNS server.

4. The domain name, along with any subdomains, is called the *fully qualified domain name (FQDN)* because it includes all the components from the top of the DNS namespace to the host.

Network services provide functionality enabling the network to operate. There are a plethora of services available, but four you need to know for the exam are DNS, DHCP, NTP, and IPAM.

Domain Name Service (DNS)

DNS performs an important function on TCP/IP-based networks. It resolves hostnames, such as www.quepublishing.com, to IP addresses, such as 209.202.161.67. Such a resolution system makes it possible for people to remember the names of and refer to frequently used hosts using easy-to-remember hostnames rather than hard-to-remember IP addresses. By default, DNS operates on port 53.

> **Note**
>
> Like other TCP/IP-based services, DNS is a platform-independent protocol. There-
> fore, it can be used on Linux, UNIX, Windows, and almost every other platform.

In the days before the Internet, the network that was to become the Internet used a text file called HOSTS to perform name resolution. The HOSTS file was regularly updated with changes and distributed to other servers. Following is a sample of some entries from a HOSTS file:

```
192.168.3.45      server1    s1          #The main file and print server
192.168.3.223     Mail       mailserver  #The email server
127.0.0.1         localhost
```

> **Note**
>
> A comment in the HOSTS file is preceded by a hash symbol (#).

As you can see, the host's IP address is listed, along with the corresponding hostname. You can add to a HOSTS file aliases of the server names, which in this example are s1 and mailserver. All the entries must be added manually, and each system to perform resolutions must have a copy of the file.

Even when the Internet was growing at a relatively slow pace, such a mechanism was both cumbersome and prone to error. It was obvious that as the network grew, a more automated and dynamic method of performing name resolution was needed. DNS became that method.

> **Tip**
>
> HOSTS file resolution is still supported by most platforms. If you need to resolve
> just a few hosts that will not change often or at all, you can still use the HOSTS file
> for this.

DNS solves the problem of name resolution by offering resolution through servers configured to act as name servers. The name servers run DNS server software, which enables them to receive, process, and reply to requests from systems that want to resolve hostnames to IP addresses. Systems that ask DNS servers for a hostname-to-IP address mapping are called *resolvers* or *DNS clients*.

Figure 2.4 shows the DNS resolution process. In this example, the client asks to reach the first server at mycoltd.com; the router turns to the DNS server for an IP address associated with that server; and after the address is returned, the client can establish a connection.

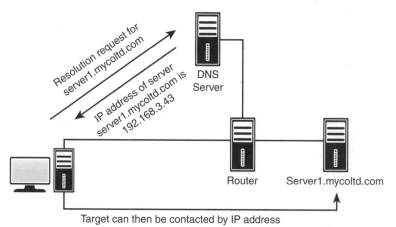

Target can then be contacted by IP address

FIGURE 2.4   **The DNS resolution process**

Because the DNS namespace (which is discussed in the following section) is large, a single server cannot hold all the records for the entire namespace. As a result, there is a good chance that a given DNS server might not resolve the request for a certain entry. In this case, the DNS server asks another DNS server if it has an entry for the host.

Note

One of the problems with DNS is that, despite all its automatic resolution capabilities, entries and changes to those entries must still be manually performed. A strategy to solve this problem is to use *Dynamic DNS (DDNS)*, a newer system that enables hosts to be dynamically registered with the DNS server. By making changes in real-time to hostnames, addresses, and related information, there is less likelihood of not finding a server or site that has been recently added or changed.

ExamAlert

You might be asked to identify the difference between DNS and DDNS.

The DNS Namespace

DNS operates in the *DNS namespace*. This space has logical divisions *hierarchically* organized. At the top level are domains such as .com (commercial) and .edu (education), as well as domains for countries, such as .uk (United Kingdom) and .de (Germany). Below the top level are subdomains or second-level domains associated with organizations or commercial companies, such as Red Hat and Microsoft. Within these domains, hosts or other subdomains can be assigned. For example, the server ftp.redhat.com would be in the redhat.com domain. Figure 2.5 shows a DNS hierarchical namespace.

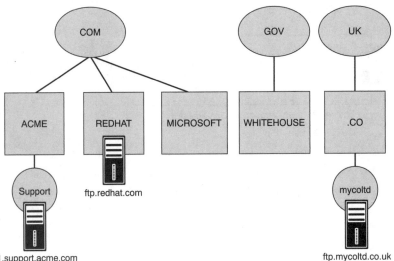

FIGURE 2.5   **A DNS hierarchical namespace**

ExamAlert

The domain name, along with any subdomains, is called the *fully qualified domain name (FQDN)* because it includes all the components from the top of the DNS namespace to the host.

Note

Many people refer to DNS as *resolving FQDNs to IP addresses*. An example of an FQDN is www.comptia.org, where www is the host, comptia is the second-level domain, and .org is the top-level domain.

The lower domains are largely open to use in whatever way the domain name holder sees fit. However, the top-level domains are relatively closely controlled. Table 2.6 lists a selection of the most widely used top-level DNS domain names. Recently, a number of top-level domains were added, mainly to accommodate the increasing need for hostnames.

TABLE 2.6 Selected Top-Level Domains in the DNS Namespace

Top-Level Domain Name	Intended Purpose
com	Commercial organizations
edu	Educational organizations/establishments
gov	U.S. government organizations/establishments
net	Network providers/centers
org	Not-for-profit and other organizations
mil	Military
arpa	Reverse DNS lookup
de	A country-specific domain—in this case, Germany*

*In addition to country-specific domains, many countries have created subdomains that follow roughly the same principles as the original top-level domains (such as co.uk and gov.nz).

Although the assignment of domain names is supposed to conform to the structure shown in Table 2.6, the assignment of names is not as closely controlled as you might think. It's not uncommon for some domain names to be used for other purposes, such as .org or .net being used for business.

> **Note**
>
> Although the primary function of DNS is to resolve hostnames to IP addresses, you can also have DNS perform IP address-to-hostname resolution. This process is called *reverse lookup*, which is accomplished by using *pointer (PTR)* records.

> **ExamAlert**
>
> For the exam, know that PTR records are used for reverse lookup functions.

Types of DNS Entries

Although the most common entry in a DNS database is an A (address) record, which maps a hostname to an IP address, DNS can hold numerous other types of entries as well. Some are the MX record, which can map entries that correspond to mail exchanger systems, and CNAME (canonical record name), which can create alias records for a system. A system can have an A record and then multiple CNAME entries for its aliases. A DNS table with all these types of entries might look like this:

```
fileserve.mycoltd.com IN   A    192.168.33.2
email.mycoltd.com      IN   A    192.168.33.7
fileprint.mycoltd.com  IN CNAME fileserver.mycoltd.com
mailer.mycoltd.com     IN   MX   10   email.mycoltd.com
```

As you can see, rather than map to an actual IP address, the CNAME and MX record entries map to another host, which DNS in turn can resolve to an IP address.

DNS Records

Each DNS name server maintains information about its zone, or domain, in a series of records, known as DNS resource records. There are several DNS resource records; each contains information about the DNS domain and the systems within it. These records are text entries stored on the DNS server. Some of the DNS resource records include the following:

- ▶ **Start of Authority (SOA):** A record of information containing data on DNS zones and other DNS records. A DNS zone is the part of a domain for which an individual DNS server is responsible. Each zone contains a single SOA record.

- ▶ **Name Server (NS):** Stores information that identifies the name servers in the domain that store information for that domain.

- ▶ **Service Locator (SRV):** This is a generalized service location record, used for newer protocols instead of creating protocol-specific records such as MX.

- ▶ **Canonical Name (CNAME):** Stores additional hostnames, or aliases, for hosts in the domain. A CNAME specifies an alias or nickname for a canonical hostname record in a *Domain Name Service (DNS)* database. CNAME records give a single computer multiple names (aliases).

- ▶ **Pointer (PTR):** A pointer to the canonical name, which is used to perform a reverse DNS lookup, in which case the name is returned when the query originates with an IP address.

> **ExamAlert**
>
> The most common type of DNS zone is the forward lookup zone, which allows DNS clients to obtain information such as IP addresses that correspond to DNS domain names. Remember that a reverse lookup zone maps from IP addresses back to DNS domain names.

▶ **IPv6 Address (AAAA):** Stores information for IPv6 (128-bit) addresses. It is most commonly used to map hostnames to an IP address for a host.

▶ **IPv4 Address (A):** Stores information for IPv4 (32-bit) addresses. It is most commonly used to map hostnames to an IP address for a host.

▶ **Text (TXT):** This field was originally created to carry human-readable text in a DNS record, but that purpose has long since passed. Today, it is more common that it holds machine-readable data, such as SPF (Sender Policy Framework), and DKIM (DomainKeys Identified Mail).

▶ **Mail Exchange (MX):** Stores information about where mail for the domain should be delivered.

> **ExamAlert**
>
> The exam objectives specifically list DNS records. You should expect to see a question about records A, MX, AAAA, CNAME, NS, SRV, TXT, or PTR.

DNS in a Practical Implementation

In a real-world scenario, whether you use DNS is almost a nonissue. If you have Internet access, you will most certainly use DNS, but you are likely to use the DNS facilities of your *Internet service provider (ISP)* rather than have your own internal DNS server—this is known as *external DNS*. However, if you operate a large, complex, multiplatform network, you might find that internal DNS servers are necessary. The major network operating system vendors know that you might need DNS facilities in your organization, so they include DNS server applications with their offerings, making third-party/cloud-hosted DNS a possibility. Google, for example, offers Cloud DNS, which is "low latency, high availability and is a cost-effective way to make your applications and services available to your users" (for more information, see https://cloud.google.com/dns/).

It is common practice for workstations to be configured with the IP addresses of two DNS servers for fault tolerance (configured via the Alternate Configuration tab in Windows, for example). The importance of DNS, particularly in environments in which the Internet is heavily used, cannot be overstated. If DNS facilities are not accessible, the Internet effectively becomes unusable, unless you can remember the IP addresses of all your favorite sites.

Windows Internet Name Service (WINS)

On Windows networks, you can use a system called WINS to enable Network Basic Input/Output System (NetBIOS) names to be resolved to IP addresses. NetBIOS name resolution is necessary on Windows networks so that systems can locate and access each other by using the NetBIOS computer name rather than the IP address. It's a lot easier for a person to remember a computer called *secretary* than to remember its IP address, 192.168.2.34. The NetBIOS name needs to be resolved to an IP address and subsequently to a MAC address (by ARP).

NetBIOS name resolution can be performed three ways on a network. The simplest way is to use a WINS server on the network that automatically performs the NetBIOS name resolution. If a WINS server is not available, NetBIOS name resolution can be performed statically using an LMHOSTS file. Using an LMHOSTS file requires that you manually configure at least one text file with the entries. As you can imagine, this can be a time-consuming process, particularly if the systems on the network frequently change. The third method, and the default, is that systems resolve NetBIOS names using broadcasts. This approach has two problems. First, the broadcasts create additional network traffic, and second, the broadcasts cannot traverse routers unless the router is configured to forward them. This means that resolutions between network segments are impossible.

Dynamic Host Configuration Protocol

One method to assign IP addresses to hosts is to use static addressing. This involves manually assigning an address from those available to you and allowing the host to always use that address. The problems with this method include the difficulty in managing addresses for a multitude of machines and efficiently and effectively issuing them.

> **ExamAlert**
>
> Be sure to know the difference between static and dynamic IP addressing as you study for the Network+ exam.

DHCP, which is defined in RFC 2131, enables ranges of IP addresses, known as *scopes* or predefined groups of addresses within *address pools* to be defined on a system running a DHCP server application. When another system configured as a DHCP client is initialized, it asks the server for an address. If all things are as they should be, the server assigns an address from the scope to the client for a predetermined amount of time, known as the *lease* or *lease time*.

At various points during the TTL of the lease time (normally the 50 percent and 85 percent points), the client attempts to renew the lease from the server. If the server cannot perform a renewal, the lease expires at 100 percent, and the client stops using the address.

In addition to an IP address and the subnet mask, the DHCP server can supply many other pieces of information; however, exactly what can be provided depends on the DHCP server implementation. In addition to the address information, the default gateway is often supplied, along with DNS information.

In addition to having DHCP supply a random address from the scope, you can configure *scope options*, such as having it supply a specific address to a client. Such an arrangement is known as a *reservation* (see Figure 2.6). Reservations are a means by which you can still use DHCP for a system but at the same time guarantee that it always has the same IP address. When based on the MAC address, this is known as *MAC reservations*. DHCP can also be configured for exclusions, also called *IP exclusions*. In this scenario, certain IP addresses are not given out to client systems.

DHCP Reservations

Reserved Addresses

Device Name	Assign IP Address	To: MAC Address	

Manually add device reservation

Add reservations by selecting from your DHCP list:

Device Name	Interface	IP Address	MAC Address	Select
Amanda's iPhone	Wireless	192.168.1.147	94:94:26:E4:81:4F	☐
Chris's iPhone	Wireless	192.168.1.134	64:9A:BE:A5:2B:24	☐
Network Device	Offline	192.168.1.136	28:EF:01:E9:8E:0E	☐
BRW0080927891B0	Wireless	192.168.1.100	00:80:92:78:91:B0	☐
ALIENBOX	LAN	192.168.1.119	00:25:64:8C:9E:BF	☐
XPS8300	LAN	192.168.1.125	78:2B:CB:A3:CF:EB	☐

Add DHCP Reservation

Ok   Cancel

FIGURE 2.6 **DHCP reservations**

The advantages of using DHCP are numerous. First, administrators do not need to manually configure each system. Second, human error, such as the assignment of duplicate IP addresses, is eliminated. Third, DHCP removes the need to reconfigure systems if they move from one subnet to another, or if you decide to make a wholesale change in the IP addressing structure. The downsides are that DHCP traffic is broadcast based and thus generates network traffic—albeit a small amount. Finally, the DHCP server software must be installed and configured on a server, which can place additional processor load (again, minimal) on that system. From an administrative perspective, after the initial configuration, DHCP is about as maintenance-free as a service can get, with only occasional monitoring normally required.

> **ExamAlert**
>
> DHCP is a protocol-dependent service and is not platform dependent. This means that you can use, for instance, a Linux DHCP server for a network with Windows clients or with Linux clients. Although the DHCP server offerings in the various network operating systems might slightly differ, the basic functionality is the same across the board. Likewise, the client configuration for DHCP servers running on a different operating system platform is the same as for DHCP servers running on the same base operating system platform.

The DHCP Process

To better understand how DHCP works, spend a few minutes looking at the processes that occur when a DHCP-enabled client connects to the network. When a system configured to use DHCP comes onto the network, it broadcasts a special packet that looks for a DHCP server. This packet is known as the DHCPDISCOVER packet. The DHCP server, which is always on the lookout for DHCPDISCOVER broadcasts, picks up the packet and compares the request with the scopes it has defined. If it finds that it has a scope for the network from which the packet originated, it chooses an address from the scope, reserves it, and sends the address, along with any other information, such as the lease duration, to the client. This is known as the DHCPOFFER packet. Because the client still does not have an IP address, this communication is also achieved via broadcast. By default, DHCP operates on ports 67 and 68.

> **ExamAlert**
>
> Remember that DHCP operates on ports 67 and 68.

When the client receives the offer, it looks at the offer to determine if it is suitable. If more than one offer is received, which can happen if more than one

DHCP server is configured, the offers are compared to see which is best. *Best* in this context can involve a variety of criteria but normally is the length of the lease. When the selection process completes, the client notifies the server that the offer has been accepted, through a packet called a DHCPREQUEST packet. At this point the server finalizes the offer and sends the client an acknowledgment. This last message, which is sent as a broadcast, is known as a DHCPACK packet. After the client system receives the DHCPACK, it initializes the TCP/IP suite and can communicate on the network.

DHCP and DNS Suffixes

In DNS, *suffixes* define the DNS servers to be used and the order in which to use them. DHCP settings can push a domain suffix search list to DNS clients. When such a list is specifically given to a client, the client uses only that list for name resolution. With Linux clients, this can occur by specifying entries in the resolve.conf file.

> ExamAlert
>
> Know that DHCP can provide DNS suffixes to clients.

DHCP Relays and IP Helpers

On a large network, the DHCP server can easily get bogged down trying to respond to all the requests. To make the job easier, *DHCP relays* help make the job easier. A DHCP relay is nothing more than an agent on the router that acts as a go-between for clients and the server. This is useful when working with clients on different subnets, because a client cannot communicate directly with the server until it has the IP configuration information assigned to it.

One level above DHCP relay is *IP helper*. These two terms are often used as synonyms, but they are not; a better way to think of it is with IP helper being a superset DHCP relay. IP helper will, by default, forward broadcasts for DHCP/BOOTP, TFTP, DNS, TACACS, the time service, and the NetBIOS name/datagram service (ports 137–139). You can disable the additional traffic (or add more), but by default IP helper will do more than a DHCP relay.

> ExamAlert
>
> Know that an IP helper can do more than a DHCP relay agent.

IP Address Management

Closely related to both DHCP and DNS, *IP Address Management (IPAM)* is a means of planning, tracking, and managing the IP addresses used in a network. IPAM integrates DNS and DHCP so that each is aware of changes in the other. It can also control reservations in DHCP and track data, such as IP addresses in use, the devices an IP is assigned to at what time, and which user an IP was assigned to. This information can be invaluable in troubleshooting connectivity problems and investigating suspected abuse. A suite of IPAM tools is available in Windows Server products. To learn more about IPAM in Windows Server visit https://technet.microsoft.com/en-us/library/hh831353(v=ws.11).aspx.

Network Time Protocol

Discussed in the ports and protocols section of this chapter, NTP is used to synchronize all participating computer systems over packet-switched, variable-latency data networks and is one of the oldest Internet protocols in current use.

Cram Quiz

1. One of the programmers has asked that DHCP always issue his workstation the same IP address. What feature of DHCP enables you to accomplish this?

   ○ **A.** Stipulation
   ○ **B.** Rider
   ○ **C.** Reservation
   ○ **D.** Provision

2. Which of the following is *not* a common packet sent during the normal DHCP process?

   ○ **A.** DHCPACK
   ○ **B.** DHCPPROVE
   ○ **C.** DHCPDISCOVER
   ○ **D.** DHCPOFFER

3. During a discussion with your ISP's technical support representative, he mentions that you might have been using the wrong FQDN. Which TCP/IP-based network service is he referring to?

   ○ **A.** DHCP
   ○ **B.** WINS
   ○ **C.** SNMP
   ○ **D.** DNS

4. Which DNS record stores additional hostnames, or aliases, for hosts in the domain?

   ○ **A.** ALSO
   ○ **B.** ALIAS
   ○ **C.** CNAME
   ○ **D.** PTR

5. Which DNS record is most commonly used to map hostnames to an IP address for a host with IPv6?

   ○ **A.** A
   ○ **B.** AAAA
   ○ **C.** MX
   ○ **D.** PTR

Cram Quiz Answers

1. **C.** Reservations are specific addresses reserved for clients.

2. **B.** DHCPPROVE is not a common packet. The other choices presented (DHCPACK, DHCPDISCOVER, and DHCPOFFER) are part of the normal process.

3. **D.** DNS is a system that resolves hostnames to IP addresses. The term *FQDN* is used to describe the entire hostname. None of the other services use FQDNs.

4. **C.** The CNAME record stores additional hostnames, or aliases, for hosts in the domain. There is not an ALSO record or ALIAS, and PTR is used for reverse lookups.

5. **B.** The AAAA record is most commonly used to map hostnames to an IP address for a host with IPv6. The A record is not used for this purpose. MX identifies the mail exchanger, and PTR is used for reverse lookup.

What's Next?

The TCP/IP suite is the most widely implemented protocol on networks today. As such, it is an important topic on the Network+ exam. Chapter 3, "Addressing, Routing, and Switching," starts by discussing one of the more complex facets of TCP/IP: addressing.

CHAPTER 3

Addressing, Routing, and Switching

This chapter covers the following official Network+ objectives:

▶ Explain the concepts and characteristics of routing and switching.

▶ Given a scenario, configure the appropriate IP addressing components.

This chapter covers CompTIA Network+ objectives 1.3 and 1.4. For more information on the official Network+ exam topics, see the "About the Network+ Exam" section in the Introduction.

Without question, the TCP/IP suite is the most widely implemented protocol on networks today. As such, it is an important topic on the Network+ exam. To pass the exam, you definitely need to understand the material presented in this chapter.

This chapter deals with the concepts that govern routing and switching. It starts, however, by discussing one of the more complex facets of TCP/IP: addressing.

IP Addressing

▶ **Given a scenario, configure the appropriate IP addressing components.**

CramSaver

If you can correctly answer these questions before going through this section, save time by skimming the Exam Alerts in this section and then completing the Cram Quiz at the end of the section.

1. How many octets does a Class A address use to represent the network portion?

2. What is the range that Class C addresses span in the first octet?

3. What are the reserved IPv4 ranges for private networks?

Answers

1. A Class A address uses only the first octet to represent the network portion, a Class B address uses two octets, and a Class C address uses three octets.

2. Class C addresses span from 192 to 223, with a default subnet mask of 255.255.255.0.

3. A private network is any network to which access is restricted. Reserved IP addresses are 10.0.0.0, 172.16.0.0 to 172.31.0.0, and 192.168.0.0.

IP addressing is one of the most challenging aspects of TCP/IP. It can leave even the most seasoned network administrators scratching their heads. Fortunately, the Network+ exam requires only a fundamental knowledge of IP addressing. The following sections look at how IP addressing works for both IPv4 and the newest version of IP: IPv6.

To communicate on a network using TCP/IP, each system must be assigned a unique address. The address defines both the number of the network to which the device is attached and the number of the node on that network. In other words, the IP address provides two pieces of information. It's a bit like a street name and house number in a person's home address.

ExamAlert

A *node* or *host* is any device connected to the network. A node might be a client computer, a server computer, a printer, a router, or a gateway.

Each device on a logical network segment must have the same network address as all the other devices on the segment. All the devices on that network segment must then have different node addresses.

In IP addressing, another set of numbers, called a subnet mask, defines which portion of the IP address refers to the network address and which refers to the node (host) address.

IP addressing is different in IPv4 and IPv6. The discussion begins by looking at IPv4.

IPv4

An IPv4 address is composed of four sets of 8 binary bits, which are called *octets*. The result is that IP addresses contain 32 bits. Each bit in each octet is assigned a decimal value. The far-left bit has a value of 128, followed by 64, 32, 16, 8, 4, 2, and 1, left to right.

Each bit in the octet can be either a 1 or a 0. If the value is 1, it is counted as its decimal value, and if it is 0, it is ignored. If all the bits are 0, the value of the octet is 0. If all the bits in the octet are 1, the value is 255, which is 128 + 64 + 32 + 16 + 8 + 4 + 2 + 1.

By using the set of 8 bits and manipulating the 1s and 0s, you can obtain any value between 0 and 255 for each octet.

Table 3.1 shows some examples of decimal-to-binary value conversions.

TABLE 3.1 **Decimal-to-Binary Value Conversions**

Decimal Value	Binary Value	Decimal Calculation
10	00001010	8 + 2 = 10
192	11000000	128 + 64 = 192
205	11001101	128 + 64 + 8 + 4 + 1 = 205
223	11011111	128 + 64 + 16 + 8 + 4 + 2 + 1 = 223

IP Address Classes

IP addresses are grouped into logical divisions called *classes*. The IPv4 address space has five address classes (A through E); however, only three (A, B, and C) assign addresses to clients. Class D is reserved for multicast addressing, and Class E is reserved for future development.

Of the three classes available for address assignments, each uses a fixed-length subnet mask to define the separation between the network and the node (host) address. A Class A address uses only the first octet to represent the network portion; a Class B address uses two octets; and a Class C address uses the first three octets. The upshot of this system is that Class A has a small number of network addresses, but each Class A address has a large number of possible host addresses. Class B has a larger number of networks, but each Class B address has a smaller number of hosts. Class C has an even larger number of networks, but each Class C address has an even smaller number of hosts. The exact numbers are provided in Table 3.2.

Be prepared for questions asking you to identify IP class ranges, such as the IP range for a Class A network.

TABLE 3.2   **IPv4 Address Classes and the Number of Available Network/ Host Addresses**

Address Class	Range	Number of Networks	Number of Hosts Per Network	Binary Value of First Octet
A	1 to 126	126	16,777,214	0xxxxxxx
B	128 to 191	16,384	65,534	10xxxxxx
C	192 to 223	2,097,152	254	110xxxxx
D	224 to 239	N/A	N/A	1110xxxx
E	240 to 255	N/A	N/A	1111xxxx

> **Note**
>
> Notice in Table 3.2 that the network number 127 is not included in any of the ranges. The 127.0.0.1 network ID is reserved for the IPv4 local loopback. The local loopback is a function of the protocol suite used in the troubleshooting process.

> **ExamAlert**
>
> For the Network+ exam, be prepared to identify into which class a given address falls. Also be prepared to identify the IPv4 loopback address. The loopback address is 127.0.0.1.

Subnet Mask Assignment

Like an IP address, a *subnet mask* is most commonly expressed in 32-bit dotted-decimal format. Unlike an IP address, though, a subnet mask performs just one function—it defines which parts of the IP address refers to the network address and which refers to the node (host) address. Each class of the IP address used for address assignment has a default subnet mask associated with it. Table 3.3 lists the default subnet masks.

TABLE 3.3 **Default Subnet Masks Associated with IP Address Classes**

Address Class	Default Subnet Mask
A	255.0.0.0
B	255.255.0.0
C	255.255.255.0

> **ExamAlert**
>
> You will likely see questions about address classes and the corresponding default subnet mask. Review Table 3.3 before taking the exam.

Subnetting

Now that you have looked at how IPv4 addresses are used, you can learn the process of subnetting. *Subnetting* is a process by which the node (host) portions of an IP address create more networks than you would have if you used the default subnet mask.

To illustrate subnetting, for example, suppose that you have been assigned the Class B address 150.150.0.0. Using this address and the default subnet mask, you could have a single network (150.150) and use the rest of the address as node addresses. This would give you a large number of possible node addresses, which in reality is probably not useful. With subnetting, you use bits from the node portion of the address to create more network addresses. This reduces the number of nodes per network, but you probably will still have more than enough.

Following are two main reasons for subnetting:

▶ It enables you to more effectively use IP address ranges.

▶ It makes IP networking more secure and manageable by providing a mechanism to create multiple networks rather than having just one. Using multiple networks confines traffic to the network that it needs to be on, which reduces overall network traffic levels. Multiple subnets also create more broadcast domains, which in turn reduces network-wide broadcast traffic. A difference exists between broadcast domains and *collision domains*: The latter is all the connected nodes, whereas the former is all the logical nodes that can reach each other. As such, collision domains are typically subsets of broadcast domains.

> **ExamAlert**
>
> Subnetting does not increase the number of IP addresses available. It increases the number of network IDs and, as a result, decreases the number of node IDs per network. It also creates more broadcast domains. Broadcasts are not forwarded by routers, so they are limited to the network on which they originate.

With *Variable Length Subnet Masking (VLSM)*, it is possible to use a different subnet mask for the same network number on different subnets. This way, a network administrator can use a long mask on networks with few hosts and a short mask on subnets with many hosts, thus allowing each subnet in a routed system to be correctly sized for the required size. The routing protocol used (EIGRP, OSPF, RIPv2, IS-IS, or BGP) must be able to advertise the mask for each subnet in the routing update, which means that it must be classless. Classless interdomain routing is discussed shortly.

Identifying the Differences Between IPv4 Public and Private Networks

IP addressing involves many considerations, not the least of which are public and private networks:

▶ A public network is a network to which anyone can connect. The best (and perhaps only pure) example of such a network is the Internet.

▶ A private network is any network to which access is restricted. A corporate network and a network in a school are examples.

> **Note**
>
> The Internet Assigned Numbers Authority (IANA) is responsible for assigning IP addresses to public networks. However, because of the workload involved in maintaining the systems and processes to do this, IANA has delegated the assignment process to a number of regional authorities. For more information, visit http://www.iana.org/numbers.

The main difference between public and private networks, other than access—a private network is tightly controlled and access to a public network is not—is that the addressing of devices on a public network must be carefully considered. Addressing on a private network has a little more latitude.

As already discussed, for hosts on a network to communicate by using TCP/IP, they must have unique addresses. This number defines the logical network that each host belongs to and the host's address on that network. On a private network with, for instance, three logical networks and 100 nodes on each network, addressing is not a difficult task. On a network on the scale of the Internet, however, addressing is complex.

If you connect a system to the Internet, you need to get a valid registered IP address. Most commonly, you obtain this address from your *Internet service provider (ISP)*. Alternatively, if you want a large number of addresses, for example, you could contact the organization responsible for address assignment in your area. You can determine who the regional numbers authority for your area is by visiting the IANA website.

Because of the nature of their business, ISPs have large blocks of IP addresses that they can assign to their clients. If you need a registered IP address, getting one from an ISP is almost certainly a simpler process than going through a regional numbers authority. Some ISP plans include blocks of registered IP addresses, working on the principle that businesses want some kind of permanent presence on the Internet. However, if you discontinue your service with the ISP, you can no longer use the provided IP address.

Private Address Ranges

To provide flexibility in addressing, and to prevent an incorrectly configured network from polluting the Internet, certain address ranges are set aside for private use. These address ranges are called *private ranges* because they are designated for use only on private networks. These addresses are special because Internet routers are configured to ignore any packets they see that use these addresses. This means that if a private network "leaks" onto the Internet, it won't get any farther than the first router it encounters. So a private address cannot be on the Internet because it cannot be routed to public networks.

Three ranges are defined in RFC 1918: one each from Classes A, B, and C. You can use whichever range you want; however, the Class A and B address ranges offer more addressing options than Class C. Table 3.4 defines the private address ranges for Class A, B, and C addresses.

TABLE 3.4 **Private Address Ranges**

Class	Address Range	Default Subnet Mask
A	10.0.0.0 to 10.255.255.255	255.0.0.0
B	172.16.0.0 to 172.31.255.255	255.255.0.0
C	192.168.0.0 to 192.168.255.255	255.255.255.0

> **ExamAlert**
>
> You can expect questions on private IP address ranges and their corresponding default subnet masks.

Classless Interdomain Routing

Classless interdomain routing (CIDR) is an IPv4 method of assigning addresses outside the standard Class A, B, and C structure. Specifying the number of bits in the subnet mask offers more flexibility than the three standard class definitions.

Using CIDR, addresses are assigned using a value known as the *slash*. The actual value of the slash depends on how many bits of the subnet mask are used to express the network portion of the address. For example, a subnet mask that uses all 8 bits from the first octet and 4 from the second would be described as /12, or "slash 12." A subnet mask that uses all the bits from the first three octets would be called /24. Why the slash? In addressing terms, the CIDR value is expressed after the address, using a slash. So, the address 192.168.2.1/24 means that the node's IP address is 192.168.2.1, and the subnet mask is 255.255.255.0.

> **Note**
>
> You can find a great CIDR calculator that can compute values from ranges at http://www.subnetcalculator.com.

> **ExamAlert**
>
> You will likely see IP addresses in their CIDR format on the exam. Be sure that you understand CIDR addressing and IPv4/IPv6 notation for the exam.

Default Gateways

Default gateways are the means by which a device can access hosts on other networks for which it does not have a specifically configured route. Most workstation configurations default to using default gateways rather than having any static routes configured. This enables workstations to communicate with other network segments or with other networks, such as the Internet.

> **ExamAlert**
>
> You will be expected to identify the purpose and function of a default gateway. You may also be asked to place the IP address of the default gateway (or other specified system) in the correct location within a performance-based question.

When a system wants to communicate with another device, it first determines whether the host is on the local network or a remote network. If the host is on a remote network, the system looks in the routing table to determine whether it has an entry for the network on which the remote host resides. If it does, it uses that route. If it does not, the data is sent to the default gateway.

> **Note**
>
> Although it might seem obvious, it's worth mentioning that the default gateway must be on the same network as the nodes that use it.

In essence, the default gateway is simply the path out of the network for a given device. Figure 3.1 shows how a default gateway fits into a network infrastructure.

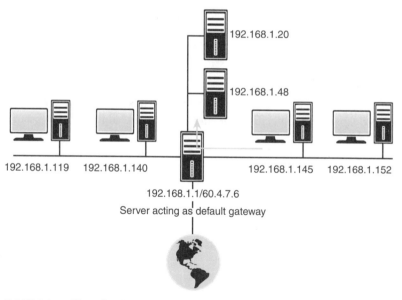

FIGURE 3.1 **The role of a default gateway**

On the network, a default gateway could be a router or a computer with network interfaces (mutihomed) for all segments to which it is connected. These interfaces have local IP addresses for the respective segments. If a system is not configured with any static routes or a default gateway, it is limited to operating on its own network segment.

> **ExamAlert**
>
> If a system is not configured with any static routes or a default gateway, it is limited to operating on its own network segment.

Virtual IP

A *virtual IP address (VIP)* is an IP address assigned to multiple applications and is often used in high availability implementations. Data packets coming in are sent to the address and that routes them to the correct network interfaces. This allows hosting of different applications and virtual appliances on servers with only one (logical) IP address.

IPv4 Address Types

IPv4 has three primary address types: unicast, broadcast, and multicast. You need to distinguish among these three types of IPv4 addresses.

Unicast Address

With a *unicast address*, a single address is specified. Data sent with unicast addressing is delivered to a specific node identified by the address. It is a point-to-point address link.

Broadcast Address

A broadcast address is at the opposite end of the spectrum from a unicast address. A *broadcast address* is an IP address that you can use to target all systems on a subnet or network instead of single hosts. In other words, a broadcast message goes to everyone on the network.

Multicast

Multicasting is a mechanism by which groups of network devices can send and receive data between the members of the group at one time, instead of separately sending messages to each device in the group. The multicast grouping is established by configuring each device with the same multicast IP address.

IPv6 Addressing

Internet Protocol version 4 (IPv4) has served as the Internet's protocol for 30 years. When IPv4 was in development more than 30 years ago, it would have been impossible for its creators to imagine or predict the future demand for IP devices and therefore IP addresses.

> **Note**
>
> There was an IPv5 after IPv4 and before IPv6, but it was an experimental protocol that never went anywhere.

Where Have All the IPv4 Addresses Gone?

IPv4 uses a 32-bit addressing scheme. This gives IPv4 a total of 4,294,967,296 possible unique addresses that can be assigned to IP devices. More than 4 billion addresses might sound like a lot, and it is. However, the number of IP-enabled devices increases daily at a staggering rate. Not all these addresses can be used by public networks. Many of these addresses are reserved and are unavailable for public use. This reduces the number of addresses that can be allocated as public Internet addresses.

The IPv6 project started in the mid-1990s, well before the threat of IPv4 limitations. Now network hardware and software are equipped for and ready to deploy IPv6 addressing. IPv6 offers a number of improvements. The most notable is its capability to handle growth in public networks. IPv6 uses a 128-bit addressing scheme, enabling a huge number of possible addresses:

340,282,366,920,938,463,463,374,607,431,768,211,456

Identifying IPv6 Addresses

As previously discussed, IPv4 uses a dotted-decimal format: 8 bits converted to its decimal equivalent and separated by periods. An example of an IPv4 address is 192.168.2.1.

Because of the 128-bit structure of the IPv6 addressing scheme, it looks quite a bit different. An IPv6 address is divided along 16-bit boundaries, and each 16-bit block is converted into a four-digit hexadecimal number and separated by colons. The resulting representation is called colon hexadecimal. Now look at how it works. Figure 3.2 shows the IPv6 address 2001:0:4137:9e50:2811:34ff: 3f57:febc from a Windows system.

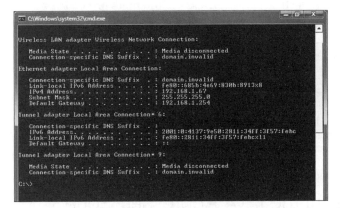

FIGURE 3.2   **An IPv6 address in a Windows dialog screen**

An IPv6 address can be simplified by removing the leading 0s within each 16-bit block. Not all the 0s can be removed, however, because each address block must have at least a single digit. Removing the 0 suppression, the address representation becomes

> 2001:0000:4137:9e50:2811:34ff:3f57:febc

Some of the IPv6 addresses you will work with have sequences of 0s. When this occurs, the number is often abbreviated to make it easier to read. In the preceding example you saw that a single 0 represented a number set in hexadecimal form. To further simplify the representation of IPv6 addresses, a contiguous sequence of 16-bit blocks set to 0 in colon hexadecimal format can be compressed to ::, known as the double colon.

For example, the IPv6 address of

> 2001:0000:0000:0000:3cde:37d1:3f57:fe93

can be compressed to

> 2001::3cde:37d1:3f57:fe93

However, there are limits on how the IPv6 0s can be reduced. 0s within the IPv6 address cannot be eliminated when they are not first in the number sequence. For instance, 2001:4000:0000:0000:0000:0000:0000:0003 cannot be compressed as 2001:4::3. This would actually appear as 2001:4000::3.

When you look at an IPv6 address that uses a double colon, how do you know exactly what numbers are represented? The formula is to subtract the number of blocks from 8 and then multiply that number by 16. For example, the address 2001:4000::3 uses three blocks: 2001, 4000, and 3. So the formula is as follows:

$$(8 - 3) \times 16 = 80$$

Therefore, the total number of bits represented by the double colon in this example is 80.

> **Note**
>
> You can remove 0s only once in an IPv6 address. Using a double colon more than once would make it impossible to determine the number of 0 bits represented by each instance of ::.

IPv6 Address Types

Another difference between IPv4 and IPv6 is in the address types. IPv4 addressing was discussed in detail earlier. IPv6 addressing offers several types of addresses, as detailed in this section.

Unicast IPv6 Addresses

As you might deduce from the name, a unicast address specifies a single interface. Data packets sent to a unicast destination travel from the sending host to the destination host. It is a direct line of communication. A few types of addresses fall under the unicast banner, as discussed next.

Global Unicast Addresses

Global unicast addresses are the equivalent of IPv4 public addresses. These addresses are routable and travel throughout the network.

Link-Local Addresses

Link-local addresses are designated for use on a single local network. Link-local addresses are automatically configured on all interfaces. This automatic configuration is comparable to the 169.254.0.0/16 APIPA automatically assigned IPv4 addressing scheme (discussed shortly). The prefix used for a link-local address is fe80::/64. On a single-link IPv6 network with no router, link-local addresses are used to communicate between devices on the link.

Site-Local Addresses

Site-local addresses are equivalent to the IPv4 private address space (10.0.0.0/8, 172.16.0.0/12, and 192.168.0.0/16). As with IPv4, in which private address ranges are used in private networks, IPv6 uses site-local addresses that do not interfere with global unicast addresses. In addition, routers do not forward site-local traffic outside the site. Unlike link-local addresses, site-local addresses are not automatically configured and must be assigned through either stateless or stateful address configuration processes. The prefix used for the site-local address is FEC0::/10.

Multicast Addresses

As with IPv4 addresses, multicasting sends and receives data between groups of nodes. It sends IP messages to a group rather than to every node on the LAN (broadcast) or just one other node (unicast).

Anycast Addresses

Anycast addresses represent the middle ground between unicast addresses and multicast addresses. Anycast delivers messages to any one node in the multicast group.

> **Note**
>
> You might encounter the terms *stateful* and *stateless* configuration. *Stateless* refers to IP autoconfiguration, in which administrators need not manually input configuration information. In a *stateful* configuration network, devices obtain address information from a server.

> **ExamAlert**
>
> Similar to stateful/stateless, *classful* and *classless* are address adjectives that are often used. Classful means that the address falls into one of the five IPv4 classes (A, B, C, D, or E), whereas classless uses the CIDR notation previously discussed.

Neighbor Discovery

IPv6 supports the Neighbor Discovery Protocol (NDP). Operating at the
network layer, it is responsible for address autoconfiguration of nodes, discovery
of other nodes on the link, determining the addresses of other nodes, duplicate
address detection, finding available routers and DNS servers, address prefix discovery, and maintaining reachability information of other active neighbor nodes.

Comparing IPv4 and IPv6 Addressing

Table 3.5 compares IPv4 and IPv6 addressing.

TABLE 3.5 **Comparing IPv4 and IPv6 Addressing**

Address Feature	IPv4 Address	IPv6 Address
Loopback address	127.0.0.1	0:0:0:0:0:0:0:1 (::1)
Network-wide addresses	IPv4 public address ranges	Global unicast IPv6 addresses
Private network addresses	10.0.0.0 172.16.0.0 192.168.0.0	Site-local address ranges (FEC0::)
Autoconfigured addresses	IPv4 automatic private IP addressing (169.254.0.0)	Link-local addresses of the FE80:: prefix

> **Note**
>
> IPv6 supports *dual stack*: This means that both IPv4 and IPv6 can run on the same network. This is extremely useful when transitioning from one to the other during the adoption and deployment phases. It also allows the network to continue to support legacy devices that may not be able to transition.

Assigning IP Addresses

Now that you understand the need for each system on a TCP/IP-based network to have a unique address, the following sections examine how those systems receive their addresses.

Static Addressing

Static addressing refers to the manual assignment of IP addresses to a system. This approach has two main problems:

▶ Statically configuring one system with the correct address is simple, but in the course of configuring, for instance, a few hundred systems, mistakes are likely. If the IP addresses are entered incorrectly, the system probably cannot connect to other systems on the network.

▶ If the IP addressing scheme for the organization changes, each system must again be manually reconfigured. In a large organization with hundreds or thousands of systems, such a reconfiguration could take a considerable amount of time. These drawbacks of static addressing are so significant that nearly all networks use dynamic IP addressing.

Dynamic Addressing

Dynamic addressing refers to the automatic assignment of IP addresses. On modern networks, the mechanism used to do this is *Dynamic Host Configuration Protocol (DHCP)*. DHCP, part of the TCP/IP suite, enables a central system to provide client systems with IP addresses. Automatically assigning addresses with DHCP alleviates the burden of address configuration and reconfiguration that occurs with static IP addressing.

The basic function of the DHCP service is to automatically assign IP addresses to client systems. To do this, ranges of IP addresses, known as *scopes*, are defined on a system running a DHCP server application. When another system configured as a DHCP client is initialized, it asks the server for an address. If all things are as they should be, the server assigns an address to the client for a predetermined amount of time, known as the *lease*, from the scope.

> **ExamAlert**
>
> As you study DHCP for the exam, make sure you know reservations, scopes, leases, options, and IP helper/DHCP relay. These topics were discussed in Chapter 2.

A DHCP server typically can be configured to assign more than just IP addresses. It often is used to assign the subnet mask, the default gateway, and *Domain Name Service (DNS)* information.

Using DHCP means that administrators do not need to manually configure each client system with a TCP/IP address. This removes the common problems associated with statically assigned addresses, such as human error. The potential problem of assigning duplicate IP addresses is also eliminated. DHCP also removes the need to reconfigure systems if they move from one subnet to another, or if you decide to make a wholesale change in the IP addressing structure.

> **ExamAlert**
>
> Even when a network is configured to use DHCP, several mission-critical network systems continue to use static addressing: DHCP server, DNS server, web server, and more. They do not have dynamic IP addressing because their IP addresses can never change. If they do, client systems may be unable to access the resources from that server.

Configuring a client for TCP/IP can be relatively complex, or it can be simple. Any complexity involved is related to the possible need to manually configure TCP/IP. The simplicity is because TCP/IP configuration can occur automatically via DHCP or through APIPA. At the least, a system needs an IP address and subnet mask to log on to a network. The default gateway and DNS server IP information is optional, but network functionality is limited without them. The following list briefly explains the IP-related settings used to connect to a TCP/IP network:

▶ **IP address:** Each system must be assigned a unique IP address so that it can communicate on the network.

▶ **Subnet mask:** Enables the system to determine what portion of the IP address represents the network address and what portion represents the node address.

▶ **Default gateway:** Enables the system to communicate on a remote network, without the need for explicit routes to be defined.

▶ **DNS server addresses:** Enables dynamic hostname resolution to be performed. It is common practice to have two DNS server addresses defined so that if one server becomes unavailable, the other can be used.

ExamAlert

At the very minimum, an IP address and subnet mask are required to connect to a TCP/IP network. With this minimum configuration, connectivity is limited to the local segment, and DNS resolution is not possible.

DHCP6 (or, more correctly, *DHCPv6*) is the IPv6 counterpart to DHCP. It issues the necessary configuration information for clients on IPv6-based networks.

BOOT Protocol (BOOTP)

BOOTP was originally created so that diskless workstations could obtain information needed to connect to the network, such as the TCP/IP address, subnet mask, and default gateway. Such a system was necessary because diskless workstations had no way to store the information.

When a system configured to use BOOTP is powered up, it broadcasts for a BOOTP server on the network. If such a server exists, it compares the MAC address of the system issuing the BOOTP request with a database of entries. From this database, it supplies the system with the appropriate information. It can also notify the workstation about a file that it must run on BOOTP.

In the unlikely event that you use BOOTP, you should be aware that, like DHCP, it is a broadcast-based system. Therefore, routers must be configured to forward BOOTP broadcasts.

Automatic Private IP Addressing

Automatic Private IP Addressing (APIPA) was introduced with Windows 98 and has been included in all subsequent Windows versions. The function of APIPA is that a system can give itself an IP address if it is incapable of receiving an address dynamically from a DHCP server. Then APIPA assigns the system an address from the 169.254.0.0 address range and configures an appropriate subnet mask (255.255.0.0). However, it doesn't configure the system with a default gateway address. As a result, communication is limited to the local network. So, if you can connect to other devices on a local network, but can't reach the Internet, for example, it is likely that your DHCP server is down and you are currently using an APIPA address.

ExamAlert

If a system that does not support APIPA cannot get an address from a DHCP server, it typically assigns itself an IP address of 0.0.0.0. Keep this in mind when troubleshooting IP addressing problems on non-APIPA platforms.

The idea behind APIPA is that systems on a segment can communicate with each other if DHCP server failure occurs. In reality, the limited usability of APIPA makes it little more than a last resort. For example, imagine that a system is powered on while the DHCP server is operational and receives an IP address of 192.168.100.2. Then the DHCP server fails. Now, if the other systems on the segment are powered on and cannot get an address from the DHCP server because it is down, they would self-assign addresses in the 169.254.0.0 address range via APIPA. The systems with APIPA addresses would talk to each other, but they couldn't talk to a system that received an address from the DHCP server. Likewise, any system that receives an IP address via DHCP cannot talk to systems with APIPA-assigned addresses. This, and the absence of a default gateway, is why APIPA is of limited use in real-world environments.

ExamAlert

Be prepared to answer APIPA questions. Know what it is and how you can tell whether you have been assigned an APIPA address and why.

Identifying MAC Addresses

Many times this book refers to MAC addresses and how certain devices use them. However, it has not yet discussed why MAC addresses exist, how they are assigned, and what they consist of.

Note

A MAC address is sometimes called a physical address because it is physically embedded in the interface (network interface card).

A MAC address is a 6-byte (48-bit) hexadecimal address that enables a NIC to be uniquely identified on the network. The MAC address forms the basis of network communication, regardless of the protocol used to achieve network connection. Because the MAC address is so fundamental to network communication, mechanisms are in place to ensure that duplicate addresses cannot be used.

To combat the possibility of duplicate MAC addresses being assigned, the *Institute of Electrical and Electronics Engineers (IEEE)* took over the assignment of MAC addresses. But rather than be burdened with assigning individual addresses, the IEEE decided to assign each manufacturer an ID and then let the manufacturer further allocate IDs. The result is that in a MAC address, the first 3 bytes define the manufacturer, and the last 3 are assigned by the manufacturer.

For example, consider the MAC address of the computer on which this book is being written: 00:D0:59:09:07:51. The first 3 bytes (00:D0:59) identify the manufacturer of the card. Because only this manufacturer can use this address, it is known as the *organizational unique identifier (OUI)*. The last 3 bytes (09:07:51) are called the *universal LAN MAC address*: They make this interface unique. You can find a complete listing of organizational MAC address assignments at http://standards.ieee.org/regauth/oui/oui.txt.

Because MAC addresses are expressed in hexadecimal, only the numbers 0 through 9 and the letters *A* through *F* can be used in them. If you get an exam question about identifying a MAC address and some of the answers contain letters and numbers other than 0 through 9 and the letters *A* through *F*, you can immediately discount those answers.

You can discover the NIC's MAC address in various ways, depending on what system or platform you work on. Table 3.6 defines various platforms and methods you can use to view an interface's MAC address.

TABLE 3.6   **Methods of Viewing the MAC Addresses of NICs**

Platform	Method
Windows	Enter `ipconfig /all` at a command prompt.
Linux/some UNIX	Enter the `ifconfig -a` command.
Cisco router	Enter the `sh int interface name` command.

ExamAlert

Be sure that you know the commands used to identify the MAC address in various operating system formats.

Just as there was fear that there would not be enough IP addresses for all the devices needed to access the Internet if we stayed with IPv4, there has also been considerable fear that there are not enough MAC addresses to assign. To deal with this, 64-bit addresses are now available. The IEEE refers to 48-bit addresses as *EUI48* (for *extended unique identifier*) and longer addresses as *EUI64*. It is projected that there are a sufficient number of 48-bit addresses to last for quite some time, but the IEEE is encouraging the adoption of the 64-bit addressing as soon as possible. The most noticeable difference between the addressing schemes is that EUI64 uses hyphens between number sets instead of colons.

ExamAlert

Be sure that you know what EUI64 is for the exam.

NAT, PAT, SNAT, and DNAT

This chapter has defined many acronyms and continues to do so with four more: NAT; PAT; SNAT; and DNAT, or port forwarding.

NAT

The basic principle of *Network Address Translation (NAT)* is that many computers can "hide" behind a single IP address. The main reason you need to do this (as pointed out earlier in the section "IP Addressing") is because there aren't enough IPv4 addresses to go around. Using NAT means that only one registered IP address is needed on the system's external interface, acting as the gateway between the internal and external networks.

Note

Don't confuse NAT with proxy servers. The proxy service is different from NAT, but many proxy server applications do include NAT functionality.

NAT enables you to use whatever addressing scheme you like on your internal networks; however, it is common practice to use the private address ranges, which were discussed earlier.

When a system is performing NAT, it funnels the requests given to it to the Internet. To the remote host, the request looks like it is originating from a single address. The system performing the NAT function keeps track of who asked for what and makes sure that when the data is returned, it is directed to the correct system. Servers that provide NAT functionality do so in different ways. For example, you can statically map a specific internal IP address to a specific external one (known as the *one-to-one NAT method*) so that outgoing requests are always tagged with the same IP address. Alternatively, if you have a group of public IP addresses, you can have the NAT system assign addresses to devices on a first-come, first-served basis. Either way, the basic function of NAT is the same.

Tunneling can be used for transmitting packets of one type (such as IPv6) over another network (such as IPv4). *6to4* is one such tunneling technology, allowing IPv6 packets to be transmitted over an IPv4 network without having to create a complex tunnel. It is often used during the transition period when a network is being updated and is not intended to be a permanent solution. Its counterpart is *4to6*.

For a more long-term solution, there is a transition technology known as *Teredo* that gives full IPv6 connectivity for IPv6-capable hosts, which are on the IPv4 Internet but lack direct native connection to an IPv6 network. The distinguishing feature of Teredo is that it can do this from behind NAT devices (such as home routers). One of the most popular Teredo implementations is *Miredo*; it is a client designed to allow full IPv6 connectivity to systems that are strictly IPv4-based.

PAT

NAT enables administrators to conserve public IP addresses and, at the same time, secure the internal network. *Port Address Translation (PAT)* is a variation on NAT. With PAT, all systems on the LAN are translated to the same IP address, but with a different port number assignment. PAT is used when multiple clients want to access the Internet. However, with not enough available public IP addresses, you need to map the inside clients to a single public IP address. When packets come back into the private network, they are routed to their destination with a table within PAT that tracks the public and private port numbers.

When PAT is used, there is a typically only a single IP address exposed to the public network, and multiple network devices access the Internet through this exposed IP address. The sending devices, IP address, and port number are not exposed. For example, an internal computer with the

IP address of 192.168.2.2 wants to access a remote web server at address 204.23.85.49. The request goes to the PAT router, where the sender's private IP and port number are modified, and a mapping is added to the PAT table. The remote web server sees the request coming from the IP address of the PAT router and not the computer actually making the request. The web server sends the reply to the address and port number of the router. When received, the router checks its table to see the packet's actual destination and forwards it.

ExamAlert

PAT enables nodes on a LAN to communicate with the Internet without revealing their IP address. All outbound IP communications are translated to the router's external IP address. Replies come back to the router, which then translates them back into the private IP address of the original host for final delivery.

SNAT

Static Network Address Translation (SNAT) is a simple form of NAT. SNAT directly maps a private IP address to a static unchanging public IP address. This enables an internal system, such as a mail server, to have an unregistered (private) IP address and still be reachable over the Internet. For example, if a network uses a private address of 192.168.2.1 for a mail server, it can be statically linked to a public IP address such as 213.23.213.85.

DNAT

To get more granular, *Destination Network Address Translation (DNAT)* can be implemented on any router to change the destination IP address on a packet (and do the inverse operation on replies). It is typically used between services located on a private network and IP addresses that are publicly accessible. It is more commonly referred to as *port forwarding*.

Note

For exam purposes, think of DNAT and port forwarding as synonyms.

Cram Quiz

1. What is the IPv6 equivalent of 127.0.0.1? (Choose two.)

   ○ **A.** 0:0:0:0:0:0:0:1

   ○ **B.** 0:0:0:0:0:0:0:24

   ○ **C.** ::1

   ○ **D.** ::24

2. Which of the following is a Class B address?

   ○ **A.** 129.16.12.200

   ○ **B.** 126.15.16.122

   ○ **C.** 211.244.212.5

   ○ **D.** 193.17.101.27

3. You are the administrator for a network with two Windows Server systems and 65 Windows desktop systems. At 10 a.m., three users call to report that they are experiencing network connectivity problems. Upon investigation, you determine that the DHCP server has failed. How can you tell that the DHCP server failure is the cause of the connectivity problems experienced by the three users?

   ○ **A.** When you check their systems, they have an IP address of 0.0.0.0.

   ○ **B.** When you check their systems, they have an IP address in the 192.168.x.x address range.

   ○ **C.** When you check their systems, they have a default gateway value of 255.255.255.255.

   ○ **D.** When you check their systems, they have an IP address from the 169.254.x.x range.

4. Which of the following address types are associated with IPv6? (Choose three.)

   ○ **A.** Broadcast

   ○ **B.** Multicast

   ○ **C.** Unicast

   ○ **D.** Anycast

5. Which of the following IP addresses is not from a private address range?

   ○ **A.** 192.168.200.117

   ○ **B.** 172.16.3.204

   ○ **C.** 127.45.112.16

   ○ **D.** 10.27.100.143

6. You have been assigned to set up a new network with TCP/IP. For the external interfaces, you decide to obtain registered IP addresses from your ISP, but for the internal network, you choose to configure systems by using one of the private address ranges. Of the following address ranges, which one would you not consider?

○ **A.** 192.168.0.0 to 192.168.255.255

○ **B.** 131.16.0.0 to 131.16.255.255

○ **C.** 10.0.0.0 to 10.255.255.255

○ **D.** 172.16.0.0 to 172.31.255.255

7. You ask your ISP to assign a public IP address for the external interface of your Windows server, which is running a proxy server application. In the email message that contains the information, the ISP tells you that you have been assigned the IP address 203.15.226.12/24. When you fill out the subnet mask field on the IP configuration dialog box on your system, what subnet mask should you use?

○ **A.** 255.255.255.255

○ **B.** 255.255.255.0

○ **C.** 255.255.240.0

○ **D.** 255.255.255.240

8. Examine the diagram shown here. What is the most likely reason that user Spencer cannot communicate with user Evan?

○ **A.** The default gateways should have different values.

○ **B.** Spencer's IP address is not a loopback address.

○ **C.** The subnet values should be the same.

○ **D.** There is no problem identifiable by the values given.

User: Evan
IP address: 192.168.1.121
Subnet mask: 255.255.255.0
Default gateway: 192.168.1.1

User: Spencer
IP address: 192.168.1.127
Subnet mask: 255.255.248.0
Default gateway: 192.168.1.1

Cram Quiz Answers

1. **A, C.** The IPv4 address 127.0.0.1 is reserved as the loopback address, and IPv6 has the same reservation. IPv6 addresses 0:0:0:0:0:0:0:0 and 0:0:0:0:0:0:0:1 are reserved as the loopback addresses. The address 0:0:0:0:0:0:0:1 can be shown using the :: notation with the 0s removed, resulting in ::1.

2. **A.** Class B addresses fall into the range 128 to 191. Answer A is the only address listed that falls into that range. Answer B is a Class A address, and answers C and D are Class C IP addresses.

3. **D.** When a Windows desktop system that is configured to obtain an IP address via DHCP fails to obtain an address, it uses APIPA to assign itself an address from the 169.254.x.x address range. An address of 0.0.0.0 normally results from a system that does not support APIPA. APIPA does not use the 192.168.x.x address range. The IP address 255.255.255.255 is the broadcast address. A DHCP failure would not lead to a system assigning itself this address.

4. **B, C, and D.** A key difference between IPv4 and IPv6 is in the address types. IPv6 addressing has three main types of addresses: unicast, multicast, and anycast. IPv4 uses broadcast addressing, but IPv6 doesn't.

5. **C.** The 127.x.x.x network range is reserved for the loopback function. It is not one of the recognized private address ranges. The private address ranges as defined in RFC 1918 are 10.x.x.x, 172.16.x.x to 172.31.x.x, and 192.168.x.x.

6. **B.** The 131.16 range is from the Class B range and is not one of the recognized private IP address ranges. All the other address ranges are valid private IP address ranges.

7. **B.** In CIDR terminology, the number of bits to be included in the subnet mask is expressed as a slash value. If the slash value is 24, the first three octets form the subnet mask, so the value is 255.255.255.0.

8. **C.** The most likely problem, given the IP values for each user's workstation, is that the subnet value is not correct on Spencer's machine and should be 255.255.255.0.

Managing TCP/IP Routing and Switching

▶ **Explain the concepts and characteristics of routing and switching.**

CramSaver

If you can correctly answer these questions before going through this section, save time by skimming the Exam Alerts in this section and then completing the Cram Quiz at the end of the section.

1. What are the most common distance-vector routing protocols?

2. What are the most common link-state protocols?

3. What is convergence?

4. What term is used when specific routes are combined into one route?

5. True or false: With the help of FSL, STP avoids or eliminates loops on Layer 2 bridges.

Answers

1. Distance-vector routing protocols include RIP, RIPv2, and EIGRP. Of these, RIPv2 would be the most popular from the exam's perspective.

2. Link-state protocols include OSPF and IS-IS.

3. Convergence represents the time it takes routers to detect change on the network.

4. The term *route aggregation* applies when specific routes are combined into one route.

5. False. With the help of Spanning Tree Algorithm (STA), STP avoids or eliminates loops on a Layer 2 bridge.

Because today's networks branch out between interconnected offices all over the world, networks may have any number of separate physical network segments connected using routers. Routers are devices that direct data between networks. Essentially, when a router receives data, it must determine the destination for the data and send it there. To accomplish this, the network router uses two key pieces of information: the gateway address and the routing tables.

The Default Gateway

A default gateway is the router's IP address, which is the pathway to any and all remote networks. To get a packet of information from one network to another, the packet is sent to the default gateway, which helps forward the packet to its destination network. Computers that live on the other side of routers are said to be on remote networks. Without default gateways, Internet communication is not possible because your computer does not have a way to send a packet destined for any other network. On the workstation, it is common for the default gateway option to be configured automatically through DHCP configuration.

Routing Tables

Before a data packet is forwarded, a chart is reviewed to determine the best possible path for the data to reach its destination. This chart is the computer's routing table. Maintaining an accurate routing table is essential for effective data delivery. Every computer on a TCP/IP network has a routing table stored locally. Figure 3.3 shows the routing table on a Windows system.

> **Note**
>
> You can use the `route print` command to view the routing table on a client system.

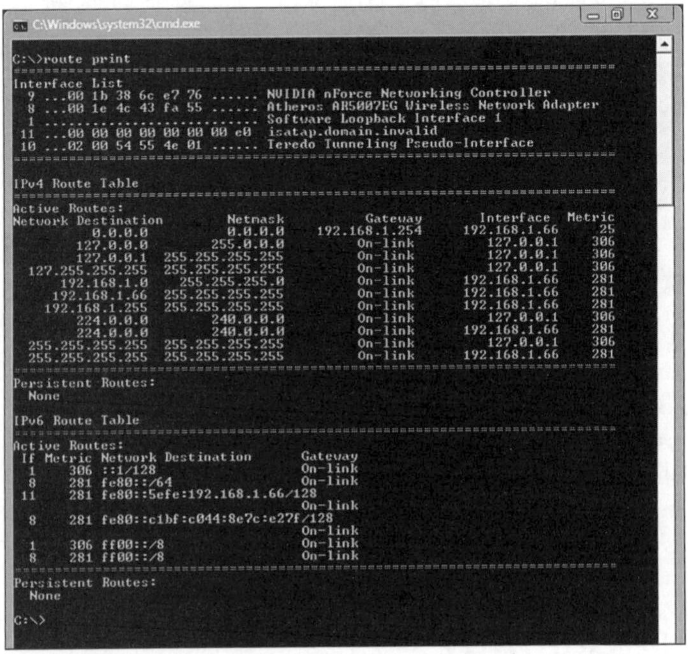

FIGURE 3.3 **The routing table on a Windows system**

As shown in Figure 3.3, the information in the routing table includes the following:

▶ **Network Destination:** The host IP address.

▶ **Netmask:** The subnet mask value for the destination parameter.

▶ **Gateway:** Where the IP address is sent. This may be a gateway server, a router, or another system acting as a gateway.

▶ **Interface:** The address of the interface that's used to send the packet to the destination.

▶ **Metric:** A measurement of the directness of a route. The lower the metric, the faster the route. If multiple routes exist for data to travel, the one with the lowest metric is chosen.

Routing tables play an important role in the network routing process. They are the means by which the data is directed through the network. For this reason, a routing table needs to be two things. It must be up to date and complete. The router can get the information for the routing table in two ways: through static routing or dynamic routing.

Static Routing

In environments that use *static routing*, routes and route information are manually entered into the routing tables. Not only can this be a time-consuming task, but also errors are more common. In addition, when a change occurs to the network's layout, or topology, statically configured routers must be manually updated with the changes. Again, this is a time-consuming and potentially error-laden task. For these reasons, static routing is suited to only the smallest environments, with perhaps just one or two routers. A far more practical solution, particularly in larger environments, is to use dynamic routing.

You can add a static route to a routing table using the route add command. To do this, specify the route, the network mask, and the destination IP address of the network card your router will use to get the packet to its destination network.

The syntax for the route add command is as follows:

```
route add 192.168.2.1 mask (255.255.255.0) 192.168.2.4
```

Adding a static address is not permanent; in other words, it will most likely be gone when the system reboots. To make it persistent (the route is still in the routing table on boot), you can use the -p switch with the command.

> **ExamAlert**
>
> The `route add` command adds a static route to the routing table. The `route add` command with the `-p` switch makes the static route persistent. You might want to try this on your own before taking the Network+ exam.

Distributed switching is typically associated with telephone networks and is nothing more than an architecture in which multiple processor-controlled switching units are distributed. In this environment, there is usually a hierarchy of switches, with a centralized host switch working with remote switches located close to concentrations of users.

Switching Methods

For systems to communicate on a network, the data needs a communication path or multiple paths on which to travel. To allow entities to communicate, these paths move the information from one location to another and back. This is the function of *switching*, which provides communication pathways between two endpoints and manages how data flows between them. Following are two of the more common switching methods used today:

▶ Packet switching

▶ Circuit switching

> **ExamAlert**
>
> You will be expected to identify the differences between packet and circuit switching methods.

Packet Switching

In packet switching, messages are broken into smaller pieces called *packets*. Each packet is assigned source, destination, and intermediate node addresses. Packets are required to have this information because they do not always use the same path or route to get to their intended destination. Referred to as *independent routing*, this is one of the advantages of packet switching. Independent routing enables better use of available bandwidth by letting packets travel different routes to avoid high-traffic areas. Independent routing also enables packets to take an alternative route if a particular route is unavailable for some reason.

> **Note**
>
> Packet switching is the most popular switching method for networks and is used on most WANs.

In a packet-switching system, when packets are sent onto the network, the sending device is responsible for choosing the best path for the packet. This path might change in transit, and the receiving device can receive the packets in a random or nonsequential order. When this happens, the receiving device waits until all the data packets are received, and then it reconstructs them according to their built-in sequence numbers.

Two types of packet-switching methods are used on networks:

▶ **Virtual-circuit packet switching:** A logical connection is established between the source and the destination device. This logical connection is established when the sending device initiates a conversation with the receiving device. The logical communication path between the two devices can remain active for as long as the two devices are available or can be used to send packets once. After the sending process has completed, the line can be closed.

▶ **Datagram packet switching:** Unlike virtual-circuit packet switching, datagram packet switching does not establish a logical connection between the sending and transmitting devices. The packets in datagram packet switching are independently sent, meaning that they can take different paths through the network to reach their intended destination. To do this, each packet must be individually addressed to determine its source and destination. This method ensures that packets take the easiest possible routes to their destination and avoid high-traffic areas. Datagram packet switching is mainly used on the Internet.

Circuit Switching

In contrast to the packet switching method, circuit switching requires a dedicated physical connection between the sending and receiving devices. The most commonly used analogy to represent circuit switching is a telephone conversation in which the parties involved have a dedicated link between them for the duration of the conversation. When either party disconnects, the circuit is broken, and the data path is lost. This is an accurate representation of how circuit switching works with network and data transmissions. The sending system establishes a physical connection, and the data is transmitted between the two. When the transmission is complete, the channel is closed.

Some clear advantages to the circuit switching technology make it well suited for certain applications, such as *public switched telephone network (PSTN)* and *Integrated Services Digital Network (ISDN)*. The primary advantage is that after a connection is established, a consistent and reliable connection exists between the sending and receiving devices. This allows for transmissions at a guaranteed rate of transfer.

Like all technologies, circuit switching has its downsides. As you might imagine, a dedicated communication line can be inefficient. After the physical connection is established, it is unavailable to any other sessions until the transmission completes. Again, using the phone call analogy, this would be like a caller trying to reach another caller and getting a busy signal. Circuit switching therefore can be fraught with long connection delays.

Comparing Switching Methods

Table 3.7 provides an overview of the various switching technologies.

TABLE 3.7 **Comparison of Switching Methods**

Switching Method	Pros	Cons	Key Features
Packet switching	Packets can be routed around network congestion. Packet switching makes efficient use of network bandwidth.	Packets can become lost while taking alternative routes to the destination. Messages are divided into packets that contain source and destination information.	The two types of packet switching are datagram and virtual circuit. Datagram packets are independently sent and can take different paths throughout the network. Virtual circuit uses a logical connection between the source and destination devices.
Circuit switching	Offers a dedicated transmission channel that is reserved until it is disconnected.	Dedicated channels can cause delays because a channel is unavailable until one side disconnects. Uses a dedicated physical link between the sending and receiving devices.	Offers the capability of storing messages temporarily to reduce network congestion.

Software-Defined Networking

Software-defined networking (SDN) is a dynamic approach to computer networking intended to allow administrators to get around the static limitations of physical architecture associated with traditional networks. This is accomplished through the implementation of technologies such as the Cisco Systems Open Network Environment.

The goal of SDN is to not only add dynamic capabilities to the network, but to also reduce IT costs through implementation of cloud architectures. SDN combines network and application services into centralized platforms that can automate provisioning and configuration of the entire infrastructure.

Dynamic Routing

In a *dynamic routing* environment, routers use special routing protocols to communicate. The purpose of these protocols is simple: They enable routers to pass on information about themselves to other routers so that other routers can build routing tables. Two types of routing protocols are used: the older distance-vector protocols and the newer link-state protocols. A third type, hybrid, combines features of these two.

> **Note**
>
> The use of any routing protocol to advertise routes that have been learned (through another protocol, through static configuration, and so on) is known as *route redistribution*.

Distance-Vector Routing

With distance-vector router communications, each router on the network communicates all the routes it knows about to the routers to which it is directly attached. In this way, routers communicate only with their router neighbors and are unaware of other routers that may be on the network.

The communication between distance-vector routers is known as *hops*. On the network, each router represents one hop, so a network using six routers has five hops between the first and last router.

The `tracert` command is used in a Windows environment to see how many hops a packet takes to reach a destination (the same functionality exists in Mac OS and Linux with the `traceroute` command). To try this at the command prompt, enter **tracert comptia.org**. Figure 3.4 shows an example of the output on a Windows workstation.

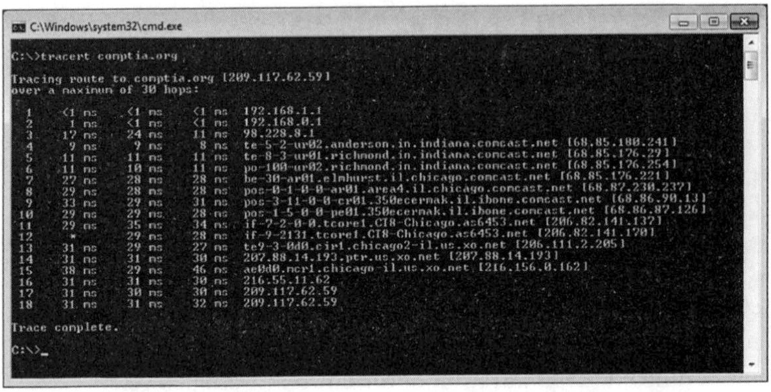

FIGURE 3.4   **The results of running** `tracert` **on a Windows system**

In addition to the `tracert` command in IPv4, you can get similar functionality in IPv6 with `tracert -6`, `traceroute6`, and `traceroute -6`.

Several distance-vector protocols are in use today, including Routing Information Protocol (RIP and RIPv2), and *Enhanced Interior Gateway Routing Protocol (EIGRP)*:

▶ **RIP:** As mentioned earlier, RIP is a distance-vector routing protocol. RIP is limited to a maximum of 15 hops. One of the downsides of the protocol is that the original specification required router updates to be transmitted every 30 seconds. On smaller networks this is acceptable; however, this can result in a huge traffic load on larger networks. The original RIP specification also did not support router authentication, leaving it vulnerable to attacks.

▶ **RIPv2:** The second version of RIP dealt with the shortcomings of the original design. Authentication was included to enable secure transmissions; also, it changed from a network-wide broadcast discovery method to a multicast method to reduce overall network traffic. However, to maintain compatibility with RIP, RIPv2 still supports a limit of 15 hops.

▶ **EIGRP:** This protocol enables routers to exchange information more efficiently than earlier network protocols. EIGRP uses its neighbors to help determine routing information. Routers configured to use EIGRP keep copies of their neighbors' routing information and query these tables to help find the best possible route for transmissions to follow. EIGRP uses *Diffusing Update Algorithm (DUAL)* to determine the best route to a destination.

ExamAlert

Be sure that you can identify the differences between the distance-vector protocols discussed here.

Distance-vector routing protocols operate by having each router send updates about all the other routers it knows about to the routers directly connected to it. The routers use these updates to compile their routing tables. The updates are sent automatically every 30 or 60 seconds. The interval depends on the routing protocol used. Apart from the periodic updates, routers can also be configured to send a *triggered update* if a change in the network topology is detected. The process by which routers learn of a change in the network topology is called *convergence*.

Routing loops can occur on networks with slow convergence. Routing loops occur when the routing tables on the routers are slow to update and a redundant communication cycle is created between routers. Two strategies can combat potential routing loops:

▶ **Split horizon:** Works by preventing the router from advertising a route back to the other router from which it was learned. This prevents two nodes from bouncing packets back and forth between them, creating a loop.

▶ **Poison reverse (also called split horizon with poison reverse):** Dictates that the route is advertised back on the interface from which it was learned, but it has a hop count of infinity, which tells the node that the route is unreachable.

ExamAlert

If a change in the routing is made, it takes some time for the routers to detect and accommodate this change. This is known as *convergence*.

Although distance-vector protocols can maintain routing tables, they have three problems:

▶ The periodic update system can make the update process slow.

▶ The periodic updates can create large amounts of network traffic—much of the time unnecessarily, because the network's topology should rarely change.

▶ Perhaps the most significant problem is that because the routers know about only the next hop in the journey, incorrect information can be propagated between routers, creating routing loops.

> **ExamAlert**
>
> Know that "next hop" in routing is the next closest router that a packet can go through.

Link-State Routing

A router that uses a link-state protocol differs from a router that uses a distance-vector protocol because it builds a map of the entire network and then holds that map in memory. On a network that uses a link-state protocol, routers send *link-state advertisements (LSAs)* that contain information about the networks to which they connect. The LSAs are sent to every router on the network, thus enabling the routers to build their network maps.

When the network maps on each router are complete, the routers update each other at a given time, just like with a distance-vector protocol; however, the updates occur much less frequently with link-state protocols than with distance-vector protocols. The only other circumstance under which updates are sent is if a change in the topology is detected, at which point the routers use LSAs to detect the change and update their routing tables. This mechanism, combined with the fact that routers hold maps of the entire network, makes convergence on a link-state-based network quickly occur.

Although it might seem like link-state protocols are an obvious choice over distance-vector protocols, routers on a link-state-based network require more powerful hardware and more RAM than those on a distance-vector-based network. Not only do the routing tables need to be calculated, but they must also be stored. A router that uses distance-vector protocols need only maintain a small database of the routes accessible by the routers to which it is directly connected. A router that uses link-state protocols must maintain a database of all the routers in the entire network.

Link-state protocols include the following:

▶ **Open Shortest Path First (OSPF):** A link-state routing protocol based on the *shortest path first (SPF)* algorithm to find the least-cost path to any destination in the network. In operation, each router using OSPF sends a list of its neighbors to other routers on the network. From this information, routers can determine the network design and the shortest path for data to travel.

▶ **Intermediate System-to-Intermediate System (IS-IS):** A link-state protocol that discovers the shortest path for data to travel using the SPF algorithm. IS-IS routers distribute topology information to other routers, enabling them to make the best path decisions.

So what's the difference between the two? OSPF (a network layer protocol) is more often used in medium to large enterprise networks because of its special tunneling features. IS-IS is more often used in large ISP networks because of its stability features and because it can support more routers.

IGP Versus EGP

Now that routing protocols have been discussed, you need to understand the difference between *interior gateway protocols (IGPs)* and *exterior gateway protocols (EGPs)*. An IGP identifies the protocols used to exchange routing information between routers within a LAN or interconnected LANs. IGP is not a protocol itself but describes a category of link-state routing protocols that support a single, confined geographic area such as a LAN. IGPs fall into two categories: distance-vector protocols, which include RIPv2, and link-state protocols, which include OSPF and IS-IS.

Whereas IGPs are geographically confined, EGPs are used to route information outside the network, such as on the Internet. On the Internet, an EGP is required. An EGP is a distance-vector protocol commonly used between hosts on the Internet to exchange routing table information. *Border Gateway Protocol (BGP)* is an example of an EGP.

Hybrid Routing Protocols

When you want the best of both worlds, distance vector and link state, you can turn to a hybrid protocol. The one hybrid protocol to know for this exam is the *Border Gateway Protocol (BGP)*. BGP can be used between gateway hosts on the Internet. BGP examines the routing table, which contains a list of known routers, the addresses they can reach, and a cost metric associated with the path to each router so that the best available route is chosen. BGP communicates between the routers using TCP. BGP supports the use of *autonomous system numbers (ASNs)*: globally unique numbers used by connected groups of IP networks that share the same routing policy.

ExamAlert

Be prepared to identify the link-state and distance-vector routing protocols used on TCP/IP networks, as well as the BGP hybrid.

Network Traffic

Network access methods govern how systems access the network media and send data. Access methods are necessary to ensure that systems on the network can communicate with each other. Without an access method, two systems could communicate at the exclusion of every other system. Access methods ensure that everyone gets an opportunity to use the network.

Several access methods are used in networks; the most popular are CSMA/CD and CSMA/CA. Look at CSMA/CD first and then CSMA/CA.

Carrier sense multiple access/collision detection (CSMA/CD), which is defined in the IEEE 802.3 standard, is the most common media access method because it is associated with 802.3 Ethernet networking, which is by far the most popular networking standard.

On a network that uses CSMA/CD, when a system wants to send data to another system, it first checks to see whether the network medium is free. It must do this because each piece of network medium used in a LAN can carry only one signal at a time. If the sending node detects that the medium is free, it transmits, and the data is sent to the destination. It seems simple.

Now, if it always worked like this, you wouldn't need the CD part of CSMA/CD. Unfortunately, in networking, as in life, things do not always go as planned. The problem arises when two systems attempt to transmit at the same time. It might seem unlikely that two systems would pick the same moment to send data, but you are dealing with communications that occur many times in a single second—and most networks have more than two machines. Imagine that 200 people are in a room. The room is silent, but then two people decide to say something at the same time. Before they start to speak, they check (listen) to see whether someone else is speaking; because no one else is speaking, they begin to talk. The result is two people speaking at the same time, which is similar to a network collision.

Collision detection works by detecting fragments of the transmission on the network media that result when two systems try to talk at the same time. The two systems wait for a randomly calculated amount of time before attempting to transmit again. This amount of time—a matter of milliseconds—is known as the *backoff* period or jam signal.

> **ExamAlert**
>
> Know that collisions do occur with CSMA. You can detect them (CD) or attempt to avoid them (CA).

When the backoff period has elapsed, the system attempts to transmit again. If the system does not succeed on the second attempt, it keeps retrying until it gives up and reports an error.

> **ExamAlert**
>
> CSMA/CD is known as a contention media access method because systems contend for access to the media.

The upside of CSMA/CD is that it has relatively low overhead, meaning that not much is involved in the workings of the system. The downside is that as more systems are added to the network, more collisions occur, and the network becomes slower. The performance of a network that uses CSMA/CD degrades exponentially as more systems are added. Its low overhead means that CSMA/CD systems theoretically can achieve greater speeds than high-overhead systems. However, because collisions take place, the chance of all that speed translating into usable bandwidth is relatively low.

> **ExamAlert**
>
> On a network that uses CSMA/CD, every node has equal access to the network media.

Despite its problems, CSMA/CD is an efficient system. As a result, rather than replace it with some other technology, workarounds have been created that reduce the likelihood of collisions. One such strategy is the use of network switches that create multiple collision domains and therefore reduce the impact of collisions on performance.

Instead of collision detection, as with CSMA/CD, the *carrier sense multiple access with collision avoidance (CSMA/CA)* access method uses signal avoidance rather than detection. In a networked environment, CSMA/CA is the access mechanism used with the 802.11 wireless standards.

On CSMA/CA networks, each computer signals its intent to transmit data signals before any data is actually sent. When a networked system detects a potential collision, it waits before sending the transmission, allowing systems to avoid transmission collisions. The CSMA/CA access method uses a random backoff time that determines how long to wait before trying to send data on the network. When the backoff time expires, the system again "listens" to verify a clear channel on which to transmit. If the medium is still busy, another backoff interval is initiated that is less than the first. The process continues until the wait time reaches zero, and the medium is clear.

CSMA/CA uses a broadcast method to signal its intention to transmit data. Network broadcasts create a considerable amount of network traffic and can cause network congestion, which could slow down the entire network. Because CSMA/CD and CSMA/CA differ only in terms of detection and avoidance, they have similar advantages and disadvantages.

ExamAlert

CSMA/CA is the access mechanism used with the 802.11 wireless standards. Know that CSMA/CA uses broadcasts.

Note

The CSMA/CA access method uses a "listen before talking" strategy. Any system wanting to transmit data must first verify that the channel is clear before transmitting, thereby avoiding potential collisions.

Routing Metrics

Following are several metrics related to routing that you should know for the exam:

▶ *Hop counts* are the number of hops necessary to reach a node. A hop count of infinity means the route is unreachable.

▶ The *maximum transmission unit (MTU)* defines the largest data unit that can be passed without fragmentation.

▶ *Bandwidth* specifies the maximum packet size permitted for Internet transmission.

▶ *Costs* are the numbers associated with traveling from point A to point B (often hops). The lower the total costs (the fewer links in the route), the more that route should be favored.

▶ *Administrative distance* is a numerical value assigned to a route based on its perceived quality. The number may be manually assigned, or assigned based on an algorithm employed by a routing protocol. The lower the number, the better the route is believed to be: 0 is the best and 255 is the worst.

▶ *Latency* is the amount of time it takes for a packet to travel from one location to another.

In the following section, we look at spanning tree protocols, but before we do, it is important to point out here that they are being replaced by *shortest path bridging (SPB)*, based on IEEE 802.1aq. The big advantage of SPB is that it allows for multiple equal cost paths, leading to faster convergence times and improving the use of mesh topologies for increased bandwidth.

Virtual Local-Area Networks

The word *virtual* is used a lot in the computing world—perhaps too often. For Virtual Local-Area Networks (VLANs), the word *virtual* does little to help explain the technology. Perhaps a more descriptive name for the VLAN concept might have been *segmented*. For now at least, use *virtual*.

> **Tip**
>
> 802.1Q is the Institute of Electrical and Electronics Engineers (IEEE) specification developed to ensure interoperability of VLAN technologies from the various vendors.

VLANs are used for network segmentation, a strategy that significantly increases the network's performance capability, removes potential performance bottlenecks, and can even increase network security. A VLAN is a group of connected computers that act as if they are on their own network segment, even though they might not be. For instance, suppose that you work in a three-story building in which the advertising employees are spread over all three floors. A VLAN can enable all the advertising personnel to be combined and access network resources as if they were connected on the same physical segment. This virtual segment can be isolated from other network segments. In effect, it would appear to the advertising group that they were on a network by themselves.

> **ExamAlert**
>
> VLANs enable you to create multiple broadcast domains on a single switch. In essence, this is the same as creating separate networks for each VLAN.

VLANs offer some clear advantages. Logically segmenting a network gives administrators flexibility beyond the restrictions of the physical network design and cable infrastructure. VLANs enable easier administration because the network can be divided into well-organized sections. Furthermore, you can increase security by isolating certain network segments from others. For example, you can segment the marketing personnel from finance or the administrators from the students. VLANs can ease the burden on overworked routers and reduce broadcast storms. Table 3.8 summarizes the benefits of VLANs.

TABLE 3.8   **Benefits of VLANs**

Advantage	Description
Increased security	With the creation of logical (virtual) boundaries, network segments can be isolated.
Increased performance	By reducing broadcast traffic throughout the network, VLANs free up bandwidth.
Organization	Network users and resources that are linked and that communicate frequently can be grouped in a VLAN.
Simplified administration	With a VLAN the network administrator's job is easier when moving users between LAN segments, recabling, addressing new stations, and reconfiguring switches and routers.

VLAN Trunking Protocol (VTP), a Cisco proprietary protocol, is used to reduce administration in the switched network. You can, for example, put all switches in the same VTP domain and reduce the need to configure the same VLAN everywhere.

Trunking falls under 802.1Q and a trunk port is one that is assigned to carry traffic for a specific switch (as opposed to an access port). The trunk port is usually fiber optic and used to interconnect switches to make a network, to interconnect LANs to make a WAN, and so on.

> **ExamAlert**
>
> IEEE 802.1Q also focuses on tagging and untagging in VLANs. *Tagging* means that the port will send out a packet with a header that has a tag number that matches its VLAN tag number. On any given port you can have just one *untagged* VLAN, and that will be the default port traffic will go to unless it is tagged to go elsewhere.

Port binding determines whether and how a port is bound. This can be done in one of three ways: static, dynamic, or ephemeral. Conversely, *port aggregation* is the combining of multiple ports on a switch, and it can be done one of three ways: auto, desirable, or on.

The *Link Aggregation Control Protocol (LACP)* is a common aggregation proto-col that allows multiple physical ports to be bound together. Most devices allow you to bind up to four, but some go up to eight.

VLAN Membership

You can use several methods to determine VLAN membership or how devices are assigned to a specific VLAN. The following sections describe the common methods to determine how VLAN membership is assigned:

▶ **Protocol-based VLANs:** With protocol-based VLAN membership, computers are assigned to VLANs using the protocol in use and the Layer 3 address. For example, this method enables a particular IP subnet to have its own VLAN.

The term *Layer 3 address* refers to one of the most important networking concepts, the Open Systems Interconnect (OSI) reference model. This conceptual model, created by the *International Organization for Standardization (ISO)* in 1978 and revised in 1984, describes a network architecture that enables data to be passed between computer systems. There are seven layers in total, which are discussed in detail in Chapter 2, "Models, Ports, Protocols, and Networking Services." In brief, Layer 3, known as the *network layer*, identifies the mechanisms by which data can be moved between two networks or systems, such as transport protocols, which in the case of TCP/IP is IP.

Although VLAN membership may be based on Layer 3 information, this has nothing to do with routing or routing functions. The IP numbers are used only to determine the membership in a particular VLAN, not to determine routing.

▶ **Port-based VLANs:** Port-based VLANs require that specific ports on a network switch be assigned to a VLAN. For example, ports 1 through 4 may be assigned to marketing, ports 5 through 7 may be assigned to sales, and so on. Using this method, a switch determines VLAN mem-bership by taking note of the port used by a particular packet. Figure 3.5 shows how the ports on a server could be used for port-based VLAN membership.

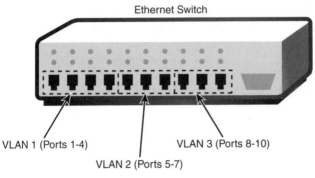

FIGURE 3.5 **Port-based VLAN membership**

▶ **MAC address-based VLANs:** The *Media Access Control (MAC)* address is a unique 12-digit hexadecimal number that is stamped into every network interface card. Every device used on a network has this unique address built in to it. It cannot be modified in any way. As you may have guessed, the MAC address type of a VLAN assigns membership according to the workstation's MAC address. To do this, the switch must keep track of the MAC addresses that belong to each VLAN. The advantage of this method is that a workstation computer can be moved anywhere in an office without needing to be reconfigured. Because the MAC address does not change, the workstation remains a member of a particular VLAN. Table 3.9 provides examples of the membership of MAC address-based VLANs.

TABLE 3.9 **MAC Address-Based VLANs**

MAC Address	VLAN	Description
44-45-53-54-00-00	1	Sales
44-45-53-54-13-12	2	Marketing
44-45-53-54-D3-01	3	Administration
44-45-53-54-F5-17	1	Sales

VLAN Segmentation

The capability to logically segment a LAN provides a level of administrative flexibility, organization, and security. Whether the LAN is segmented using the protocol, MAC address, or port, the result is the same: The network is segmented. The segmentation is used for several reasons, including security, organization, and performance. To give you a better idea of how this works, Figure 3.6 shows a network that doesn't use a VLAN.

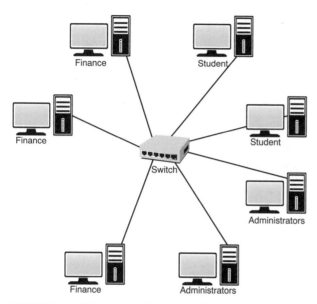

FIGURE 3.6   **Network configuration without using a VLAN**

In Figure 3.6, all systems on the network can see each other. That is, the students can see the finance and administrator computers. Figure 3.7 shows how this network may look using a VLAN.

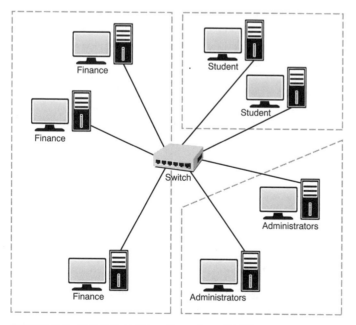

FIGURE 3.7   **Network configuration using a VLAN**

The Spanning Tree Protocol

An Ethernet network can have only a single active path between devices on a network. When multiple active paths are available, switching loops can occur. Switching loops are the result of having more than one path between two switches in a network. *Spanning Tree Protocol (STP)* is designed to prevent these loops from occurring.

STP is used with network bridges and switches. With the help of *Spanning Tree Algorithm (STA)*, STP avoids or eliminates loops on a Layer 2 bridge.

> **Note**
>
> As a heads up, talking about STP refers to Layer 2 of the OSI model. Both bridges and most switches work at Layer 2; routers work at Layer 3, as do Layer 3 switches.

STA enables a bridge or switch to dynamically work around loops in a network's topology. Both STA and STP were developed to prevent loops in the network and provide a way to route around any failed network bridge or ports. If the network topology changes, or if a switch port or bridge fails, STA creates a new spanning tree, notifies the other bridges of the problem, and routes around it. STP is the protocol, and STA is the algorithm STP uses to correct loops.

If a particular port has a problem, STP can perform a number of actions, including blocking the port, disabling the port, or forwarding data destined for that port to another port. It does this to ensure that no redundant links or paths are found in the spanning tree and that only a single active path exists between any two network nodes.

STP uses *bridge protocol data units (BPDUs)* to identify the status of ports and bridges across the network. BPDUs are simple data messages exchanged between switches. BPDUs contain information on ports and provide the status of those ports to other switches. If a BPDU message finds a loop in the network, it is managed by shutting down a particular port or bridge interface.

Redundant paths and potential loops can be avoided within ports in several ways:

- ▶ **Blocking:** A blocked port accepts BPDU messages but does not forward them.

- ▶ **Disabled:** The port is offline and does not accept BPDU messages.

- ▶ **Forwarding:** The port is part of the active spanning tree topology and forwards BPDU messages to other switches.

▶ **Learning:** In a learning state, the port is not part of the active spanning tree topology but can take over if another port fails. Learning ports receive BPDUs and identify changes to the topology when made.

▶ **Listening:** A listening port receives BPDU messages and monitors for changes to the network topology.

Most of the time, ports are in either a forwarding or blocked state. When a disruption to the topology occurs or a bridge or switch fails for some reason, listening and learning states are used.

> **ExamAlert**
>
> STP actively monitors the network, searching for redundant links. When it finds some, it shuts them down to prevent switching loops. STP uses STA to create a topology database to find and then remove the redundant links. With STP operating from the switch, data is forwarded on approved paths, which limits the potential for loops.

Interface Configuration and Switch Management

Aside from VLAN trunking (802.1Q), binding, and a number of other possibilities previously discussed in this chapter, when you configure a switch interface there are often other options that you can choose or tweak. These include the following:

▶ **Tag versus untag VLANs:** Tagging should be used if you are trunking. Because trunking combines VLANs, you need a way to identify which packet belongs to which VLAN; this is easily accomplished by placing a VLAN header (a *tag*) in the data packet. The only VLAN that is not tagged in a trunk is the *native VLAN*, and frames are transmitted to it unchanged.

▶ **Default VLAN:** The *default VLAN* is mandatory (cannot be deleted) and is used for communication between switches (such as configuring STP). In the Cisco world, the default VLAN is VLAN 1.

▶ **Port mirroring:** There are a number of reasons why port mirroring can be used (duplicating the data for one port and sending it to another). One of the most common is to monitor the traffic. This can be done locally or remotely—the latter using a remote protocol such as *Remote Switched Port Analyzer (RSPAN)* instead of *Switched Port Analyzer (SPAN)*.

▶ **Authentication, accounting, and authorization (AAA):** AAA overrides can also be configured for network security parameters as needed. AAA is the primary method for access control and often uses RADIUS, TACACS+, or Kerberos to accomplish integrated security.

▶ **Usernames/passwords:** It is possible to configure, without AAA, local username authentication using a configured username and password. This does not provide the same level of access control as AAA does and is not recommended.

▶ **Virtual consoles and terminals:** The console port (often called the *virtual console* or *VC*) is often a serial or parallel port, and it is possible for virtual ports to connect to physical ports. The *virtual terminal* (vt or vty) is a remote port connected to through Telnet or a similar utility and, as an administrator, you will want to configure an access list to limit who can use it.

ExamAlert

Know that the simplest way to protect a virtual terminal interface is to configure a username and password for it and prevent unauthorized logins.

▶ **Other:** Other common configuration parameters include the speed, whether duplexing will be used or not, IP addressing, and the default gateway.

Trunking

In computer networking, the term *trunking* refers to the use of multiple network cables or ports in parallel to increase the link speed beyond the limits of any one cable or port. Sound confusing? If you have network experience, you might have heard the term *link aggregation*, which is essentially the same thing. It is using multiple cables to increase the throughput. The higher-capacity trunking link is used to connect switches to form larger networks.

Note

Aggregation is a popular term anytime multiples are combined. The term route aggregation applies when specific routes are combined into one route, and this is accomplished in BGP with the aggregate-address command.

VLAN trunking is the application of trunking to the virtual LAN—now common with routers, firewalls, VMware hosts, and wireless access points. VLAN trunking provides a simple and cheap way to offer a nearly unlimited number of virtual network connections. The requirements are only that the switch, the network adapter, and the OS drivers all support VLANs. The *VLAN Trunking Protocol (VTP)* is a proprietary protocol from Cisco for just such a purpose.

Port Mirroring

You need some way to monitor network traffic and monitor how well a switch works. This is the function of *port mirroring*. To use port mirroring, administrators configure a copy of all inbound and outbound traffic to go to a certain port. A protocol analyzer examines the data sent to the port and therefore does not interrupt the flow of regular traffic.

> **ExamAlert**
>
> Port mirroring enables administrators to monitor the traffic outbound and inbound to the switch.

Port Authentication

Port authentication is what it sounds like—authenticating users on a port-by-port basis. One standard that specifies port authentication is the 802.1X standard, often associated with wireless security. Systems that attempt to connect to a LAN port must be authenticated. Those who are authenticated can access the LAN; those who are not authenticated get no further.

Power over Ethernet

The purpose of Power over Ethernet (PoE) is pretty much described in its name. Essentially, PoE is a technology defined by 802.3af that enables electrical power to transmit over twisted-pair Ethernet cable. This was enhanced/extended in 2009 by 802.3at (also known as *PoE+*) to be able to provide more power (increasing from 12.95W to 25.5W) and raising the maximum current (from 350mA to 600mA).

The power transfers, along with data, to provide power to remote devices. These devices may include remote switches, wireless access points, *Voice over IP (VoIP)* equipment, and more.

One of the key advantages of PoE is the centralized management of power. For instance, without PoE, all remote devices need to be independently powered.

In the case of a power outage, each of these devices requires an *uninterruptible power supply (UPS)* to continue operating. A UPS is a battery pack that enables devices to operate for a period of time. With PoE supplying power, a UPS is required only in the main facility. In addition, centralized power management enables administrators to power remote equipment up or down.

DMZ

An important firewall-related concept is the *demilitarized zone (DMZ)*, some-times called a *perimeter network*. A DMZ is part of a network where you place servers that must be accessible by sources both outside and inside your net-work. However, the DMZ is not connected directly to either network, and it must always be accessed through the firewall. The military term DMZ is used because it describes an area that has little or no enforcement or policing.

Using DMZs gives your firewall configuration an extra level of flexibility, pro-tection, and complexity. By using a DMZ, you can create an additional step that makes it more difficult for an intruder to gain access to the internal net-work. Although it is not impossible for an intruder to gain access to the internal network through a DMZ, it is difficult.

> **ExamAlert**
>
> Be prepared to identify the purpose of a DMZ.

MAC Address Table

It was mentioned earlier that the MAC (Media Access Control) address is a unique 12-digit hexadecimal number that is stamped into every network interface card. This value can be used by a switch to "switch" frames between LAN ports efficiently. When the switch receives a frame, it associates the MAC address of the sending network device with the LAN port on which it was received and dynamically builds a *MAC address table* by using the source address of the frames received. Then, when the switch receives a frame for a MAC des-tination address not listed in its address table, it floods the frame to all LAN ports of the same VLAN except the port that received the frame.

When a destination station replies, the switch adds the MAC source address and port ID to this address table. Now that it knows the value, the switch can then forward all subsequent frames to a single LAN port without flooding all LAN ports.

> **ExamAlert**
>
> For the exam, know that all Ethernet switching ports maintain MAC address tables.

Switch Management

Devices can be managed several ways: using *Simple Network Management Protocol (SNMP)*, *Windows Management Instrumentation (WMI)*, or *Intelligent Platform Management Interface (IPMI)*. If the monitoring of devices is done remotely, this is known as *out-of-band management*; otherwise, it is known as *in-band management*.

> **ExamAlert**
>
> For the exam, associate in-band management with local management (the most common method) and out-of-band management with remote.

Managed and Unmanaged

If the switch has any configuration interface or options, it is said to be *managed*. If it does not have any configuration interface or options, it is said to be *unmanaged*. Although not always the case, it is generally such that unmanaged devices are less-expensive plug-and-play devices intended for a home or small office.

Quality of Service

Quality of Service (QoS) describes the strategies used to manage and increase the flow of network traffic. QoS features enable administrators to predict bandwidth use, monitor that use, and control it to ensure that bandwidth is available to the applications that need it. These applications generally can be broken into two categories:

▶ **Latency sensitive:** These applications need bandwidth for quick delivery where network lag time impacts their effectiveness. This includes voice and video transfer. For example, *Voice over IP (VoIP)* would be difficult to use if there were a significant lag time in the conversation.

▶ **Latency insensitive:** Controlling bandwidth also involves managing latency-insensitive applications. This includes bulk data transfers such as huge backup procedures and *File Transfer Protocol (FTP)* transfers.

With bandwidth limited, and networks becoming increasingly congested, it becomes more difficult to deliver latency-sensitive traffic. If network traffic continues to increase and you cannot always increase bandwidth, the choice is to prioritize traffic to ensure timely delivery. This is where QoS comes into play. QoS ensures the delivery of applications, such as videoconferencing (and related video applications), VoIP telephony, and unified communications without adversely affecting network throughput. QoS achieves more efficient use of network resources by differentiating between latency-insensitive traffic such as fax data and latency-sensitive streaming media.

Two important components of QoS are DSCP and CoS. *Differentiated services code point* (also known as *Diffserv*) is an architecture that specifies a simple and coarse-grained mechanism for classifying and managing network traffic and providing QoS on modern networks. *Class of service (CoS)* is a parameter that is used in data and voice to differentiate the types of payloads being transmitted.

One important strategy for QoS is priority queuing. Essentially, traffic is placed in order based of its importance of delivery time. All data is given access, but the more important and latency-sensitive data is given higher priority.

> **ExamAlert**
>
> Be sure that you understand QoS and the methods used to ensure QoS on networks. Know that it is used with high-bandwidth applications such as VoIP, video applications, and unified communications.

Traffic Shaping

The demand for bandwidth on networks has never been higher. Internet and intranet applications demand a large amount of bandwidth. Administrators must ensure that despite all these demands, adequate bandwidth is available for mission-critical applications while few resources are dedicated to spam or peer-to-peer downloads. To do this, you need to monitor network traffic to ensure that data flows as you need it to.

The term *traffic shaping* describes the mechanisms used to control bandwidth usage on the network. With this, administrators can control who uses bandwidth, for what purpose, and what time of day bandwidth can be used. Traffic shaping establishes priorities for data traveling to and from the Internet and within the network.

A packet shaper essentially performs two key functions: monitoring and shaping. Monitoring includes identifying where usage is high and the time of day.

After that information is obtained, administrators can customize or shape bandwidth usage for the best needs of the network.

Access Control Lists

When it comes to computing, many things serve a similar function and go by the name of an *access control list (ACL)*. When it comes to websites, determining which ones users can or cannot access is usually done through a list of allowed or nonallowed websites. When it comes to routing and switching, an ACL provides rules that are applied to port numbers or IP addresses that are available on a host or other Layer 3 device, each with a list of hosts and/or networks permitted to use the service.

Although these two uses of ACL may seem disparate, in both cases, the ACL is the list of what is allowed by the entity trying to access. An alternative approach that can serve the same purpose is to reverse the situation and deny access to all entities (pages or ports, depending on the case) except those that appear in an "allowed" list. This approach has high administrative overhead and can greatly limit the productive benefits available.

> **ExamAlert**
>
> Remember that the ACL is a list of allowed or nonallowed services, ports, websites, and the like.

Cram Quiz

1. Which of the following best describes the function of the default gateway?

   - ○ **A.** It provides the route for destinations outside the local network.
   - ○ **B.** It enables a single Internet connection to be used by several users.
   - ○ **C.** It identifies the local subnet and formulates a routing table.
   - ○ **D.** It is used to communicate in a multiple-platform environment.

2. What is the term used for the number of hops necessary to reach a node?

   - ○ **A.** Jump list
   - ○ **B.** Link stops
   - ○ **C.** Connections
   - ○ **D.** Hop count

3. Which of the following enables administrators to monitor the traffic outbound and inbound to the switch?

    ◯ **A.** Spanning Tree Algorithm

    ◯ **B.** Trunking

    ◯ **C.** HSRP

    ◯ **D.** Port mirroring

4. Which of the following is the IEEE specification developed to ensure interoperability of VLAN technologies from the various vendors?

    ◯ **A.** 802.1z

    ◯ **B.** 802.1s

    ◯ **C.** 802.1Q

    ◯ **D.** 802.1X

5. Which of the following is a proprietary protocol from Cisco used to reduce administration in the switched network?

    ◯ **A.** VTP

    ◯ **B.** VNMP

    ◯ **C.** VCPN

    ◯ **D.** VNMC

6. Which of the following is PoE+ also known as?

    ◯ **A.** 802.3aa

    ◯ **B.** 802.3ac

    ◯ **C.** 802.3af

    ◯ **D.** 802.3at

Cram Quiz Answers

1. **A.** The default gateway enables systems on one local subnet to access those on another. Answer B does not accurately describe the role of the default gateway. Answers C and D do not describe the main function of a default gateway, which is to provide the route for destinations outside the local network.

2. **D.** The hop count is the number of hops necessary to reach a node.

3. **D.** Port mirroring enables administrators to monitor the traffic outbound and inbound to the switch.

4. **C.** 802.1Q is the IEEE specification developed to ensure interoperability of VLAN technologies from the various vendors.

5. **A.** *VLAN Trunking Protocol (VTP)* is used to reduce administration in the switched network.

6. **D.** IEEE 802.3at is more commonly known as PoE+.

What's Next?

Chapter 4, "Network Components and Devices," introduces you to commonly used networking devices. All but the most basic of networks require devices to provide connectivity and functionality. Understanding how these networking devices operate and identifying the functions they perform are essential skills for any network administrator and are requirements for a Network+ candidate.

CHAPTER 4

Network Components and Devices

This chapter covers the following official Network+ objectives:

▶ Given a scenario, determine the appropriate placement of networking devices on a network and install/configure them.

▶ Explain the purposes and use cases for advanced network devices.

This chapter covers CompTIA Network+ objectives 2.2 and 2.3. For more information on the official Network+ exam topics, see the "About the Network+ Exam" section in the Introduction.

All but the most basic of networks require devices to provide connectivity and functionality. Understanding how these networking devices operate and identifying the functions they perform are essential skills for any network administrator and are requirements for a Network+ candidate.

This chapter introduces commonly used networking devices. You are not likely to encounter all the devices mentioned in this chapter on the exam, but you can expect to work with at least some of them.

Common Network Devices

▶ **Given a scenario, determine the appropriate placement of networking devices on a network and install/configure them.**

CramSaver

If you can correctly answer these questions before going through this section, save time by skimming the Exam Alerts in this section and then completing the Cram Quiz at the end of the section.

1. What is the difference between an active and a passive hub?

2. What is the major difference between a hub and a switch?

3. What are the types of ports found on hubs and switches?

Answers

1. Hubs can be either active or passive. Hubs are considered active when they regenerate a signal before forwarding it to all the ports on the device.

2. Rather than forwarding data to all the connected ports, a switch forwards data only to the port on which the destination system is connected.

3. Hubs and switches have two types of ports: *Medium-Dependent Interface (MDI)* and *Medium-Dependent Interface Crossed (MDI-X)*.

The best way to think about this chapter is as a catalog of networking devices. The first half looks at devices that you can commonly find in a network of any substantial size. The devices are discussed in alphabetical order to simplify study and include everything from access points to VPN concentrators.

ExamAlert

Remember that this objective begins with "Given a scenario." That means that you may receive a drag and drop, matching, or "live OS" scenario where you have to click through to complete a specific objective-based task.

Firewall

A *firewall* is a networking device, either hardware or software based, that controls access to your organization's network. This controlled access is designed to protect data and resources from an outside threat. To do this, firewalls typically are placed at a network's entry/exit points—for example, between an internal network and the Internet. After it is in place, a firewall can control access into and out of that point.

Although firewalls typically protect internal networks from public networks, they are also used to control access between specific network segments within a network. An example is placing a firewall between the Accounts and Sales departments.

As mentioned, firewalls can be implemented through software or through a dedicated hardware device. Organizations implement software firewalls through *network operating systems (NOSs)* such as Linux/UNIX, Windows Servers, and Mac OS servers. The firewall is configured on the server to allow or block certain types of network traffic. In small offices and for regular home use, a firewall is commonly installed on the local system and is configured to control traffic. Many third-party firewalls are available.

Hardware firewalls are used in networks of all sizes today. Hardware firewalls are often dedicated network devices that can be implemented with little configuration. They protect all systems behind the firewall from outside sources. Hardware firewalls are readily available and often are combined with other devices today. For example, many broadband routers and wireless access points have firewall functionality built in. In such a case, the router or AP might have a number of ports available to plug systems into.

> **ExamAlert**
>
> Remember that a firewall can protect internal networks from public networks and control access between specific network segments.

Router

In a common configuration, routers create larger networks by joining two network segments. A *small office/home office (SOHO)* router connects a user to the Internet. A SOHO router typically serves 1 to 10 users on the system. A router can be a dedicated hardware device or a computer system with more than one network interface and the appropriate routing software. All modern network operating systems include the functionality to act as a router.

> **Note**
>
> Routers normally create, add, or divide networks or network segments at the network layer of the OSI reference model because they normally are IP-based devices. Chapter 2, "Models, Ports, Protocols, and Networking Services," covers the OSI reference model in greater detail.

A router derives its name from the fact that it can route data it receives from one network to another. When a router receives a packet of data, it reads the packet's header to determine the destination address. After the router has determined the address, it looks in its routing table to determine whether it knows how to reach the destination; if it does, it forwards the packet to the next hop on the route. The next hop might be the final destination, or it might be another router. Figure 4.1 shows, in basic terms, how a router works.

> **Note**
>
> You can find more information on network routing in Chapter 3.

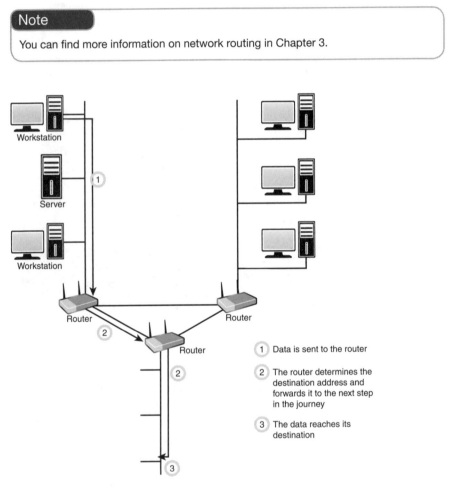

FIGURE 4.1   **How a router works**

A router works at Layer 3 (the network layer) of the OSI model.

Switch

Like hubs, *switches* are the connectivity points of an Ethernet network. Devices connect to switches via twisted-pair cabling, one cable for each device. The difference between hubs and switches is in how the devices deal with the data they receive. Whereas a hub forwards the data it receives to all the ports on the device, a switch forwards it to only the port that connects to the destination device. It does this by the MAC address of the devices attached to it and then by matching the destination MAC address in the data it receives. Figure 4.2 shows how a switch works. In this case, it has learned the MAC addresses of the devices attached to it; when the workstation sends a message intended for another workstation, it forwards the message on and ignores all the other workstations.

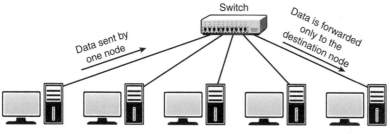

FIGURE 4.2   **How a switch works**

By forwarding data to only the connection that should receive it, the switch can greatly improve network performance. By creating a direct path between two devices and controlling their communication, the switch can greatly reduce the traffic on the network and therefore the number of collisions. As you might recall, collisions occur on Ethernet networks when two devices attempt to transmit at the same time. In addition, the lack of collisions enables switches to communicate with devices in full-duplex mode. In a full-duplex configuration, devices can send data to and receive data from the switch at the same time. Contrast this with half-duplex communication, in which communication can occur in only one direction at a time. Full-duplex transmission speeds are double that of a standard half-duplex connection. So, a 100 Mbps connection becomes 200 Mbps, and a 1000 Mbps connection becomes 2000 Mbps, and so on.

The net result of these measures is that switches can offer significant performance improvements over hub-based networks, particularly when network use is high.

Irrespective of whether a connection is at full or half duplex, the method of switching dictates how the switch deals with the data it receives. The following is a brief explanation of each method:

▶ **Cut-through:** In a cut-through switching environment, the packet begins to be forwarded as soon as it is received. This method is fast, but it creates the possibility of errors being propagated through the network because no error checking occurs.

▶ **Store-and-forward:** Unlike cut-through, in a store-and-forward switching environment, the entire packet is received and error-checked before being forwarded. The upside of this method is that errors are not propagated through the network. The downside is that the error-checking process takes a relatively long time, and store-and-forward switching is considerably slower as a result.

▶ **Fragment-free:** To take advantage of the error checking of store-and-forward switching, but still offer performance levels nearing that of cut-through switching, fragment-free switching can be used. In a fragment-free switching environment, enough of the packet is read so that the switch can determine whether the packet has been involved in a collision. As soon as the collision status has been determined, the packet is forwarded.

Hub and Switch Cabling

In addition to acting as a connection point for network devices, hubs and switches can be connected to create larger networks. This connection can be achieved through standard ports with a special cable or by using special ports with a standard cable.

The ports on a hub to which computer systems are attached are called *Medium-Dependent Interface Crossed (MDI-X)*. The crossed designation is derived from the fact that two of the wires within the connection are crossed so that the send signal wire on one device becomes the receive signal of the other. Because the ports are crossed internally, a standard or straight-through cable can be used to connect devices.

Another type of port, called a *Medium-Dependent Interface (MDI)* port, is often included on a hub or switch to facilitate the connection of two switches or hubs. Because the hubs or switches are designed to see each other as an extension of the network, there is no need for the signal to be crossed. If a hub or switch does not have an MDI port, hubs or switches can be connected by using a cable between two MDI-X ports. The crossover cable uncrosses the internal crossing. Auto MDI-X ports on more modern network device interfaces can detect whether the connection would require a crossover, and automatically choose the MDI or MDI-X configuration to properly match the other end of the link.

> **ExamAlert**
>
> In a crossover cable, wires 1 and 3 and wires 2 and 6 are crossed.

A switch can work at either Layer 2 (the data link layer) or Layer 3 (the network layer) of the OSI model.

Hub

At the bottom of the networking food chain, so to speak, are hubs. Hubs are used in networks that use twisted-pair cabling to connect devices. Hubs also can be joined to create larger networks. *Hubs* are simple devices that direct data packets to all devices connected to the hub, regardless of whether the data package is destined for the device. This makes them inefficient devices and can create a performance bottleneck on busy networks.

In its most basic form, a hub does nothing except provide a pathway for the electrical signals to travel along. Such a device is called a *passive* hub. Far more common nowadays is an *active* hub, which, as well as providing a path for the data signals, regenerates the signal before it forwards it to all the connected devices. In addition, an active hub can buffer data before forwarding it. However, a hub does not perform any processing on the data it forwards, nor does it perform any error checking.

Hubs come in a variety of shapes and sizes. Small hubs with five or eight connection ports are commonly called *workgroup hubs*. Others can accommodate larger numbers of devices (normally up to 32). These are called *high-density devices*.

> **ExamAlert**
>
> Because hubs don't perform any processing, they do little except enable communication between connected devices. For today's high-demand network applications, something with a little more intelligence is required. That's where switches come in.

A basic hub works at Layer 1 (the physical layer) of the OSI model.

Bridge

A *bridge*, as the name implies, connects two networks. Bridging is done at the first two layers of the OSI model and differs from routing in its simplicity. With routing, a packet is sent to where it is intended to go, whereas with bridging, it is sent away from this network. In other words, if a packet does not belong on this network, it is sent across the bridge with the assumption that it belongs there rather than here.

If one or more segments of the bridged network are wireless, the device is known as a *wireless bridge*.

Modems

A modem (short for modulator/demodulator) is a device that converts the digital signals generated by a computer into analog signals that can travel over conventional phone lines. The modem at the receiving end converts the signal back into a format that the computer can understand. Modems can be used as a means to connect to an ISP or as a mechanism for dialing up a LAN.

Modems can be internal add-in expansion cards or integrated with the motherboard, external devices that connect to a system's serial or USB port, or proprietary devices designed for use on other devices, such as portables and handhelds.

Wireless Access Point

The term *access point* can technically be used for either a wired or wireless connection, but in reality it is almost always associated only with a wireless-enabling device. Wireless *access points (APs)* are a transmitter and receiver (transceiver) device used to create a *wireless LAN (WLAN)*. APs typically are a separate network device with a built-in antenna, transmitter, and adapter. APs use the wireless infrastructure network mode to provide a connection point between WLANs and a wired Ethernet LAN. APs also usually have several ports, giving you a way to expand the network to support additional clients.

Depending on the size of the network, one or more APs might be required. Additional APs are used to allow access to more wireless clients and to expand the range of the wireless network. Each AP is limited by a transmission range—the distance a client can be from an AP and still obtain a usable signal. The actual distance depends on the wireless standard used and the obstructions and environmental conditions between the client and the AP.

> **ExamAlert**
>
> An AP can operate as a bridge connecting a standard wired network to wireless devices or as a router passing data transmissions from one access point to another.

Saying that an AP is used to extend a wired LAN to wireless clients does not give you the complete picture. A wireless AP today can provide different services in addition to just an access point. Today, the APs might provide many ports that can be used to easily increase the network's size. Systems can be added to and removed from the network with no effect on other systems on the network. Also, many APs provide firewall capabilities and *Dynamic Host Configuration Protocol (DHCP)* service. When they are hooked up, they give client systems a private IP address and then prevent Internet traffic from accessing those systems. So, in effect, the AP is a switch, DHCP server, router, and firewall.

APs come in all shapes and sizes. Many are cheaper and are designed strictly for home or small office use. Such APs have low-powered antennas and limited expansion ports. Higher-end APs used for commercial purposes have high-powered antennas, enabling them to extend how far the wireless signal can travel.

> **Note**
>
> APs are used to create a wireless LAN and to extend a wired network. APs are used in the infrastructure wireless topology.

An AP works at Layer 2 (the data link layer) of the OSI model.

Media Converter

When you have two dissimilar types of network media, a *media converter* is used to allow them to connect. They are sometimes referred to as couplers. Depending on the conversion being done, the converter can be a small device, barely larger than the connectors themselves, or a large device within a sizable chassis.

Reasons for not using the same media throughout the network, and thus reasons for needing a converter, can range from cost (gradually moving from coax to fiber), disparate segments (connecting the office to the factory), or needing to run a particular media in a setting (the need for fiber to reduce EMI problems in a small part of the building).

Figure 4.3 shows an example of a media converter. The one shown converts between 10/100/1000TX and 1000LX (with an SC-type connector).

FIGURE 4.3 **A common media converter**

The following converters are commonly implemented and are ones that CompTIA has previously included on the Network+ exam.

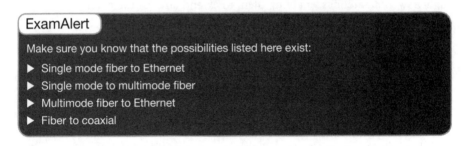

ExamAlert

Make sure you know that the possibilities listed here exist:

▶ Single mode fiber to Ethernet

▶ Single mode to multimode fiber

▶ Multimode fiber to Ethernet

▶ Fiber to coaxial

Wireless Range Extender

A wireless range extender (also called a repeater or booster), can amplify a wireless signal to make it stronger. This increases the distance that the client system can be placed from the access point and still be on the network. The extender needs to be set to the same channel as the AP for the repeater to take the transmission and repeat it. This is an effective strategy to increase wireless transmission distances.

> **ExamAlert**
>
> Carefully read troubleshooting question scenarios to be sure the transmission from the AP is getting to the repeater first, and then the repeater is duplicating the signal and passing it on.

VoIP Endpoint

In the world of Voice over IP (VoIP), an *endpoint* is any final destination for a voice call. That final destination can be to a physical device (such as a physical telephone handset), a software application, or a server. Endpoints are used with the Session Initiation Protocol (SIP). To illustrate some of the possibilities, Cisco publishes an 18-page endpoint product matrix (available at https://www.cisco.com/c/dam/en/us/products/collateral/collaboration-endpoints/sales-tool-c96-739424.pdf.

Network Devices Summary

The information in this chapter is important for the Network+ exam. To summarize the coverage of network devices to this point, Table 4.1 lists some of the key points about each device. You should learn this information well.

TABLE 4.1 **Network Devices Summary**

Device	Description	Key Points
Hub	Connects devices on an Ethernet twisted-pair network	A hub does not perform any tasks besides signal regeneration.
Switch	Connects devices on a twisted-pair network	A switch forwards data to its destination by using the MAC address embedded in each packet.
Router	Connects networks	A router uses the software-configured network address to make forwarding decisions.
Modem	Provides serial communication capabilities across phone lines	Modems modulate the digital signal into analog at the sending end and perform the reverse function at the receiving end.
Firewall	Provides controlled data access between networks	Firewalls can be hardware or software based. They are an essential part of a network's security strategy.
Bridge	The simplest way to connect two networks	Operates on Layers 1 and 2 of the OSI model and has largely been replaced in most networks by switches.

Device	Description	Key Points
Media Converter	Used to change from one media to another	Commonly used in conjunction with fiber.
Wireless Access Point	Used to create a wireless LAN and to extend a wired network	Use the wireless infrastructure network mode to provide a connection point between WLANs and a wired Ethernet LAN.
Wireless Extender	Used to extend the distance of a wireless network	The extender is also known as a repeater as it amplifies what it receives and retransmits it.
VoIP Endpoint	The receiving item for a VoIP network	This can be a handset, application, or server.

ExamAlert

You will be expected to know the function of the devices mentioned in this chapter. Review Table 4.1. Make sure that you understand each device and how and why it is used on the network.

Cram Quiz

1. Users are complaining that the network's performance is unsatisfactory. It takes a long time to pull files from the server, and, under heavy loads, workstations can become disconnected from the server. The network is heavily used, and a new videoconferencing application is about to be installed. The network is a 1000BASE-T system created with Ethernet hubs. Which device are you most likely to install to alleviate the performance problems?

   ○ **A.** Switch

   ○ **B.** Router

   ○ **C.** Media converter

   ○ **D.** Firewall

2. Which of the following devices forwards data packets to all connected ports?

   ○ **A.** Router

   ○ **B.** Switch

   ○ **C.** Content filter

   ○ **D.** Hub

3. Which of the following devices passes data based on the MAC address?

- ○ **A.** Hub
- ○ **B.** Switch
- ○ **C.** MSAU
- ○ **D.** Router

Cram Quiz Answers

1. A. Replacing Ethernet hubs with switches can yield significant performance improvements. Of the devices listed, switches are also the only ones that can be substituted for hubs. A router is used to separate networks, not as a connectivity point for workstations. A media converter is used to connect two dissimilar types of network media. A firewall is not a solution to the problem presented.

2. D. Hubs are inefficient devices that send data packets to all connected devices. Switches pass data packets to the specific destination device. This method significantly increases network performance.

3. B. When determining the destination for a data packet, the switch learns the MAC address of all devices attached to it and then matches the destination MAC address in the data it receives. None of the other devices listed passes data based solely on the MAC address.

Advanced Networking Devices

▶ **Explain the purposes and use cases for advanced networking devices.**

CramSaver

If you can correctly answer these questions before going through this section, save time by skimming the Exam Alerts in this section and then complete the Cram Quiz at the end of the section.

1. What can distribute incoming data to specific application servers and help distribute the load?

2. True or false: A multilayer switch operates as both a router and a switch.

3. Your company is looking to add a hardware device to the network that can increase redundancy and data availability as it increases performance by distributing the workload. What use case might this example technology apply to?

Answers

1. A content switch can distribute incoming data to specific application servers and help distribute the load.

2. True. A multilayer switch operates as both a router and a switch.

3. A load balancer can be either a software or hardware component, and it increases redundancy and data availability as it increases performance by distributing the workload.

In addition to the networking devices discussed previously, CompTIA wants you to be aware of 12 others for the Network+ exam. The exam expects you to be able to explain the purposes and identify actual use cases for the advanced networking devices covered in this section.

ExamAlert

Notice that this objective contains the wording "use cases": this is new to the Network+ exam objectives and means that you should expect questions which contain phrasing such as "Common use cases for this technology/device are..."

Multilayer Switch

It used to be that networking devices and the functions they performed were separate. Bridges, routers, hubs, and more existed but were separate devices. Over time, the functions of some individual network devices became integrated into a single device. This is true of *multilayer switches*.

A multilayer switch is one that can operate at both Layer 2 and Layer 3 of the OSI model, which means that the multilayer device can operate as both a switch and a router. Also called a Layer 3 switch, the multilayer switch is a high-performance device that supports the same routing protocols that routers do. It is a regular switch directing traffic within the LAN; in addition, it can forward packets between subnets.

> **ExamAlert**
>
> A multilayer switch operates as both a router and a switch.

A content switch is another specialized device. A content switch is not as common on today's networks, mostly due to cost. A content switch examines the network data it receives, decides where the content is intended to go, and forwards it. The content switch can identify the application that data is targeted for by associating it with a port. For example, if data uses the Simple Mail Transfer Protocol (SMTP) port, it could be forwarded to an SMTP server.

Content servers can help with load balancing because they can distribute requests across servers and target data to only the servers that need it, or distribute data between application servers. For example, if multiple mail servers are used, the content switch can distribute requests between the servers, thereby sharing the load evenly. This is why the content switch is sometimes called a load-balancing switch.

> **ExamAlert**
>
> A content switch can distribute incoming data to specific application servers and help distribute the load.

Wireless Controller

Wireless controllers are often used with branch/remote office deployments for wireless authentication. When an AP boots, it authenticates with a controller before it can start working as an AP. This is often used with *VLAN pooling*, in which multiple interfaces are treated as a single entity (usually for load balancing).

Load Balancer

Network servers are the workhorses of the network. They are relied on to hold and distribute data, maintain backups, secure network communications, and more. The load of servers is often a lot for a single server to maintain. This is where load balancing comes into play. *Load balancing* is a technique in which the workload is distributed among several servers. This feature can take networks to the next level; it increases network performance, reliability, and availability.

> **ExamAlert**
>
> Remember that load balancing increases redundancy and therefore data availability. Also, load balancing increases performance by distributing the workload.

A load balancer can be either a hardware device or software specially configured to balance the load.

> **Note**
>
> Multilayer switches and DNS servers can serve as load balancers.

IDS/IPS

An *intrusion detection system (IDS)* is a passive detection system. The IDS can detect the presence of an attack and then log that information. It also can alert an administrator to the potential threat. The administrator then analyzes the situation and takes corrective measures if needed.

A variation on the IDS is the *Intrusion Prevention System (IPS)*, which is an active detection system. With IPS, the device continually scans the network, looking for inappropriate activity. It can shut down any potential threats. The IPS looks for any known signatures of common attacks and automatically tries to prevent those attacks. An IPS is considered an active/reactive security measure because it actively monitors and can take steps to correct a potential security threat.

Following are several variations on IDSs/IPSs:

▶ **Behavior based:** A *behavior-based system* looks for variations in behavior such as unusually high traffic, policy violations, and so on. By looking for deviations in behavior, it can recognize potential threats and quickly respond.

▶ **Signature based:** A signature-based system, also commonly known as *misuse-detection system (MD-IDS/MD-IPS)*, is primarily focused on evaluating attacks based on attack signatures and audit trails. Attack signatures describe a generally established method of attacking a system. For example, a TCP flood attack begins with a large number of incomplete TCP sessions. If the MD-IDS knows what a TCP flood attack looks like, it can make an appropriate report or response to thwart the attack. This IDS uses an extensive database to determine the signature of the traffic.

▶ **Network-based intrusion detection/prevention system (NIDS or NIPS):** The system examines all network traffic to and from network systems. If it is software, it is installed on servers or other systems that can monitor inbound traffic. If it is hardware, it may be connected to a hub or switch to monitor traffic.

▶ **Host-based intrusion detection/prevention system (HIDS or HIPS):** This refers to applications such as spyware or virus applications that are installed on individual network systems. The system monitors and creates logs on the local system.

ExamAlert

The four types of IDS/IPS tested on the exam are behavior based, signature based, network based, and host based.

Proxy Server

Proxy servers typically are part of a firewall system. They have become so integrated with firewalls that the distinction between the two can sometimes be lost.

However, proxy servers perform a unique role in the network environment—a role that is separate from that of a firewall. For the purposes of this book, a proxy server is defined as a server that sits between a client computer and the Internet and looks at the web page requests the client sends. For example, if a client computer wants to access a web page, the request is sent to the proxy server rather than directly to the Internet. The proxy server first determines whether the request is intended for the Internet or for a web server locally. If the request is intended for the Internet, the proxy server sends the request *as if it originated the request*. When the Internet web server returns the information, the proxy server returns the information to the client. Although a delay might be induced by the extra step of going through the proxy server, the process is largely transparent to the client that originated the request. Because each request a client sends to the Internet is channeled through the proxy server, the proxy server can provide certain functionality over and above just forwarding requests.

One of the most notable extra features is that proxy servers can greatly improve network performance through a process called *caching*. When a caching proxy server answers a request for a web page, the server makes a copy of all or part of that page in its cache. Then, when the page is requested again, the proxy server answers the request from the cache rather than going back to the Internet. For example, if a client on a network requests the web page www.comptia.org, the proxy server can cache the contents of that web page. When a second client computer on the network attempts to access the same site, that client can grab it from the proxy server cache, and accessing the Internet is unnecessary. This greatly increases the response time to the client and can significantly reduce the bandwidth needed to fulfill client requests.

Nowadays, speed is everything, and the capability to quickly access information from the Internet is a crucial concern for some organizations. Proxy servers and their capability to cache web content accommodate this need for speed.

An example of this speed might be found in a classroom. If a teacher asks 30 students to access a specific *uniform resource locator (URL)* without a proxy server, all 30 requests would be sent into cyberspace and subjected to delays or other issues that could arise. The classroom scene with a proxy server is quite different. Only one request of the 30 finds its way to the Internet; the other 29 are filled by the proxy server's cache. Web page retrieval can be almost instantaneous.

However, this caching has a potential drawback. When you log on to the Internet, you get the latest information, but this is not always so when information is retrieved from a cache. For some web pages, it is necessary to go directly to the Internet to ensure that the information is up to date. Some proxy servers can update and renew web pages, but they are always one step behind.

The second key feature of proxy servers is allowing network administrators to filter client requests. If a server administrator wants to block access to certain websites, a proxy server enables this control, making it easy to completely disallow access to some websites. This is okay, but what if it were necessary to block numerous websites? This is when maintaining proxy servers gets a bit more complicated.

Determining which websites users can or cannot access is usually done through something called an *access control list (ACL)*. Chapter 3 discussed how an ACL can be used to provide rules for which port numbers or IP addresses are allowed access. An ACL can also be a list of allowed or nonallowed websites; as you might imagine, compiling such a list can be a monumental task. Given that millions of websites exist, and new ones are created daily, how can you target and disallow access to the "questionable" ones? One approach is to reverse the situation and deny access to all pages except those that appear in an "allowed" list. This approach has high administrative overhead and can greatly limit the productive benefits available from Internet access.

Understandably, it is impossible to maintain a list that contains the locations of all sites with questionable content. In fairness, that is not what proxy servers were designed to do. However, by maintaining a list, proxy servers can better provide a greater level of control than an open system. Along the way, proxy servers can make the retrieval of web pages far more efficient.

A *reverse proxy server* is one that resides near the web servers and responds to requests. These are often used for load balancing purposes because each proxy can cache information from a number of servers.

VPN Concentrator

A *VPN concentrator* can be used to increase remote-access security. This device can establish a secure connection (tunnel) between the sending and receiving network devices. VPN concentrators add an additional level to VPN security. Not only can they create the tunnel, they also can authenticate users, encrypt the data, regulate the data transfer, and control traffic.

The concentrator sits between the VPN client and the VPN server, creates the tunnel, authenticates users using the tunnel, and encrypts data traveling through the tunnel. When the VPN concentrator is in place, it can establish a secure connection (tunnel) between the sending and receiving network devices.

VPN concentrators add an additional level to VPN security. Depending on the exact concentrator, they can do the following:

- ▶ Create the tunnel.

- ▶ Authenticate users who want to use the tunnel.

- ▶ Encrypt and decrypt data.

▶ Regulate and monitor data transfer across the tunnel.

▶ Control inbound and outbound traffic as a tunnel endpoint or router.

The VPN concentrator invokes various standard protocols to accomplish these functions.

AAA/RADIUS Server

Among the potential issues network administrators face when implementing remote access are utilization and the load on the remote-access server. As a network's remote-access implementation grows, reliance on a single remote-access server might be impossible, and additional servers might be required. *RADIUS* can help in this scenario.

> **ExamAlert**
>
> RADIUS is a protocol that enables a single server to become responsible for all remote-access authentication, authorization, and auditing (or accounting) services; this is referred to as *AAA*.

RADIUS functions as a client/server system. The remote user dials in to the remote-access server, which acts as a RADIUS client, or *network access server (NAS)*, and connects to a RADIUS server. The RADIUS server performs authentication, authorization, and auditing (or accounting) functions and returns the information to the RADIUS client (which is a remote-access server running RADIUS client software); the connection is either established or rejected based on the information received.

> **Note**
>
> To learn more about AAA/RADIUS, visit www.cisco.com/c/en/us/td/docs/ios/12_2/security/configuration/guide/fsecur_c/scfrad.html.

UTM Appliances and NGFW/Layer 7 Firewalls

A firewall can employ a variety of methods to ensure security. In addition to the role just described, modern firewall applications can perform a range of other functions, often through the addition of add-on modules directed at the application layer (Layer 7) of the OSI model; they are then often referred to as *Unified Threat Management (UTM)* devices or *Next Generation Firewalls (NGFW)*. UTMs can include the following functionality:

▶ **Content filtering:** Most firewalls can be configured to provide some level of content filtering. This can be done for both inbound and outbound content. For instance, the firewall can be configured to monitor inbound content, restricting certain locations or particular websites. Firewalls can also limit outbound traffic by prohibiting access to certain websites by maintaining a list of URLs and IP addresses. This is often done when organizations want to control employee access to Internet sites.

▶ **Signature identification:** A signature is a unique identifier for a particular application. In the antivirus world, a signature is an algorithm that uniquely identifies a specific virus. Firewalls can be configured to detect certain signatures associated with malware or other undesirable applications and block them before they enter the network.

▶ **Virus scanning services:** As web pages are downloaded, content within the pages can be checked for viruses. This feature is attractive to companies concerned about potential threats from Internet-based sources.

▶ **Network Address Translation (NAT):** To protect the identity of machines on the internal network, and to allow more flexibility in internal TCP/IP addressing structures, many firewalls translate the originating address of data into a different address. This address is then used on the Internet. The most common type of NAT is *Port Address Translation (PAT)*, enabling multiple devices on the network to share one single public address (or a few). NAT is a popular function because it works around the limited availability of TCP/IP addresses in IPv4. When the migration to IPv6 becomes complete, the need for NAT will lessen.

▶ **URL filtering:** By using a variety of methods, the firewall can choose to block certain websites from being accessed by clients within the organization. This blocking allows companies to control what pages can be viewed and by whom.

▶ **Bandwidth management:** Although it is required in only certain situations, bandwidth management can prevent a certain user or system from hogging the network connection. The most common approach to bandwidth management is to divide the available bandwidth into sections and then make a certain section available to a user or system.

▶ **Other:** Although the preceding functions are the most common, UTMs can also be used for network intrusion IDS/IPS, VPN, data loss prevention (DLP), and load balancing, as well as to enable logging and monitoring features.

These functions are not strictly firewall activities. However, the flexibility offered by a firewall, coupled with its placement at the edge of a network, makes a firewall the ideal base for controlling access to external resources.

> **ExamAlert**
>
> You can expect to see exam questions on the types of firewalls and their characteristics. For example, you should know the differences between software and hardware firewalls and understand stateful inspection versus stateless packet filtering firewalls.

VoIP PBX and Gateway

When telephone technology is married with information technology, the result is called telephony. There has been a massive move from landlines to *Voice over IP (VoIP)* for companies to save money. One of the biggest issues with the administration of this is security. By having both data and VoIP on the same line, they are both vulnerable in the case of an attack. Standard telephone systems should be replaced with a securable *PBX*.

A *VoIP gateway*, also sometimes called a PBX gateway, can be used to convert between the legacy telephony connection and a VoIP connection using SIP (Session Initiation Protocol). This is referred to as a "digital gateway" because the voice media are converted in the process.

> **ExamAlert**
>
> Be sure that you know that by having both data and VoIP on the same line, they are both vulnerable in the case of an attack.

Content Filter

A *content filter* is any software that controls what a user is allowed to peruse and is most often associated with websites. Using a content filter, an employer can block access to pornographic sites to all users, some users, or even just an individual user. The filter can be applied as software on client machines (known as client-side filters), on a proxy server on the network (a server-side filter), at the Internet service provider (ISP), or even within the search engine itself. The latter is most commonly used on home machines.

Cram Quiz

1. Which of the following can serve as load balancers?

   ○ **A.** IDS and DNS servers

   ○ **B.** Multilayer switches and IPS

   ○ **C.** Multilayer switches and DNS servers

   ○ **D.** VoIP PBXs and UTM appliances

2. Which of the following is the best answer for a device that continually scans the network, looking for inappropriate activity?

   ○ **A.** IPS

   ○ **B.** NGFW

   ○ **C.** VCPN

   ○ **D.** AAA

3. Which of the following is the best answer for any software that controls what a user is allowed to peruse and is most often associated with websites?

   ○ **A.** IDS

   ○ **B.** Proxy server

   ○ **C.** RADIUS server

   ○ **D.** Content filter

4. You are wanting to add a protocol to the network that enables a single server to become responsible for all remote-access authentication, authorization, and auditing (or accounting) services. Which use case is the best example of this?

   ○ **A.** VPN

   ○ **B.** RADIUS

   ○ **C.** UTM

   ○ **D.** VoIP

Cram Quiz Answers

1. **C.** Multilayer switches and DNS servers can serve as load balancers.

2. **A.** An intrusion prevention system (IPS) is a device that continually scans the network, looking for inappropriate activity.

3. **D.** A content filter is any software that controls what a user is allowed to peruse and is most often associated with websites.

4. **B.** RADIUS is a protocol that enables a single server to become responsible for all remote-access authentication, authorization, and auditing (or accounting) services.

What's Next?

Chapter 5, "WAN Technologies," looks at wide-area networks (WANs) and reviews the characteristics of various WAN technologies. Many of today's network environments are not restricted to a single location or LAN. Instead, many networks span great distances, making WAN knowledge essential for the network administrator.

CHAPTER 5
WAN Technologies

This chapter covers the following official Network+ objective:

▶ Compare and contrast WAN technologies.

This chapter covers CompTIA Network+ objective 2.5. For more information on the official Network+ exam topics, see the "About the Network+ Exam" section in the Introduction.

If you think of networking as something that can be represented on a plane, there would be two ends of the spectrum. At one end of the spectrum, there would be small networks of only a few nodes and devices connected together. At the other end of the spectrum is the *wide-area network (WAN)*: an amalgamation of multiple *local-area networks (LANs)* creating an entity that is only as strong as its weakest link.

This chapter focuses mostly on the WAN end of the spectrum, but also covers such small network practices such as dial-up connectivity. It also looks at best practices and safety practices associated with networking today.

WAN Technologies

▶ **Compare and contrast WAN technologies.**

CramSaver

If you can correctly answer these questions before going through this section, save time by skimming the Exam Alerts in this section and then completing the Cram Quiz at the end of the section.

1. What are T-lines used for, and what is the maximum speed of T1 and T3?

2. What are the X.25 transmission speed restrictions?

3. What is the difference between circuit switching and packet switching technologies?

Answers

1. T-carrier lines create point-to-point network connections for private networks. T1 lines offer transmission speeds of up to 1.544 Mbps, whereas T3 lines offer transmission speeds of 44.736 Mbps.

2. X.25 is restricted to transmission rates of 56 Kbps or 64 Kbps with digital implementations.

3. Circuit switching networking offers a dedicated transmission channel that is reserved until it is disconnected. Packet switching enables packets to be routed around network congestion.

Many of today's network environments are not restricted to a single location or LAN. Instead, many networks span great distances, becoming *wide-area networks (WANs)*. When they do, hardware and software are needed to connect these networks. This section reviews the characteristics of various WAN technologies.

Integrated Services Digital Network

ISDN has long been an alternative to the slower modem WAN connections but at a higher cost. ISDN enables the transmission of voice and data over the same physical connection.

ISDN connections are considerably faster than regular modem connections. To access ISDN, a special phone line is required. This line usually is paid for through a monthly subscription. You can expect these monthly costs to be significantly higher than those for traditional dial-up modem connections.

To establish an ISDN connection, you dial the number associated with the receiving computer, much as you do with a conventional phone call or modem dial-up connection. A conversation between the sending and receiving devices is then established. The connection is dropped when one end disconnects or hangs up. The line pickup of ISDN is fast, enabling a connection to be established, or brought up, much more quickly than a conventional phone line.

ISDN has two defined interface standards: *Basic Rate Interface (BRI)* and *Primary Rate Interface (PRI)*.

BRI

BRI ISDN uses three separate channels—two bearer (B) channels of 64 Kbps each and a delta channel of 16 Kbps. B channels can be divided into four D channels, which enable businesses to have eight simultaneous Internet connections. The B channels carry the voice or data, and the D channels are used for signaling.

> **Note**
>
> BRI ISDN channels can be used separately using 64 Kbps transfer or combined to provide 128 Kbps transfer rates.

PRI

PRI is a form of ISDN that generally is carried over a T1 line and can provide transmission rates of up to 1.544 Mbps. PRI is composed of 23 B channels, each providing 64 Kbps for data/voice capacity, and one 64 Kbps D channel, which is used for signaling.

Comparing BRI and PRI ISDN

Table 5.1 compares BRI to PRI ISDN.

> **ExamAlert**
>
> ISDN is considered a leased line because access to ISDN is leased from a service provider.

TABLE 5.1 **BRI to PRI ISDN Comparison**

Characteristic	BRI	PRI
Speed	128 Kbps	1.544 Mbps
Channels	2B+D	23B+D
Transmission carrier	ISDN	T1

> **Note**
>
> It is recommended that you know how PRI compares to BRI and their basic characteristics shown in Table 5.1.

Leased Lines

T-carrier lines are high-speed dedicated digital lines that can be leased from telephone companies. This creates an always-open, always-available line between you and whomever you choose to connect to when you establish the service.

T-carrier lines can support both voice and data transmissions and are often used to create point-to-point private networks. Because they are a dedicated link, they can be a costly WAN option. Four types of T-carrier lines are available:

▶ **T1:** Offers transmission speeds of 1.544 Mbps and can create point-to-point dedicated digital communication paths. T1 lines have commonly been used for connecting LANs. In North America, DS (digital signal) notation is used with T-lines to describe the circuit. For all practical purposes, DS1 is synonymous with T1.

▶ **T2:** Offers transmission speeds of 6.312 Mbps. It accomplishes this by using 96 64 Kbps B channels.

▶ **T3:** Offers transmission speeds of up to 44.736 Mbps, using 672 64 Kbps B channels. Digital signal 3 (DS3) is a more accurate name in North America, but T3 is what most refer to the link as.

> **ExamAlert**
>
> When you take the exam, think of DS3 and T3 as synonymous.

▶ **T4:** Offers impressive transmission speeds of up to 274.176 Mbps by using 4,032 64 Kbps B channels.

> **ExamAlert**
>
> Of these T-carrier lines, the ones commonly associated with networks and the ones most likely to appear on the exam are the T1 and T3 lines.

> **Note**
>
> Because of the cost of a T-carrier solution, you can lease portions of a T-carrier service. This is known as *fractional T*. You can subscribe and pay for service based on 64 Kbps channels.

T-carrier is the designation for the technology used in the United States and Canada. In Europe, they are called E-carriers, and in Japan, J-carriers. Table 5.2 describes the T/E/J carriers.

TABLE 5.2 **Comparing T/E/J Carriers**

Name	Transmission Speed
T1	1.544 Mbps
T1C	3.152 Mbps
T2	6.312 Mbps
T3	44.736 Mbps
T4	274.176 Mbps
J0	64 Kbps
J1	1.544 Mbps
J1C	3.152 Mbps
J2	6.312 Mbps
J3	32.064 Mbps
J3C	97.728 Mbps
J4	397.200 Mbps
E0	64 Kbps
E1	2.048 Mbps
E2	8.448 Mbps
E3	34.368 Mbps
E4	139.264 Mbps
E5	565.148 Mbps

> **ExamAlert**
>
> Ensure that you review the speeds of the T1, T3, E1, and E3 carriers.

T3 Lines

For a time, the speeds offered by T1 lines were sufficient for all but a few organizations. As networks and the data they support expanded, T1 lines did not provide enough speed for many organizations. T3 service answered the call by providing transmission speeds of 44.736 Mbps.

T3 lines are dedicated circuits that provide high capacity; generally, they are used by large companies, ISPs, and long-distance companies. T3 service offers all the strengths of a T1 service (just a whole lot more), but the cost associated with T3 limits its use to the few organizations that have the money to pay for it.

Fiber, SONET, and OCx Levels

In 1984, the U.S. Department of Justice and AT&T reached an agreement stating that AT&T was a monopoly that needed to be divided into smaller, directly competitive companies. This created a challenge for local telephone companies, which were faced with the task of connecting to an ever-growing number of independent long-distance carriers, each of which had a different interfacing mechanism. Bell Communications Research answered the challenge by developing *Synchronous Optical Network (SONET)*, a fiber-optic WAN technology that delivers voice, data, and video at speeds starting at 51.84 Mbps. Bell's main goals in creating SONET were to create a standardized access method for all carriers within the newly competitive U.S. market and to unify different standards around the world. SONET is capable of transmission speeds from 51.84 Mbps to 2.488 Gbps and beyond.

One of Bell's biggest accomplishments with SONET was that it created a new system that defined data rates in terms of *Optical Carrier (OCx)* levels. Table 5.3 lists the OCx levels you should be familiar with.

> **ExamAlert**
>
> Before taking the exam, review the information provided in Table 5.3. Be sure that you are familiar with OC-3 and OC-192 specific transmission rates.

TABLE 5.3 **OCx Levels and Transmission Rates**

OCx Level	Transmission Rate
OC-1	51.84 Mbps
OC-3	155.52 Mbps
OC-12	622.08 Mbps

OCx Level	Transmission Rate
OC-24	1.244 Gbps
OC-48	2.488 Gbps
OC-96	4.976 Gbps
OC-192	9.953 Gbps
OC-768	39.813 Gbps

Note

Optical carrier (OCx) levels represent the range of digital signals that can be carried on SONET fiber-optic networks. Each OCx level defines the speed at which it operates.

Synchronous Digital Hierarchy (SDH) is the European counterpart to SONET.

ExamAlert

When you take the exam, equate SDH with SONET.

A *passive optical network (PON)* is one in which unpowered optical splitters are used to split the fiber so it can service a number of locations, and it brings the fiber either to the curb, the building, or the home. It is known as a passive system because there is no power to the components and consists of an *optical line termination (OLT)* at the split and a number of *optical network units (ONUs)* at the end of each run (typically near the end user). It can be combined with wavelength division multiplexing and is then known as WDM-PON.

A form of multiplexing optical signals is *dense wavelength-division multiplexing (DWDM)*. This method replaces SONET/SDH regenerators with *erbium doped fiber amplifiers (EDFAs)* and can also amplify the signal and enable it to travel a greater distance. The main components of a DWDM system include the following:

▶ Terminal multiplexer

▶ Line repeaters

▶ Terminal demultiplexer

Note

Chapter 6, "Cabling Solutions," discusses several other methods of multiplexing.

> **ExamAlert**
>
> Make sure that you understand that DWDM works with SONET/SDH.

An alternative to DWDM is *coarse wavelength-division multiplexing (CWDM)*. This method is commonly used with television cable networks. The main thing to know about it is that it has relaxed stabilization requirements; thus, you can have vastly different speeds for download than upload.

> **ExamAlert**
>
> Make sure that you associate CWDM with television cabling.

Frame Relay

To understand *Frame Relay*, it is important to understand some ancient history and X.25. X.25 was one of the original packet-switching technologies, but today it has been replaced in most applications by Frame Relay. Various telephone companies, along with network providers, developed X.25 in the mid-1970s to transmit digital data over analog signals on copper lines. Because so many entities had their hands in the development and implementation of X.25, it works well on many kinds of networks with different types of traffic. X.25 is one of the oldest standards, and therein lies both its greatest advantage and its greatest disadvantage. On the upside, X.25 is a global standard that can be found all over the world. On the downside, its maximum transfer speed is 56 Kbps—which is reasonable when compared to other technologies in the mid-1970s but slow and cumbersome today. However, in the 1980s a digital version of X.25 was released, increasing throughput to a maximum of 64 Kbps. This, too, is slow by today's standards.

Because X.25 is a packet-switching technology, it uses different routes to get the best possible connection between the sending and receiving device at a given time. As conditions on the network change, such as increased network traffic, so do the routes that the packets take. Consequently, each packet is likely to take a different route to reach its destination during a single communication session. The device that makes it possible to use the X.25 service is called a *packet assembler/disassembler (PAD)*, which is required at each end of the X.25 connection.

At its core, Frame Relay is a WAN protocol that operates at the physical and data link layers of the OSI model. Frame Relay enables data transmission for intermittent traffic between LANs and between endpoints in a WAN.

Frame Relay was designed to provide standards for transmitting data packets in high-speed bursts over digital networks, using a public data network service. Frame Relay is a packet-switching technology that uses variable-length packets. Essentially, Frame Relay is a streamlined version of X.25. It uses smaller packet sizes and fewer error-checking mechanisms than X.25; consequently, it has less overhead than X.25.

A Frame Relay connection is built by using *permanent virtual circuits (PVCs)* that establish end-to-end communication. This means that Frame Relay is not dependent on the best-route method of X.25. Frame Relay can be implemented on several WAN technologies, including 56 Kbps, T1, T3, and ISDN lines.

To better understand how it works, look at some of the components of Frame Relay technology. All devices in the Frame Relay WAN fall into two primary categories:

▶ **Data terminal equipment (DTE):** In the Frame Relay world, the term *DTE* refers to terminating equipment located within a company's network. Termination equipment includes such hardware as end-user systems, servers, routers, bridges, and switches.

▶ **Data circuit-terminating equipment (DCE):** DCE refers to the equipment owned by the carrier. This equipment provides the switching services for the network and therefore is responsible for actually transmitting the data through the WAN.

As previously mentioned, Frame Relay uses virtual circuits to create a communication channel. These virtual circuits establish a bidirectional communication link between DTE devices. Two types of virtual circuits are used with Frame Relay:

▶ **Permanent virtual circuit (PVC):** A permanent dedicated virtual link shared in a Frame Relay network, replacing a hard-wired dedicated end-to-end line.

▶ **Switched virtual circuit (SVC):** Represents a temporary virtual circuit established and maintained only for the duration of a data transfer session.

Figure 5.1 shows the components of a Frame Relay network.

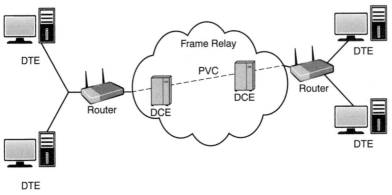

FIGURE 5.1   **A Frame Relay network**

Asynchronous Transfer Mode

Introduced in the early 1990s, *Asynchronous Transfer Mode (ATM)* was heralded as a breakthrough technology for networking because it was an end-to-end solution, ranging in use from a desktop to a remote system. Although it was promoted as both a LAN and WAN solution, ATM did not live up to its hype due to associated implementation costs and a lack of standards. The introduction of Gigabit Ethernet, which offered great transmission speeds and compatibility with existing network infrastructure, further dampened the momentum of the ATM bandwagon. ATM has, however, found a niche with some ISPs and is also commonly used as a network backbone. It provides functionality that combines the benefits of both packet switching and circuit switching.

ATM is a packet-switching technology that provides transfer speeds ranging from 1.544 Mbps to 622 Mbps. It is well suited for a variety of data types, such as voice, data, and video. Using fixed-length packets, or *cells*, that are 53 bytes long, ATM can operate more efficiently than variable-length-packet packet-switching technologies such as Frame Relay. Having a fixed-length packet allows ATM to be concerned only with the header information of each packet. It does not need to read every bit of a packet to determine its beginning and end. ATM's fixed cell length also makes it easily adaptable to other technologies as they develop. Each cell has 48 bytes available for data, with 5 bytes reserved for the ATM header.

ATM is a circuit-based network technology because it uses a virtual circuit to connect two networked devices. Like Frame Relay, ATM is a circuit-based network technology that also uses PVCs and SVCs. PVCs and SVCs were discussed in the preceding section.

ATM is compatible with the most widely used and implemented networking media types available today, including single-mode and multimode fiber, coaxial cable, unshielded twisted-pair, and shielded twisted-pair. Although ATM can be used over various media, the limitations of some of the media types make them impractical choices for deployment in an ATM network. ATM can also operate over other media, including FDDI, T1, T3, SONET, OC-3, and Fibre Channel.

Copper Versus Fiber

The WAN technology used is often based on the infrastructure on which it is built, and the infrastructure—in turn—is based on the WAN technology that you want to deploy. The symbiotic relationship between the technology and the media is one of great interdependence.

The two most common media in use with WANs are copper and fiber. Both are explored in much more detail in the next chapter, "Cabling Solutions," but Table 5.4 provides an overview of the technologies discussed so far and the media that support them.

TABLE 5.4 **Comparing WAN Technologies**

WAN Technology	Speed	Supported Media	Switching Method Used	Key Characteristics
ISDN	BRI: 64 Kbps to 128 Kbps PRI: 64 Kbps to 1.5 Mbps	Copper/ fiber-optic	Can be used for circuit-switching or packet-switching connections	ISDN can be used to transmit all types of traffic, including voice, video, and data. BRI uses 2B+D channels; PRI uses 23B+D channels. B channels are 64 Kbps. ISDN uses the public network and requires dial-in access.
T-carrier (T1, T3)	T1: 1.544 Mbps T3: 44.736 Mbps	Copper/ fiber-optic	Circuit switching	T-carrier is used to create point-to-point network connections for private networks.
ATM	1.544 Mbps to 622 Mbps	Copper/ fiber-optic	Cell switching	ATM uses fixed cells that are 53 bytes long.

WAN Technology	Speed	Supported Media	Switching Method Used	Key Characteristics
X.25	56 Kbps/ 64 Kbps	Copper/ fiber-optic	Packet switching	X.25 is limited to 56 Kbps. X.25 provides a packet-switching network over standard phone lines.
Frame Relay	56 Kbps to 1.544 Mbps	Copper/ fiber-optic	PVCs and SVCs	Frame Relay is a packet-oriented protocol, and it uses variable-length packets.
SONET/OCx	51.8 Mbps to 2.4 Gbps	Fiber-optic	N/A	SONET defines synchronous data transfer over optical cable.

ExamAlert

For the Network+ exam, be sure that you can identify the characteristics of the various WAN technologies from Table 5.4.

Other WAN Technologies

Table 5.4 lists the most popular WAN technologies used today, but you should be aware of several others as well:

▶ **PPP:** Point-to-Point Protocol is a data link protocol that is used to establish a connection between two nodes. PPP works with *plain old telephone service (POTS)*, ISDN, fiber links such as SONET, and other faster connections, such as T1. PPP does not provide data security, but it does provide authentication using the *Challenge Handshake Authentication Protocol (CHAP)*. A PPP connection allows remote users to log on to the network and have access as though they were local users on the network. PPP by itself does not provide for any encryption services for the channel. As you might have guessed, the unsecure nature of PPP makes it largely unsuitable for WAN connections. To counter this issue, other protocols have been created that take advantage of PPP's flexibility and build on it. For example, PPP can be used with the *Encryption Control Protocol (ECP)*.

You should make sure that all your PPP connections use secure channels, dedicated connections, or high-speed connections.

▶ **PPPoE:** Point-to-Point Protocol over Ethernet offers the capability to encapsulate PPP frames inside Ethernet frames. It was first utilized to tunnel packets over a DSL connection to an ISP's IP network. Although it has been around for many years, it is still widely used by DSL Internet providers.

Note

PPPoE is not used by cable (or fiber) Internet providers.

ExamAlert

Be sure you understand the WAN technology characteristics of service for MPLS, PPPoE, PPP, DMVPN and SIP trunk.

▶ **Multilink PPP:** Building off of PPP, Multilink PPP allows you to configure multiple links to act as one, thus increasing the speed of the connection. This technology has gained popularity with the cloud, but still suffers from problems inherent with PPP.

▶ **MPLS (Multiprotocol Label Switching):** Used in high-performance-based telecom networks, MPLS is a technology that uses short path labels instead of longer network addresses to direct data from one node to another. These "labels" are used to identify shorter virtual links between nodes instead of endpoints. MPLS supports technologies such as ATM, Frame Relay, DSL, T1, and E1.

▶ **GSM/CDMA:** The *Global System for Mobile Communications (GSM)* can work with *code division-multiple access (CDMA)* to provide various means of cell phone coverage. The methods that can be used include LTE/4G, HSPA+, 3G, or Edge.

▶ **DMVPN:** The Dynamic Multipoint Virtual Private Network offers the capability to create a dynamic-mesh VPN network without having to preconfigure all the possible tunnel endpoints. The hubs are statically configured, and then it dynamically builds out a hub-and-spoke network by finding, and accepting, new spokes, thus requiring no additional configuration on the hubs or the spokes.

▶ **Metro-Ethernet (Metropolitan Ethernet):** This is nothing more than an Ethernet-based MAN (metropolitan-area network). Various levels of deployment can be implemented, but all have limitations based on the underlying technology.

▶ **SIP Trunk:** With SIP trunking, the Session Initiation Protocol is used as a streaming media service with Voice over Internet Protocol (VoIP) to provide telephone services and unified communications. It requires the use of SIP-based private branch exchanges (IP-PBX) and Unified Communications software applications, such as voice, video, and other streaming media applications (desktop sharing, shared whiteboard, web conferencing, and the like).

Cram Quiz

1. Your company currently uses a standard communication link to transfer files between LANs. Until now, the transfer speeds have been sufficient for the amount of data that needs to be transferred. Recently, a new application was purchased that requires a minimum transmission speed of 1.5 Mbps. You have been given the task to find the most cost-effective solution to accommodate the new application. Which of the following technologies would you use?

   ○ **A.** T3

   ○ **B.** X.25

   ○ **C.** T1

   ○ **D.** BRI ISDN

2. Which of the following best describes the process to create a dedicated circuit between two communication endpoints and direct traffic between those two points?

   ○ **A.** Multiplexing

   ○ **B.** Directional addressing

   ○ **C.** Addressing

   ○ **D.** Circuit switching

3. Which of the following statements are true of ISDN? (Choose the two best answers.)

   ○ **A.** BRI ISDN uses 2 B+1 D channels.

   ○ **B.** BRI ISDN uses 23 B+1 D channels.

   ○ **C.** PRI ISDN uses 2 B+1 D channels.

   ○ **D.** PRI ISDN uses 23 B+1 D channels.

4. You have been hired to establish a WAN connection between two offices: one in Vancouver and one in Seattle. The transmission speed can be no less than 2 Mbps. Which of the following technologies could you choose?

   ○ **A.** T1

   ○ **B.** PPPoE

   ○ **C.** T3

   ○ **D.** ISDN

5. On an ISDN connection, what is the purpose of the D channel?

   ○ **A.** It carries the data signals.

   ○ **B.** It carries signaling information.

   ○ **C.** It enables multiple channels to be combined to provide greater bandwidth.

   ○ **D.** It provides a temporary overflow capacity for the other channels.

6. Which of the following circuit-switching strategies does ATM use? (Choose the two best answers.)

   ○ **A.** SVC

   ○ **B.** VCD

   ○ **C.** PVC

   ○ **D.** PCV

7. Due to recent cutbacks, your boss approaches you and demands an alternative to the company's costly dedicated T1 line. Only small amounts of data require transfer over the line. Which of the following are you likely to recommend?

   ○ **A.** ISDN

   ○ **B.** FDDI

   ○ **C.** A public switched telephone network

   ○ **D.** X.25

8. Which of the following technologies requires a logical connection between the sending and receiving devices?

   ○ **A.** Circuit switching

   ○ **B.** Virtual-circuit packet switching

   ○ **C.** Message switching

   ○ **D.** High-density circuit switching

9. Which technology uses short path labels instead of longer network addresses to direct data from one node to another?

- ○ **A.** MPLS
- ○ **B.** Metropolitan Ethernet
- ○ **C.** DMVPN
- ○ **D.** PPP

Cram Quiz Answers

1. **C.** A T1 line has a transmission capability of 1.544 Mbps and is considerably cheaper than a T3 line. X.25 and BRI ISDN cannot provide the required transmission speed.

2. **D.** Circuit switching is the process of creating a dedicated circuit between two communications endpoints and directing traffic between those two points. None of the other answers are valid types of switching.

3. **A, D.** BRI ISDN uses 2 B+1 D channels, which are two 64 Kbps data channels, and PRI ISDN uses 23 B+1 D channels. The D channel is 16 Kbps for BRI and 64 Kbps for PRI.

4. **C.** The only possible answer capable of transfer speeds above 2 Mbps is a T3 line. None of the other technologies listed can provide the transmission speed required.

5. **B.** The D channel on an ISDN link carries signaling information, whereas the B, or bearer, channels carry the data.

6. **A, C.** ATM uses two types of circuit switching: PVC and SVC. VCD and PCV are not the names of switching methods.

7. **C.** When little traffic will be sent over a line, a public switched telephone network (PSTN) is the most cost-effective solution, although it is limited to 56 Kbps. All the other WAN connectivity methods accommodate large amounts of data and are expensive compared to the PSTN.

8. **B.** When virtual-circuit switching is used, a logical connection is established between the source and the destination device.

9. **A.** Used in high-performance-based telecom networks, MPLS is a technology that uses short path labels instead of longer network addresses to direct data from one node to another. Metropolitan Ethernet is nothing more than an Ethernet-based MAN (metropolitan-area network). DMVPN offers the capability to create a dynamic-mesh VPN network without having to preconfigure all the possible tunnel endpoints. PPP is a data link protocol that is used to establish a connection between two nodes. PPP works with *plain old telephone service (POTS)*, ISDN, fiber links such as SONET, and other faster connections, such as T1.

Internet Access Technologies

▶ **Compare and contrast WAN technologies.**

CramSaver

If you can correctly answer these questions before going through this section, save time by skimming the Exam Alerts in this section and then completing the Cram Quiz at the end of the section.

1. What is VHDSL commonly used for?

2. True or false: DSL using regular phone lines transfers data over the same copper wire.

3. What is the difference between a one-way and a two-way satellite system?

4. What hardware is located at the demarcation point?

Answers

1. VHDSL supports high-bandwidth applications such as VoIP and HDTV.

2. True. DSL using regular phone lines transfers data over the same copper wire.

3. A *one-way satellite system* requires a satellite card and a satellite dish installed at the end user's site. This system works by sending outgoing requests on one link using a phone line, with inbound traffic returning on the satellite link. A *two-way satellite system*, in contrast, provides data paths for both upstream and downstream data.

4. The hardware at the demarcation point is the smart jack, also known as the network interface device (NID).

Internet access has become an integral part of modern business. You can obtain Internet access in several ways. Which type you choose often depends on the cost and what technologies are available in your area. This section explores some of the more common methods of obtaining Internet access.

Note

The term *broadband* often refers to high-speed Internet access. Both DSL and cable modems are common broadband Internet technologies. Broadband routers and broadband modems are network devices that support both DSL and cable.

DSL Internet Access

Digital subscriber line (DSL) is an Internet access method that uses a standard phone line to provide high-speed Internet access. DSL is most commonly associated with high-speed Internet access. Because it is a relatively inexpensive Internet access, it is often found in homes and small businesses. With DSL, a different frequency can be used for digital and analog signals, which means that you can talk on the phone while you upload data.

For DSL services, two types of systems exist: *asymmetric digital subscriber line (ADSL)* and *high-rate digital subscriber line (HDSL)*. ADSL provides a high data rate in only one direction. It enables fast download speeds but significantly slower upload speeds. ADSL is designed to work with existing analog telephone service (POTS) service. With fast download speeds, ADSL is well suited for home-use Internet access where uploading large amounts of data isn't a frequent task.

In contrast to ADSL, HDSL provides a bidirectional high-data-rate service that can accommodate services such as videoconferencing that require high data rates in both directions. A variant of HDSL is *very high-rate digital subscriber line (VHDSL)*, which provides an HDSL service at very high data transfer rates.

DSL arrived on the scene in the late 1990s and brought with it a staggering number of flavors. Together, all these variations are known as *xDSL*:

▶ **Asymmetric DSL (ADSL):** Probably the most common of the DSL varieties is ADSL, which uses different channels on the line. One channel is used for POTS and is responsible for analog traffic. The second channel provides upload access, and the third channel is used for downloads. With ADSL, downloads are faster than uploads, which is why it is called *asymmetric* DSL.

> **Note**
>
> ADSL2 made some improvements in the data rate and increased the distance from the telephone exchange that the line can run. ADSL2+ doubled the downstream bandwidth and kept all the features of ADSL2. Both ADSL2 and ADSL2+ are compatible with legacy ADSL equipment.

▶ **Symmetric DSL (SDSL):** Offers the same speeds for uploads and downloads, making it most suitable for business applications such as web hosting, intranets, and e-commerce. It is not widely implemented in the home/small business environment and cannot share a phone line.

▶ **ISDN DSL (IDSL):** A symmetric type of DSL commonly used in environments in which SDSL and ADSL are unavailable. IDSL does not support analog phones.

▶ **Rate-adaptive DSL (RADSL):** A variation on ADSL that can modify its transmission speeds based on signal quality. RADSL supports line sharing.

▶ **Very high bit rate DSL (VHDSL or VDSL):** An asymmetric version of DSL and, as such, can share a telephone line. VHDSL supports high-bandwidth applications such as VoIP and HDTV. VHDSL can achieve data rates up to approximately 10 Mbps, making it the fastest available form of DSL. To achieve high speeds, VHDSL uses fiber-optic cabling.

▶ **High bit rate DSL (HDSL):** A symmetric technology that offers identical transmission rates in both directions. HDSL does not allow line sharing with analog phones.

Why are there are so many DSL variations? The answer is quite simply that each flavor of DSL is aimed at a different user, business, or application. Businesses with high bandwidth needs are more likely to choose a symmetric form of DSL, whereas budget-conscious environments such as home offices are likely to choose an option that enables phone line sharing at the expense of bandwidth. In addition, some of the DSL variants are older technologies. Although the name persists, they have been replaced with newer DSL implementations. When you work in a home/small office environment, you should expect to work with an ADSL system.

Table 5.5 summarizes the maximum speeds of the various DSL options. Maximum speeds are rarely obtained.

TABLE 5.5 **DSL Speeds**

DSL Variation	Upload Speed*	Download Speed*
ADSL	1 Mbps	3 Mbps
ADSL2	1.3 Mbps	12 Mbps
ADSL2+	1.4 Mbps	24 Mbps
SDSL	1.5 Mbps	1.5 Mbps
IDSL	144 Kbps	144 Kbps
RADSL	1 Mbps	7 Mbps
VHDSL	1.6 Mbps	13 Mbps
HDSL	768 Kbps	768 Kbps

*Speeds may vary greatly, depending on the technologies used and the quality of the connection.

> **ExamAlert**
>
> For the exam, focus on ADSL as you study, but be able to put it in perspective with other varieties.

> **Note**
>
> DSL using regular phone lines transfers data over the same copper wire. The data and voice signals are sent over different frequencies, but sometimes the signals interfere with each other. This is why you use DSL filters. A DSL filter works by minimizing this interference, making for a faster and cleaner DSL connection.

DSL Troubleshooting Procedures

Troubleshooting DSL is similar to troubleshooting any other Internet connection. The following are a few things to check when users are experiencing problems with a DSL connection:

▶ **Physical connections:** The first place to look when troubleshooting a DSL problem is the network cable connections. From time to time, these cables can come loose or inadvertently be detached, and they are often overlooked as the cause of a problem. DSL modems typically have a minimum of three connections: one for the DSL line, one for the local network, and one for the power. Make sure that they are all plugged in appropriately.

▶ **The network interface card (NIC):** While you are checking the cable at the back of the system, take a quick look to see whether the network card LED is lit. If it is not, something could be wrong with the card. It might be necessary to swap out the network card and replace it with one that is known to be working.

▶ **Drivers:** Ensure that the network card is installed and has the correct drivers. Many times, simply using the most up-to-date driver can resolve connectivity issues.

▶ **Protocol configuration:** The device you are troubleshooting might not have a valid IP address. Confirm the IP address by using the appropriate tool for the operating system (and version of IP whether it be IPv4 or IPv6) being used—for example, `ipconfig` or `ifconfig`. If the system requires the automatic assignment of an IP address, confirm that the system is automatically set to obtain an IP address. It might be necessary to use the `ipconfig /release` and `ipconfig /renew` commands to get a new IP address.

▶ **DSL LEDs:** Each DSL box has an LED on it. The light sequences are often used to identify connectivity problems or problems with the box itself. Refer to the manufacturer's website for specific information about error codes and LEDs, but remember the basics. A link light should be on to indicate that the physical connection is complete, and a flashing LED indicates that the connection is active.

> **ExamAlert**
>
> When troubleshooting remote connectivity on a cable or DSL modem, use the LEDs that are always present on these devices to aid in your troubleshooting process.

Ultimately, if none of these steps cures or indicates the cause of the problem, you might have to call the DSL provider for assistance.

Cable Broadband

Cable broadband Internet access is an always-on Internet access method available in areas that have digital cable television. Cable Internet access is attractive to many small businesses and home office users because it is both inexpensive and reliable. Most cable providers do not restrict how much use is made of the access, but they do control the speed. Connectivity is achieved by using a device called a *cable modem*. It has a coaxial connection for connecting to the provider's outlet and an *unshielded twisted-pair (UTP)* connection for connecting directly to a system or to a hub, switch, or router.

Cable providers often supply the cable modem, with a monthly rental agreement. Many cable providers offer free or low-cost installation of cable Internet service, which includes installing a network card in a PC. Some providers also do not charge for the network card. Cable Internet costs are comparable to DSL subscription.

Most cable modems offer the capability to support a higher-speed Ethernet connection for the home LAN than is achieved. The actual speed of the connection can vary somewhat, depending on the utilization of the shared cable line in your area.

> **ExamAlert**
>
> A cable modem generally is equipped with a *medium-dependent interface crossed (MDI-X)* port, so you can use a straight-through UTP cable to connect the modem to a system.

One of the biggest disadvantages of cable access (by DSL providers, at least) is that you share the available bandwidth with everyone else in your cable area. As a result, during peak times, performance of a cable link might be poorer than in low-use periods. In residential areas, busy times are evenings and weekends, and particularly right after school. In general, though, performance with cable systems is good, and in low-usage periods, it can be fast.

> **Note**
>
> The debate between cable and DSL has gone on for years. Although cable modem technology delivers *shared bandwidth* within the local neighborhood, its speeds are theoretically higher but influenced by this shared bandwidth. DSL delivers *dedicated local bandwidth* but is sensitive to distance that impacts overall performance. With the monthly costs about the same, the decision of which to use is often based on the package and bundle specials offered by local providers.

Cable Troubleshooting Procedures

In general, cable Internet access is a low-maintenance system with few problems. When problems do occur, you can try various troubleshooting measures:

▶ **Check the user's end:** Before looking at the cable modem, make sure that the system is configured correctly and that all cables are plugged in. If a hub, switch, or router is used to share the cable Internet access among a group of computers, make sure that the device is on and correctly functioning.

▶ **Check the physical connections:** Like DSL modems, cable modems have three connections: one for the cable signal, one for the local network, and one for the power. Make sure that they are all appropriately plugged in.

▶ **Ensure that the protocol configuration on the system is valid:** If an IP address is assigned via *Dynamic Host Configuration Protocol (DHCP)*, the absence of an address is a sure indicator that connectivity is at fault. Try obtaining a new IP address by using the appropriate command for the operating system platform you use. If the IP addresses are statically configured, make sure that they are correctly set. Trying to use any address other than that specified by the ISP might prevent a user from connecting to the network.

▶ **Check the indicator lights on the modem:** Most cable modems have indicator lights that show the modem's status. Under normal conditions, a single light labeled Ready or Online should be lit. Most cable providers give the user a modem manual that details the functions of the lights and what they indicate in certain states. Generally, any red light is bad. Flashing LEDs normally indicate traffic on the connection.

▶ **Cycle the power on the modem:** Cycling the power on the modem is a surefire way to reset it.

▶ **Call the technical support line:** If you are sure that the connectors are all in place and the configuration of the system is correct, the next step is to call the technical support line of the cable provider. If the provider experiences problems that affect many users, you might get a message while you're on hold, informing you of that. If not, you eventually get to speak to someone who can help you troubleshoot the problem. One of the good things about cable access is that the cable company can remotely monitor and reset the modem. The cable company should tell you whether the modem is correctly functioning.

Unless the modem is faulty, which is not that common, by this point the user should be back on the Internet, or at least you should fully understand why the user cannot connect. If the problem is with the cable provider's networking equipment, you and the user simply have to wait for the system to come back on.

Broadband Security Considerations

Whether you use DSL or cable Internet access, keep a few things in mind. Each of these technologies offers always-on service. This means that even when you are away from your computer, it still connects to the Internet. As you can imagine, this creates a security risk. The longer you are online, the better the chances that someone can remotely access your system.

The operating systems in use today all have some security holes that attackers wait to exploit. These attacks often focus on technologies such as email or open TCP/UDP ports. Combining OS security holes with an always-on Internet technology is certainly a dangerous mix.

Today, DSL and cable Internet connections must be protected by mechanisms such as firewalls. The firewall offers features such as packet filtering and *Network Address Translation (NAT)*. The firewall can be a third-party software application installed on the system, or it can be a hardware device.

In addition to a firewall, it is equally important to ensure that the operating system you use is completely up to date in terms of updates and security patches.

Today's client systems typically offer automatic update features that alert you when a new security update or patch is available.

If you diligently follow a few security measures, both DSL and cable Internet can provide safe Internet access.

Dial-up

Although it's somewhat slow, one means to connect to the Internet or a remote network from a remote location where broadband access is not available may still be the good old telephone line and a modem: either an internal PCIe or external USB one. Because the same line used for a household phone is used for dial-up access, it is called the *plain old telephone system (POTS)* method of access. Although many parts of the world are served by broadband providers offering services such as those discussed so far in this chapter, some people still must (or choose to) connect with a dial-up modem.

Internet access through a phone system requires two things: a modem and a dial-up access account through an ISP. Dial-up modems are devices that convert the digital signals generated by a computer system into analog signals that can travel across a phone line. A computer can have either an internal or external modem. External USB modems tend to be less problematic to install and troubleshoot because they don't require reconfiguration of the host system. Internal modems use one of the serial port assignments (that is, a COM port) and therefore must be configured not to conflict with other devices.

The second piece of the puzzle, the dial-up ISP account, can easily be obtained by contacting one of the many local, regional, or national ISPs. Most ISPs offer a range of plans normally priced based on the amount of time the user is allowed to spend online. Almost without exception, ISPs offer 56 Kbps access, the maximum possible under current standards. Most ISPs also provide email accounts, access to newsgroup servers, and often small amounts of web space.

It is a good idea to carefully research an ISP choice. Free services exist, but they generally restrict users to a certain number of online hours per month or use extensive banner advertising to pay for the services.

Another big consideration for dial-up Internet access is how many lines the ISP has. ISPs never have the same number of lines as subscribers; instead, they work on a first-come, first-served basis for dial-up clients. This means that sometimes users get busy signals when they try to connect. Before signing up for a dial-up Internet access account, ask the company what its ratio of lines to subscribers is, and use that figure as part of your comparison criteria.

With a modem and an ISP account, you are ready to connect. But what happens if things don't go as you plan? Welcome to the interesting and sometimes challenging world of troubleshooting dial-up connections.

Dial-up Troubleshooting Procedures

Troubleshooting a dial-up connection problem can be tricky and time-consuming because you must consider many variables. Of the remote connectivity mechanisms discussed in this chapter, you are far more likely to have problems with a POTS connection than with any of the others. The following are some places to start your troubleshooting under various conditions.

> **Note**
>
> In some cases, users may not even use an ISP; instead, they may directly dial another system on the corporate network. In that case, all the troubleshooting steps in this section apply. The exception is that you must rely on the technical support capabilities of the person responsible for the remote system rather than the ISP if you have a problem.

If the user cannot dial out, try the following:

▶ **Check physical connections:** The most common problem with modem connections is that something has become unplugged; modems rarely fail after they initially work. For an external modem, you also need to verify that the modem has power and that it is connected to the correct COM port.

▶ **Check that the line has a dial tone:** You can do this by plugging a normal phone into the socket to see whether you can dial out. Also, a modem generally has a speaker, and you can set up the modem to use the speaker so that you can hear what is going on.

If the user can dial out but cannot connect to the network, try the following:

▶ **Make sure that the user is dialing the correct number:** This suggestion sounds obvious, but sometimes numbers change or are incorrectly entered.

▶ **Call the ISP:** You can call the ISP to determine whether it is having problems.

▶ **Check the modem speaker:** Find out whether you get busy signals from the ISP by turning on the modem speaker.

If the user can dial out and can get a connection but is then disconnected, try the following:

▶ **Make sure that the modem connection is correctly configured:** The most common modem configuration is 8 data bits, 1 stop bit, and no parity (commonly called *eight-one-none*).

▶ **Check the username and password:** Make sure that the correct username and password combination is configured for the dial-up connection.

▶ **Verify that the connection settings are correct:** Pay particular attention to things such as the IP address. Nearly all ISPs assign IP addresses through DHCP, and trying to connect with a statically configured IP address is not permitted.

▶ **Make sure that the user has not exceeded a preset connection time limit:** Some ISPs restrict the number of monthly access hours. If the user has such a plan, check to ensure that some time credit is left.

▶ **Try specifying a lower speed for the connection:** Modems are designed to negotiate a connection speed with which both devices are comfortable. Sometimes, during the negotiation process, the line can be dropped. Initially setting a lower speed might get you a connection. You can then increase the modem speed to accommodate a better connection.

The Public Switched Telephone Network

The Public Switched Telephone Network (PSTN), often considered a POTS, is the entire collection of interconnected telephone wires throughout the world. Discussions of the PSTN include all the equipment that goes into connecting two points, such as the cable, the networking equipment, and the telephone exchanges.

ExamAlert

Although PSTN is not specifically listed as an exam objective, you need to know how it compares with other technologies. Know that if money is a major concern, the PSTN is the method of choice for creating a WAN.

The modern PSTN is largely digital, with analog connections existing primarily between homes and local phone exchanges. Modems are used to convert the computer system's digital signals into analog so that they can be sent over the analog connection.

Using the PSTN to establish WAN connections is a popular choice, although the significant drawback is the limited transfer speeds. Transfer on the PSTN is limited to 56 Kbps with a modem and 128 Kbps with an ISDN connection, and it is difficult to share large files or videoconferencing at such speeds. However, companies that need to send only small amounts of data remotely can use the PSTN as an inexpensive alternative for remote access, particularly when other resources such as the Internet are unavailable.

Satellite Internet Access

Many people take DSL and cable Internet access for granted, but these technologies are not offered everywhere. Many rural areas do not have cable Internet access. For areas where cheaper broadband options are unavailable, a limited number of Internet options are available. One of the primary options is Internet via satellite.

Satellite access provides a viable Internet access solution for those who cannot get other methods of broadband. Satellite Internet offers an always-on connection with download speeds considerably faster than an old dial-up connection. Satellite Internet access does have a few drawbacks, though, such as cost and high latency. *Latency* is the time it takes for the signal to travel back and forth from the satellite.

Although satellite Internet is slower and costlier than DSL or cable, it offers some attractive features, the first of which is its portability. Quite literally, wherever you go, you have Internet access with no phone lines or other cables. For businesses with remote users and clients, the benefit is clear. But the technology has a far-reaching impact; it is not uncommon to see *recreational vehicles (RVs)* with a satellite dish on the roof. They have 24/7 unlimited access to the Internet as they travel.

Many companies offer satellite Internet services; a quick Internet search reveals quite a few. These Internet providers offer different Internet packages that vary greatly in terms of price, access speeds, and service. Some target businesses, whereas others aim for the private market.

Two different types of broadband Internet satellite services are deployed: one-way and two-way systems. A *one-way satellite system* requires a satellite card and a satellite dish installed at the end user's site. This system works by sending outgoing requests on one link using a phone line, with inbound traffic returning on the satellite link. A *two-way satellite system*, in contrast, provides data paths for both upstream and downstream data. Like a one-way system, a two-way system uses a satellite card and a satellite dish installed at the end user's site; bidirectional communication occurs directly between the end user's node and the satellite.

Home satellite systems are asymmetric; that is, download speeds are faster than upload speeds. A home satellite system is likely to use a modem for the uplink traffic, with downloads coming over the satellite link. The exact speeds you can expect with satellite Internet depend on many factors. As with other wireless technologies, atmospheric conditions can significantly affect the performance of satellite Internet access. One additional consideration for satellite Internet is increased *propagation time*—how long it takes the signal to travel back and forth from the satellite. In networking terms, this time is long and therefore is an important consideration for business applications.

Home Satellite Troubleshooting Procedures

Your ability to troubleshoot satellite Internet connections might be limited. Home satellite Internet is a line-of-sight wireless technology, and the installation configuration must be precise. Because of this requirement, many satellite companies insist that the satellite be set up and configured by trained staff members. If you install a satellite system in a way that does not match the manufacturer's recommendations, you might void any warranties.

Given this limitation, troubleshooting satellite connections often requires you to concentrate less on connectivity issues and more on physical troubleshooting techniques. Perhaps more than for any other Internet technology, calls to technical support occur early in the troubleshooting process. Satellite Internet has a few aspects that you should be aware of:

▶ **Rain fade:** Refers to signal loss due to moisture interference. The general rule is that the smaller the dish, the more susceptible it is to rain fade. Homes and small businesses use small dishes.

▶ **Latency:** Refers to the time lapse between sending or requesting information and the time it takes to return. As you might expect, satellite communication experiences high latency due to the distance it has to travel.

▶ **Line-of-sight:** Despite the distance, satellite is basically a line-of-sight technology. This means that the path between the satellite dish and the satellite should be as unobstructed as possible.

Wireless Internet Access

Not too long ago, it would have been inconceivable to walk into your local coffee shop with your laptop under your arm and surf the Web while drinking a latte. Putting aside that beverages and laptops don't mix, wireless Internet access has become common.

Wireless Internet access is provided by an ISP providing public wireless Internet access known as *hotspots*. Hotspots offer Internet access for mobile network devices such as laptops, handheld computers, and cell phones in airports, coffee shops, conference rooms, and so on. A hotspot is created using one or many wireless access points near the hotspot location.

Client systems might need to install special application software for billing and security purposes; others require no configuration other than obtaining the network name (*service set identifier* [*SSID*]). Hotspots do not always require a fee for service, because companies use them as a marketing tool to lure Internet users to their businesses.

Hotspots are not everywhere, but finding them is not difficult. Typically, airports, hotels, and coffee shops advertise that they offer Internet access for customers or clients. In addition, ISPs list their hotspot sites online so that they are easily found.

Establishing a connection to a wireless hotspot is a straightforward process. If not equipped with built-in wireless capability, laptops require an external wireless adapter card. With the physical requirements of the wireless card taken care of, connect as follows:

1. When you arrive at the hotspot site, power up your laptop or other mobile device. In some instances, you might need to reboot your system to clear out old configuration settings if it was on standby.

2. The card might automatically detect the network. If this is the case, configuration settings, such as the SSID, are automatically detected, and the wireless Internet is available. If Internet access is free, there is little else to do; if it is a paid-for service, you need to enter a method of payment. One thing to remember is to verify that you use encryption for secure data transfer.

3. If for some reason the wireless settings are not automatically detected, you need to open your wireless NIC's configuration utility and manually set the configurations. These can include setting the mode to infrastructure, inputting the correct SSID, and setting the level of encryption used.

In addition to using an ISP, some companies, such as hotels and cafes, provide wireless Internet access by connecting a wireless router to a DSL or cable Internet connection. The router becomes the wireless access point to which the users connect, and it enables clients to connect to the Internet through the broadband connection. The technology is based on the 802.11 standards, typically 802.11n/ac today, and client systems require only an internal or external wireless adapter.

> **Note**
>
> Want more information on wireless? Chapter 7, "Wireless Solutions," covers wireless technologies in detail.

Termination Points

To work properly, a network must have termination points. These endpoints stop the signal and prevent it from living beyond its needed existence. For the exam, CompTIA wants you to be familiar with a number of termination-related topics, all of which are discussed in the sections that follow.

Demarc, Demarc Extension, and Smart Jacks

A network's *demarcation point* is the connection point between the operator's part of the network and the customer's portion of the network. This point is important for network administrators because it distinguishes the portion of the network that the customer is responsible for from the section the owner is responsible for. For example, for those who have high-speed Internet, the boundary between the customer's premises and the ISP typically is mounted on the wall on the side of the home. However, high-speed service providers support everything from the cable modem back to their main distribution center. This is why, if a modem fails, it is replaced by the ISP and not by the customer. This is true for the wiring to that point as well.

Knowing the location of the demarcation point is essential because it marks the point between where the customer (or administrator) is responsible and where the owner is. It also identifies the point at which the customer is responsible should a problem occur, and who should pay for that problem. The ISP is responsible for ensuring that the network is functional up to the demarcation point. The customer/administrator is responsible for ensuring that everything from that point is operational.

The demarcation point is the point at which the ISP places its services in your network. There is not always a choice of where this demarcation is placed. This means that a company might have six floors of offices, and the demarcation point is in the basement—impractical for the network. This is when you need a demarcation extension, which extends the demarcation point to a more functional location. This might sound simple, but it involves knowledge of cabling distances and other infrastructure needs. The demarcation extension might be the responsibility of the administrator, or for a fee, owners might provide extension services.

As you might imagine, you need some form of hardware at the demarcation point. This is the *smart jack*, also known as the *network interface device (NID)*. The smart jack performs several primary functions:

▶ **Loopback feature:** The loopback feature is built in to the smart jack. Like the Ethernet loopback cable, it is used for testing purposes. In this case, the loopback feature enables remote testing so that technicians do not always need to be called to visit the local network to isolate problems.

▶ **Signal amplification:** The smart jack can amplify signals. This feature is similar to that of the function of repeaters in an Ethernet network.

▶ **Surge protection:** Lightning and other environmental conditions can cause electrical surges that can quickly damage equipment. Many smart jacks include protection from environmental situations.

▶ **Remote alarms:** Smart jacks typically include an alarm that allows the owner to identify if something goes wrong with the smart jack and therefore the connections at the demarcation point.

ExamAlert

Demarcation point is the telephone company or ISP term for where their facilities or wires end and where yours begin.

CSUs/DSUs

A *channel service unit/data service unit (CSU/DSU)* acts as a translator between the LAN data format and the WAN data format. Such a conversion is necessary because the technologies used on WAN links are different from those used on LANs. Some consider a CSU/DSU a type of digital modem. But unlike a normal modem, which changes the signal from digital to analog, a CSU/DSU changes the signal from one digital format to another.

A CSU/DSU has physical connections for the LAN equipment, normally via a serial interface, and another connection for a WAN.

ExamAlert

Traditionally, the CSU/DSU has been in a box separate from other networking equipment. However, the increasing use of WAN links means that some router manufacturers are now including CSU/DSU functionality in routers or are providing the expansion capability to do so.

Verify Wiring Installation and Termination

After a segment of network cable has been placed where it needs to go, whether run through the plenum or connecting a patch cable, the final task is wiring termination. Termination is the process to connect the network cable to the wall jack, plug, or patch panel. Termination generally is a straightforward process. You can quickly see if the wiring and termination worked if the LED on the connected network card is lit. Also, if you connect a client system, you can ping other devices on the network if all works.

> **Note**
>
> Cabling topics, such as patch cables and plenums, are discussed in Chapter 6, "Cabling Solutions."

If you run the wiring and complete termination, but a system cannot access the network and the link light is not lit, you should look for a few things when troubleshooting the wiring installation and termination.

Verify that the termination and wiring installation link light on the device (switch/NIC) is not lit:

▶ If you connect a patch cable to a PC or a switch, and no link light is lit, verify that the patch cable is good by switching it with a known working one.

▶ If it is a homemade patch cable, ensure that the RJ-45 connector is properly attached.

▶ Ensure that the RJ-45 connector is properly seated in the wall jack and NIC or switch port.

▶ If no link light is lit when you connect to a switch, change to another port on the switch. Sometimes a single port can be faulty.

▶ Verify that the correct patch cable is used. It is possible that a rollover cable or crossover cable has been accidentally used.

▶ Verify that the cables used are the correct standard. For example, the patch cable should be a 568A or 568B.

If the link light on a device is lit and intermittent problems occur, check the following:

▶ Try replacing the cable with a known working one.

▶ Verify where the network cable is run. Ensure that a plenum-rated cable is used if it runs through ceilings or ductwork.

▶ Look for heavy bends or partial breaks in the network cable.

▶ Verify that shielded cabling is used in areas of potentially high interference.

▶ Check the length of the cable run. Remember, the total run of cable should be about 100 meters. If the patch cable or the cable between the wall jack and the wiring closet is too long, intermittent signals can occur.

Cram Quiz

1. Which of the following technologies require dial-up access? (Choose the best answer.)

　　○　**A.** Fiber

　　○　**B.** ISDN

　　○　**C.** Packet switching

　　○　**D.** DMVPN

2. Which of the following is an advantage of ISDN over a public switched telephone network?

　　○　**A.** ISDN is more reliable.

　　○　**B.** ISDN is cheaper.

　　○　**C.** ISDN is faster.

　　○　**D.** ISDN uses 53 Kbps fixed-length packets.

3. Which of the following is the time lapse between sending or requesting information and the time it takes to return?

　　○　**A.** Echo

　　○　**B.** Attenuation

　　○　**C.** Bandwidth

　　○　**D.** Latency

4. What is the speed usually offered with dial-up service?

　　○　**A.** 1 Gbps

　　○　**B.** 256 Kbps

　　○　**C.** 144 Kbps

　　○　**D.** 56 Kbps

5. What device acts as a translator between the LAN data format and the WAN data format?

   ○ **A.** SIP Trunk

   ○ **B.** PRI

   ○ **C.** MPLS

   ○ **D.** CSU/DSU

Cram Quiz Answers

1. **B.** ISDN requires a dial-up connection to establish communication sessions.

2. **C.** One clear advantage that ISDN has over the PSTN is its speed. ISDN can combine 64 Kbps channels for faster transmission speeds than the PSTN can provide. ISDN is no more or less reliable than the PSTN. ISDN is more expensive than the PSTN.

3. **D.** Latency refers to the time lapse between sending or requesting information and the time it takes to return.

4. **D.** Almost without exception, ISPs offer 56 Kbps access, the maximum possible under current dial-up standards.

5. **D.** A channel service unit/data service unit (CSU/DSU) acts as a translator between the LAN data format and the WAN data format. Such a conversion is necessary because the technologies used on WAN links are different from those used on LANs.

What's Next?

For the Network+ exam, and for routinely working with an existing network or implementing a new one, you need to identify the characteristics of network media and their associated cabling. Chapter 6, "Cabling Solutions," focuses on the media and connectors used in today's networks and what you are likely to find in wiring closets.

CHAPTER 6

Cabling Solutions

This chapter covers the following official Network+ objectives:

▶ Given a scenario, deploy the appropriate cabling solution.

▶ Given a scenario, troubleshoot common wired connectivity and performance issues.

This chapter covers CompTIA Network+ objectives 2.1 and 5.3. For more information on the official Network+ exam topics, see the "About the Network+ Exam" section in the Introduction.

When working with an existing network or implementing a new one, you need to identify the characteristics of network media and their associated cabling. This chapter focuses on the media and connectors used in today's networks and how they fit into wiring closets.

General Media Considerations

▶ **Given a scenario, deploy the appropriate cabling solution.**

CramSaver

If you can correctly answer these questions before going through this section, save time by skimming the Exam Alerts in this section and then completing the Cram Quiz at the end of the section.

1. What are the two main types of twisted-pair wiring used today?

2. What is the name of the wiring standard that offers a minimum of 500 MHz of bandwidth and specifies transmission distances up to 100 meters with 10 Gbps?

3. What is the difference between RJ-11 and RJ-45 connectors?

4. What are the two most common connectors used with fiber-optic cabling?

5. What are F-type connectors used for?

Answers

1. The two main types of twisted-pair cabling in use today are unshielded twisted-pair (UTP) and shielded twisted-pair (STP).

2. Category 6a (Cat 6a) offers improvements over Category 6 (Cat 6) by offering a minimum of 500 MHz of bandwidth. It specifies transmission distances up to 100 meters with 10 Gbps networking speeds.

3. RJ-11 connectors are used with standard phone lines and are similar in appearance to RJ-45 connectors used in networking. However, RJ-11 connectors are smaller. RJ-45 connectors are used with UTP cabling.

4. Fiber-optic cabling uses a variety of connectors, but SC and ST are more commonly used than others. ST connectors offer a twist-type attachment, whereas SCs have a push-on connector. LC and MTRJ are other types of fiber-optic connectors. In environments where vibration can be a problem, FC connectors can be used and feature a threaded body.

5. F-type connectors are used to connect coaxial cable to devices such as Internet modems.

In addition to identifying the characteristics of network media and their associated cabling, the Network+ exam requires knowledge of some general terms and concepts that are associated with network media. Before looking at the individual media types, it is a good idea to first have an understanding of some general media considerations.

Broadband Versus Baseband Transmissions

Networks employ two types of signaling methods/modulation techniques:

▶ **Baseband transmissions:** Baseband transmissions use digital signaling over a single wire. Communication on baseband transmissions is bidirectional, allowing signals to be sent and received, but not at the same time. To send multiple signals on a single cable, baseband uses something called *time-division multiplexing (TDM)*. TDM divides a single channel into time slots. The key thing about TDM is that it does not change how baseband transmission works—only how data is placed on the cable.

▶ **Broadband transmissions:** In terms of LAN network standards, broadband transmissions use analog transmissions. For broadband transmissions to be sent and received, the medium must be split into two channels. (Alternatively, two cables can be used: one to send and one to receive transmissions.) Multiple channels are created using *frequency-division multiplexing (FDM)*. FDM allows broadband media to accommodate traffic going in different directions on a single medium at the same time.

Simplex, Half-Duplex, and Full-Duplex Modes

Simplex, half-duplex, and full-duplex modes are referred to as *dialog modes*, and they determine the direction in which data can flow through the network media:

▶ Simplex mode enables one-way communication of data through the network, with the full bandwidth of the cable used for the transmitting signal. One-way communication is of little use on LANs, making it unusual at best for network implementations.

▶ Far more common is half-duplex mode, which accommodates transmitting and receiving on the network, but not at the same time. Many networks are configured for half-duplex communication.

▶ The preferred dialog mode for network communication is full-duplex mode. To use full-duplex, both the network card and the hub or switch must support full duplexing. Devices configured for full duplexing can simultaneously transmit and receive. This means that 100 Mbps network cards theoretically can transmit at 200 Mbps using full-duplex mode.

Data Transmission Rates

One of the more important media considerations is the supported data transmission rate or speed. Different media types are rated to certain maximum speeds, but whether they are used to this maximum depends on the networking standard used and the network devices connected to the network.

> **Note**
>
> The transmission rate of media is sometimes incorrectly called the *bandwidth*. But the term *bandwidth* refers to the width of the range of electrical frequencies or the number of channels that the medium can support.

Transmission rates normally are measured by the number of data bits that can traverse the medium in a single second. In the early days of data communications, this measurement was expressed in bits per second (bps), but today's networks are measured in *megabits per second (Mbps)* and *gigabits per second (Gbps)*.

The different network media vary greatly in the transmission speeds they support. Many of today's application-intensive networks require more than the 10 Mbps or 100 Mbps offered by the older networking standards. In some cases, even 1 Gbps, which is found in many modern LANs, is not enough to meet current network needs. For this reason, many organizations now deploy 10 Gbps implementations.

Types of Network Media

Whatever type of network is used, some type of network medium is needed to carry signals between computers. Two types of media are used in networks: cable-based media, such as twisted-pair, and the media types associated with wireless networking, such as radio waves.

In networks using cable-based media, there are two basic choices:

▶ Copper

▶ Fiber-optic

Copper wire is used with both twisted-pair and coaxial cables to conduct the signals electronically; fiber-optic cable uses a glass or plastic conductor and transmits the signals as light.

For many years, coaxial was the cable of choice for most LANs. Today, twisted-pair has proven to be the cable medium of choice, thus retiring coaxial to the confines of storage closets. Fiber-optic cable has seen a rise in popularity, but cost slowed its adoption to the home (although it is common today). It is widely used as a network backbone where segment length and higher speeds are needed and is common in server room environments as a server-to-switch connection method and in building-to-building connections in *metropolitan-area networks (MANs)*.

The following sections summarize the characteristics of each of these cable types.

Twisted-Pair Cabling

Twisted-pair cabling has been around for a long time. It was originally created for voice transmissions and has been widely used for telephone communication. Today, in addition to telephone communication, twisted-pair is the most widely used medium for networking.

The popularity of twisted-pair can be attributed to the fact that it is lighter, more flexible, and easier to install than coaxial or fiber-optic cable. It is also cheaper than other media alternatives and can achieve greater speeds than its coaxial competition. These factors make twisted-pair the ideal solution for most network environments.

Two main types of twisted-pair cabling are in use today: *unshielded twisted-pair (UTP)* and *shielded twisted-pair (STP)*. UTP is significantly more common than

STP and is used for most networks. Shielded twisted-pair is used in environments in which greater resistance to EMI and attenuation is required. The greater resistance comes at a price, however. The additional shielding, plus the need to ground that shield (which requires special connectors), can significantly add to the cost of a cable installation of STP.

STP provides the extra shielding by using an insulating material that is wrapped around the wires within the cable. This extra protection increases the distances that data signals can travel over STP but also increases the cost of the cabling. Figure 6.1 shows UTP and STP cabling.

UTP Cable   Shielding

                                STP Cable

FIGURE 6.1 **UTP and STP cabling**

There are several categories of twisted-pair cabling. The early categories are most commonly associated with voice transmissions. The categories are specified by the *Electronic Industries Association/Telecommunications Industry Association (EIA/TIA)*. EIA/TIA is an organization that focuses on developing standards for electronic components, electronic information, telecommunications, and Internet security. These standards are important to ensure uniformity of components and devices.

> **Note**
>
> When learning about cabling, you need to understand the distinction between hertz and bits per second in relation to bandwidth. When you talk about bandwidth and a bits-per-second rating, you refer to a rate of data transfer.

EIA/TIA has specified a number of categories of twisted-pair cable, some of which are now obsolete. Those still in use today include the following:

▶ **Category 3:** Data-grade cable that can transmit data up to 10 Mbps with a possible bandwidth of 16 MHz. For many years, Category 3 was the cable of choice for twisted-pair networks. As network speeds pushed the 100 Mbps speed limit, Category 3 became ineffective.

▶ **Category 5:** Data-grade cable that typically was used with Fast Ethernet operating at 100 Mbps with a transmission range of 100 meters. Although Category 5 was a popular media type, this cable is an outdated standard. Newer implementations use the 5e or greater standards. Category 5 provides a minimum of 100 MHz of band-width. Category 5, despite being used primarily for 10/100 Ethernet networking, can go faster. The IEEE 802.11ae standard specifies 1000 Mbps over Category 5 cable.

▶ **Category 5e:** Data-grade cable used on networks that run at 10/100 Mbps and even up to 1000 Mbps. Category 5e cabling can be used up to 100 meters, depending on the implementation and standard used. Category 5e cable provides a minimum of 100 MHz of bandwidth.

▶ **Category 6:** High-performance UTP cable that can transmit data up to 10 Gbps. Category 6 has a minimum of 250 MHz of bandwidth and specifies cable lengths up to 100 meters with 10/100/1000 Mbps transfer, along with 10 Gbps over shorter distances. Category 6 cable typically is made up of four twisted pairs of copper wire, but its capabilities far exceed those of other cable types. Category 6 twisted-pair uses a longitudinal separator, which separates each of the four pairs of wires from each other. This extra construction significantly reduces the amount of crosstalk in the cable and makes the faster transfer rates possible.

▶ **Category 6a:** Also called augmented 6. Offers improvements over Category 6 by offering a minimum of 500 MHz of bandwidth. It specifies transmission distances up to 100 meters with 10 Gbps networking speeds.

▶ **Category 7:** The big advantage to this cable is that shielding has been added to individual pairs and to the cable as a whole to greatly reduce cross-talk. It is rated for transmission of 600 MHz and is backward compatible with Category 5 and Category 6. Category 7 differs from the other cables in this group in that it is not recognized by the EIA/TIA and that it is shielded twisted pair while all others listed as exam objectives are unshielded.

ExamAlert

On the exam, you might see these as Cat 3, Cat 5, Cat 5e, Cat 6, Cat 6a, and Cat 7. Remember their characteristics, such as cable length, speed, and bandwidth.

Tip

If you work on a network that is a few years old, you might need to determine which category of cable it uses. The easiest way to do this is to read the cable. The category number should be clearly printed on it.

Table 6.1 summarizes the categories and the speeds they support in common network implementations.

TABLE 6.1 **Twisted-Pair Cable Categories**

Category	Common Application
3	16 Mbps
5	100 Mbps
5e	1000 Mbps
6	10/100/1000 Mbps plus 10 Gbps
6a	10 Gbps and beyond networking
7	10 Gbps and beyond networking

> **Note**
>
> The numbers shown in Table 6.1 refer to speeds these cables are commonly used to support. Ratified standards for these cabling categories might actually specify lower speeds than those listed, but cable and network component manufacturers are always pushing the performance envelope in the quest for greater speeds. The ratified standards define minimum specifications. For more information on cabling standards, visit the TIA website at http://www.tiaonline.org/.

Coaxial Cables

Coaxial cable, or *coax* as it is commonly called, has been around for a long time. Coax found success in both TV signal transmission and network implementations. As shown in Figure 6.2, coax is constructed with a copper core at the center (the main wire) that carries the signal, insulation (made of plastic), ground (braided metal shielding), and insulation on the outside (an outer plastic covering).

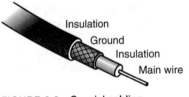

Insulation
Ground
Insulation
Main wire

FIGURE 6.2 **Coaxial cabling**

Coaxial cable is constructed in this way to add resistance to *attenuation* (the loss of signal strength as the signal travels over distance), *crosstalk* (the degradation of a signal caused by signals from other cables running close to it), and EMI.

Two types of coax are used in networking: thin coax, also known as thinnet or 10BASE2, and thick coax, also known as *thicknet*. Neither is particularly popular anymore, but you are most likely to encounter thin coax. Thick coax was used primarily for backbone cable. It could be run through plenum spaces because it offered significant resistance to EMI and crosstalk and could run in lengths up to 500 meters. Thick coax offers speeds up to 10 Mbps, far too slow for today's network environments.

Thin coax is much more likely to be seen than thick coax in today's networks, but it isn't common. Thin coax is only .25 inches in diameter, making it fairly easy to install. Unfortunately, one of the disadvantages of all thin coax types is that they are prone to cable breaks, which increase the difficulty when installing and troubleshooting coaxial-based networks.

Several types of thin coax cable exist, each of which has a specific use. Table 6.2 summarizes these categories.

ExamAlert

For the exam, you should focus on RG-59 and RG-6.

TABLE 6.2 **Thin Coax Categories**

Cable Type	Description
RG-59	Used to generate low-power video connections. The RG-59 cable cannot be used over long distances because of its high-frequency power losses. In such cases, RG-6 cables are used instead.
RG-6	Often used for cable TV and cable modems.

Fiber-Optic Cables

In many ways, fiber-optic media addresses the shortcomings of copper-based media. Because fiber-based media use light transmissions instead of electronic pulses, threats such as EMI, crosstalk, and attenuation become nonissues. Fiber is well suited for the transfer of data, video, and voice transmissions. In addition, fiber-optic is the most secure of all cable media. Anyone trying to access data signals on a fiber-optic cable must physically tap into the medium. Given the composition of the cable, this is a particularly difficult task.

Unfortunately, despite the advantages of fiber-based media over copper, it still does not enjoy the popularity of twisted-pair cabling. The moderately difficult installation and maintenance procedures of fiber often require skilled technicians with specialized tools. Furthermore, the cost of a fiber-based solution limits the number of organizations that can afford to implement it. Another sometimes hidden drawback of implementing a fiber solution is the cost of retrofitting existing network equipment. Fiber is incompatible with most electronic network equipment. This means you have to purchase fiber-compatible network hardware.

> **ExamAlert**
>
> Fiber-optic cable, although still more expensive than other types of cable, is well suited for high-speed data communications. It eliminates the problems associated with copper-based media, such as near-end crosstalk, EMI, and signal tampering.

As shown in Figure 6.3, fiber-optic cable is composed of a core (glass fiber) that is surrounded by *cladding* (silica). A silicone coating is next, followed by a buffer jacket. There are strength members next and then a protective sheath (polyurethane outer jacket) surrounds everything.

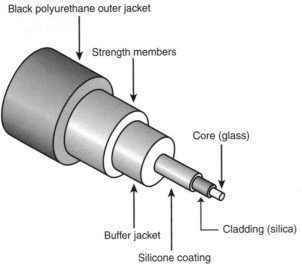

FIGURE 6.3 **Fiber-optic cabling**

Two types of fiber-optic cable are available:

▶ **Multimode fiber:** Many beams of light travel through the cable, bouncing off the cable walls. This strategy actually weakens the signal, reducing the length and speed at which the data signal can travel.

▶ **Single-mode fiber:** Uses a single direct beam of light, thus allowing for greater distances and increased transfer speeds.

Some common types of fiber-optic cable include the following:

▶ 62.5-micron core/125-micron cladding multimode

▶ 50-micron core/125-micron cladding multimode

▶ 8.3-micron core/125-micron cladding single mode

In the ever-increasing search for bandwidth that can keep pace with the demands of modern applications, fiber-optic cables are sure to continue to play a key role.

> **ExamAlert**
>
> Understanding the types of fiber optics available, as well as their advantages and limitations, is important for real-world applications as well as the Network+ exam.

Plenum Versus PVC Cables

A plenum is the mysterious space that resides between the false, or drop, ceiling and the true ceiling. This space typically is used for air conditioning and heating ducts. It might also hold a myriad of cables, including telephone, electrical, and networking. The cables that occupy this space must be plenum-rated rather than the standard PVC cables. Plenum cables are coated with a nonflammable material, often Teflon or Kynar, and they do not give off toxic fumes if they catch fire. As you might imagine, plenum-rated cables cost more than regular (PVC-based) cables, but they are mandatory when cables are not run through a conduit. As a bonus, plenum-rated cables suffer from less attenuation than non-plenum cables.

> **ExamAlert**
>
> Cables run through the plenum areas must have two important characteristics: They must be fire resistant, and they must not produce toxic fumes if exposed to intense heat.

Types of Media Connectors

A variety of connectors are used with the associated network media. Media connectors attach to the transmission media and allow the physical connection into the computing device. For the Network+ exam, you need to identify the connectors associated with a specific medium. The following sections describe the connectors and associated media.

BNC Connectors

BNC connectors are associated with coaxial media and 10BASE2 networks. BNC connectors are not as common as they previously were, but they still are used on some networks, older network cards, and older hubs. Common BNC connectors include a barrel connector, T-connector, and terminators. Figure 6.4 shows two terminators (top and bottom) and two T-connectors (left and right).

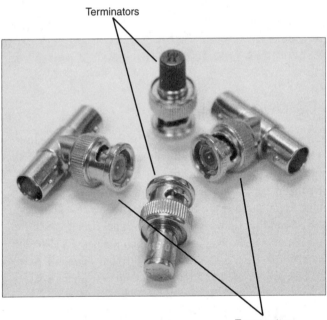

Terminators

T-connectors

FIGURE 6.4 **BNC connectors**

ExamAlert

Connectors are sometimes referred to as couplers. For exam purposes, consider the two words to be synonyms.

RJ-11 Connectors

RJ-11 (Registered Jack) connectors are small plastic connectors used on telephone cables. They have capacity for six small pins. However, in many cases, not all the pins are used. For example, a standard telephone connection uses only two pins, and a cable used for a *digital subscriber line (DSL)* modem connection uses four.

RJ-11 connectors are somewhat similar to RJ-45 connectors, which are discussed next, although they are a little smaller. Both RJ-11 and RJ-45 connectors have a small plastic flange on top of the connector to ensure a secure connection. Figure 6.5 shows two views of an RJ-11 connector.

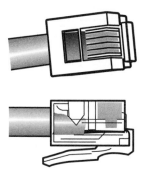

FIGURE 6.5 **RJ-11 connectors**

RJ-45 Connectors

RJ-45 connectors, as shown in Figure 6.6, are the ones you are most likely to encounter in your network travels. RJ-45 connectors are used with twisted-pair cabling, the most prevalent network cable in use today. RJ-45 connectors resemble the aforementioned RJ-11 phone jacks, but they support up to eight wires instead of the six supported by RJ-11 connectors. RJ-45 connectors are also larger than RJ-11 connectors.

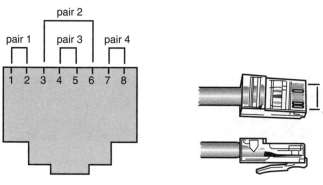

FIGURE 6.6 **RJ-45 connectors**

F-Type Connectors and RG-59 and RG-6 Cables

F-type connectors, as shown in Figure 6.7, are screw-on connections used to attach coaxial cable to devices. This includes RG-59 and RG-6 cables. In the world of modern networking, F-type connectors are most commonly associated with connecting Internet modems to cable or satellite *Internet service providers' (ISP)* equipment. However, F-type connectors are also used to connect to some proprietary peripherals.

FIGURE 6.7   **F-type connector**

F-type connectors have a "nut" on the connection that provides something to grip as the connection is tightened by hand. If necessary, this nut can also be lightly gripped with pliers to aid disconnection.

> **ExamAlert**
>
> For the Network+ exam, you will be expected to identify the connectors discussed in this chapter by their appearance.

Fiber Connectors

A variety of connectors are associated with fiber cabling, and there are several ways of connecting them. These include bayonet, snap-lock, and push-pull connectors. Figure 6.8 shows the fiber connectors identified in the Network+ objectives.

> **ExamAlert**
>
> As with the other connectors discussed in this section, be prepared to identify fiber connectors by their appearance and by how they are physically connected.

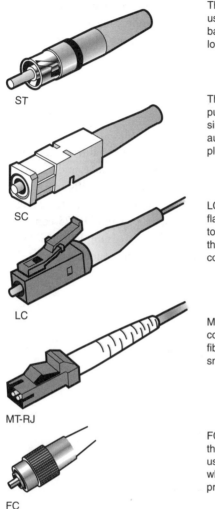

The ST connector uses a half-twist bayonet type of lock.

ST

The SC uses a push-pull connector similar to common audio and video plugs and sockets.

SC

LC connectors have a flange on top, similar to an RJ-45 connector, that aids secure connection.

LC

MT-RJ is a popular connector for two fibers in a very small form factor.

MT-RJ

FC connectors have a threaded body and are used in environments where vibration is a problem.

FC

FIGURE 6.8 **Fiber connectors**

Within the various types of connectors (ST, SC, LC, MT-RJ, and so on), you can choose to purchase ones that are either angle polished connectors (APC) or ultra polished connectors (UPC). The biggest difference between these two is the "angle" present in APC. UPC connectors have an endface polished at a zero-degree angle (flat), whereas APC is eight degrees. As a general rule, the more polished (UPC) gives less insertion loss.

MT-RJ (standing for either Mechanical Transfer Registered Jack or Media Termination Recommended Jack) is popular for duplex multimode connections. It is often written with the dash between the letters, but CompTIA prefers to use MTRJ in their objectives and on the exam.

RS-232 Standard Connectors (DB-9 and DB-25)

Recommended Standard (RS-232) is a TIA/EIA standard for serial transmission between computers and peripheral devices such as modems, mice, and keyboards. The RS-232 standard was introduced way back in the 1960s and is still used today. However, peripheral devices are more commonly connected using USB or wireless connections. RS-232 commonly uses a 25-pin DB-25 connector or a nine-pin DB-9 connector. Figure 6.9 shows an example of RS-232 standard connectors with the numbers identifying the pin sequences used by all.

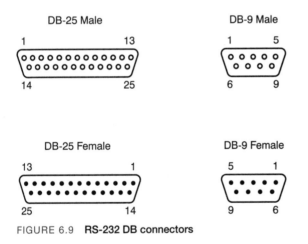

FIGURE 6.9 **RS-232 DB connectors**

Serial connectors need to attach to a serial cable. Serial cables often use four to six wires to attach to the connectors. Similar to other cable types, they can come in both an unshielded and shielded type. Shielding reduces interference and EMI for the cable. The distance that a length of serial cable can run varies somewhat. It depends on the characteristics of the serial port and the quality of the serial cable. The RS-232 standard specifies serial cable distances up to 50 feet and a transfer speed up to 20 Kbps. Other serial standards increase this range and speed.

Universal Serial Bus (USB) Connectors

USB ports are now an extremely common sight on desktop and mobile computer systems. USB is associated more with connecting consumer peripherals such as smartphones, MP3 players, and digital cameras than with networking. However, many manufacturers now make wireless network cards that plug directly into a USB port. Most desktop and mobile computers have between two and four USB ports, but USB hubs are available that provide additional ports if required.

A number of connectors are associated with USB ports, but the three most popular are Type A, Type B, and Type C. Type A connectors were traditionally the more common and used on PCs, whereas many peripheral devices used Type B connectors. In recent years, Type C (commonly called USB-C) has increased in popularity. Type C is a 24-pin USB connector that has a horizontally symmetrical "reversible" connector. Figure 6.10 shows the three types of USB connectors.

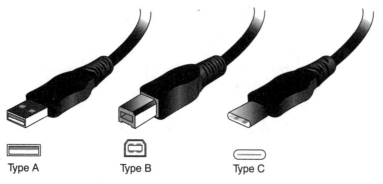

Type A   Type B   Type C

FIGURE 6.10   **Type A, B, and C connectors**

Transceivers

On routers, *small form-factor pluggable (SFP)* modules and *gigabit interface converter (GBIC)* modules are often used to link a gigabit Ethernet port with a fiber network (often 1000BASE-X). Both SFPs and GBICs exist for technologies other than fiber (Ethernet and SONET/SDH are usual), but connecting to fiber has become the most common use.

> **Note**
>
> *SFP+* is an enhanced small form-factor pluggable module that is a newer version of SFP that supports data rates up to 16 Gbps. Quad Small Form-factor Pluggable (QSFP) is a different transceiver that is both compact and hot-pluggable that has been jointly developed by many networking vendors.

Fiber transceivers are *bidirectional* and capable of operating in *duplex* mode. With either an SFP or GBIC, there is a *receiver port (RX)* and *transmitter port (TX)*. These devices are static-sensitive as well as dust-sensitive, and dirty connectors can cause intermittent problems. Care should be taken to not remove them more often than absolutely necessary to keep from shortening their life. After a module goes bad, they can be swapped for a new one to resolve the problem.

> **Note**
>
> Cisco has a great post on the care and maintenance of SFPs at www.cisco.com/en/US/products/hw/modules/ps4999/products_tech_note09186a00807a30d6.shtml.

Signal loss can occur not only from unclean connectors, but also from *connector mismatch*. Improper alignment and differences in core diameters contribute to signal loss.

When troubleshooting an SFP or GBIC, you want to make sure that you do not have a *cable mismatch* or a *bad cable/transceiver*. As simple as it may sound, it is important to verify that you are using a single-mode fiber with a single-mode interface and a multimode fiber cable for a multimode interface. Such a *fiber type mismatch* can cause the physical link to go completely down but does not always do so, thus making troubleshooting it difficult.

Media Couplers/Converters

When you have two dissimilar types of network media, a *media converter* is used to allow them to connect. They are sometimes referred to as couplers. Depending on the conversion being done, the converter can be a small device barely larger than the connectors themselves or a large device within a sizable chassis.

Reasons for not using the same media throughout the network, and thus reasons for needing a converter, can range from cost (gradually moving from coax to fiber), disparate segments (connecting the office to the factory), or needing to run a particular media in a setting (the need for fiber to reduce EMI problems in a small part of the building).

Figure 6.11 shows an example of a media converter. The one shown converts between 10/100/1000TX and SFP.

FIGURE 6.11   **A common media converter**

The following converters are commonly implemented and ones that CompTIA includes on the Network+ exam.

> **ExamAlert**
>
> Make sure you know that the possibilities listed here exist.
>
> ▶ Single mode fiber to Ethernet
> ▶ Single mode to multimode fiber
> ▶ Multimode fiber to Ethernet
> ▶ Fiber to coaxial

568A and 568B Wiring Standards

568A and 568B are telecommunications standards from TIA and EIA. These 568 standards specify the pin arrangements for the RJ-45 connectors on UTP or STP cables. The number 568 refers to the order in which the wires within the cable are terminated and attached to the connector.

The *TIA/EIA 568A* and *568B* standards (often referred to as *T568A* and *T568B* for termination standard) are similar; the difference is the order in which the pins are terminated. The signal is the same for both. Both are used for patch cords in an Ethernet network.

Network media might not always come with connectors attached, or you might need to make custom length cables. This is when you need to know something about how these standards actually work. Before you can crimp on the connectors, you need to know in which order the individual wires will be attached to the connector. Figure 6.12 shows the pin number assignments for the T568A and T568B standards.

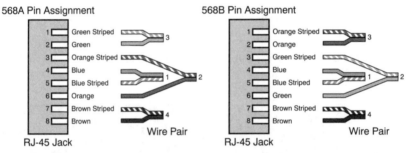

FIGURE 6.12 **Pin assignments for the T568A and T568B standards**

Straight-Through Versus Crossover Cables

Two types of cables are used to connect devices to hubs and switches: crossover cables and straight-through cables. The difference between the two types is that in a crossover cable, two of the wires are crossed; in a straight-through cable, all the wires run straight through.

Specifically, in a crossover cable, wires 1 and 3 and wires 2 and 6 are crossed. Wire 1 at one end becomes wire 3 at the other end, wire 2 at one end becomes wire 6 at the other end, and vice versa in both cases. You can see the differences between the two cables in Figures 6.13 and 6.14. Figure 6.13 shows the pinouts for a straight-through cable, and Figure 6.14 shows the pinouts for a crossover cable.

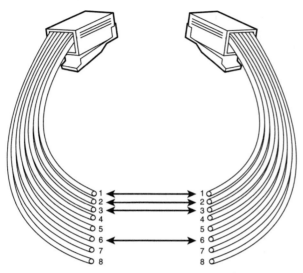

FIGURE 6.13   **Pinouts for a straight-through twisted-pair cable**

Note

Auto MDI-X ports on newer interfaces detect whether the connection requires a crossover and automatically choose the MDI or MDI-X configuration to match the other end of the link.

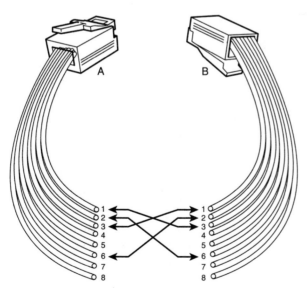

FIGURE 6.14   **Pinouts for a crossover twisted-pair cable**

To make a crossover Ethernet cable, you need to use both the 568A and 568B standards. One end of the cable can be wired according to the 568A standard and the other with the 568B standard.

A T1 crossover cable, the pinouts of which are shown in Figure 6.15, is used to connect two T1 CSU/DSU devices in a back-to-back configuration. RJ-45 connectors are used on both ends.

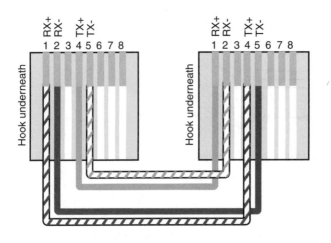

PRI (T1) CrossOver/Loopback Cable

FIGURE 6.15   Pinouts for a T1 crossover cable

Rollover and Loopback Cables

The rollover cable is a Cisco proprietary cable used to connect a computer system to a router or switch console port. The rollover cable resembles an Ethernet UTP cable; however, it is not possible to use it on anything but Cisco equipment. Like UTP cable, the rollover cable has eight wires inside and an RJ-45 connectors on each end that connect to the router and the computer port.

As far as pinouts are concerned, pin 1 on one end of the rollover cable connects to pin 8 at the other end of the cable. Similarly, pin 2 connects to pin 7, and so on. The ends are simply reversed. As soon as one end of the rollover cable is connected to the PC and the other to the Cisco terminal, the Cisco equipment can be accessed from the computer system using a program such as PuTTY.

> **ExamAlert**
>
> Remember that the rollover cable is a proprietary cable used to connect a PC to a Cisco router.

A loopback cable, also known as a *plug*, is used to test and isolate network problems. If made correctly, the loopback plug causes the link light on a device such as a *network interface card (NIC)* to come on. This is a quick and cheap way to test simple network cabling problems. The loopback plug redirects outgoing data signals to the system. The system then believes that it is both sending and receiving data.

The loopback cable is basically a troubleshooting tool used to test the device to see if it is sending and receiving properly. It uses UTP cable and RJ-45 connectors.

> **ExamAlert**
>
> Know that a loopback cable is a basic troubleshooting tool.

Components of Wiring Distribution

So far, this chapter has examined various types of media and the associated connectors. This section looks at wiring in the closet, the place in networks where you connect the cables and networking devices. These rooms have many names, including the wiring closet, the telecommunications room, and the *network operations center (NOC)*. These telecommunications rooms contain the key network devices, such as the hubs, routers, switches, and servers. These rooms also contain the network media, such as patch cables that connect network devices to horizontal cables and the rest of the network.

Network Cross-Connects

The cable that runs throughout a network can be divided into two distinct sections:

▶ **Horizontal cabling:** Connects client systems to the network.

▶ **Vertical (backbone) cabling:** Runs between floors to connect different locations on the network.

Both of these cable types have to be consolidated and distributed from a location—a wiring closet.

Following are three types of cable distribution:

▶ **Vertical or main cross-connect:** The location where outside cables enter the building for distribution. This can include Internet and phone cabling.

▶ **Horizontal cross-connect:** The location where the vertical and horizontal connections meet.

▶ **Intermediate cross-connect:** Typically used in larger networks. Provides an intermediate cross-connect between the main and horizontal cross-connects.

The term *cross-connect* refers to the point where the cables running throughout the network meet and are connected.

Horizontal Cabling

Within the telecommunications room, horizontal cabling connects the telecommunications room to the end user, as shown in Figure 6.16. Specifically, the horizontal cabling extends from the telecommunications outlet, or a network outlet with RJ-45 connectors, at the client end. It includes all cable from that outlet to the telecommunications room to the horizontal cross-connect—the distribution point for the horizontal cable. The horizontal cross-connect includes all connecting hardware, such as patch panels and patch cords. The horizontal cross-connect is the termination point for all network horizontal cables.

Horizontal cabling runs within walls and ceilings and therefore is called *permanent cable* or *structure cable*. The length of cable running from the horizontal connects and the telecommunication outlet on the client side should not exceed 90 meters. Patch cables used typically should not exceed 5 meters. This is because of the 100-meter distance limitation of most UTP cable.

> **Note**
>
> Horizontal wiring includes all cabling run from the wall plate or network connection to the telecommunications closet. The outlets, cable, and cross-connects in the closet are all part of the horizontal wiring, which gets its name because the cable typically runs horizontally above ceilings or along the floor.

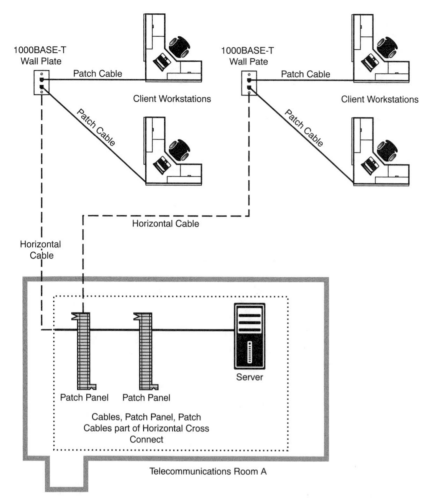

FIGURE 6.16   **Horizontal cabling**

Vertical Cables

Vertical cable, or backbone cable, refers to the media used to connect telecommunications rooms, server rooms, and remote locations and offices. Vertical cable may be used to connect locations outside the local LAN that require high-speed connections. Therefore, vertical cable is often fiber-optic cable or high-speed UTP cable. Figure 6.17 shows the relationship between horizontal cable and vertical cable.

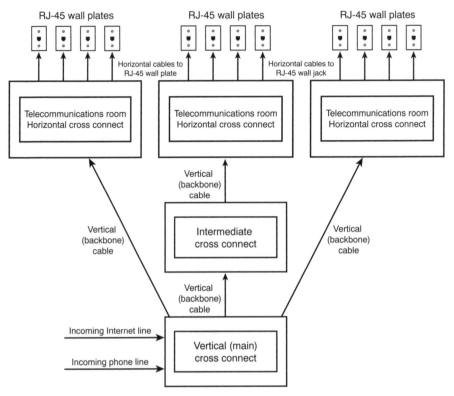

FIGURE 6.17 **Vertical and horizontal cabling**

Patch Panels

If you have ever looked in a telecommunications room, you have probably seen a distribution block, more commonly called a patch panel. A *patch panel* is a freestanding or wall-mounted unit with a number of RJ-45 port connections on the front. In a way, it looks like a wall-mounted hub without the *light-emitting diodes (LEDs)*. The patch panel provides a connection point between network equipment, such as hubs and switches, and the ports to which PCs are connected, which normally are distributed throughout a building.

> **Note**
>
> Not all environments use patch panels. In some environments, cables run directly between systems and a hub or switch. This is an acceptable method of connectivity, but it is not as easy to make tidy as a structured cabling system that uses a patch panel system and wall or floor sockets.

Also found in a wiring closet is the punchdown block. The wires from a telephony or UTP cable are attached to the punchdown block using a *punchdown tool*. To use the punchdown tool, you place the wires in the tip of the tool and push it into the connectors attached to the punchdown block. The wire insulation is stripped, and the wires are firmly embedded into the metal connector. Because the connector strips the insulation on the wire, it is known rather grandiosely as an *insulation displacement connector (IDC)*. Figure 6.18 shows a punchdown tool placing wires into an IDC of a patch panel.

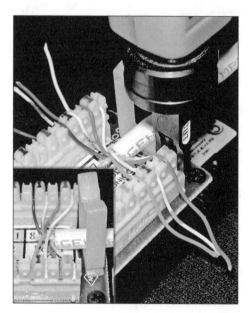

FIGURE 6.18   **Punchdown tool inserting wires into an IDC**

Using a punchdown tool is much faster than using wire strippers to prepare each individual wire and then twisting the wire around a connection pole or tightening a screw to hold the wire in place. In many environments, cable tasks are left to a specialized cable contractor. In others, the administrator is the one who must connect wires to a patch panel.

ExamAlert

Punchdown tools are used to attach twisted-pair network cable to connectors within a patch panel. Specifically, they connect twisted-pair wires to the IDC.

Fiber Distribution Panels

Just as a patch panel is used to provide a connection point between network equipment, so too is a *fiber distribution panel (FDP)*. The difference between the two is that the FDP is a cabinet intended to provide space for termination, storage, and splicing of fiber connections.

ExamAlert

As you study for the exam, make sure you can identify the following exam objectives discussed here and following: termination points, 66 block, 110 block, patch panel, and fiber distribution panel.

---

66 and 110 Blocks (T568A, T568B)

Two main types of punchdown blocks are used: type 66 and type 110. Type 66 is an older design used to connect wiring for telephone systems and other low-speed network systems and is not as widely used as type 110. The 66 block has 50 rows of IDC contacts to accommodate 25-pair twisted-pair cable. Block 66 was used primarily for voice communication. Although it was approved for Category 5 and greater, it is not really suitable for anything greater than 10BASE-T due to crosstalk problems. However, specialized CAT5e certified 66 blocks are available that do meet CAT5e termination standards.

In the network wiring closet, the 110 block is used to connect network cable to patch panels. 110 connections can also be used at the other end of the network cable at the RJ-45 wall jack. 110 blocks are preferred over the older 66 blocks, the 110 block improves on the 66 block by supporting higher frequencies and less crosstalk. Therefore, it supports higher-speed networks and higher grade twisted-pair cable. The termination will be T568A or T568B, depending on which wiring standard is used.

MDF and IDF Wiring Closets

The preceding section looked at wiring closets. Two types of wiring closets are *main distribution frame (MDF)* and *intermediate distribution frame (IDF)*. The main wiring closet for a network typically holds the majority of the network gear, including routers, switches, wiring, servers, and more. This is also typically the wiring closet where outside lines run into the network. This main wiring closet is known as the MDF. One of the key components in the MDF is a primary patch panel. The network connector jacks attached to this patch panel lead out to the building for network connections.

In some networks, multiple wiring closets are used. When this is the case, the MDF connects to these secondary wiring closets, or IDFs, using a backbone cable. This backbone cable may be UTP, fiber, or even coaxial. In today's high-speed networks, UTP Gigabit Ethernet or high-speed fiber are the media of choice. Figure 6.19 shows the relationship between the MDF and the IDF.

ExamAlert

Be prepared to identify the difference between an IDF and an MDF.

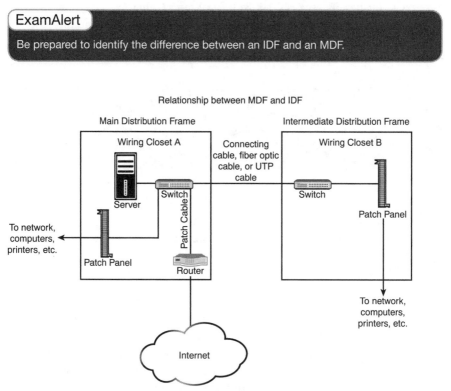

FIGURE 6.19 **The relationship between MDFs and IDFs**

Ethernet Deployment Standards

A number of IEEE standards relate to networking and cover everything from implementation to security. The 802.3 standards relate to Ethernet deployment, and many of the early ones have become outdated. Make sure that you are familiar with the information that follows for the most popular standards presently before you take the Network+ exam.

100BaseT

At one time, 10 Mbps networks were considered fast enough, but those days are long gone. Today, companies and home users alike demand more bandwidth than that and three Fast Ethernet (100BaseT) standards are specified in the

IEEE 802.3u standard: 100BASE-T4, 100BASE-TX, and 100BASE-FX—not all of which you need to know for the Network+ exam objectives.

As its name suggests, 100BASE-TX transmits network data at speeds up to 100 Mbps. 100BASE-TX is most often implemented with UTP cable, but it can use STP; therefore, it suffers from the same 100-meter distance limitations as other UTP-based networks. 100BASE-TX uses Category 5, or higher, UTP cable, and it uses independent transmit and receive paths and therefore can support full-duplex operation. 100BASE-TX is the most common implementation of the Fast Ethernet standard.

> **ExamAlert**
>
> Hyphens have no meaning when it comes to wiring standards; 100Base-T is the same as 100BaseT. Although the most recent iteration of the exam objectives leaves the hyphen out, know that both notations mean the same thing.

> **Tip**
>
> Repeaters are sometimes needed when you connect segments that use 100BASE-TX, or 100BASE-FX.

100BASE-FX is the IEEE standard for running Fast Ethernet over fiber-optic cable. Due to the expense of fiber implementations, 100BASE-FX is largely limited to use as a network backbone. 100BASE-FX can use two-strand multimode fiber or single-mode fiber media. The maximum segment length for half-duplex multimode fiber is 412 meters, but this maximum increases to an impressive 10,000 meters for full-duplex single-mode fiber. 100BASE-FX often uses SC or ST fiber connectors. Table 6.3 summarizes the characteristics of the 802.3u Fast Ethernet specifications.

TABLE 6.3   **Summary of 802.3u Fast Ethernet Characteristics**

Characteristic	100BASE-TX	100BASE-FX
Transmission method	Baseband	Baseband
Speed	100 Mbps	100 Mbps
Distance	100 meters	412 meters (multimode half duplex); 10,000 meters (single mode full duplex)
Cable type	Category UTP, STP	Fiber optic
Connector type	RJ-45	SC, ST

1000BaseT

1000BaseT, sometimes called 1000BASE-T or 1000BASE-TX, is a Gigabit Ethernet standard, and it is given the IEEE 802.3ab designation. The 802.3ab standard specifies Gigabit Ethernet over Category 5 or better UTP cable. The standard allows for full-duplex transmission using the four pairs of twisted cable. To reach speeds of 1000 Mbps over copper, a data transmission speed of 250 Mbps is achieved over each pair of twisted-pair cable. Table 6.4 summarizes the characteristics of 1000BaseT.

TABLE 6.4 **Summary of 1000BaseT Characteristics**

Characteristic	Description
Transmission method	Baseband
Speed	1000 Mbps
Total distance/segment	75 meters
Cable type	Category 5 or better
Connector type	RJ-45

10GBaseT

The 802.3an standard brings 10-gigabit speed to regular copper cabling. Although transmission distances may not be that of fiber, it allows a potential upgrade from 1000 Gbps networking to 10 Gbps networking using the current wiring infrastructure.

The 10GBaseT standard specifies 10 Gbps transmissions over UTP or STP twisted-pair cables. The standard calls for a cable specification of Category 6 or Category 6a. With Category 6, the maximum transmission range is 55 meters; with the augmented Category 6a cable, transmission range increases to 100 meters. Category 6 and 6a cables are specifically designed to reduce attenuation and crosstalk, making 10 Gbps speeds possible. 802.3an specifies regular RJ-45 networking connectors. Table 6.5 outlines the characteristics of the 802.3an standard.

TABLE 6.5 **Summary of 802.3an Characteristics**

Characteristic	Descriptions
Transmission method	Baseband
Speed	10 Gbps
Total distance/segment	100 meters Category 6a cable; 55 meters Category 6 cable
Cable type	Category 6, 6a UTP or STP
Connector	RJ-45

1000BaseLX and 1000BaseSX

Both 1000BaseLX and 1000BaseSX are Gigabit Ethernet standards for fiber.

1000BaseLX is a fiber standard for Gigabit Ethernet that utilizes single-mode fiber. It can also run over multimode fiber with a maximum segment length of 550m.

1000BaseSX is intended for use with multimode fiber and has a maximum length of 220 meters for default installations (550 meters is possible with the right optics and terminations). This standard is popular for intrabuilding links in office buildings.

Cram Quiz

1. Which of following connectors is commonly used with fiber cabling?

   ○ **A.** RJ-45

   ○ **B.** BNC

   ○ **C.** SC

   ○ **D.** RJ-11

2. What kind of cable would you associate with an F-type connector?

   ○ **A.** Fiber optic

   ○ **B.** UTP

   ○ **C.** Coaxial

   ○ **D.** STP

3. Which of the following is not a type of fiber-optic connector used in network implementations?

   ○ **A.** MTRJ

   ○ **B.** SC

   ○ **C.** BNC

   ○ **D.** LC

4. Which of the following fiber connectors uses a twist-type connection method?

   ○ **A.** ST

   ○ **B.** SC

   ○ **C.** BNC

   ○ **D.** SA

5. Which of the following is a fiber standard for Gigabit Ethernet that utilizes single-mode fiber?

  ○ **A.** 1000BaseSX

  ○ **B.** TIA/EIA 568a

  ○ **C.** RG-6

  ○ **D.** 1000BaseLX

6. In a crossover cable, which wire is wire 1 crossed with?

  ○ **A.** 2

  ○ **B.** 3

  ○ **C.** 4

  ○ **D.** 5

7. What are the two main types of punchdown blocks? (Choose two.)

  ○ **A.** 110

  ○ **B.** 220

  ○ **C.** 66

  ○ **D.** 12

8. Which of the following are cables that are specifically coated with a nonflammable material and do not give off toxic fumes if they catch fire?

  ○ **A.** SFP and GBIC

  ○ **B.** Cat 5e, Cat 6, Cat 6a

  ○ **C.** FDP

  ○ **D.** Plenum-rated

Cram Quiz Answers

1. **C.** SC connectors are used with fiber-optic cable. RJ-45 connectors are used with UTP cable, BNC is used for thin coax cable, and RJ-11 is used for regular phone connectors.

2. **C.** F-type connectors are used with coaxial cables. They are not used with fiber-optic, unshielded twisted-pair (UTP), or shielded twisted-pair (STP) cabling.

3. **C.** BNC is a connector type used with coaxial cabling. It is not used as a connector for fiber-optic cabling. MTRJ, SC, and LC are all recognized types of fiber-optic connectors.

4. **A.** ST fiber connectors use a twist-type connection method. SC connectors use a push-type connection method. The other choices are not valid fiber connectors.

5. **D.** 1000BaseLX is a fiber standard for Gigabit Ethernet that utilizes single-mode fiber. 1000BaseSX is intended for use with multimode fiber and has a maximum

length of 220 meters for default installations. TIA/EIA 568A (and 568B) are telecommunications standards that specify the pin arrangements for the RJ-45 connectors on UTP or STP cables. RG-6 is a common type of coaxial cable often used for cable TV and cable modems.

6. **B.** In a crossover cable, wires 1 and 3 and wires 2 and 6 are crossed.

7. **A, C.** The two main types of punchdown blocks are type 66 and type 110. Type 66 is an older design used to connect wiring for telephone systems and other low-speed network systems and is not as widely used as type 110.

8. **D.** Plenum-rated cables are coated with a nonflammable material, often Teflon or Kynar, and they do not give off toxic fumes if they catch fire. On routers, SFP modules and GBIC modules are often used to link a gigabit Ethernet port with a fiber network. Cat 5, Cat 5e, Cat 6, Cat 6a are general categories of twisted-pair cabling. FDP is an acronym for fiber distribution panel: a cabinet intended to provide space for termination, storage, and splicing of fiber connections.

Troubleshooting Common Wired Connectivity Issues

▶ **Given a scenario, troubleshoot common wired connectivity and performance issues.**

CramSaver

If you can correctly answer these questions before going through this section, save time by skimming the Exam Alerts in this section and then completing the Cram Quiz at the end of the section.

1. What is the correct term for delay time on a satellite-based network?

2. What are two types of crosstalk?

Answers

1. Latency is the time of the delay.

2. Two types of crosstalk are near end (NEXT) and far end crosstalk (FEXT).

When administering a wired network, you should be aware of a number of performance issues and common connectivity problems. Some of the topics lumped within this objective are more knowledge/definitions than actionable items, but make sure you are familiar with the following.

ExamAlert

Remember that this objective begins with "Given a scenario." That means that you may receive a drag and drop, matching, or "live OS" scenario where you have to click through to complete a specific objective-based task.

Attenuation

Attenuation refers to the weakening of data signals as they travel through a medium. Network media vary in their resistance to attenuation. Coaxial cable generally is more resistant than *unshielded twisted-pair (UTP)*; *shielded twisted-pair (STP)* is slightly more resistant than UTP; and fiber-optic cable does not suffer from attenuation. That's not to say that a signal does not weaken as it travels over fiber-optic cable, but the correct term for this weakening is *chromatic dispersion* rather than attenuation.

You must understand attenuation or chromatic dispersion and the maximum distances specified for network media. Exceeding a medium's distance without using repeaters can cause hard-to-troubleshoot network problems. A repeater is a network device that amplifies data signals as they pass, enabling them to travel farther. Most attenuation-related or chromatic dispersion-related difficulties on a network require using a network analyzer to detect them.

All media have recommended lengths at which the cable can be run. This is because data signals weaken as they travel farther from the point of origin. If the signal travels far enough, it can weaken so much that it becomes unusable. The weakening of data signals as they traverse the medium is called attenuation. The measurement of it is done in decibels; thus, attenuation is also known as *dB loss*.

All copper-based cabling is particularity susceptible to attenuation. When cable lengths have to be run farther than the recommended lengths, signal repeaters can be used to boost the signal as it travels. If you work on a network with intermittent problems, and you notice that cable lengths are run too far, attenuation may be the problem.

> **ExamAlert**
>
> For the Network+ objective referencing cable problems associated with distance, think of attenuation.

Latency

One of the biggest problems with satellite access is trouble with *latency* (the time lapse between sending or requesting information and the time it takes to return). Satellite communication experiences high latency due to the distance it has to travel as well as weather conditions.

The current average latency with satellite is 638ms. Attempts have been made to reduce latency by using satellites in lower orbit (thus a shorter distance to travel), but they usually offer service at lower rates of speed and thus have not been an ideal solution.

While latency is not restricted solely to satellites, it is one of the easiest forms of transmission to associate with it. In reality, latency can occur with almost any form of transmission.

Jitter

Closely tied to latency, which was discussed earlier, *jitter* differs in that the length of the delay between received packets differs. While the sender continues to transmit packets in a continuous stream and space them evenly apart, the delay between packets received varies instead of remaining constant. This can be caused by network congestion, improper queuing, or configuration errors.

Crosstalk

Whether it is coaxial cable or UTP, copper-based cabling is susceptible to crosstalk. *Crosstalk* happens when the signal in one cable gets mixed up with the signal in another cable. This can happen when cables are run too closely together. Cables use shielding to help reduce the impact of crosstalk. If shielded cable is not used, cables should be separated from each other. Crosstalk can also occur when one wire pair within the twisted-pair cable interferes with the signals on other wires. Crosstalk can be a result of insufficient cable shielding, disparity between signal levels in adjacent circuits, and twisted terminations at connection points. There are two types of crosstalk interference: *near end (NEXT)* and *far end crosstalk (FEXT)*.

> **ExamAlert**
>
> Remember that fiber-optic uses optical signals, not electrical, giving it a greater resistance to EMI and crosstalk.

Near End Crosstalk (NEXT)

NEXT refers to interference between adjacent wire pairs within the twisted-pair cable at the near end of the link (the end closest to the origin of the data signal). NEXT occurs when an outgoing data transmission leaks over to an incoming transmission. In effect, the incoming transmission overhears the signal sent by a transmitting station at the near end of the link. The result is that a portion of the outgoing signal is coupled back into the received signal.

Far End Crosstalk (FEXT)

FEXT occurs when a receiving station overhears a data signal being sent by a transmitting station at the other end of a transmission line. FEXT identifies the interference of a signal through a wire pair to an adjacent pair at the farthest end from the interfering source (the end where the signal is received).

> **Note**
>
> As mentioned previously, crosstalk occurs when the signals sent through media interfere with data signals on adjacent wires. Within the twisted-pair cable, each wire pair is twisted to help reduce crosstalk; the tighter the twist, the more effective the cable is at managing crosstalk. This is one reason to buy high-quality cable.

EMI

Depending on where network cabling (commonly called *media*) is installed, *interference* can be a major consideration. Two types of media interference can adversely affect data transmissions over network media: *electromagnetic interference (EMI)* and crosstalk (discussed earlier).

EMI is a problem when cables are installed near electrical devices, such as air conditioners or fluorescent light fixtures. If a network medium is placed close enough to such a device, the signal within the cable might become corrupt. Network media vary in their resistance to the effects of EMI. Standard *unshielded twisted-pair (UTP)* cable is susceptible to EMI, whereas fiber cable, with its light transmissions, is resistant to EMI. When deciding on a particular medium, consider where it will run and the impact EMI can have on the installation.

EMI can reduce or corrupt signal strength. This can happen when cables are run too close to everyday office fixtures, such as computer monitors, fluorescent lights, elevators, microwaves, and anything else that creates an electromagnetic field. Again, the solution is to carefully run cables away from such devices. If they have to be run through EMI areas, shielded cabling or fiber cabling is needed.

Open/Short

In addition to the common issue of miswiring, other problems that can occur with cables (and that can be checked with a multifunction cable tester) include *open/short* faults. An open fault means that the cables are not making a full circuit; this can be due to a cut in the cable (across all or some of the wires). A short fault means that the data attempts to travel on wires other than those for which it is intended; this can be caused by miswiring or a twist in the cabling at a cut allowing the bare wires to touch.

> **ExamAlert**
>
> You should expect questions asking you what tool can be used to identify an open/short fault.

Incorrect Pin-Out

Most splits in a cable are intentional—enabling you to run the wiring in multiple directions with the use of a splitter. Depending on the type of cabling in question, it is not uncommon for each split to reduce the strength of the signal. It is also not uncommon for splitters to go bad. You want to split the cable as few times as possible and check the splitter if a problem in a run that was normally working suddenly occurs.

If the split is unintentional, you are often dealing with an open/short, which was the subject of the previous discussion.

Incorrect Cable Types

An incorrect cable type—using a crossover cable instead of a standard cable, for instance—will keep the host from being able to communicate on the network. A cable tester can be used to diagnose individual cabling issues, and the solution is to swap the incorrect cable with one suited for the purpose you are intending to use it for.

Bad Port

On the router, the port configuration dictates what traffic is allowed to flow through. The router can be configured to enable individual port traffic in, out, or both and is referred to as *port forwarding*. If a port is blocked (such as 80 for HTTP or 21 for FTP), the data will not be allowed through, and users will be affected.

> **ExamAlert**
>
> Think of port configuration and port forwarding as the same when it comes to the router.

A condition known as a *black hole* can occur when a router does not send back an expected message that the data has been received. It is known as a black hole from the view that data is being sent, but is essentially being lost.

This condition occurs when the packet the router receives is larger than the configured size of the *maximum transmission unit (MTU)* and the Don't Fragment flag is configured on that packet. When this occurs, the router is supposed to send a "Destination Unreachable" message back to the host. If the packet is not received, the host does not know that the packet did not go through.

Although there are several solutions to this problem, the best is to verify whether a mismatch has occurred between the maximum size packet clients can send and that the router can handle. You can use ping to check that packets of a particular size can move through the router by using the -1 parameter to set a packet size and the -f parameter to set the Do Not Fragment bit.

Transceiver Mismatch

When troubleshooting an SFP or GBIC, you want to make sure that you do not have a bad, or mismatched, transceiver. As simple as it may sound, it is important to verify that you are using a single-mode fiber with a single-mode interface and a multimode fiber cable for a multimode interface. Such a fiber type mismatch can cause the physical link to go completely down but does not always do so, thus making troubleshooting it difficult.

TX/RX Reversed

Two primary types of cables can be used in an Ethernet network: a straight-through cable (as the name implies, all wires run straight through and are the same on both ends) and a crossover cable. In a crossover cable, two pairs of the wires are reversed; these are the TX and RX pairs (transmit and receive).

A crossover cable is intended to be used in specific applications only (such as to directly network two PCs without using a hub or switch) and will cause problems when used where a straight-through cable is called for (as a general rule, in all fixed wiring).

Duplex/Speed Mismatch

When configuring a client for the network, you must be aware of two settings: port speed and duplex settings. These are adjusted in Windows in the Network Properties area. Speed and duplex mismatches can slow data rates to a crawl and prevent high-bandwidth applications (such as voice or streaming video) from being possible.

You have several choices for port speed and duplex settings. You can choose Auto Negotiation to detect the setting that the network uses. You also can choose one of the other settings to match the network configuration, such as 100 Mbps Half Duplex. If you work with a client system that is unable to log on to a network, you might need to ensure that the duplex setting and port speeds are correctly set for the network.

Damaged Cables

Damaged or bad wiring could be a patch cable (easy to replace) or the in-wall wiring (more difficult to replace). If you suspect wiring to be the faulty component, you can diagnose rather quickly by taking the device that is having trouble connecting to another location and/or bringing a working machine to this environment.

> **Note**
>
> Never assume that the cable you use is good until you test it and confirm that it is good. Sometimes cables break, and bad media can cause network problems.

You can use a multifunction cable tester to troubleshoot most wiring problems. You must check for cable continuity, as well as for shorts.

Bent Pins

Bent pins on a network cable or socket can result in very little or no contact being made on those connections. If the problem is with the cable, you can replace the cable. If the problem is with the client machine, it can be difficult to fix because most Ethernet ports are soldered directly to the motherboard. Often, the solution is to abandon that port and use a USB/Ethernet adapter to allow the client to continue to connect to the network.

Bottlenecks

Network bottlenecks often lead to network breakdowns. Because of that, you want to always be scanning for them and identify them before they have the opportunity to bring your system down. A number of tools are useful in checking connectivity. One of the simplest might be `traceroute`, which provides a lot of useful information, including the IP address of every router connection it passes through and, in many cases, the name of the router. (This depends on the router's configuration.) `traceroute` also reports the length, in milliseconds, of the round-trip the packet made from the source location to the router and back.

> **Note**
>
> The `traceroute` utility/command is usually associated with Linux and Mac OS, and `tracert` performs the same function in Microsoft Windows.

After a bottleneck has been identified, it is imperative to monitor it and plan to eliminate it as soon as possible.

VLAN Mismatch

VLANs provide a method to segment and organize the network. Computer systems can be located anywhere on the network but communicate as if they are on the same segment. For example, networks with VLANs can be segmented according to an organization's departments, such as sales, finance, and secretaries, or can be segmented according to usage, security permissions, and more.

Segmenting the network offers some clear advantages. It provides increased security because devices can communicate only with other systems in the VLAN. Users can see only the systems in their VLAN segment. This can help control broadcast traffic and makes it easier to move end systems around the network.

Problems can arise when users are moved or otherwise connected to the wrong VLAN. Administrators have to ensure that the user system is plugged into the correct VLAN port. For example, suppose a network is using port-based VLANs to assign ports 1 through 8 to marketing, ports 9 through 18 to sales, and so on. Plugging a sales client into port 6 would make that sales client part of the marketing network. This sounds simple, but if the documentation is not up-to-date, and you work with a new network, this can be tricky to identify.

One of the keys to preventing VLAN assignment errors is to clearly document the VLAN arrangement. If systems are moved, you need to know how to reconnect them and forward them to the correct VLAN port.

> **ExamAlert**
>
> VLAN assignment is one of the troubleshooting topics you should expect to see a question about on the exam.

Another consideration to keep in mind is that membership to a VLAN can be assigned both statically and dynamically. In static VLAN assignment, the switch ports are assigned to a specific VLAN. New systems added are assigned to the VLAN associated with that particular port. For example, if you plug a new system into port 8, the user becomes part of the administrator's network. So you must ensure that you have the right port assigned to users.

Dynamic VLAN assignment requires specific software to control VLAN distribution. Using a VLAN server, administrators can dynamically assign VLAN membership based on criteria such as a MAC address or a username/

password combination. As a system tries to access the network, it queries the VLAN server database to ask for VLAN membership information. The server responds and logs the system on to the appropriate VLAN network. When correctly configured, dynamic assignment reduces the human error associated with static VLAN assignment.

Network Connection LED Status Indicators

Hubs and switches provide light-emitting diodes (LEDs) that provide information on the port status. For instance, by using the LEDs, you can determine whether there is a jabbering network card, whether there is a proper connection to the network device, and whether there are too many collisions on the network.

Cram Quiz

1. Which of the following describes the loss of signal strength as a signal travels through a particular medium?

   ○ **A.** Attenuation
   ○ **B.** Crosstalk
   ○ **C.** EMI
   ○ **D.** Chatter

2. A user calls to report that he is experiencing periodic problems connecting to the network. Upon investigation, you find that the cable connecting the user's PC to the switch is close to a fluorescent light fixture. What condition is most likely causing the problem?

   ○ **A.** Crosstalk
   ○ **B.** EMI
   ○ **C.** Attenuation
   ○ **D.** Faulty cable

3. Which of the following is similar to latency but differs in that the length of the delay between received packets differs?

   ○ **A.** Slack
   ○ **B.** Jitter
   ○ **C.** Stretch
   ○ **D.** Lax

4. With a crossover cable, which two pairs are reversed?

- ○ **A.** RX and SX
- ○ **B.** TX and RX
- ○ **C.** SX and TX
- ○ **D.** SX and CX

Cram Quiz Answers

1. **A.** The term used to describe the loss of signal strength for media is *attenuation*. Crosstalk refers to the interference between two cables, EMI is electromagnetic interference, and chatter is not a valid media interference concern.

2. **B.** EMI is a type of interference that is often seen when cables run too close to electrical devices. Crosstalk is when two cables interfere with each other. Attenuation is a loss of signal strength. Answer D is incorrect also. It may be that a faulty cable is causing the problem. However, the question asked for the most likely cause. Because the cable is running near fluorescent lights, the problem is more likely associated with EMI.

3. **B.** Jitter is when the length of the delay between received packets differs.

4. **B.** In a crossover cable, two pairs of the wires are reversed; these are the TX and RX pairs (transmit and receive).

What's Next?

This chapter focused on wiring solutions. Chapter 7, "Wireless Solutions," looks at wireless solutions. Client systems communicate with a wireless access point using wireless LAN adapters. Such adapters are built in to or can be added to laptop, handheld, or desktop computers. Wireless LAN adapters provide the communication point between the client system and the airwaves via an antenna.

CHAPTER 7

Wireless Solutions

This chapter covers the following official Network+ objectives:

▶ Given a scenario, implement the appropriate wireless technologies and configurations.

▶ Given a scenario, troubleshoot common wireless connectivity and performance issues.

This chapter covers CompTIA Network+ objectives 1.6 and 5.4. For more information on the official Network+ exam topics, see the "About the Network+ Exam" section in the Introduction.

One of the bigger changes in the networking world since the Network+ exam first came into being is in wireless networking technologies. Networks of all shapes and sizes incorporate wireless segments into their networks. Home wireless networking has also grown significantly in the past few years.

Wireless networking enables users to connect to a network using radio waves instead of wires. Network users within range of a wireless *access point (AP)* can move around an office or any other location within range of a hotspot freely, without needing to plug into a wired infrastructure. The benefits of wireless networking clearly have led to its continued growth.

This chapter explores the many facets of wireless networking, starting with some of the concepts and technologies that make wireless networking possible.

Understanding Wireless Basics

▶ **Given a scenario, implement the appropriate wireless technologies and configurations.**

CramSaver

If you can correctly answer these questions before going through this section, save time by skimming the Exam Alerts in this section and then completing the Cram Quiz at the end of the section.

1. How many nonoverlapping channels are supported by 802.11a?

2. What are the ranges the 802.11b and 802.11g standards operate in?

3. True or false: Linux users can use the `iwconfig` command to view the state of their wireless network.

Answers

1. 802.11a supports up to eight nonoverlapping channels.

2. 802.11b and 802.11g standards operate in the 2.4 to 2.497 GHz range.

3. True. Linux users can use the `iwconfig` command to view the state of their wireless network.

Note

One of the topics that objective 1.6 includes is the 802.11 wireless standards, but they are not discussed in this chapter because they were included in the first chapter. If you need a refresher on these topologies, review Chapter 1, "Introduction to Networking Technologies."

ExamAlert

Remember that this objective begins with "Given a scenario." That means that you may receive a drag and drop, matching, or "live OS" scenario where you have to click through to complete a specific objective-based task.

Wireless Channels and Frequencies

Radio frequency (RF) channels are an important part of wireless communication. A *channel* is the band of RF used for the wireless communication. Each IEEE wireless standard specifies the channels that can be used. The 802.11a standard specifies radio frequency ranges between 5.15 and 5.875 GHz. In contrast,

802.11b and 802.11g standards operate in the 2.4 to 2.497 GHz range. 802.11n can operate in either 2.4 GHz/5 GHz ranges, and 802.11ac operates in the 5 GHz range. IEEE wireless standards are discussed in detail later in this chapter.

> **Note**
>
> *Hertz (Hz)* is the standard of measurement for radio frequency. Hertz is used to measure the frequency of vibrations and waves, such as sound waves and electromagnetic waves. One hertz is equal to one cycle per second. RF is measured in *kilohertz (KHz)*, 1,000 cycles per second; *megahertz (MHz)*, one million cycles per second; or *gigahertz (GHz)*, one billion cycles per second.

As far as channels are concerned, 802.11a has a wider frequency band, enabling more channels and therefore more data throughput. As a result of the wider band, 802.11a supports up to eight nonoverlapping channels. 802.11b/g standards use the smaller band and support only up to three nonoverlapping channels.

It is recommended that nonoverlapping channels be used for communication. In the United States, 802.11b/g use 11 channels for data communication, as mentioned; three of these—channels 1, 6, and 11—are nonoverlapping. Most manufacturers set their default channel to one of the nonoverlapping channels to avoid transmission conflicts. With wireless devices you can select which channel your WLAN operates on to avoid interference from other wireless devices that operate in the 2.4 GHz frequency range.

When troubleshooting a wireless network, be aware that overlapping channels can disrupt the wireless communications. For example, in many environments, APs are inadvertently placed close together—perhaps two APs in separate offices located next door to each other or between floors. Signal disruption results if channel overlap exists between the APs. The solution is to try to move the AP to avoid the overlap problem, or to change channels to one of the other nonoverlapping channels. For example, you could switch from channel 6 to channel 11.

Typically, you would change the channel of a wireless device only if it overlapped with another device. If a channel must be changed, it must be changed to another, nonoverlapping channel. Table 7.1 shows the channel ranges for 802.11b/g wireless standards. Table 7.2 shows the channel ranges for 802.11a. 802.11n added the option of using both channels used by 802.11a and b/g and operating at 2.4 GHz/5 GHz. As such, you can think of 802.11n as an amendment that improved upon the previous 802.11 standards by adding *multiple-input multiple-output (MIMO)* antennas and a huge increase in the data rate. 802.11n devices are still available, but they have largely been superseded today by 802.11ac, which became an approved standard in January 2014, and can be thought of as an extension of 802.11n.

> **ExamAlert**
>
> When troubleshooting a wireless problem in Windows, you can use the `ipconfig` command to see the status of IP configuration. Similarly, the `ifconfig` command can be used in Linux. In addition, Linux users can use the `iwconfig` command to view the state of your wireless network. Using `iwconfig`, you can view such important information as the link quality, AP MAC address, data rate, and encryption keys, which can be helpful in ensuring that the parameters in the network are consistent.

> **Note**
>
> IEEE 802.11b/g wireless systems communicate with each other using radio frequency signals in the band between 2.4 GHz and 2.5 GHz. Neighboring channels are 5 MHz apart. Applying two channels that allow the maximum channel separation decreases the amount of channel crosstalk and provides a noticeable performance increase over networks with minimal channel separation.

Tables 7.1 and 7.2 outline the available wireless channels. When deploying a wireless network, it is recommended that you use channel 1, grow to use channel 6, and add channel 11 when necessary, because these three channels do not overlap.

> **ExamAlert**
>
> 802.11n and 802.11ac are the standards most common today, and you will be hard pressed to purchase (or even find) older technologies. It is, however, recommended that you know the older technologies for the exam.

TABLE 7.1 **RF Channels for 802.11b/g**

Channel	Frequency Band
1	2412 MHz
2	2417 MHz
3	2422 MHz
4	2427 MHz
5	2432 MHz
6	2437 MHz
7	2442 MHz
8	2447 MHz
9	2452 MHz
10	2457 MHz
11	2462 MHz

Note

One thing to remember when looking at Table 7.1 is that the RF channels listed (2412 for channel 1, 2417 for 2, and so on) are actually the center frequency that the transceiver within the radio and AP uses. There is only a 5 MHz separation between the center frequencies, and an 802.11b signal occupies approximately 30 MHz of the frequency spectrum. As a result, data signals fall within about 15 MHz of each side of the center frequency and overlap with several adjacent channel frequencies. This leaves you with only three channels (channels 1, 6, and 11 for the United States) that you can use without causing interference between APs.

TABLE 7.2 **RF Channels for 802.11a**

Channel	Frequency
36	5180 MHz
40	5200 MHz
44	5220 MHz
48	5240 MHz
52	5260 MHz
56	5280 MHz
60	5300 MHz
64	5320 MHz

As mentioned, channels 1, 6, and 11 do not overlap. On a non-MIMO setup (such as with 802.11a, b, or g), always try to use one of these three channels. Similarly, if you use 802.11n with 20 MHz channels, stay with channels 1, 6, and 11.

ExamAlert

Understand the importance of channels 1, 6, and 11 as you study for the exam.

ExamAlert

For the exam, you should know the values in Table 7.2.

Cellular Access

The *Global System for Mobile Communications (GSM)* can work with *code division-multiple access (CDMA)* to provide various means of cell phone coverage. GSM also uses *time-division multiple access (TDMA)* to provide multiuser access by chopping up the channel into sequential time slices. Each user of the channel takes turns to transmit and receive signals. The individual methods that can be used include LTE/4G, HSPA+, 3G, or Edge.

Speed, Distance, and Bandwidth

When talking about wireless transmissions, you need to distinguish between *throughput* and *data rate*. From time to time these terms are used interchangeably, but technically speaking, they are different. As shown later in this chapter, each wireless standard has an associated speed. For instance, 802.11n lists a theoretical speed of up to 600 Mbps, and 802.11ac lists speeds up to a whopping 1300 Mbps. This represents the speed at which devices using this standard can send and receive data. However, in network data transmissions, many factors prevent the actual speeds from reaching this end-to-end theoretical maximum. For instance, data packets include overhead such as routing information, checksums, and error recovery data. Although this might all be necessary, it can impact overall speed.

The number of clients on the network can also impact the data rate; the more clients, the more collisions. Depending on the network layout, collisions can have a significant impact on end-to-end transmission speeds. Wireless network signals degrade as they pass through obstructions such as walls or doors; the signal speed deteriorates with each obstruction.

All these factors leave you with the actual throughput of wireless data transmissions. Goodput represents the actual speed to expect from wireless transmissions (what is often thought of as throughput). In practical application, wireless transmissions are approximately one-half or less of the data rate. Depending on the wireless setup, the transmission rate could be much less than its theoretical maximum.

> ## ExamAlert
>
> Data rate refers to the theoretical maximum of a wireless standard, such as 600 Mbps or 1300 Mbps. Throughput refers to the actual speeds achieved after all implementation and interference factors.

> **Note**
>
> Speed is always an important factor in the design of any network, and *high through-put (ht)* is a goal that has been around for a while. A number of the 802.11 standards offer a high throughput connection type, such as *802.11a-ht* and *802.11g-ht*. Although these implementations are better with the ht than without, it is true that today you will achieve better results with 802.11ac.

Channel Bonding

With channel bonding, you can use two channels at the same time. As you might guess, the ability to use two channels at once increases performance. Bonding can help increase wireless transmission rates from the 54 Mbps offered with the 802.11g standards to a theoretical maximum of 600 Mbps with 802.11n. 802.11n uses the OFDM transmission strategy.

MIMO/MU-MIMO/Unidirectional/Omnidirectional

A wireless antenna is an integral part of overall wireless communication. Antennas come in many shapes and sizes, with each one designed for a specific purpose. Selecting the right antenna for a particular network implementation is a critical consideration, and one that could ultimately decide how successful a wireless network will be. In addition, using the right antenna can save you money on networking costs because you need fewer antennas and APs.

> **ExamAlert**
>
> *Multiple input, multiple output (MIMO)* and *multiuser multiple input, multiple output (MU-MIMO)* are advanced antenna technologies that are key in wireless standards such as 802.11n, 802.11ac, HSPA+, WiMAX, and LTE.

Many small home network adapters and APs come with a nonupgradable antenna, but higher-grade wireless devices require you to choose an antenna. Determining which antenna to select takes careful planning and requires an understanding of what range and speed you need for a network. The antenna is designed to help wireless networks do the following:

▶ Work around obstacles

▶ Minimize the effects of interference

▶ Increase signal strength

▶ Focus the transmission, which can increase signal speed

The following sections explore some of the characteristics of wireless antennas.

Antenna Ratings

When a wireless signal is low and is affected by heavy interference, it might be possible to upgrade the antenna to create a more solid wireless connection. To determine an antenna's strength, refer to its *gain value*. But how do you determine the gain value?

> **ExamAlert**
>
> For the exam, know that an antenna's strength is its gain value.

Suppose that a huge wireless tower is emanating circular waves in all directions. If you could see these waves, you would see them forming a sphere around the tower. The signals around the antenna flow equally in all directions, including up and down. An antenna that does this has a 0dBi gain value and is called an *isotropic antenna*. The isotropic antenna rating provides a base point for measuring actual antenna strength.

> **Note**
>
> The *dB* in dBi stands for decibels, and the *i* stands for the hypothetical isotropic antenna.

An antenna's gain value represents the difference between the 0dBi isotropic and the antenna's power. For example, a wireless antenna advertised as 15dBi is 15 times stronger than the hypothetical isotropic antenna. The higher the decibel figure, the higher the gain.

When looking at wireless antennas, remember that a higher gain value means stronger send and receive signals. In terms of performance, the general rule is that every 3dB of gain added doubles an antenna's effective power output.

Antenna Coverage

When selecting an antenna for a particular wireless implementation, you need to determine the type of coverage the antenna uses. In a typical configuration, a wireless antenna can be either *omnidirectional* or *unidirectional*. Which one you choose depends on the wireless environment.

An omnidirectional antenna is designed to provide a 360-degree dispersed wave pattern. This type of antenna is used when coverage in all directions from the antenna is required. Omnidirectional antennas are advantageous when a broad-based signal is required. For example, if you provide an even signal in all directions, clients can access the antenna and its associated AP from various locations. Because of the dispersed nature of omnidirectional antennas, the signal is weaker overall and therefore accommodates shorter signal distances. Omnidirectional antennas are great in an environment that has a clear line of sight between the senders and receivers. The power is evenly spread to all points, making omnidirectional antennas well suited for home and small office applications.

> **ExamAlert**
>
> Omnidirectional antennas provide wide coverage but weaker signal strength in any one direction than a directional antenna.

Unidirectional antennas are designed to focus the signal in a particular direction. This focused signal enables greater distances and a stronger signal between two points. The greater distances enabled by unidirectional antennas give you a viable alternative for connecting locations, such as two offices, in a point-to-point configuration.

Unidirectional antennas are also used when you need to tunnel or thread a signal through a series of obstacles. This concentrates the signal power in a specific direction and enables you to use less power for a greater distance than an omnidirectional antenna. Table 7.3 compares omnidirectional and unidirectional wireless antennas.

TABLE 7.3 **Comparing Omnidirectional and Unidirectional Antennas**

Characteristic	Omnidirectional	Unidirectional	Advantage/Disadvantage
Wireless area coverage	General coverage area	Focused coverage area	Omnidirectional allows 360-degree coverage, giving it a wide coverage area. Unidirectional provides a targeted path for signals to travel.
Wireless transmission range	Limited	Long point-to-point range	Omnidirectional antennas provide a 360-degree coverage pattern and, as a result, far less range. Unidirectional antennas focus the wireless transmission; this focus enables greater range.
Wireless coverage shaping	Restricted	The unidirectional wireless range can be increased and decreased.	Omnidirectional antennas are limited to their circular pattern range. Unidirectional antennas can be adjusted to define a specific pattern, wider or more focused.

> **Note**
>
> In the wireless world, *polarization* refers to the direction in which the antenna radiates wavelengths. This direction can be vertical, horizontal, or circular. Today, vertical antennas are perhaps the most common. As far as the configuration is concerned, the sending and receiving antennas should be set to the same polarization.

Site Surveys

As more networks go wireless, you need to pay special attention to issues associated with them. Wireless survey tools can be used to create heat maps showing the quantity and quality of wireless network coverage in areas. They can also allow you to see access points (including rogues) and security settings. These can be used to help you design and deploy an efficient network, and they can also be used (by you or others) to find weaknesses in your existing network (often marketed for this purpose as wireless analyzers).

Establishing Communications Between Wireless Devices

When you work with wireless networks, you must have a basic understanding of the communication that occurs between wireless devices. If you use an infrastructure wireless network design, the network has two key parts: the wireless client, also known as the *station (STA)*, and the AP. The AP acts as a *bridge* (or wireless bridge) between the STA and the wired network.

ExamAlert

When a single AP is connected to the wired network and to a set of wireless stations, it is called a *basic service set (BSS)*. An *extended service set (ESS)* describes the use of multiple BSSs that form a single subnetwork. Ad hoc mode is sometimes called an *independent basic service set (IBSS)*.

As with other forms of network communication, before transmissions between devices can occur, the wireless AP and the client must begin to talk to each other. In the wireless world, this is a two-step process involving *association* and *authentication*.

The association process occurs when a wireless adapter is turned on. The client adapter immediately begins scanning the wireless frequencies for wireless APs or, if using ad hoc mode, other wireless devices. When the wireless client is configured to operate in infrastructure mode, the user can choose a wireless AP with which to connect. This process may also be automatic, with the AP selection based on the SSID, signal strength, and frame error rate. Finally, the wireless adapter switches to the assigned channel of the selected wireless AP and negotiates the use of a port.

If at any point the signal between the devices drops below an acceptable level, or if the signal becomes unavailable for any reason, the wireless adapter initiates another scan, looking for an AP with stronger signals. When the new AP is located, the wireless adapter selects it and associates with it. This is known as *re-association*.

ExamAlert

The 802.11 standards enable a wireless client to roam between multiple APs. An AP transmits a beacon signal every so many milliseconds. It includes a time stamp for client synchronization and an indication of supported data rates. A client system uses the beacon message to identify the strength of the existing connection to an AP. If the connection is too weak, the *roaming* client attempts to associate itself with a new AP. This enables the client system to roam between distances and APs.

With the association process complete, the authentication process begins. After the devices associate, keyed security measures are applied before communication can take place. On many APs, authentication can be set to either *shared key authentication* or *open authentication*. The default setting for older APs typically is open authentication. Open authentication enables access with only the SSID and/or the correct WEP key for the AP. The problem with open authentication is that if you do not have other protection or authentication mechanisms in place, your wireless network is totally open to intruders. When set to shared key mode, the client must meet security requirements before communication with the AP can occur.

After security requirements are met, you have established IP-level communication. This means that wireless standard requirements have been met, and Ethernet networking takes over. There is basically a switch from 802.11 to 802.3 standards. The wireless standards create the physical link to the network, enabling regular networking standards and protocols to use the link. This is how the physical cable is replaced, but to the networking technologies there is no difference between regular cable media and wireless media.

Several components combine to enable wireless communications between devices. Each of these must be configured on both the client and the AP:

▶ **Service set identifier (SSID):** Whether your wireless network uses infrastructure mode or ad hoc mode, an SSID is required. The SSID is a configurable client identification that enables clients to communicate with a particular base station. Only client systems configured with the same SSID as the AP can communicate with it. SSIDs provide a simple password arrangement between base stations and clients in a BSS network. ESSIDs are used for the ESS wireless network.

▶ **Wireless channel:** As stated earlier in the chapter, RF channels are an important part of wireless communications. A channel is the frequency band used for the wireless communication. Each standard specifies the channels that can be used. The 802.11a standard specified radio frequency ranges between 5.15 GHz and 5.875 GHz. In contrast, the 802.11b and 802.11g standards operate in the 2.4 GHz to 2.497 GHz ranges. 802.11n can operate in either 2.4 GHz or 5 GHz range, and 802.11ac is at 5 GHz. Fourteen channels are defined in the IEEE 802.11 channel set, 11 of which are available in North America.

▶ **Security features:** IEEE 802.11 provides security using two methods: authentication and encryption. Authentication verifies the client system. In infrastructure mode, authentication is established between an AP and each station. Wireless encryption services must be the same on the client and the AP for communication to occur.

Configuring the Wireless Connection

Wireless connection configuration is fairly straightforward. Figure 7.1 shows an example of a simple wireless router. In addition to providing wireless access, it also includes a four-port wired switch.

FIGURE 7.1   **A wireless broadband router for a small network**

Most of the broadband routers similar to the one shown in Figure 7.1 differ based upon the following features:

▶ **Wireless bands:** The routers can provide only 2.4 GHz, only 5 GHz, or be either selectable (choosing one of the two) or simultaneous (using both).

▶ **Switch speed:** The ports on the switch can usually support either Fast Ethernet (10/100 Mbps) or Gigabit Ethernet (10/100/1000 Mbps).

▶ **Security supported:** The SSID, security mode, and passphrase may be configurable for each band, and some routers include a push-button feature for accessing setup. Some enable you to configure MAC address filtering and guest access. MAC address filtering enables you to limit access to only those specified hosts. Guest access uses a different password and network name and enables visitors to use the Internet without having access to the rest of the network (thus avoiding your data and computers).

▶ **Antenna:** The antenna may be a single external pole, two poles or even more, or be entirely internal. The model shown in Figure 7.1 uses an internal antenna, as shown in Figure 7.2.

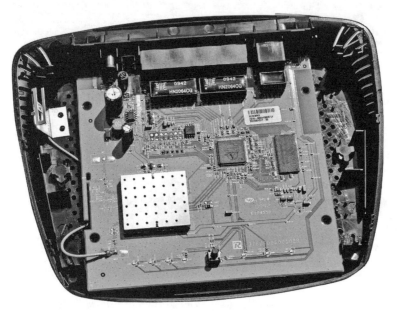

FIGURE 7.2 **The antenna is the wire and metal component on the left**

> **Note**
>
> The wireless antenna for a laptop, all-in-one desktop system, or mobile device is often built in to the areas around the screen.

The settings for a wireless router are typically clearly laid out. You can adjust many settings for troubleshooting or security reasons. For example, most newer *small office/home office (SOHO)* wireless routers offer useful configuration setup screens for administering firewall, *demilitarized zone (DMZ)*, apps and gaming, parental controls, guest access, and diagnostic settings (as illustrated in Figure 7.3). Following are some of the basic settings that can be adjusted on a wireless AP:

▶ **SSID:** This name is used for anyone who wants to access the Internet through this wireless AP. The SSID is a configurable client identification that enables clients to communicate with a particular base station. In an application, only clients configured with the same SSID can communicate with base stations having the same SSID. SSID provides a simple password arrangement between base stations and clients.

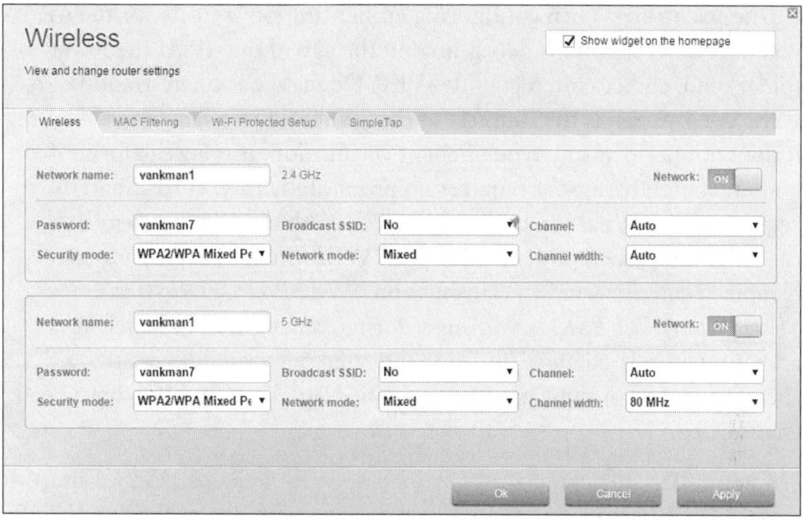

FIGURE 7.3   **Common configuration parameters for a wireless router**

As far as troubleshooting is concerned, if a client cannot access a base station, ensure that both use the same SSID. Incompatible SSIDs are sometimes found when clients move computers, such as laptops or other mobile devices, between different wireless networks. They obtain an SSID from one network. If the system is not rebooted, the old SSID does not enable communication with a different base station.

▶ **Channel:** To access this network, all systems must use this channel. If needed, you can change the channel using the drop-down menu. The menu lists channels 1 through 11.

▶ **SSID broadcast:** In their default configuration, wireless APs typically broadcast the SSID name into the air at regular intervals. This feature is intended to allow clients to easily discover the network and roam between WLANs. The problem with SSID broadcasting is that it makes it a little easier to get around security. SSIDs are not encrypted or protected in any way. Anyone can snoop and get a look at the SSID and attempt to join the network if not secured.

Note

For SOHO use, *roaming* is not needed. This feature can be disabled for home use to improve the security of your WLAN. As soon as your wireless clients are manually configured with the right SSID, they no longer require these broadcast messages.

▶ **Authentication:** When configuring authentication security for the AP, you have several options depending on the age of the AP. At the lower (older) end, choices often include WEP-Open, WEP-Shared, and WPA-PSK. WEP-Open is the simplest of the authentications methods because it does not perform any type of client verification. It is a weak form of authentication because it requires no proof of identity. WEP-Shared requires that a WEP key be configured on both the client system and the AP. This makes authentication with WEP-Shared mandatory, so it is more secure for wireless transmission. *Wi-Fi Protected Access with Pre-Shared Key (WPA-PSK)* is a stronger form of encryption in which keys are automatically changed and authenticated between devices after a specified period of time, or after a specified number of packets have been transmitted.

On newer APs, the choices usually include WPA Personal, WPA Enterprise, WPA2 Personal, and WPA2 Enterprise, with one of the two WPA2 choices as the default. Other choices can include WPA2/WPA Mixed Mode and RADIUS.

▶ **Wireless mode:** To access the network, the client must use the same wireless mode as the AP. Today, most users configure the network for 802.11n or 802.11ac for faster speeds.

▶ **DTIM period (seconds):** Wireless transmissions can broadcast to all systems—that is, they can send messages to all clients on the wireless network. Multiple broadcast messages are known as *multicast* or *broadcast traffic*. *Delivery Traffic Indication Message (DTIM)* is a feature used to ensure that when the multicast or broadcast traffic is sent, all systems are awake to hear the message. The DTIM setting specifies how often the DTIM is sent within the beacon frame. For example, if the DTIM setting by default is 1, this means that the DTIM is sent with every beacon. If the DTIM is set to 3, the DTIM is sent every three beacons as a DTIM wake-up call.

▶ **Maximum connection rate:** The transfer rate typically is set to Auto by default. This enables the maximum connection speed. However, it is possible to decrease the speed to increase the distance that the signal travels and boost signal strength caused by poor environmental conditions.

▶ **Network type:** This is where the network can be set to use the ad hoc or infrastructure network design.

It is easy to fall into the trap of thinking of wireless devices as being laptops connecting to the AP. Over the years, however, the number and type of mobile devices that need to connect to the network has expanded tremendously. In addition to the laptops and tablets, gaming devices, media devices, and cell phones now all connect for wireless access. Although they might all seem different, they require the same information to connect.

Unfortunately, they all bring security concerns as well. *Bring your own device (BYOD)* policies are highly recommended for every organization. Administrators can implement *mobile device management (MDM)* and *mobile application management (MAM)* products to help with the management and administration issues with these devices.

> **ExamAlert**
>
> Know that devices on networks today include such things as PCs, cell phones, laptops, tablets, gaming devices, and media devices.

Cram Quiz

1. Which of the following wireless protocols operate at 2.4 GHz? (Select three.)
   - ○ **A.** 802.11a
   - ○ **B.** 802.11b
   - ○ **C.** 802.11g
   - ○ **D.** 802.11n
   - ○ **E.** 802.11ac

2. Under what circumstance would you change the default channel on an access point?
   - ○ **A.** When channel overlap occurs between APs
   - ○ **B.** To release and renew the SSID
   - ○ **C.** To increase WPA2 security settings
   - ○ **D.** To decrease WPA2 security settings

3. A client on your network has had no problems accessing the wireless network in the past, but recently she moved to a new office. Since the move, she cannot access the network. Which of the following is most likely the cause of the problem?
   - ○ **A.** The SSIDs on the client and the AP are different.
   - ○ **B.** The SSID has been erased.
   - ○ **C.** The client has incorrect broadcast settings.
   - ○ **D.** The client system has moved too far from the AP.

4. You are installing a wireless network solution, and you require a standard that can operate using either 2.4 GHz or 5 GHz frequencies. Which of the following standards would you choose?

   ○ **A.** 802.11a
   ○ **B.** 802.11b
   ○ **C.** 802.11g
   ○ **D.** 802.11n
   ○ **E.** 802.11ac

5. You are installing a wireless network solution that uses a feature known as MU-MIMO. Which wireless networking standard are you using?

   ○ **A.** 802.11a
   ○ **B.** 802.11b
   ○ **C.** 802.11n
   ○ **D.** 802.11ac

Cram Quiz Answers

1. **B, C, D.** Wireless standards specify an RF range on which communications are sent. The 802.11b and 802.11g standards use the 2.4 GHz range. 802.11a and 802.11ac use the 5 GHz range. 802.11n can operate at 2.4 GHz and 5 GHz.

2. **A.** Ordinarily, the default channel used with a wireless device is adequate; however, you might need to change the channel if overlap occurs with another nearby AP. The channel should be changed to another, nonoverlapping channel. Changing the channel would not impact the WPA2 security settings.

3. **D.** An AP has a limited distance that it can send data transmissions. When a client system moves out of range, it cannot access the AP. Many strategies exist to increase transmission distances, including RF repeaters, amplifiers, and buying more powerful antennas or wireless APs. The problem is not likely related to the SSID or broadcast settings, because the client had access to the network before, and no settings were changed.

4. **D.** The IEEE standard 802.11n can use either the 2.4 GHz or 5 GHz radio frequencies. 802.11a uses 5 GHz, and 802.11b and 802.11g use 2.4 GHz. 802.11ac operates at 5 GHz.

5. **D.** MU-MIMO is used by the 802.11ac standard and makes multiuser MIMO possible (increasing the range and speed of wireless networking). MIMO, itself, enables the transmission of multiple data streams traveling on different antennas in the same channel at the same time.

Troubleshooting Wireless Issues

▶ **Given a scenario, troubleshoot common wireless connectivity and performance issues.**

CramSaver

If you can correctly answer these questions before going through this section, save time by skimming the Exam Alerts in this section and then completing the Cram Quiz at the end of the section.

1. You have noticed that connections between nodes on one network are inconsistent and suspect there may be another network using the same channel. What should you try first?

2. True or false: Weather conditions should not have a noticeable impact on wireless signal integrity.

Answers

1. If connections are inconsistent, try changing the channel to another, non-overlapping channel.

2. False. Weather conditions can have a huge impact on wireless signal integrity.

ExamAlert

Remember that this objective begins with "Given a scenario." That means that you may receive a drag and drop, matching, or "live OS" scenario where you have to click through to complete a specific objective-based task.

Poor communication between wireless devices has many different potential causes. Some of these problems, such as latency and jitter, are similar to those that exist with wired connections and were discussed in the previous chapter. Others are characteristic only of wireless connectivity and are discussed in the following sections.

To put a lot of information into a format that is coherent, the discussion starts with a review checklist of wireless troubleshooting and then moves into some individual topics:

▶ **Signal loss:** The cause of signal loss, known as *attenuation*, can be anything from distance to obstacles to interference. The *signal-to-noise ratio* should be examined to measure the desired signal against the background noise interfering with it. Look for signs of saturation with either the device or the bandwidth.

> **ExamAlert**
>
> Signal-to-noise ratio can be used to measure that which the name implies.

▶ **Wireless enabled:** Some laptops make it incredibly easy to turn wireless on and off. A user may accidentally press a button that he is not aware of and then suddenly not be able to access the network. Although this is a simple problem to fix, it is one that you need to identify as quickly as possible. Figure 7.4 shows the wireless light on an HP laptop. This light is also a button that toggles wireless on and off. When the light is blue, wireless is enabled, and when it is not blue (orange), it is disabled.

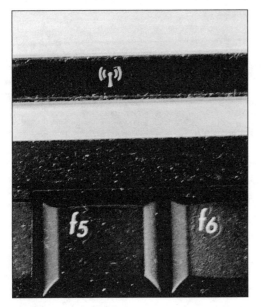

FIGURE 7.4 **A light also serves as a button, enabling wireless to be quickly turned on and off**

▶ **Untested updates:** Never apply untested updates to the network. This is especially true with AP updates, which should always be tested in nonproduction environments before being applied to live machines.

▶ **Wrong wireless standard:** Make sure that the standard you are using supports the rates and attributes you are striving for. This is particularly important in terms of throughput, frequency, distance, and channels.

▶ **Auto transfer rate:** By default, wireless devices are configured to use the strongest, fastest signal. If you experience connectivity problems between wireless devices, try using the lower transfer rate in a fixed mode to achieve a more stable connection. For example, you can manually choose the wireless transfer rate. Also, instead of using the highest transfer rate available, try a lesser speed. The higher the transfer rate, the shorter the connection distance.

▶ **AP placement and configuration:** If signal strength is low, try moving the AP to a new location. Moving it just a few feet can make a difference. You can also try to *bounce* a signal, as needed, off of reflective surfaces. The configuration of the AP should take into account the use of *Lightweight Access Point Protocol (LWAPP)*, which can allow you to monitor the network and reduce the amount of time needed to configure and troubleshoot it—and whether the authentication/configuration will be done at the AP (known as *thick*) or it will be passed on up (known as *thin*).

> **Note**
>
> Anytime an AP is doing key functions—authentication, filtering, QoS enforcement, and so on—it is said to be *thick*. If it is not doing these key functions—even though it might be doing others—it is usually said to be *thin*. Although there is no 100% sure method of distinguishing what a vendor will label thick or thin, one good rule is to question whether the AP is dependent on another device (thin) or not (thick).

▶ **Antenna:** The default antenna shipped with wireless devices may not be powerful enough for a particular client system. Better-quality antennas can be purchased for some APs, which can boost the distance the signal can go. Make sure you do not use the wrong antenna type or have other incompatibilities.

▶ **Environmental obstructions:** Wireless RF communications are weakened if they have to travel through obstructions such as metal studs, window film, and concrete walls. Wireless site surveys can be performed to troubleshoot RF signal loss issues as well as assist in planning optimal locations for new wireless networks.

▶ **Conflicting devices:** Any device that uses the same frequency range as the wireless device can cause interference. For example, 2.4 GHz phones, appliances, or Bluetooth devices can cause interference with devices using the 802.11g or single-band 802.11n wireless standards.

▶ **Wireless channels:** If connections are inconsistent, try changing the channel to another, nonoverlapping channel. Make certain you do not have mismatched channels between devices.

▶ **Protocol issues:** If an IP address is not assigned to the wireless client, a wrong SSID or incorrect WEP/WPA/WPA2 settings can prevent a system from obtaining IP information.

▶ **SSID:** The SSID number used on the client system must match the one used on the AP. You might need to change it if you are switching a laptop or other wireless device between different WLANs.

▶ **Encryption type:** If encryption is enabled on the connecting system, the encryption type must match what is set in the AP. For example, if the AP uses WPA2-AES, the connecting system must also use WPA2-AES.

Most router configuration interfaces allow you to run basic diagnostics through them, as illustrated in Figure 7.5. You can also usually change the security settings and configure the firewall, as shown in Figure 7.6.

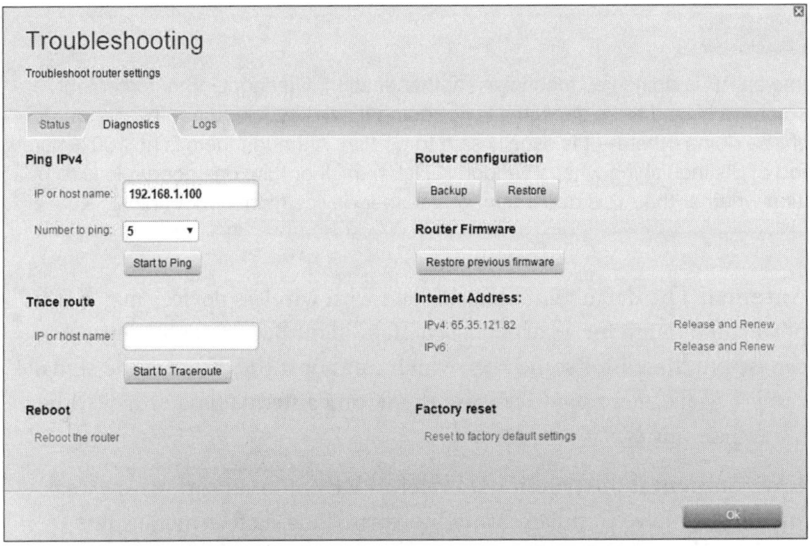

FIGURE 7.5 **Wireless router diagnostic options**

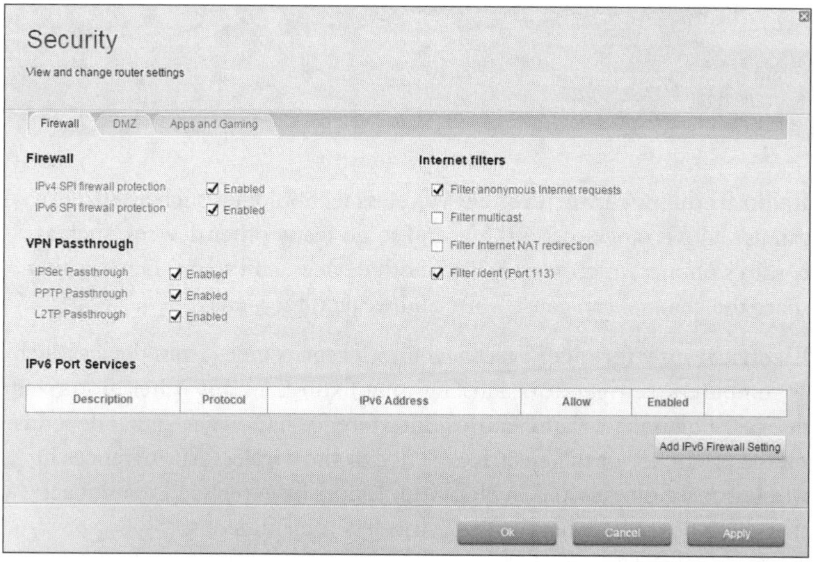

FIGURE 7.6   **Configuring security settings**

Factors Affecting Wireless Signals

Because wireless signals travel through the atmosphere, they are susceptible
to different types of interference than are standard wired networks. Interference weakens wireless signals and therefore is an important consideration when
working with wireless networking.

Interference

Wireless interference is an important consideration when you plan a wireless
network. Interference is, unfortunately, inevitable, but the trick is to minimize
the levels of interference. Wireless LAN communications typically are based on
radio frequency signals that require a clear and unobstructed transmission path.

The following are some factors that cause interference:

▶ **Physical objects:** Trees, masonry, buildings, and other physical structures are some of the most common sources of interference. The *density*
of the materials used in a building's construction determines the number of walls the RF signal can pass through and still maintain adequate
coverage. Concrete and steel walls are particularly difficult for a signal
to pass through. These structures weaken or at times completely prevent
wireless signals.

> **ExamAlert**
>
> Be sure that you understand that physical objects are a common source of interference. A wireless site survey can be used to test for interference.

▶ **Radio frequency interference:** Wireless technologies such as 802.11n can use an RF range of 2.4 GHz, and so do many other devices, such as cordless phones, microwaves, Bluetooth devices, and so on. Devices that share the channel can cause noise and weaken the signals.

▶ **Electrical interference:** Electrical interference comes from devices such as computers, refrigerators, fans, lighting fixtures, or any other motorized devices. The impact that electrical interference has on the signal depends on the proximity of the electrical device to the wireless AP. Advances in wireless technologies and in electrical devices have reduced the impact that these types of devices have on wireless transmissions.

▶ **Environmental factors:** Weather conditions can have a huge impact on wireless signal integrity. Lightning, for example, can cause electrical interference, and fog can weaken signals as they pass through.

Reflection, Refraction, and Absorption

It can be a blurry line differentiating between interference and reflection when it comes to wireless networking. The key difference between them is that interference is a conflict with something else (usually another signal), whereas reflection is a problem caused by a bouncing of the same signal off of an object. A subset of this is refraction, which involves a change in direction of the wave as a result of its traveling at different speeds at different points. Put in simple terms, reflection happens when the signal hits a piece of metal and cannot pass through, and refraction happens when the signal goes through a body of water.

If the wave is completely swallowed by the object it hits (not reflected, or refracted), then it is said to be absorbed. Where security is concerned, items known to absorb wireless signals can be used to prevent the signal from traveling beyond an established perimeter. Shielding paint (sometimes called RF paint) can be used for this purpose, as can copper plates and aluminum sheets.

Many wireless implementations are found in the office or at home. Even when outside interference such as weather is not a problem, every office has plenty of wireless obstacles. Table 7.4 highlights a few examples to be aware of when implementing a wireless network indoors.

TABLE 7.4 **Wireless Obstacles Found Indoors**

Obstruction	Obstacle Severity	Sample Use
Wood/wood paneling	Low	Inside a wall or hollow door
Drywall	Low	Inside walls
Furniture	Low	Couches or office partitions
Clear glass	Low	Windows
Tinted glass	Medium	Windows
People	Medium	High-volume traffic areas that have considerable pedestrian traffic
Ceramic tile	Medium	Walls
Concrete blocks	Medium/high	Outer wall construction
Mirrors	High	Mirror or reflective glass
Metals	High	Metal office partitions, doors, metal office furniture
Water	High	Aquariums, rain, fountains

ExamAlert

Be sure that you understand the severity of obstructions given in Table 7.4.

Troubleshooting AP Coverage

Like any other network medium, APs have a limited transmission distance. This limitation is an important consideration when you decide where an AP should be placed on the network. When troubleshooting a wireless network, pay close attention to how far the client systems are from the AP.

ExamAlert

Distance limitations from the AP are among the first things to check when troubleshooting AP coverage.

When faced with a problem in which client systems cannot consistently access the AP, you could try moving the AP to better cover the area, but then you may disrupt access for users in other areas. So what can be done to troubleshoot AP coverage?

Depending on the network environment, the quick solution may be to throw money at the problem and purchase another access point, cabling, and other hardware to expand the transmission area. However, you can try a few things before installing another wireless AP. The following list starts with the least expensive solution and progresses to the most expensive:

▶ **Increase transmission power:** Some APs have a setting to adjust the transmission power output (power levels). By default, most of these settings are set to the maximum output; however, this is worth verifying just in case. You can decrease the transmission power if you are trying to reduce the dispersion of radio waves beyond the immediate network. Increasing the power gives clients stronger data signals and greater transmission distances.

▶ **Relocate the AP:** When wireless client systems suffer from connectivity problems, the solution may be as simple as relocating the AP. You could relocate it across the room, a few feet away, or across the hall. Finding the right location will likely take a little trial and error.

▶ **Adjust or replace antennas:** If the AP distance is insufficient for some network clients, it might be necessary to replace the default antenna used with both the AP and the client with higher-end antennas. Upgrading an antenna can make a big difference in terms of transmission range. Unfortunately, not all APs have replaceable antennas.

▶ **Signal amplification:** *Radio frequency (RF)* amplifiers add significant distance to wireless signals. An RF amplifier increases the strength and readability of the data transmission. The amplifier improves both the received and transmitted signals, resulting in an increase in wireless network performance.

▶ **Use a repeater:** Before installing a new AP, you might want to think about a wireless repeater. When set to the same channel as the AP, the repeater takes the transmission and repeats it. So, the AP transmission gets to the repeater, and then the repeater duplicates the signal and passes it on. This is an effective strategy to increase wireless transmission distances.

ExamAlert

Be prepared to answer questions on AP coverage and possible reasons to relocate or replace APs.

Cram Quiz

1. You purchase a new wireless AP that uses no security by default. You change the security settings to use 128-bit encryption. How must the client systems be configured?

   - ○ **A.** All client systems must be set to 128-bit encryption.
   - ○ **B.** The client system inherits security settings from the AP.
   - ○ **C.** Wireless security does not support 128-bit encryption.
   - ○ **D.** The client wireless security settings must be set to autodetect.

2. You experience connectivity problems with your SOHO network. What can you change in an attempt to solve this problem?

   - ○ **A.** Shorten the SSID.
   - ○ **B.** Remove all encryption.
   - ○ **C.** Lower the transfer rate.
   - ○ **D.** Raise the transfer rate.

Cram Quiz Answers

1. **A.** On a wireless connection between an AP and the client, each system must be configured to use the same wireless security settings. In this case, they must both be configured to use 128-bit encryption.

2. **C.** If you experience connectivity problems between wireless devices, try using the lower transfer rate in a fixed mode to achieve a more stable connection. For example, you can manually choose the wireless transfer rate. The higher the transfer rate, the shorter the connection distance.

What's Next?

Chapter 8, "Cloud Computing and Virtualization," focuses on the definitions of cloud computing and virtualization at the level you need to know them for the Network+ exam.

CHAPTER 8

Cloud Computing and Virtualization

This chapter covers the following official Network+ objectives:

▶ Summarize cloud concepts and their purposes.

▶ Explain the purposes of virtualization and network storage technologies.

This chapter covers CompTIA Network+ objectives 1.7 and 2.4. For more information on the official Network+ exam topics, see the "About the Network+ Exam" section in the Introduction.

The term *cloud computing* is used everywhere these days, even by those who have no idea what it means. Being a Network+ candidate, it is important to be versed in the definitions of cloud computing, and virtualization, and able to discuss it with others using a common vernacular.

This chapter focuses on the definitions of cloud computing and virtualization at the level you need to know them for the Network+ exam. If you want to go further with the technology, consider the newly created Cloud+ certification from CompTIA.

Cloud Concepts

▶ **Summarize cloud concepts and their purposes.**

CramSaver

If you can correctly answer these questions before going through this section, save time by skimming the Exam Alerts in this section and then completing the Cram Quiz at the end of the section.

1. In which cloud delivery model are resources owned by the organization, and that organization acts as both the provider and the consumer?

2. With which cloud service model can consumers deploy, but not manage or control, any of the underlying cloud infrastructure (but they can have control over the deployed applications)?

3. What are some of the characteristics of cloud computing?

Answers

1. In a private cloud model, the cloud is owned by the organization and it acts as both the provider and the consumer.

2. With the Platform as a Service (PaaS) cloud service model, consumers can deploy, but not manage or control, any of the underlying cloud infrastructure (but they can have control over the deployed applications).

3. Regardless of the service model used, the characteristics include on-demand self-service, broad network access, resource pooling, rapid elasticity, and measured service.

The best way to think about this chapter is as an introduction to cloud computing and an agreement on the definition of what the terms associated with it really mean. The *National Institute of Standards and Technology (NIST)* defines three service models in Special Publication 800-145: Software as a Service (SaaS); Platform as a Service (PaaS); and Infrastructure as a Service (IaaS). It also defines four possible delivery models: private, public, community, and hybrid.

This chapter looks at each of these seven terms and what they mean as defined by the NIST and agreed upon by the computing community. Know that it is possible to mix and match the service models with the platform models so that you can have public IaaS, or private PaaS, and so on and that you utilize a Cloud Access Security Broker (CASB)—a software program—to sit between the cloud service users and cloud applications to monitor activity and enforce established security policies.

> **Note**
>
> The CASB can offer services beyond just monitoring users' actions, but must always be able to enforce compliance with security policies.

Software as a Service

According to the NIST, Software as a Service (SaaS) is defined as follows: "The capability provided to the consumer is to use the provider's applications running on a cloud infrastructure. The applications are accessible from various client devices through either a thin client interface, such as a web browser (for example, web-based email), or a program interface. The consumer does not manage or control the underlying cloud infrastructure including network, servers, operating systems, storage, or even individual application capabilities, with the possible exception of limited user-specific application configuration settings."

The words used are significant and the ones to focus on in this definition are that consumers can *use* the provider's applications and that they do not *manage or control* any of the underlying cloud infrastructure. Figure 8.1 depicts the responsibility of each party in the SaaS model.

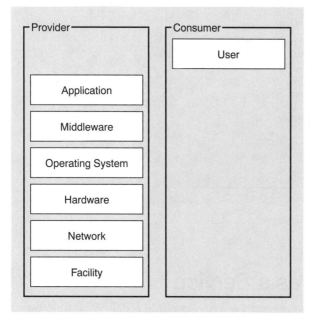

FIGURE 8.1   **The SaaS service model**

Platform as a Service

According to the NIST, *Platform as a Service (PaaS)* is defined as follows: "The capability provided to the consumer is to deploy onto the cloud infrastructure consumer-created or acquired applications created using programming languages, libraries, services and tools supported by the provider. The consumer does not manage or control the underlying cloud infrastructure including network, servers, operating systems, or storage, but has control over the deployed applications and possible configuration settings for the application-hosting environment."

The important words to focus on in this definition are that consumers can *deploy*, that they do not *manage or control* any of the underlying cloud infrastructure, but they can have *control over the deployed applications*. Figure 8.2 depicts the responsibility of each party in the PaaS model.

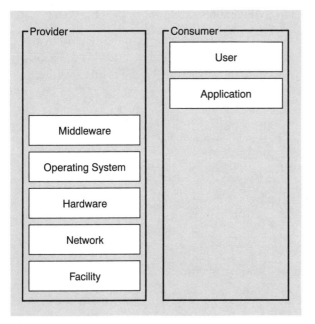

FIGURE 8.2   **The PaaS service model**

Infrastructure as a Service

According to the NIST, *Infrastructure as a Service (IaaS)* is defined as follows: "The capability provided to the consumer is to provision processing, storage, networks, and other fundamental computing resources where the consumer is able to deploy and run arbitrary software, which can include operating systems and applications. The consumer does not manage or control the underlying cloud infrastructure but has control over operating systems, storage, and deployed applications; and possible limited control of select networking components (e.g., host firewalls)."

The words to focus on are that the consumer can *provision*, is able to *deploy and run*, but still does not *manage or control* the underlying cloud infrastructure, but now can be responsible for some aspects. Figure 8.3 depicts the responsibility of each party in the IaaS model.

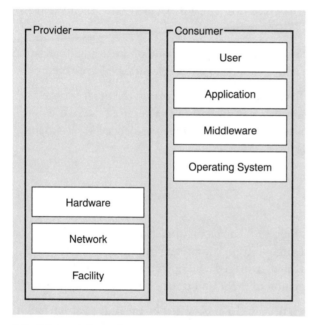

FIGURE 8.3 **The IaaS service model**

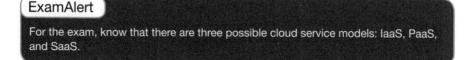

Note

Regardless of the service model used, the characteristics of each of them are that they include on-demand self-service, broad network access, resource pooling, rapid elasticity, and measured service.

After you have a service model selected, both CompTIA and the NIST recognize the different delivery models, which are discussed next.

ExamAlert

For the exam, know that there are three possible cloud service models: IaaS, PaaS, and SaaS.

Other Types of Services

The CompTIA objectives specifically list IaaS, PaaS, and SaaS as the three they test on. These are the most popular models in use today, but virtually anything can have "aaS" tacked to the end of it and its subscription referenced "as a Service." This is important because three models appear in the official acronym list that do not appear in the objectives. For that reason, be sure you know what the acronyms stand for and a brief definition. The three are as follows:

▶ **CaaS:** Communication as a Service is outsourced communications leased from a vendor(s) such as Voice over IP (VoIP), videoconferencing apps, and so on.

▶ **DaaS:** Desktop as a Service is an implementation of desktop virtualization that does not require you to build and manage your own infrastructure.

▶ **MaaS:** Mobility as a Service is much different from the other service models and is also known as Transportation as a Service (TaaS). It is the use of other forms of transportation—on an as-needed basis—than company-owned vehicles.

Private Cloud

A *private cloud* is defined as follows: "The cloud infrastructure is provisioned for exclusive use by a single organization comprising multiple consumers (e.g., business units). It may be owned, managed, and operated by the organization, a third party, or some combination of them, and it may exist on or off premises."

Under most circumstances, a private cloud is owned by the organization, and it acts as both the provider and the consumer. It has a security-related advantage in not needing to put its data on the Internet.

Public Cloud

A *public cloud* is defined as follows: "The cloud infrastructure is provisioned for open use by the general public. It may be owned, managed, and operated by a business, academic, or government organization, or some combination of them. It exists on the premises of the cloud provider."

Under most circumstances, a public cloud is owned by the cloud provider, and it uses a pay-as-you-go model. A good example of a public cloud is webmail or online document sharing/collaboration.

Hybrid Cloud

A *hybrid cloud* is defined as follows: "The cloud infrastructure is a composition of two or more distinct cloud infrastructures (private, community, or public) that remain unique entities, but are bound together by standardized or proprietary technology that enables data and application portability (e.g., cloud bursting for load balancing between clouds)."

A hybrid can be any combination of other delivery models. Not only are public and private listed in the definition, but also community. CompTIA no longer includes the community cloud delivery model on the Network+ exam (but does require you to know it for its cloud-focused certifications). For real-world purposes, you should know that the key to distinguishing between a community cloud and other types of cloud delivery is that it serves a *similar* group. There must be joint interests and limited enrollment.

> **Note**
>
> A common reason for using cloud computing is to be able to offload traffic to resources from a cloud provider if your own servers become too busy. This is known as *cloud bursting*, and it requires load-balancing/prioritizing technologies such as *quality of service (QoS)* protocols to make it possible.

> **ExamAlert**
>
> For the exam, you should know that the most deployed cloud delivery models are private, public, and hybrid.

Connectivity Methods

Most cloud providers offer a number of methods that clients can employ to connect to them. It is important, before making an investment in infrastructure, to check with your provider and see what methods it recommends and supports. One of the most common is to use an IPsec, hardware VPN connection between your network(s) and the cloud providers. This method offers the capability to have a managed VPN endpoint that includes automated multidata center redundancy and failover.

A dedicated direct connection is another, simpler, method. You can combine the dedicated network connection(s) with the hardware VPN to create a combination that offers an IPsec-encrypted private connection while also reducing network costs.

Amazon Web Services (AWS) is one of the most popular cloud providers on the market. They allow the two connectivity methods discussed (calling the dedicated connection "AWS Direct Connect") and a number of others that are variations, or combinations, of these two.

Security Implications and Considerations

Security is one of the most important issues to discuss with your cloud provider. Cloud computing holds great promise when it comes to scalability, cost savings, rapid deployment, and empowerment. As with any technology where so much is removed from your control, though, risks are involved. Each risk should be considered carefully to identify ways to help mitigate it. Naturally, the responsibilities of both the organization and the cloud provider vary depending on the service model chosen, but ultimately the organization is accountable for the security and privacy of the outsourced service.

Software and services not necessary for the implementation should be removed or at least disabled. Patches and firmware updates should be kept current, and log files should be carefully monitored. You should find the vulnerabilities in the implementation before others do and work with your service provider(s) to close any holes.

When it comes to data storage on the cloud, encryption is one of the best ways to protect it (keeping it from being of value to unauthorized parties), and VPN routing and forwarding can help. Backups should be performed regularly (and encrypted and stored in safe locations), and access control should be a priority.

> **Note**
>
> For a good discussion of cloud computing and data protection, visit
> http://whoswholegal.com/news/features/article/18246/cloud-computing-data-protection.

The Relationship Between Resources

Just as the cloud holds such promise for running applications, balancing loads, and a plethora of other options, it also offers the ability to store more and more data on it and to let a provider worry about scaling issues instead of local administrators. From an economic perspective, this can be a blessing. From an administrative point, though, it can present some issues. Redundancy that occurs from having data in more than one location (local and remote) can be wonderful when you need to recover data, but problematic when you want to make sure you are always working with the most recent version. To minimize problems, be sure that files are kept current, and synchronization between local and remote files is always running.

Cram Quiz

1. With which cloud service model can consumers use the provider's applications but not manage or control any of the underlying cloud infrastructure?

   ○ **A.** SaaS

   ○ **B.** PaaS

   ○ **C.** IaaS

   ○ **D.** GaaS

2. Which of the following involves offloading traffic to resources from a cloud provider if your own servers become too busy?

   ○ **A.** Ballooning

   ○ **B.** Cloud bursting

   ○ **C.** Bridging

   ○ **D.** Harvesting

3. Which of the following does the NIST define as a composition of two or more distinct cloud infrastructures?

   ○ **A.** Private cloud

   ○ **B.** Public cloud

   ○ **C.** Community cloud

   ○ **D.** Hybrid cloud

Cram Quiz Answers

1. **A.** With the SaaS cloud service model, consumers are able to use the provider's applications, but they do not manage or control any of the underlying cloud infrastructure.

2. **B.** A common reason for using cloud computing is to be able to offload traffic to resources from a cloud provider if your own servers become too busy. This is known as *cloud bursting*.

3. **D.** The hybrid cloud delivery model is a composition of two or more distinct cloud infrastructures (public, private, and so on).

Virtualization and Storage-Area Networks

▶ **Explain the purposes of virtualization and network storage technologies.**

CramSaver

If you can correctly answer these questions before going through this section, save time by skimming the Exam Alerts in this section and then completing the Cram Quiz at the end of the section.

1. What technology sends very large Ethernet frames that are less processor intensive?

2. True or false: Virtual NICs have MAC addresses assigned to them.

Answers

1. The goal of jumbo frames is to send very large Ethernet frames that are less processor intensive.

2. True. Virtual NICs (VNICs) have MAC addresses assigned to them.

Cloud computing and virtualization are two items that go together like ketchup and mustard on a hot dog; it is possible to use one without the other, but they are often used together. In the first half of this chapter, you learned the definitions for cloud computing; now you learn the principles of virtualization and storage-area networks.

Virtualization

Cloud computing is built on virtualization; it is the foundation on which cloud computing stands. At the core of virtualization is the *hypervisor* (the software/hardware combination that makes it possible). There are two methods of implementation: Type I (known as *bare metal*) and Type II (known as *hosted*). Type I is independent of the operating system and boots before the OS, whereas Type II is dependent on the operating system and cannot boot until the OS is up; it needs the OS to stay up so that it can operate. Figure 8.4 depicts the Type I model while Figure 8.5 depicts the Type II model. From a performance and scalability standpoint, Type I is considered superior to Type II.

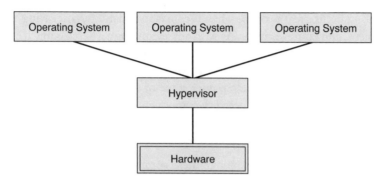

FIGURE 8.4   **The Type I hypervisor model**

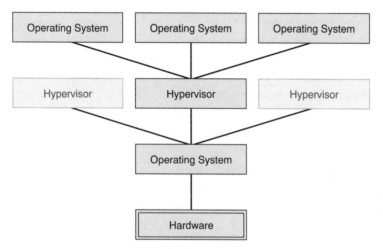

FIGURE 8.5   **The Type II hypervisor model**

Tip

The machine on which virtualization software is running is known as a *host*, and the virtual machines are known as *guests*.

Note

Whereas once it was the case that hypervisors were the only way to have virtualization, containers are now thought by most to be their successor. These are not tested on in this iteration of the Network+ exam, but you should know for the real world that the use of containers (a piece of software bundled with everything that it needs to run—code, runtime, system tools, system libraries, and so on) are becoming more common.

Cloud computing holds great promise when it comes to scalability, cost saving, rapid deployment, and empowerment. As with any technology where so much is removed from your control, however, risks are involved. Each risk should be considered and thought through to identify ways to help mitigate them. Data segregation, for example, can help reduce some of the risks associated with multitenancy. Common virtual network components include *virtual network interface cards (VNICs)*, virtual routers and switches, shared memory, virtual CPUs, and storage (shared or clustered).

In the following sections, we look at some of these components used to create the virtual environment.

Virtual Routers and Switches

Just as physical routers establish communication by maintaining tables about destinations and local connections, a *virtual router* works similarly but is software only. Remember that a router contains information about the systems connected to it and where to send requests if the destination is not known. These routing tables grow as connections are made through the router. Routing can occur within the network (interior) or outside it (exterior). The routes, themselves, can be configured as static or dynamic.

A *virtual switch*, similarly, is a software program that allows one virtual machine (VM) to communicate with another. The virtual switch allows the VM to use the hardware of the host OS (the NIC) to connect to the Internet.

Switches are multiport devices that improve network efficiency. A switch typically contains a small amount of information about systems in a network— a table of MAC addresses as opposed to IP addresses. Switches improve network efficiency over routers because of the virtual circuit capability. Switches also improve network security because the virtual circuits are more difficult to examine with network monitors. The switch maintains limited routing information about nodes in the internal network, and it allows connections to systems such as a hub or a router.

Virtual Firewall

A *virtual firewall (VF)* is either a network firewall service or an appliance running entirely within the virtualized environment. Regardless of which implementation, a VF serves the same purpose as a physical one: packet filtering and monitoring. The firewall can also run in a guest OS VM.

One key to a VF is to not overlook the contribution from *Network Address Translation (NAT)*. This allows an organization to present a single address (or set of addresses) to the Internet for all computer connections—it acts as a proxy between the local-area network (which can be using private IP addresses) and the Internet. NAT effectively hides your network from the world, making it much harder to determine what systems exist on the other side of the router.

> **Tip**
>
> Not only can NAT save IP addresses, but it can also act as a firewall.

Virtual Versus Physical NICs

A NIC card within a machine can be either virtual or physical and will be configured the same. Existing on the virtual network, it must have an IP address, a MAC address, a default gateway, a subnet mask value, and can have a connection that is bridged or not. A VNIC is software only but allows interaction with other devices on network. (The VLAN makes it possible for VNICs to communicate with other network devices.)

> **ExamAlert**
>
> For the exam, you should be able to differentiate between the various virtualization components: switches, routers, firewalls, and NICs.

When talking about virtual networking, it is important to note that so much of what is discussed is software based. Never forget that the goal of virtualization is to emulate physical environments and devices without actually having those physical elements.

Storage-Area Networks

When it comes to data storage in the cloud, encryption is one of the best ways to protect it (keeping it from being of value to unauthorized parties), and VPN routing and forwarding can help. Backups should be performed regularly (and encrypted and stored in safe locations), and access control should be a priority.

The consumer retains the ultimate responsibility for compliance. Per NIST SP 800-144, "The main issue centers on the risks associated with moving important applications or data from within the confines of the organization's computing center to that of another organization (i.e., a public cloud), which is readily available for use by the general public. The responsibilities of both the organization and the cloud provider vary depending on the service model. Reducing cost and increasing efficiency are primary motivations for moving towards a public cloud, but relinquishing responsibility for security should not be. Ultimately, the organization is accountable for the choice of public cloud and the security and privacy of the outsourced service." For more information, see http://nvlpubs.nist.gov/nistpubs/Legacy/SP/nistspecialpublication800-144.pdf.

Shared storage can be done on *storage-area networks (SANs)*, *network-attached storage (NAS)*, and so on; the virtual machine sees only a "physical disk." With clustered storage, you can use multiple devices to increase performance. A handful of technologies exist in this realm, and the following are those that you need to know for the Network+ exam.

> **Tip**
>
> Look to CompTIA's Cloud+ certification for more specialization in cloud and virtualization technologies.

iSCSI

The *Small Computer System Interface (SCSI)* standard has long been the language of storage. *Internet Small Computer System Interface (iSCSI)* expands this through Ethernet, allowing IP to be used to send SCSI commands.

Logical unit numbers (LUNs) came from the SCSI world and carry over, acting as unique identifiers for devices. Both NAS and SAN use "targets" that hold up to eight devices.

Using iSCSI for a virtual environment gives users the benefits of a file system without the difficulty of setting up Fibre Channel. Because iSCSI works both at the hypervisor level and in the guest operating system, the rules that govern the size of the partition in the OS are used rather than those of the virtual OS (which are usually more restrictive).

The disadvantage of iSCSI is that users can run into IP-related problems if configuration is not carefully monitored.

Jumbo Frames

One of the biggest issues with networking is that data of various sizes is crammed into packets and sent across the medium. Each time this is done, headers are created (more data to process), along with any filler needed, creating additional overhead. To get around this, the concept of *jumbo frames* is used to allow for very large Ethernet frames; by sending a lot of data at once, the number of packets is reduced, and the data sent is less processor intensive.

Fibre Channel and FCoE

Instead of using an older technology and trying to adhere to legacy standards, Fibre Channel (FC) is an option providing a higher level of performance than anything else. It utilizes FCP, the Fiber Channel Protocol, to do what needs to be done, and *Fiber Channel over Ethernet (FCoE)* can be used in high-speed (10 GB and higher) implementations.

The big advantage of Fibre Channel is its scalability. FCoE encapsulates FC over the Ethernet portions of connectivity, making it easy to add into an existing network. As such, FCoE is an extension to FC intended to extend the scalability and efficiency associated with Fibre Channel.

Network-Attached Storage

Storage is always a big issue, and the best answer is always a SAN. Unfortunately, a SAN can be costly and difficult to implement and maintain. That is where *network-attached storage (NAS)* comes in. NAS is easier than SAN and uses TCP/IP. It offers file level access, and a client sees the shared storage as a file server.

> **Note**
>
> On a VLAN, multipathing creates multiple paths to the storage resources and can be used to increase availability *and* add fault tolerance.

> **ExamAlert**
>
> For the exam, you should know the difference between NAS and SAN technologies and how to apply them.

InfiniBand

One high-speed technology on the market, and supported by the InfiniBand Trade Association, is *InfiniBand (IB)*. This standard promises high through-put and low latency, making it ideal for use in high-performance computing connections (both within the computer and between computers). Both Mellanox and Intel manufacture InfiniBand host bus adapters and network switches, and Oracle Corporation has introduced a line of products as well.

> **Note**
>
> InfiniBand is designed to be scalable and uses a switched fabric network topology.

> **ExamAlert**
>
> For the exam, you should know that InfiniBand competes with Fibre Channel and a number of proprietary technologies.

Cram Quiz

1. Logical unit numbers (LUNs) came from the SCSI world and use "targets" that hold up to how many devices?

   ○ **A.** 4

   ○ **B.** 6

   ○ **C.** 8

   ○ **D.** 128

2. Which of the following technologies creates multiple paths to the storage resource?

   ○ **A.** Multilisting

   ○ **B.** Multihoming

   ○ **C.** Multitenancy

   ○ **D.** Multipathing

3. Which of the following types of virtualization is known as bare metal?

   ○ **A.** Type 0

   ○ **B.** Type I

   ○ **C.** Type II

   ○ **D.** Type III

Cram Quiz Answers

1. **C.** LUNs came from the SCSI world and carry over, acting as unique identifiers for devices. Both NAS and SAN use "targets" that hold up to eight devices.

2. **D.** On a VLAN, multipathing creates multiple paths to the storage resources and can be used to increase availability *and* add fault tolerance.

3. **B.** There are two methods of implementation: Type I (known as bare metal) and Type II (known as hosted). Type I is independent of the operating system and boots before the OS, whereas Type II is dependent on the operating system and cannot boot until the OS is up, and it needs the OS to stay up.

What's Next?

Chapter 9, "Network Operations," focuses on two important topics: network management and network optimization technologies and techniques.

CHAPTER 9

Network Operations

This chapter covers the following official Network+ objectives:

▶ Given a scenario, use appropriate documentation and diagrams to manage the network.

▶ Compare and contrast business continuity and disaster recovery concepts.

▶ Explain common scanning, monitoring, and patching processes and summarize their expected outputs.

▶ Given a scenario, use remote access methods.

▶ Identify policies and best practices.

This chapter covers CompTIA Network+ objectives 3.1, 3.2, 3.3, 3.4, and 3.5. For more information on the official Network+ exam topics, see the "About the Network+ Exam" section in the Introduction.

This chapter focuses on two important parts of the role of a network administrator: documentation and the tools to use to monitor or optimize connectivity. Documentation, although not glamorous, is an essential part of the job. This chapter looks at several aspects of network documentation.

Documentation Management

▶ **Given a scenario, use appropriate documentation and diagrams to manage the network.**

▶ **Identify policies and best practices.**

CramSaver

If you can correctly answer these questions before going through this section, save time by skimming the Exam Alerts in this section and then completing the Cram Quiz at the end of the section.

1. Which network topology focuses on the direction in which data flows within the physical environment?

2. In computing, what are historical readings used as a measurement for future calculations referred to as?

3. True or false: Both logical and physical network diagrams provide an overview of the network layout and function.

Answers

1. The logical network refers to the direction in which data flows on the network within the physical topology. The logical diagram is not intended to focus on the network hardware but rather on how data flows through that hardware.

2. Keeping and reviewing baselines is an essential part of the administrator's role.

3. True. Both logical and physical network diagrams provide an overview of the network layout and function.

ExamAlert

Remember that this objective begins with "Given a scenario." That means that you may receive a drag and drop, matching, or "live OS" scenario where you have to click through to complete a specific objective-based task.

Administrators have several daily tasks, and new ones often crop up. In this environment, tasks such as documentation sometimes fall to the background.

It's important that you understand why administrators need to spend valuable time writing and reviewing documentation. Having a well-documented network offers a number of advantages:

▶ **Troubleshooting:** When something goes wrong on the network, including the wiring, up-to-date documentation is a valuable reference to guide the troubleshooting effort. The documentation saves you money and time in isolating potential problems.

▶ **Training new administrators:** In many network environments, new administrators are hired, and old ones leave. In this scenario, documentation is critical. New administrators do not have the time to try to figure out where cabling is run, what cabling is used, potential trouble spots, and more. Up-to-date information helps new administrators quickly see the network layout.

▶ **Working with contractors and consultants:** Consultants and contractors occasionally may need to visit the network to make recommendations for the network or to add wiring or other components. In such cases, up-to-date documentation is needed. If documentation is missing, it would be much more difficult for these people to do their jobs, and more time and money would likely be required.

▶ **Inventory management:** Knowing what you have, where you have it, and what you can turn to in the case of an emergency is both constructive and helpful.

Quality network documentation does not happen by accident; rather, it requires careful planning. When creating network documentation, you must keep in mind who you are creating the documentation for and that it is a communication tool. Documentation is used to take technical information and present it in a manner that someone new to the network can understand. When planning network documentation, you must decide what you need to document.

> **Note**
>
> Imagine that you have just taken over a network as administrator. What information would you like to see? This is often a clear gauge of what to include in your network documentation.

All networks differ and so does the documentation required for each network. However, certain elements are always included in quality documentation:

▶ **Network topology:** Networks can be complicated. If someone new is looking over the network, it is critical to document the entire topology. This includes both the wired and wireless topologies used on the network. Network topology documentation typically consists of a diagram or series of diagrams labeling all critical components used to create the network. These diagrams utilize common symbols for components such as firewalls, hubs, routers, and switches. Figure 9.1, for example, shows standard figures for, from left to right, a firewall, a hub, a router, and a switch.

FIGURE 9.1   Diagram symbols for a firewall, a hub, a router, and a switch

▶ **Wiring layout and rack diagrams:** Network wiring can be confusing. Much of it is hidden in walls and ceilings, making it hard to know where the wiring is and what kind is used on the network. This makes it critical to keep documentation on network wiring up to date. Diagram what is on each rack and any unusual configurations that might be employed.

▶ **IDF/MDF documentation:** It is not enough to show that there is an intermediate distribution frame (IDF) and/or main distribution frame (MDF) in your building. You need to thoroughly document any and every free-standing or wall-mounted rack and the cables running between them and the end user devices.

▶ **Server configuration:** A single network typically uses multiple servers spread over a large geographic area. Documentation must include schematic drawings of where servers are located on the network and the services each provides. This includes server function, server IP address, operating system (OS), software information, and more. Essentially, you need to document all the information you need to manage or administer the servers.

▶ **Network equipment:** The hardware used on a network is configured in a particular way—with protocols, security settings, permissions, and more. Trying to remember these would be a difficult task. Having up-to-date documentation makes it easier to recover from a failure.

▶ **Network configuration, performance baselines, and key applications:** Documentation also includes information on all current network configurations, performance baselines taken, and key applications used on the network, such as up-to-date information on their updates, vendors, install dates, and more.

▶ **Detailed account of network services:** Network services are a key ingredient in all networks. Services such as Domain Name Service (DNS), Dynamic Host Configuration Protocol (DHCP), Remote Access Services (RAS), and more are an important part of documentation. You should describe in detail which server maintains these services, the backup servers for these services, maintenance schedules, how they are structured, and so on.

▶ **Standard operating procedures/work instructions:** Finally, documentation should include information on network policy and procedures. This includes many elements, ranging from who can and cannot access the server room, to network firewalls, protocols, passwords, physical security, cloud computing use, mobile device use, and so on.

ExamAlert

Be sure that you know the types of information that should be included in network documentation.

Wiring and Port Locations

Network wiring schematics are an essential part of network documentation, particularly for midsize to large networks, where the cabling is certainly complex. For such networks, it becomes increasingly difficult to visualize network cabling and even harder to explain it to someone else. A number of software tools exist to help administrators clearly document network wiring in detail.

Several types of wiring schematics exist. They can be general, as shown in Figure 9.2, or they can be very specific, indicating the actual type of wiring used, the operating system on each machine, and so on. The more generalized they are, the less they need updating, whereas very specific schematics often need to be changed regularly. Table 9.1 represents another way of documenting data.

ExamAlert

For the exam, be familiar with the look of a general wiring schematic such as the one shown in Figure 9.2.

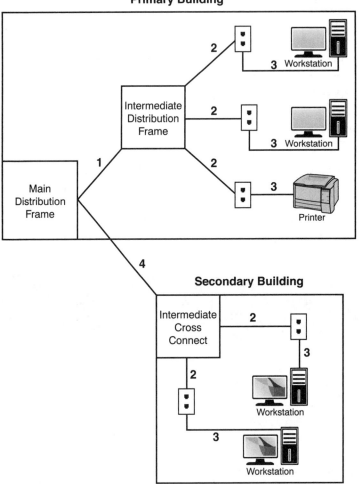

FIGURE 9.2 **A general wiring schematic**

TABLE 9.1 **Wiring Details**

Cable	Description	Installation Notes
1	Category 6 plenum-rated cable	Cable runs 50 feet from the MDF to IDF. Cable placed through the ceiling and through a mechanical room. Cable was installed 02/26/2017, upgrading a non-plenum Category 5e cable.
2	Category 6a plenum cable	Horizontal cable runs 45 feet to 55 feet from IDF to wall jack. Replaced Category 5 cable February 2017. Section of cable run through the ceiling and over fluorescent lights.

Cable	Description	Installation Notes
3	Category 5e UTP cable	All patch cable connectors were attached in-house. Patch cable connecting the printer runs 45 feet due to printer placement.
4	8.3-micron core/ 125-micron clad- ding single mode	Connecting fiber cable runs 2 kilometers between the primary and secondary buildings.

Figure 9.2 provides a simplified look at network wiring schematics. Imagine how complicated these diagrams would look on a network with 1,000, 2,000, or even 6,000 computers. Quality network documentation software makes this easier; however, the task of network wiring can be a large one for administrators. Administrators need to ensure that someone can pick up the wiring documentation diagrams and have a good idea of the network wiring.

> **Caution**
>
> Reading schematics and determining where wiring runs are an important part of the administrator's role. Expect to see a schematic on your exam.

Port locations should be carefully recorded and included in the documentation as well. SNMP can be used directly to map ports on switches and other devices; it is much easier, however, to use software applications that incorporate SNMP and use it to create ready-to-use documentation. A plethora of such programs are available; some are free and many are commercial products.

Troubleshooting Using Wiring Schematics

Some network administrators do not take the time to maintain quality documentation. This will haunt them when it comes time to troubleshoot some random network problems. Without any network wiring schematics, the task will be frustrating and time-consuming. The information shown in Figure 9.2 might be simplified, but you could use that documentation to evaluate the network and make recommendations.

> **Caution**
>
> When looking at a wiring schematic, pay close attention to where the cable is run and the type of cable used if the schematic indicates this. If a correct cable is not used, a problem could occur.

Physical and Logical Network Diagrams

In addition to the wiring schematics, documentation should include diagrams of the physical and logical network design. Recall from Chapter 1, "Introduction to Networking Technologies," that network topologies can be defined on a physical or a logical level. The *physical topology* refers to how a network is physically constructed—how it looks. The *logical topology* refers to how a network looks to the devices that use it—how it functions.

Network infrastructure documentation isn't reviewed daily; however, this documentation is essential for someone unfamiliar with the network to manage or troubleshoot the network. When it comes to documenting the network, you need to document all aspects of the infrastructure. This includes the physical hardware, physical structure, protocols, and software used.

The physical documentation of the network should include the following elements:

▶ **Cabling information:** A visual description of all the physical communication links, including all cabling, cable grades, cable lengths, WAN cabling, and more.

▶ **Servers:** The server names and IP addresses, types of servers, and domain membership.

▶ **Network devices:** The location of the devices on the network. This includes the printers, hubs, switches, routers, gateways, and more.

▶ **Wide-area network:** The location and devices of the WAN and components.

▶ **User information:** Some user information, including the number of local and remote users.

As you can see, many elements can be included in the physical network diagram. Figure 9.3 shows a physical segment of a network.

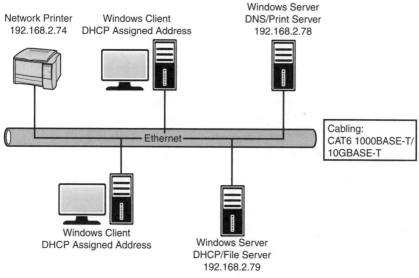

FIGURE 9.3 **A physical network diagram**

> **Caution**
>
> You should recognize the importance of maintaining documentation that includes network diagrams, asset management, IP address utilization, vendor documentation, and internal operating procedures, policies, and standards.

Networks are dynamic, and changes can happen regularly, which is why the physical network diagrams also must be updated. Networks have different policies and procedures on how often updates should occur. Best practice is that the diagram should be updated whenever significant changes to the network occur, such as the addition of a switch or router, a change in protocols, or the addition of a new server. These changes impact how the network operates, and the documentation should reflect the changes.

> **Caution**
>
> There are no hard-and-fast rules about when to change or update network documentation. However, most administrators will want to update whenever functional changes to the network occur.

The logical network refers to the direction in which data flows on the network within the physical topology. The logical diagram is not intended to focus on the network hardware but rather on how data flows through that hardware. In practice, the physical and logical topologies can be the same. In the case of the bus physical topology, data travels along the length of the cable from one computer to the next. So, the diagram for the physical and logical bus would be the same.

This is not always the case. For example, a topology can be in the physical shape of a star, but data is passed in a logical ring. The function of data travel is performed inside a switch in a ring formation. So the physical diagram appears to be a star, but the logical diagram shows data flowing in a ring formation from one computer to the next. Simply put, it is difficult to tell from looking at a physical diagram how data is flowing on the network.

In today's network environments, the star topology is a common network implementation. Ethernet uses a physical star topology but a logical bus topology. In the center of the physical Ethernet star topology is a switch. It is what happens inside the switch that defines the logical bus topology. The switch passes data between ports as if they were on an Ethernet bus segment.

In addition to data flow, logical diagrams may include additional elements, such as the network domain architecture, server roles, protocols used, and more. Figure 9.4 shows how a logical topology may look in the form of network documentation.

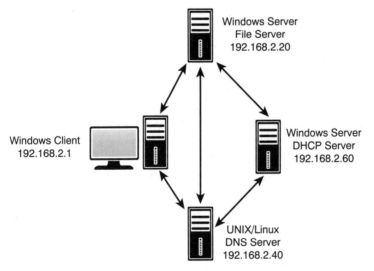

FIGURE 9.4 **A logical topology diagram**

> **Caution**
>
> The logical topology of a network identifies the logical paths that data signals travel over the network.

Baselines

Baselines play an integral part in network documentation because they let you monitor the network's overall performance. In simple terms, a *baseline* is a measure of performance that indicates how hard the network is working and where network resources are spent. The purpose of a baseline is to provide a basis of comparison. For example, you can compare the network's performance results taken in March to results taken in June, or from one year to the next. More commonly, you would compare the baseline information at a time when the network is having a problem to information recorded when the network was operating with greater efficiency. Such comparisons help you determine whether there has been a problem with the network, how significant that problem is, and even where the problem lies.

To be of any use, baselining is not a one-time task; rather, baselines should be taken periodically to provide an accurate comparison. You should take an initial baseline after the network is set up and operational, and then again when major changes are made to the network. Even if no changes are made to the network, periodic baselining can prove useful as a means to determine whether the network is still operating correctly.

All *network operating systems (NOSs)*, including Windows, Mac OS, UNIX, and Linux, have built-in support for network monitoring. In addition, many third-party software packages are available for detailed network monitoring. These system-monitoring tools provided in a NOS give you the means to take performance baselines, either of the entire network or for an individual segment within the network. Because of the different functions of these two baselines, they are called a system baseline and a component baseline.

To create a network baseline, network monitors provide a graphical display of network statistics. Network administrators can choose a variety of network measurements to track. They can use these statistics to perform routine troubleshooting tasks, such as locating a malfunctioning network card, a downed server, or a *denial-of-service (DoS)* attack.

> **Note**
>
> *Graphing*, and the process of seeing data visually, can be much more helpful in identifying trends than looking at raw data and log files.

Collecting network statistics is a process called *capturing*. Administrators can capture statistics on all elements of the network. For baseline purposes, one of the most common statistics to monitor is bandwidth usage. By reviewing bandwidth statistics, administrators can see where the bulk of network bandwidth is used. Then they can adapt the network for bandwidth use. If too much bandwidth is used by a particular application, administrators can actively control its bandwidth usage. Without comparing baselines, however, it is difficult to see what is normal network bandwidth usage and what is unusual.

> **Caution**
>
> Remember that baselines need to be taken periodically and under the same conditions to be effective. They are used to compare current performance with past performance to help determine whether the network is functioning properly or if troubleshooting is required.

Policies, Procedures, Configurations, and Regulations

Well-functioning networks are characterized by documented policies, procedures, configurations, and regulations. Because they are unique to every network, policies, procedures, configurations, and regulations should be clearly documented.

Policies

By definition, policies refer to an organization's documented rules about what is to be done, or not done, and why. Policies dictate who can and cannot access particular network resources, server rooms, backup media, and more.

Although networks might have different policies depending on their needs, some common policies include the following:

▶ **Network usage policy:** Defines who can use network resources such as PCs, printers, scanners, and remote connections. In addition, the usage policy dictates what can be done with these resources after they are accessed. No outside systems will be networked without permission from the network administrator.

▶ **Internet usage policy:** This policy specifies the rules for Internet use on the job. Typically, usage should be focused on business-related tasks. Incidental personal use is allowed during specified times.

▶ **Bring your own device (BYOD) policy:** This policy specifies the rules for employees' personally owned mobile devices (smartphones, laptops, tablets, and so on) that they bring into the workplace and use to interact with privileged company information and applications. Two things the policy needs to address are onboarding and offboarding. *Onboarding* the mobile device is the procedures gone through to get it ready to go on the network (scanning for viruses, adding certain apps, and so forth). *Offboarding* is the process of removing company-owned resources when it is no longer needed (often done with a wipe or factory reset). *Mobile device management (MDM)* and *mobile application management (MAM)* tools (usually third party) are used to administer and leverage both employee-owned and company-owned mobile devices and applications.

ExamAlert

For the exam, be familiar with onboarding and offboarding.

▶ **Email usage policy:** Email must follow the same code of conduct as expected in any other form of written or face-to-face communication. All emails are company property and can be accessed by the company. Personal emails should be immediately deleted.

▶ **Personal software policy:** No outside software should be installed on network computer systems. All software installations must be approved by the network administrator. No software can be copied or removed from a site. Licensing restrictions must be adhered to.

▶ **Password policy:** Detail how often passwords must be changed and the minimum level of security for each (number of characters, use of alphanumeric character set, and so on).

▶ **User account policy:** All users are responsible for keeping their password and account information secret. All staff are required to log off and sometimes lock their systems after they finish using them. Attempting to log on to the network with another user account is considered a serious violation.

▶ **International export controls:** A number of laws and regulations govern what can and cannot be exported when it comes to software and hardware to various countries. Employees should take every precaution to make sure they are adhering to the letter of the law.

▶ **Data loss prevention:** Losses from employees can quickly put a company in the red. It should be understood that it is every employee's responsibility to make sure all preventable losses are prevented.

- ▶ **Incident response policies:** When an incident occurs, all employees should understand it is their responsibility to be on the lookout for it and report it immediately to the appropriate party.

- ▶ **Non Disclosure Agreements (NDAs):** NDAs are the oxygen that many companies need to thrive. Employees should understand the importance of them to continued business operations and agree to follow them to the letter, and spirit, of the law.

- ▶ **Safety procedures and policies:** Safety is everyone's business, and all employees should know how to do their job in the safest manner while also looking out for other employees and customers alike.

- ▶ **Ownership policy:** The company owns all data, including users' email, voice mail, and Internet usage logs, and the company reserves the right to inspect these at any time. Some companies even go so far as controlling how much personal data can be stored on a workstation.

This list is just a snapshot of the policies that guide the behavior for administrators and network users. Network policies should be clearly documented and available to network users. Often, these policies are reviewed with new staff members or new administrators. As they are updated, they are rereleased to network users. Policies are regularly reviewed and updated.

> **Note**
>
> You might be asked about network policies. Network policies dictate network rules and provide guidelines for network conduct. Policies are often updated and reviewed and are changed to reflect changes to the network and perhaps changes in business requirements.

Password-Related Policies

Although biometrics and smart cards are becoming more common, they still have a long way to go before they attain the level of popularity that username and password combinations enjoy. Usernames and passwords do not require any additional equipment, which practically every other method of authentication does; the username and password process is familiar to users, easy to implement, and relatively secure. For that reason, they are worthy of more detailed coverage than the other authentication systems previously discussed.

> **Note**
>
> Biometrics are not as ubiquitous as username/password combinations, but they are coming up quickly. Some smartphones, for example, offer the ability to use a fingerprint scanner and/or gestures to access the system instead of username and password. Features such as these are expected to become more common with future releases.

Passwords are a relatively simple form of authentication in that only a string of characters can be used to authenticate the user. However, how the string of characters is used and which policies you can put in place to govern them make usernames and passwords an excellent form of authentication.

Password Policies

All popular network operating systems include password policy systems that enable the network administrator to control how passwords are used on the system. The exact capabilities vary between network operating systems. However, generally they enable the following:

- ▶ **Minimum length of password:** Shorter passwords are easier to guess than longer ones. Setting a minimum password length does not prevent a user from creating a longer password than the minimum; however, each network operating system has a limit on how long a password can be.

- ▶ **Password expiration:** Also known as the maximum password age, password expiration defines how long the user can use the same password before having to change it. A general practice is that a password be changed every 30 days. In high-security environments, you might want to make this value shorter, but you should generally not make it any longer. Having passwords expire periodically is a crucial feature because it means that if a password is compromised, the unauthorized user will not indefinitely have access.

- ▶ **Prevention of password reuse:** Although a system might cause a password to expire and prompt the user to change it, many users are tempted to use the same password again. A process by which the system remembers the last 10 passwords, for example, is most secure because it forces the user to create completely new passwords. This feature is sometimes called enforcing password history.

▶ **Prevention of easy-to-guess passwords:** Some systems can evaluate the password provided by a user to determine whether it meets a required level of complexity. This prevents users from having passwords such as *password*, *12345678*, their name, or their nickname.

ExamAlert

You must identify an effective password policy. For example, a robust password policy would include forcing users to change their passwords on a regular basis.

Password Strength

No matter how good a company's password policy, it is only as effective as the passwords created within it. A password that is hard to guess, or strong, is more likely to protect the data on a system than one that is easy to guess, or weak.

If you are using only numbers and letters—and the OS is not case sensitive—36 possible combinations exist for each entry, and the total number of possibilities is 36^6. That might seem like a lot, but to a password-cracking program, it's not much security. A password that uses eight case-sensitive characters, with letters, numbers, and special characters, has so many possible combinations that a standard calculator cannot display the actual number.

There has always been a debate over how long a password should be. It should be sufficiently long that it is hard to break but sufficiently short that the user can easily remember it (and type it). In a normal working environment, passwords of eight characters are sufficient. Certainly, they should be no fewer than six characters. In environments in which security is a concern, passwords should be 10 characters or more.

Users should be encouraged to use a password that is considered strong. A strong password has at least eight characters; has a combination of letters, numbers, and special characters; uses mixed case; and does not form a proper word. Examples are 3Ecc5T0h and e1oXPn3r. Such passwords might be secure, but users are likely to have problems remembering them. For that reason, a popular strategy is to use a combination of letters and numbers to form phrases or long words. Examples include d1eTc0La and tAb1eT0p. These passwords might not be quite as secure as the preceding examples, but they are still strong and a whole lot better than the name of the user's pet.

Procedures

Network procedures differ from policies in that they describe how tasks are to be performed. For example, each network administrator has backup procedures specifying the time of day backups are done, how often they are done, and where they are stored. A network is full of a number of procedures for practical reasons and, perhaps more important, for security reasons.

Administrators must be aware of several procedures when on the job. The number and exact type of procedures depends on the network. The network's overall goal is to ensure uniformity and ensure that network tasks follow a framework. Without this procedural framework, different administrators might approach tasks differently, which could lead to confusion on the network.

Network procedures might include the following:

- ▶ **Backup procedures:** Backup procedures specify when they are to be performed, how often a backup occurs, who does the backup, what data is to be backed up, and where and how it will be stored. Network administrators should carefully follow backup procedures.

- ▶ **Procedures for adding new users:** When new users are added to a network, administrators typically have to follow certain guidelines to ensure that the users have access to what they need, but no more. This is called the *principle of least privilege*.

- ▶ **Privileged user agreement:** Administrators and authorized users who have the ability to modify secure configurations and perform tasks such as account setup, account termination, account resetting, auditing, and so on need to be held to high standards.

- ▶ **Security procedures:** Some of the more critical procedures involve security. Security procedures are numerous but may include specifying what the administrator must do if security breaches occur, security monitoring, security reporting, and updating the OS and applications for potential security holes.

- ▶ **Network monitoring procedures:** The network needs to be constantly monitored. This includes tracking such things as bandwidth usage, remote access, user logons, and more.

- ▶ **Software procedures/system life cycle:** All software must be periodically monitored and updated. Documented procedures dictate when, how often, why, and for whom these updates are done. When assets are disposed of, asset disposal procedures should be followed to properly document and log their removal.

▶ **Procedures for reporting violations:** Users do not always follow outlined network policies. This is why documented procedures should exist to properly handle the violations. This might include a verbal warning upon the first offense, followed by written reports and account lockouts thereafter.

▶ **Remote-access and network admission procedures:** Many workers remotely access the network. This remote access is granted and maintained using a series of defined procedures. These procedures might dictate when remote users can access the network, how long they can access it, and what they can access. *Network admission control (NAC)*— also referred to as *network access control*—determines who can get on the network and is usually based on 802.1X guidelines.

Change Management Documentation

Change management procedures might include the following:

▶ **Document reason for a change:** Before making any change at all, the first question to ask is *why*. A change requested by one user may be based on a misunderstanding of what technology can do, may be cost prohibitive, or may deliver a benefit not worth the undertaking.

▶ **Change request:** An official request should be logged and tracked to verify what is to be done and what has been done. Within the realm of the change request should be the configuration procedures to be used, the rollback process that is in place, potential impact identified, and a list of those who need to be notified.

▶ **Approval process:** Changes should not be approved on the basis of who makes the most noise, but rather who has the most justified reasons. An official process should be in place to evaluate and approve changes prior to actions being undertaken. The approval can be done by a single administrator or a formal committee based on the size of your organization and the scope of the change being approved.

▶ **Maintenance window:** After a change has been approved, the next question to address is when it is to take place. Authorized downtime should be used to make changes to production environments.

▶ **Notification of change:** Those affected by a change should be notified after the change has taken place. The notification should not be just of the change but should include any and all impact to them and identify who they can turn to with questions.

▶ **Documentation:** One of the last steps is always to document what has been done. This should include documentation on network configurations, additions to the network, and physical location changes.

These represent just a few of the procedures that administrators must follow on the job. It is crucial that all these procedures are well documented, accessible, reviewed, and updated as needed to be effective.

Configuration Documentation

One other critical form of documentation is configuration documentation. Many administrators believe they could never forget the configuration of a router, server, or switch, but it often happens. Although it is often a thankless, time-consuming task, documenting the network hardware and software configurations is critical for continued network functionality.

Two primary types of network configuration documentation are required: software documentation and hardware documentation. Both include all configuration information so that should a computer or other hardware fail, both the hardware and software can be replaced and reconfigured as quickly as possible. The documentation is important because often the administrator who configured the software or hardware is unavailable, and someone else has to re-create the configuration using nothing but the documentation. To be effective in this case, the documentation must be as current as possible. Older configuration information might not help.

> **Note**
>
> Organizing and completing the initial set of network documentation is a huge task, but it is just the beginning. Administrators must constantly update all documentation to keep it from becoming obsolete. Documentation is perhaps one of the less-glamorous aspects of the administrator's role, but it is one of the most important.

Regulations

The terms *regulation* and *policy* are often used interchangeably; however, there is a difference. As mentioned, policies are written by an organization for its employees. Regulations are actual legal restrictions with legal consequences. These regulations are set not by the organizations but by applicable laws in the area. Improper use of networks and the Internet can certainly lead to legal violations and consequences. The following is an example of network regulation from an online company:

"Transmission, distribution, uploading, posting or storage of any material in violation of any applicable law or regulation is prohibited. This includes, without limitation, material protected by copyright, trademark, trade secret or other intellectual property right used without proper authorization, material kept in violation of state laws or industry regulations such as social security numbers or credit card numbers, and material that is obscene, defamatory, libelous, unlawful, harassing, abusive, threatening, harmful, vulgar, constitutes an illegal threat, violates export control laws, hate propaganda, fraudulent material or fraudulent activity, invasive of privacy or publicity rights, profane, indecent or otherwise objectionable material of any kind or nature. You may not transmit, distribute, or store material that contains a virus, 'Trojan Horse,' adware or spyware, corrupted data, or any software or information to promote or utilize software or any of Network Solutions services to deliver unsolicited email. You further agree not to transmit any material that encourages conduct that could constitute a criminal offense, gives rise to civil liability or otherwise violates any applicable local, state, national or international law or regulation."

> **ExamAlert**
>
> For the exam and for real-life networking, remember that regulations often are enforceable by law.

Labeling

One of the biggest problems with documentation is in the time that it takes to do it. To shorten this time, it is human nature to take shortcuts and use code or shorthand when labeling devices, maps, reports, and the like. Although this can save time initially, it can render the labels useless if a person other than the one who created the labels looks at them or if a long period of time has passed since they were created and the author cannot remember what the label now means.

To prevent this dilemma, it is highly recommended that standard labeling rules be created by each organization and enforced at all levels.

Cram Quiz

You have been given a physical wiring schematic that shows the following:

Description	Installation Notes
Category 5E 350 MHz plenum-rated cable	Cable runs 50 feet from the MDF to the IDF.
	Cable placed through the ceiling and through a mechanical room.
	Cable was installed 01/15/2018, upgrading a nonplenum cable.
Category 5E 350 MHz nonplenum cable	Horizontal cable runs 45 feet to 55 feet from the IDF to a wall jack.
	Cable 6 replaced Category 5e cable February 2018.
	Section of cable run through ceiling and over fluorescent lights.
Category 6a UTP cable	Patch cable connecting printer runs 15 feet due to printer placement.
8.3-micron core/125-micron	Connecting fiber cable runs 2 kilometers cladding single mode between the primary and secondary buildings.

1. Given this information, what cable recommendation might you make, if any?

   O A. Nonplenum cable should be used between the IDF and MDF.

   O B. The horizontal cable run should use plenum cable.

   O C. The patch cable connecting the printer should be shorter.

   O D. Leave the network cabling as is.

2. You have been called in to inspect a network configuration. You are given only one network diagram, shown in the following figure. Using the diagram, what recommendation might you make?

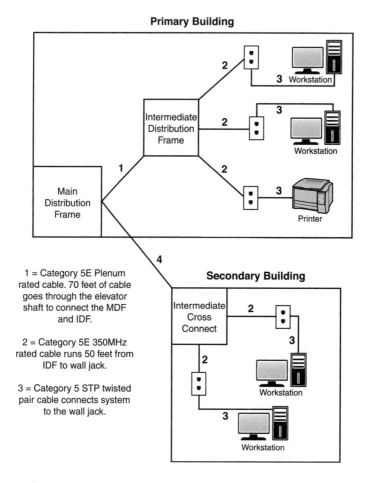

Primary Building

2

3 Workstation

Intermediate
Distribution
Frame

3

2

Workstation

1

2

Main
Distribution
Frame

3

Printer

4

1 = Category 5E Plenum rated cable. 70 feet of cable goes through the elevator shaft to connect the MDF and IDF.

2 = Category 5E 350MHz rated cable runs 50 feet from IDF to wall jack.

3 = Category 5 STP twisted pair cable connects system to the wall jack.

Secondary Building

Intermediate
Cross
Connect

2

3

2

Workstation

3

Workstation

○ **A.** Cable 1 does not need to be plenum rated.

○ **B.** Cable 2 should be STP cable.

○ **C.** Cable 3 should be STP cable.

○ **D.** None. The network looks good.

3. Hollis is complaining that the network cabling in her office is outdated and should be changed. What should she do to have the cabling evaluated and possibly changed?

   ○ **A.** Tell her supervisor that IT needs to get on the ball.

   ○ **B.** Tell your supervisor that IT needs to get on the ball.

   ○ **C.** Purchase new cabling at the local electronics store.

   ○ **D.** Complete a change request.

Cram Quiz Answers

1. **B.** In this scenario, a section of horizontal cable runs through the ceiling and over fluorescent lights. This cable run might be a problem because such devices can cause EMI. Alternatively, plenum cable is used in this scenario. STP may have worked as well.

2. **B.** In this diagram, Cable 1 is plenum rated and should be fine. Cable 3 is patch cable and does not need to be STP rated. Cable 2, however, goes through walls and ceilings. Therefore, it would be recommended to have a better grade of cable than regular UTP. STP provides greater resistance to EMI.

3. **D.** An official change request should be logged and tracked to verify what is to be done and what has been done. Within the realm of the change request should be the configuration procedures to be used, the rollback process that is in place, potential impact identified, and a list of those that need to be notified.

Business Continuity and Disaster Recovery

▶ **Compare and contrast business continuity and disaster recovery concepts.**

▶ **Identify policies and best practices.**

CramSaver

If you can correctly answer these questions before going through this section, save time by skimming the Exam Alerts in this section and then completing the Cram Quiz at the end of the section.

1. What is the difference between an incremental backup and a differential backup?

2. What are hot, warm, and cold sites used for?

3. True or false: Acceptable use policies define what controls are required to implement and maintain the security of systems, users, and networks.

Answers

1. With incremental backups, all data that has changed since the last full or incremental backup is backed up. The restore procedure requires several backup iterations: the media used in the latest full backup and all media used for incremental backups since the last full backup. An incremental backup uses the archive bit and clears it after a file is saved to disk. With a differential backup, all data changed since the last full backup is backed up. The restore procedure requires the latest full backup media and the latest differential backup media. A differential backup uses the archive bit to determine which files must be backed up but does not clear it.

2. Hot, warm, and cold sites are designed to provide alternative locations for network operations if a disaster occurs.

3. False. Security policies define what controls are required to implement and maintain the security of systems, users, and networks. *Acceptable use policies (AUPs)* describe how the employees in an organization can use company systems and resources: both software and hardware.

Even the most fault-tolerant networks can fail, which is an unfortunate fact. When those costly and carefully implemented fault-tolerance strategies fail, you are left with disaster recovery.

Disaster recovery can take many forms. In addition to disasters such as fire, flood, and theft, many other potential business disruptions can fall under the banner of disaster recovery. For example, the failure of the electrical supply to your city block might interrupt the business functions. Such an event, although not a disaster per se, might invoke the disaster recovery methods.

The cornerstone of every disaster recovery strategy is the preservation and recoverability of data. When talking about preservation and recoverability, you must talk about backups. Implementing a regular backup schedule can save you a lot of grief when fault tolerance fails or when you need to recover a file that has been accidentally deleted. When it's time to design a backup schedule, you can use three key types of backups: full, differential, and incremental.

Backups
Full Backups

The preferred method of backup is the *full backup* method, which copies all files and directories from the hard disk to the backup media. There are a few reasons why doing a full backup is not always possible. First among them is likely the time involved in performing a full backup.

> **ExamAlert**
>
> During a recovery operation, a full backup is the fastest way to restore data of all the methods discussed here, because only one set of media is required for a full restore.

Depending on the amount of data to be backed up, however, full backups can take an extremely long time when you are backing up and can use extensive system resources. Depending on the configuration of the backup hardware, this can considerably slow down the network. In addition, some environments have more data than can fit on a single medium. This makes doing a full backup awkward because someone might need to be there to change the media.

The main advantage of full backups is that a single set of media holds all the data you need to restore. If a failure occurs, that single set of media should be all that is needed to get all data and system information back. The upshot of all this is that any disruption to the network is greatly reduced.

Unfortunately, its strength can also be its weakness. A single set of media holding an organization's data can be a security risk. If the media were to fall into the wrong hands, all the data could be restored on another computer. Using passwords on backups and using a secure offsite and onsite location can minimize the security risk.

Differential Backups

Companies that don't have enough time to complete a full backup daily can use the *differential backup*. Differential backups are faster than a full backup because they back up only the data that has changed since the last full backup. This means that if you do a full backup on a Saturday and a differential backup on the following Wednesday, only the data that has changed since Saturday is backed up. Restoring the differential backup requires the last full backup and the latest differential backup.

Differential backups know what files have changed since the last full backup because they use a setting called the archive bit. The archive bit flags files that have changed or have been created and identifies them as ones that need to be backed up. Full backups do not concern themselves with the archive bit because all files are backed up, regardless of date. A full backup, however, does clear the archive bit after data has been backed up to avoid future confusion. Differential backups notice the archive bit and use it to determine which files have changed. The differential backup does not reset the archive bit information.

Incremental Backups

Some companies have a finite amount of time they can allocate to backup procedures. Such organizations are likely to use *incremental backups* in their backup strategy. Incremental backups save only the files that have changed since the last full or incremental backup. Like differential backups, incremental backups use the archive bit to determine which files have changed since the last full or incremental backup. Unlike differentials, however, incremental backups clear the archive bit, so files that have not changed are not backed up.

> **ExamAlert**
>
> Both full and incremental backups clear the archive bit after files have been backed up.

The faster backup time of incremental backups comes at a price—the amount of time required to restore. Recovering from a failure with incremental backups requires numerous sets of media—all the incremental backup media sets and the one for the most recent full backup. For example, if you have a full backup from Sunday and an incremental for Monday, Tuesday, and Wednesday, you need four sets of media to restore the data. Each set in the rotation is an additional step in the restore process and an additional failure point. One damaged incremental media set means that you cannot restore the data. Table 9.2 summarizes the various backup strategies.

TABLE 9.2 **Backup Strategies**

Backup Type	Advantage	Disadvantage	Data Backed Up	Archive Bit
Full	Backs up all data on a single media set. Restoring data requires the fewest media sets.	Depending on the amount of data, full backups can take a long time.	All files and directories are backed up.	Does not use the archive bit, but resets it after data has been backed up.
Differential	Faster backups than a full backup.	The restore process takes longer than just a full backup. Uses more media sets than a full backup.	All files and directories that have changed since the last full backup.	Uses the archive bit to determine the files that have changed, but does not reset the archive bit.
Incremental	Faster backup times	Requires multiple disks; restoring data takes more time than the other backup methods.	The files and directories that have changed since the last full or incremental backup.	Uses the archive bit to determine the files that have changed, and resets the archive bit.

ExamAlert

Review Table 9.2 before taking the Network+ exam.

Snapshots

In addition to the three types of backups previously discussed, there are also *snapshots*. Whereas a backup can take a long time to complete, the advantage of a snapshot—an image of the state of a system at a particular point in time—is that it is an instantaneous copy of the system. This is often accomplished by splitting a mirrored set of disks or by creating a copy of a disk block when it is written in order to preserve the original and keep it available.

Snapshots are popular with virtual machine implementations. You can take as many snapshots as you want (provided you have enough storage space) in order to be able to revert a machine to a "saved" state. Snapshots contain a copy of the virtual machine settings (hardware configuration), information on all virtual disks attached, and the memory state of the machine at the time of the snapshot. This makes the snapshots additionally useful for virtual machine cloning, allowing the machine to be copied once—or multiple times—for testing.

Backup Best Practices

Many details go into making a backup strategy a success. The following are issues to consider as part of your backup plan:

▶ **Offsite storage:** Consider storing backup media sets offsite so that if a disaster occurs in a building, a current set of media is available offsite. The offsite media should be as current as any onsite and should be secure.

▶ **Label media:** The goal is to restore the data as quickly as possible. Trying to find the media you need can prove difficult if it is not marked. Furthermore, this can prevent you from recording over something you need to keep.

▶ **Verify backups:** Never assume that the backup was successful. Seasoned administrators know that checking backup logs and performing periodic test restores are part of the backup process.

▶ **Cleaning:** You need to occasionally clean the backup drive. If the inside gets dirty, backups can fail.

Using Uninterruptible Power Supplies

No discussion of fault tolerance can be complete without a look at power-related issues and the mechanisms used to combat them. When you design a fault-tolerant system, your planning should definitely include *uninterruptible power supplies (UPSs)*. A UPS serves many functions and is a major part of server consideration and implementation.

On a basic level, a UPS, also known as a *battery backup*, is a box that holds a battery and built-in charging circuit. During times of good power, the battery is recharged; when the UPS is needed, it's ready to provide power to the server.

Most often, the UPS is required to provide enough power to give the administrator time to shut down the server in an orderly fashion, preventing any potential data loss from a dirty shutdown.

Why Use a UPS?

Organizations of all shapes and sizes need UPSs as part of their fault tolerance strategies. A UPS is as important as any other fault-tolerance measure. Three key reasons make a UPS necessary:

▶ **Data availability:** The goal of any fault-tolerance measure is data availability. A UPS ensures access to the server if a power failure occurs—or at least as long as it takes to save a file.

▶ **Protection from data loss:** Fluctuations in power or a sudden power-down can damage the data on the server system. In addition, many servers take full advantage of caching, and a sudden loss of power could cause the loss of all information held in cache.

▶ **Protection from hardware damage:** Constant power fluctuations or sudden power-downs can damage hardware components within a computer. Damaged hardware can lead to reduced data availability while the hardware is repaired.

Power Threats

In addition to keeping a server functioning long enough to safely shut it down, a UPS safeguards a server from inconsistent power. This inconsistent power can take many forms. A UPS protects a system from the following power-related threats:

▶ **Blackout:** A total failure of the power supplied to the server.

▶ **Spike:** A short (usually less than 1 second) but intense increase in voltage. Spikes can do irreparable damage to any kind of equipment, especially computers.

▶ **Surge:** Compared to a spike, a surge is a considerably longer (sometimes many seconds) but usually less intense increase in power. Surges can also damage your computer equipment.

▶ **Sag:** A short-term voltage drop (the opposite of a spike). This type of voltage drop can cause a server to reboot.

▶ **Brownout:** A drop in voltage that usually lasts more than a few minutes.

Many of these power-related threats can occur without your knowledge; if you don't have a UPS, you cannot prepare for them. For the cost, it is worth buying a UPS, if for no other reason than to sleep better at night.

Alternatives to UPS

Power management is not limited only to the use of UPSs. In addition, to these devices, you should employ *power generators* to be able to keep your systems up and running when the electrical provider is down for an extended period of time. *Redundant circuits* and *dual power supplies* should also be used for key equipment.

Hot, Warm, and Cold Sites

A disaster recovery plan might include the provision for a recovery site that can be quickly brought into play. These sites fall into three categories: hot, warm, and cold. The need for each of these types of sites depends largely on the business you are in and the funds available. Disaster recovery sites represent the ultimate in precautions for organizations that need them. As a result, they do not come cheaply.

The basic concept of a disaster recovery site is that it can provide a base from which the company can be operated during a disaster. The disaster recovery site normally is not intended to provide a desk for every employee. It's intended more as a means to allow key personnel to continue the core business functions.

In general, a cold recovery site is a site that can be up and operational in a relatively short amount of time, such as a day or two. Provision of services, such as telephone lines and power, is taken care of, and the basic office furniture might be in place. But there is unlikely to be any computer equipment, even though the building might have a network infrastructure and a room ready to act as a server room. In most cases, cold sites provide the physical location and basic services.

Cold sites are useful if you have some forewarning of a potential problem. Generally, cold sites are used by organizations that can weather the storm for a day or two before they get back up and running. If you are the regional office of a major company, it might be possible to have one of the other divisions take care of business until you are ready to go. But if you are the only office in the company, you might need something a little hotter.

For organizations with the dollars and the desire, hot recovery sites represent the ultimate in fault-tolerance strategies. Like cold recovery sites, hot sites are designed to provide only enough facilities to continue the core business function, but hot recovery sites are set up to be ready to go at a moment's notice.

A hot recovery site includes phone systems with connected phone lines. Data networks also are in place, with any necessary routers and switches plugged in and turned on. Desks have installed and waiting desktop PCs, and server areas are replete with the necessary hardware to support business-critical functions. In other words, within a few hours, the hot site can become a fully functioning element of an organization.

The issue that confronts potential hot-recovery site users is that of cost. Office space is expensive in the best of times, but having space sitting idle 99.9 percent of the time can seem like a tremendously poor use of money. A popular strategy to get around this problem is to use space provided in a disaster recovery facility, which is basically a building, maintained by a third-party company, in which various businesses rent space. Space is usually apportioned according to how much each company pays.

Sitting between the hot and cold recovery sites is the warm site. A warm site typically has computers but is not configured ready to go. This means that data might need to be upgraded or other manual interventions might need to be performed before the network is again operational. The time it takes to get a warm site operational lands right in the middle of the other two options, as does the cost.

> **ExamAlert**
>
> A hot site mirrors the organization's production network and can assume network operations at a moment's notice. Warm sites have the equipment needed to bring the network to an operational state but require configuration and potential database updates. A cold site has the space available with basic services but typically requires equipment delivery.

High Availability and Recovery Concepts

When an incident occurs, it is too late to consider policies and procedures then; this must be done well ahead of time. *Business continuity* should always be of the utmost concern. Business continuity is primarily concerned with the processes, policies, and methods that an organization follows to minimize the impact of a system failure, network failure, or the failure of any key component needed for operation. *Business continuity planning (BCP)* is the process of implementing policies, controls, and procedures to counteract the effects of losses, outages, or failures of critical business processes. BCP is primarily a management tool that ensures that *critical business functions (CBFs)* can be performed when normal business operations are disrupted.

Critical business functions refer to those processes or systems that must be made operational immediately when an outage occurs. The business can't function without them, and many are information intensive and require access to both technology and data. When you evaluate your business's sustainability, realize that disasters do indeed happen. If possible, build infrastructures that don't have a *single point of failure (SPOF)* or connection. If you're the administrator for a small company, it is not uncommon for the SPOF to be a router/gateway, but you must identify all *critical nodes* and *critical assets*. The best way to remove an SPOF from your environment is to add in redundancy.

Know that every piece of equipment can be rated in terms of mean time between failures (MTBF) and mean time to recovery (MTTR). The MTBF is the measurement of the anticipated or predicted incidence of failure of a system or component between inherent failures, whereas the MTTR is the measurement of how long it takes to repair a system or component after a failure occurs.

Some technologies that can help with availability are the following:

▶ **Fault tolerance** is the capability to withstand a fault (failure) without losing data. This can be accomplished through the use of RAID, backups, and similar technologies. Popular fault-tolerant RAID implementations include RAID 1, RAID 5, and RAID 10.

▶ **Load balancing** is a technique in which the workload is distributed among several servers. This feature can take networks to the next level; it increases network performance, reliability, and availability. A load balancer can be either a hardware device or software specially configured to balance the load.

ExamAlert

Remember that load balancing increases redundancy and therefore data availability. Also, load balancing increases performance by distributing the workload.

▶ **NIC teaming** is the process of combining multiple network cards for performance and redundancy (fault tolerance) reasons. This can also be called bonding, balancing, or aggregation.

▶ **Port aggregation** is the combining of multiple ports on a switch; it can be done one of three ways: auto, desirable, or on.

▶ **Clustering** is a method of balancing loads and providing fault tolerance.

Use *vulnerability scanning* and *penetration testing* to find the weaknesses in your systems before others do. Make sure that *end user awareness and training* is a priority when it comes to identifying problems and that you stress *adherence to standards and policies*. Those policies should include the following:

▶ **Standard business documents:** Many of these have been discussed in previous chapters, but they include *service-level agreements (SLAs), memorandums of understanding (MOUs), master license agreements (MLAs)*, and *statements of work (SOWs)*. An SLA, in particular, is an agreement between you or your company and a service provider, typically a technical support provider. SLAs are also usually part of network availability and other agreements. They stipulate the performance you can expect or demand by outlining the expectations a vendor has agreed to meet. They define what is possible to deliver and provide the contract to make sure what is delivered is what was promised.

▶ **Acceptable use policy:** *Acceptable use policies (AUPs)* describe how the employees in an organization can use company systems and resources: both software and hardware. This policy should also outline the consequences for misuse. In addition, the policy (also known as a *use policy*) should address installation of personal software on company computers and the use of personal hardware, such as USB devices.

▶ **Network policies:** Similar to AUPs, these describe acceptable uses for the network resources.

▶ **Security policies:** *Security policies* define what controls are required to implement and maintain the security of systems, users, and networks. This policy should be used as a guide in system implementations and evaluations. One of particular note is a *consent to monitoring policy* in which employees and other network users acknowledge that they know they're being monitored and consent to it.

▶ **BYOD policies:** *Bring your own device (BYOD)* policies define what personally owned mobile devices (laptops, tablets, and smartphones) employees are allowed to bring to their workplace and use. *Mobile device management (MDM)* and *mobile application management (MAM)* systems can be used to help enterprises manage and secure the use of those mobile devices in the workplace.

ExamAlert

As you study for the exam, three topics to pay attention to are adherence to standards and policies, vulnerability scanning, and penetration testing.

All these policies are important, but those that relate to first responders and deal with data breaches are of elevated importance.

Cram Quiz

1. Which two types of backup methods clear the archive bit after the backup has been completed? (Choose two.)

   ○ **A.** Full

   ○ **B.** Differential

   ○ **C.** Incremental

   ○ **D.** GFS

2. You come to work on Thursday morning to find that the server has failed and you need to restore the data from backup. You finished a full backup on Sunday and incremental backups on Monday, Tuesday, and Wednesday. How many media sets are required to restore the backup?

   ○ **A.** Four

   ○ **B.** Two

   ○ **C.** Three

   ○ **D.** Five

3. Which of the following recovery sites might require the delivery of computer equipment and an update of all network data?

   ○ **A.** Cold site

   ○ **B.** Warm site

   ○ **C.** Hot site

   ○ **D.** None of the above

4. As part of your network administrative responsibilities, you have completed your monthly backups. As part of backup best practices, where should the media be stored?

   ○ **A.** In a secure location in the server room

   ○ **B.** In a secure location somewhere in the building

   ○ **C.** In an offsite location

   ○ **D.** In a secure offsite location

5. As network administrator, you have been tasked with designing a disaster recovery plan for your network. Which of the following might you include in a disaster recovery plan?

   ○ **A.** RAID 5

   ○ **B.** Offsite media storage

   ○ **C.** Mirrored hard disks

   ○ **D.** UPS

6. Which type of recovery site mirrors the organization's production network and can assume network operations on a moment's notice?

   ○ **A.** Warm site

   ○ **B.** Hot site

   ○ **C.** Cold site

   ○ **D.** Mirrored site

7. Which of the following are used to find weaknesses in your systems before others do? (Choose two.)

   ○ **A.** Data breachers

   ○ **B.** Vulnerability scanners

   ○ **C.** Penetration testers

   ○ **D.** First responders

8. Which of the following is a type of policy in which employees and other network users give consent to be monitored?

   ○ **A.** Consent to monitoring

   ○ **B.** Acceptable use

   ○ **C.** Memorandum of Understanding

   ○ **D.** Service-Level Agreement

Cram Quiz Answers

1. **A, C.** The archive bit is reset after a full backup and an incremental backup. Answer B is incorrect because the differential backup does not reset the archive bit. Answer D is wrong because GFS is a rotation strategy, not a backup method.

2. **A.** Incremental backups save all files and directories that have changed since the last full or incremental backup. To restore, you need the latest full backup and all incremental media sets. In this case, you need four sets of media to complete the restore process.

3. **A.** A cold site provides an alternative location but typically not much more. A cold site often requires the delivery of computer equipment and other services. A hot site has all network equipment ready to go if a massive failure occurs. A warm site has most equipment ready but still needs days or weeks to have the network up and running.

4. **D.** Although not always done, it is a best practice to store backups in a secure offsite location in case of fire or theft. Answer A is incorrect because if the server room is damaged by fire or flood, the backups and the data on the server can be compromised by the same disaster. Similarly, answer B is incorrect because storing the backups onsite does not eliminate the threat of a single disaster destroying the data on the server and backups. Answer C is incorrect because of security reasons. The offsite media sets must be secured.

5. **B.** Offsite storage is part of a disaster recovery plan. The other answers are considered fault-tolerance measures because they are implemented to ensure data availability.

6. **B.** A hot site mirrors the organization's production network and can assume network operations at a moment's notice. Answer A is incorrect because warm sites have the equipment needed to bring the network to an operational state but require configuration and potential database updates. Answer C is incorrect because cold sites have the space available with basic services but typically require equipment delivery. Answer D is incorrect because a mirrored site is not a valid option.

7. **B, C.** Use vulnerability scanning and penetration testing to find the weaknesses in your systems before others do. Answer A is incorrect because data breaches are invalid. Answer D is incorrect because first responders are typically those who are first on the scene after an incident.

8. **A.** A consent to monitoring policy is one in which employees and other network users acknowledge that they know they're being monitored and consent to it. Answer B is incorrect because acceptable use policies describe how the employees in an organization can use company systems and resources. Answers C and D are incorrect because a Memorandum of Understanding and Service-Level Agreements are standard business documents.

Monitoring Network Performance

▶ **Explain common scanning, monitoring and patching processes and summarize their expected outputs.**

CramSaver

If you can correctly answer these questions before going through this section, save time by skimming the Exam Alerts in this section and then completing the Cram Quiz at the end of the section.

1. What can be used to capture network data?

2. True or false: Port scanners detect open and often unsecured ports.

3. True or false: Interface monitoring tools can be used to create "heat maps" showing the quantity and quality of wireless network coverage in areas.

4. True or false: Always test updates on a lab machine before rolling out on production machines.

5. What is it known as when you roll a system back to a previous version of a driver or firmware?

Answers

1. Packet sniffers can be used by both administrators and hackers to capture network data.

2. True. Port scanners detect open and often unsecured ports.

3. False. Wireless survey tools can be used to create heat maps showing the quantity and quality of wireless network coverage in areas.

4. True. Always test updates on a lab machine before rolling out on production machines.

5. This is known as *downgrading* and is often necessary when dealing with legacy systems and implementations.

When networks were smaller and few stretched beyond the confines of a single location, network management was a simple task. In today's complex, multisite, hybrid networks, however, the task of maintaining and monitoring network devices and servers has become a complicated but essential part of the network administrator's role. Nowadays, the role of network administrator often stretches beyond the physical boundary of the server room and reaches every node and component on the network. Whether an organization has 10 computers on a single segment or a multisite network with several thousand devices attached, the network administrator must monitor all network devices, protocols, and usage—preferably from a central location.

Given the sheer number and diversity of possible devices, software, and systems on any network, it is clear why network management is such a significant consideration. Despite that a robust network management strategy can improve administrator productivity and reduce downtime, many companies choose to neglect network management because of the time involved in setting up the system or because of the associated costs. If these companies understood the potential savings, they would realize that neglecting network management provides false economies.

Network management and network monitoring are essentially methods to control, configure, and monitor devices on a network. Imagine a scenario in which you are a network administrator working out of your main office in Spokane, Washington, and you have satellite offices in New York, Dallas, Vancouver, and London. Network management allows you to access systems in the remote locations or have the systems notify you when something goes awry. In essence, network management is about seeing beyond your current boundaries and acting on what you see.

Network management is not one thing. Rather, it is a collection of tools, systems, and protocols that, when used together, enables you to perform tasks such as reconfiguring a network card in the next room or installing an application in the next state.

Common Reasons to Monitor Networks

The capabilities demanded from network management vary somewhat among organizations, but essentially, several key types of information and functionality are required, such as fault detection and performance monitoring. Some of the types of information and functions that network management tools can provide include the following:

▶ **Utilization:** Once upon a time, it was not uncommon for a network to have to limp by with scarce resources. Administrators would constantly have to trim logs and archive files to keep enough storage space available to service print jobs. Those days are gone, and any such hint of those conditions would be unacceptable today. To keep this from happening, one of the keys is to manage utilization and stay on top of problems before they escalate. Five areas of utilization to monitor are as follows:

  ▶ **Bandwidth/throughput:** There must be enough bandwidth to serve all users, and you need to be alert for bandwidth hogs. You want to look for top talkers (those that transmit the most) and top listeners (those that receive the most) and figure out why they are so popular.

▶ **Storage space:** Free space needs to be available for all users, and quotas may need to be implemented.

▶ **Network device CPU:** Just as a local machine will slow when the processor is maxed out, so will the network.

▶ **Network device memory:** It is next to impossible to have too much memory. Balance loads to optimize the resources you have to work with.

▶ **Wireless channel utilization:** Akin to bandwidth utilization is channel utilization in the wireless realm. As a general rule, a wireless network starts experiencing performance problems when channel utilization reaches 50% of the channel capacity.

▶ **Fault detection:** One of the most vital aspects of network management is knowing if anything is not working or is not working correctly. Network management tools can detect and report on a variety of faults on the network. Given the number of possible devices that constitute a typical network, determining faults without these tools could be an impossible task. In addition, network management tools might not only detect the faulty device, but also shut it down. This means that if a network card is malfunctioning, you can remotely disable it. When a network spans a large area, fault detection becomes even more invaluable because it enables you to be alerted to network faults and to manage them, thereby reducing downtime.

ExamAlert

Most of this discussion involves your being alerted to some condition. Those alerts can generally be sent to you through email or SMS to any mobile device.

▶ **Performance monitoring:** Another feature of network management is the ability to monitor network performance. Performance monitoring is an essential consideration that gives you some crucial information. Specifically, performance monitoring can provide network usage statistics and user usage trends. This type of information is essential when you plan network capacity and growth. Monitoring performance also helps you determine whether there are any performance-related concerns, such as whether the network can adequately support the current user base.

▶ **Security monitoring:** Good server administrators have a touch of paranoia built into their personality. A network management system enables you to monitor who is on the network, what they are doing, and how long they have been doing it. More important, in an environment in which corporate networks are increasingly exposed to outside sources, the ability to identify and react to potential security threats is a priority. Reading log files to learn of an attack is a poor second to knowing that an attack is in progress and being able to react accordingly. *Security information and event management (SIEM)* products provide notifications and real-time analysis of security alerts and can help you head off problems quickly.

▶ **Link status:** You should regularly monitor link status to make sure that connections are up and functioning. Breaks should be found and identified as quickly as possible to repair them or find workarounds. A number of link status monitors exist for the purpose of monitoring connectivity, and many can reroute (per a configured script file) when a down condition occurs.

▶ **Interface monitoring:** Just as you want to monitor for a link going down, you also need to know when there are problems with an interface. Particular problems to watch for include errors, utilization problems (unusually high, for example), discards, packet drops, resets, and problems with speed/duplex. An *interface monitoring tool* is invaluable for troubleshooting problems here.

▶ **Maintenance and configuration:** Want to reconfigure or shut down the server located in Australia? Reconfigure a local router? Change the settings on a client system? Remote management and configuration are key parts of the network management strategy, enabling you to centrally manage huge multisite locations.

▶ **Environmental monitoring:** It is important to monitor the server room, and other key equipment, for temperature and humidity conditions. Humidity control prevents the buildup of static electricity and when the level drops much below 50%, electronic components become vulnerable to damage from electrostatic shock. *Environmental monitoring tools* can alert you to any dangers that arise here.

ExamAlert

For the exam, recognize the role humidity plays in controlling electrostatic shock.

▶ **Power monitoring:** A consistent flow of reliable energy is needed to keep a network up and running. A wide array of *power monitoring tools* are available to help identify and log problems that you can then begin to resolve.

▶ **Wireless monitoring:** As more networks go wireless, you need to pay special attention to issues associated with them. *Wireless survey tools* can be used to create heat maps showing the quantity and quality of wireless network coverage in areas. They can also allow you to see access points (including rogues) and security settings. These can be used to help you design and deploy an efficient network, and they can also be used (by you or others) to find weaknesses in your existing network (often marketed for this purpose as *wireless analyzers*).

Many tools are available to help monitor the network and ensure that it is properly functioning. Some tools, such as a packet sniffer, can be used to monitor traffic by administrators and those who want to obtain data that does not belong to them. The following sections look at several monitoring tools.

SNMP Monitors

An SNMP management system is a computer running a special piece of software called a *network management system (NMS)*. These software applications can be free, or they can cost thousands of dollars. The difference between the free applications and those that cost a great deal of money normally boils down to functionality and support. All NMS applications, regardless of cost, offer the same basic functionality. Today, most NMS applications use graphical maps of the network to locate a device and then query it. The queries are built in to the application and are triggered by pointing and clicking. You can actually issue SNMP requests from a command-line utility, but with so many tools available, this is unnecessary.

> **Note**
>
> Some people call SNMP managers or NMSs *trap managers*. This reference is misleading, however, because an NMS can do more than just accept trap messages from agents.

Using SNMP and an NMS, you can monitor all the devices on a network, including switches, hubs, routers, servers, and printers, as well as any device that supports SNMP, from a single location. Using SNMP, you can see the amount of free disk space on a server in Jakarta or reset the interface on a router in Helsinki—all from the comfort of your desk in San Jose. Such power, though, brings with it some considerations. For example, because an NMS enables you to reconfigure network devices, or at least get information from them, it is common practice to implement an NMS on a secure workstation platform, such as a Linux or Windows server, and to place the NMS PC in a secure location.

Management Information Bases (MIB)

Although the SNMP trap system might be the most commonly used aspect of SNMP, manager-to-agent communication is not a one-way street. In addition to reading information from a device using the SNMP commands Get and Get Next, SNMP managers can issue the Set command. If you have a large sequence of Get Next commands to perform, you can use the Walk command to automatically move through them. The purpose of this command is to save a manager's time: you issue one command on the root node of a subtree and the command "walks" through, getting the value of every node in the subtree.

To demonstrate how SNMP commands work, imagine that you and a friend each have a list on which the following four words are written: four, book, sky, and table. If you, as the manager, ask your friend for the first value, she, acting as the agent, can reply "four." This is analogous to an SNMP Get command. Now, if you ask for the next value, she would reply "book." This is analogous to an SNMP Get Next command. If you then say "set green," and your friend changes the word *book* to *green*, you have performed the equivalent of an SNMP Set command. Sound simplistic? Well, if you can imagine expanding the list to include 100 values, you can see how you could navigate and set any parameter in the list, using just those commands. The key, though, is to make sure that you and your friend have the same list—which is where *Management Information Bases (MIBs)* come in.

SNMP uses databases of information called MIBs to define what parameters are accessible, which of the parameters are read-only, and which can be set. MIBs are available for thousands of devices and services, covering every imaginable need.

To ensure that SNMP systems offer cross-platform compatibility, MIB creation is controlled by the *International Organization for Standardization (ISO)*. An organization that wants to create MIBs can apply to the ISO. The ISO then assigns the organization an ID under which it can create MIBs as it sees fit.

The assignment of numbers is structured within a conceptual model called the *hierarchical name tree*.

Packet Sniffers

Packet sniffers are commonly used on networks and are also referred to as *packet/network analyzers*. They are either a hardware device or software that basically eavesdrops on transmissions traveling throughout the network, and can be helpful in performing *packet flow monitoring*. The packet sniffer quietly captures data and saves it to be reviewed later. Packet sniffers can also be used on the Internet to capture data traveling between computers. Internet packets often have long distances to travel, going through various servers, routers, and gateways. Anywhere along this path, packet sniffers can quietly sit and collect data. Given the capability of packet sniffers to sit and silently collect data packets, it is easy to see how they could be exploited.

You should use two key defenses against packet sniffers to protect your network:

▶ Use a switched network, which most today are. In a switched network, data is sent from one computer system and is directed from the switch only to intended targeted destinations. In an older network using traditional hubs, the hub does not switch the traffic to isolated users but to all users connected to the hub's ports. This shotgun approach to network transmission makes it easier to place a packet sniffer on the network to obtain data.

▶ Ensure that all sensitive data is encrypted as it travels. Ordinarily, encryption is used when data is sent over a public network such as the Internet, but it may also be necessary to encrypt sensitive data on a LAN. Encryption can be implemented in a number of ways. For example, connections to web servers can be protected using the *Secure Sockets Layer (SSL)* protocol and HTTPS. Communications to mail servers can also be encrypted using SSL. For public networks, the IPsec protocol can provide end-to-end encryption services.

Note

Chapter 10, "Network Security," provides more information about encryption protocols.

Throughput Testing

In the networking world, *throughput* refers to the rate of data delivery over a communication channel. In this case, throughput testers test the rate of data delivery over a network. Throughput is measured in *bits per second (bps)*. Testing throughput is important for administrators to make them aware of exactly what the network is doing. With throughput testing, you can tell whether a high-speed network is functioning close to its expected throughput.

A throughput tester is designed to quickly gather information about network functionality—specifically, the average overall network throughput. Many software-based throughput testers are available online—some for free and some for a fee. Figure 9.5 shows a software-based throughput tester.

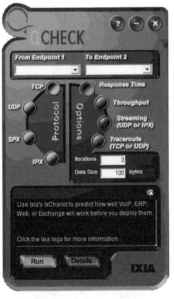

FIGURE 9.5 **A software throughput tester**

As you can see, throughput testers do not need to be complicated to be effective. A throughput tester tells you how long it takes to send data to a destination point and receive an acknowledgment that the data was received. To use the tester, enter the beginning point and then the destination point. The tester sends a predetermined number of data packets to the destination and then reports on the throughput level. The results typically display in *kilobits per second (Kbps)*, *megabits per second (Mbps)*, or *gigabits per second (Gbps)*. Table 9.3 shows the various data rate units.

TABLE 9.3 **Data Rate Units**

Data Transfer	Abbreviation	Rate
Kilobits per second	Kbps or Kbit/s	1,000 bits per second
Megabits per second	Mbps or Mbit/s	1,000,000 bits per second
Gigabits per second	Gbps or Gbit/s	1,000,000,000 bits per second
Kilobytes per second	KBps	1,000 bytes per second, or 8 kilobits per second
Megabytes per second	MBps	1,000,000 bytes per second, or 8 megabits per second
Gigabytes per second	GBps	1,000,000,000 bytes per second, or 8 gigabits per second

Administrators can periodically conduct throughput tests and keep them on file to create a picture of network performance. If you suspect a problem with the network functioning, you can run a test to compare with past performance to see exactly what is happening.

One thing worth mentioning is the difference between throughput and bandwidth. These terms are often used interchangeably, but they have different meanings. When talking about measuring throughput, you measure the amount of data flow under real-world conditions—measuring with possible electromagnetic interference (EMI) influences, heavy traffic loads, improper wiring, and even network collisions. Take all this into account, take a measurement, and you have the network throughput. Bandwidth, in contrast, refers to the maximum amount of information that can be sent through a particular medium under ideal conditions.

> **Note**
>
> Be sure that you know the difference between throughput and bandwidth.

Port Scanners

A *port scanner* is an application written to probe a host (usually a server) for open ports. This can be done by an administrator for legitimate purposes—to verify security policies on the network—or by attackers to find vulnerabilities to exploit. Port scanners are discussed in more detail in Chapter 11, "Network Troubleshooting."

Vulnerability Scanners

In a vulnerability test, you run a software program that contains a database of known vulnerabilities against your system to identify weaknesses. It is highly recommended that you obtain such a vulnerability scanner and run it on your network to check for any known security holes. It is always preferable for you to find them on your own network before someone outside the organization does by running such a tool against you.

The vulnerability scanner may be a port scanner (such as Nmap: https://nmap.org/), a network enumerator, a web application, or even a worm, but in all cases it runs tests on its target against a gamut of known vulnerabilities.

Although Nessus and Retina are two of the better-known vulnerability scanners, SAINT and OpenVAS (which was originally based on Nessus) are also widely used.

> **ExamAlert**
>
> For the exam, CompTIA wants you to know that Nessus and Nmap are two popular vulnerability scanners.

Network Performance, Load, and Stress Testing

To test the network, administrators often perform three distinct types of tests:

▶ Performance tests

▶ Load tests

▶ Stress tests

These test names are sometimes used interchangeably. Although some overlap exists, they are different types of network tests, each with different goals.

Performance Tests

A *performance test* is, as the name suggests, all about measuring the network's current performance level. The goal is to take ongoing performance tests and evaluate and compare them, looking for potential bottlenecks. For performance tests to be effective, they need to be taken under the same type of network load each time, or the comparison is invalid. For example, a performance test taken at 3 a.m. will differ from one taken at 3 p.m.

> **Note .**
>
> The goal of performance testing is to establish baselines for the comparison of network functioning. The results of a performance test are meaningless unless you can compare them to previously documented performance levels.

Load Tests

Load testing has some overlap with performance testing. Sometimes called *volume* or *endurance testing*, load tests involve artificially placing the network under a larger workload. For example, the network traffic might be increased throughout the entire network. After this is done, performance tests can be done on the network with the increased load. Load testing is sometimes done to see if bugs exist in the network that are not currently visible but that may become a problem as the network grows. For example, the mail server might work fine with current requirements. However, if the number of users in the network grew by 10%, you would want to determine whether the increased load would cause problems with the mail server. Load tests are all about finding a potential problem before it happens.

Performance tests and load tests are actually quite similar; however, the information outcomes are different. Performance tests identify the current level of network functioning for measurement and benchmarking purposes. Load tests are designed to give administrators a look into the future of their network load and to see if the current network infrastructure can handle it.

> **Note**
>
> Performance tests are about network functioning today. Load tests look forward to see whether performance may be hindered in the future by growth or other changes to the network.

Stress Tests

Whereas load tests do not try to break the system under intense pressure, stress tests sometimes do. They push resources to the limit. Although these tests are not done often, they are necessary and—for administrators, at least—entertaining. Stress testing has two clear goals:

▶ It shows you exactly what the network can handle. Knowing a network's breaking point is useful information when you consider network expansion.

▶ It enables administrators to test their backup and recovery procedures. If a test knocks out network resources, administrators can verify that their recovery procedures work. Stress testing enables administrators to observe network hardware failure.

Stress tests assume that someday something will go wrong, and administrators will know exactly what to do when it happens.

Performance Metrics

Whether the testing being done is related to performance, load, or stress, you have to choose the metrics you want to monitor and focus on. Although a plethora of options are available, the most common four are the following:

▶ **Error rate:** This identifies the frequency of errors.

▶ **Utilization:** This shows the percentage of resources being utilized.

▶ **Packet drops:** How many packets of data on the network fail to reach their destination.

▶ **Bandwidth/throughput:** The capability to move data through a channel as related to the total capability of the system to identify bottlenecks, throttling, and other issues.

Tracking Event Logs

In a network environment, all NOSs and most firewalls, proxy servers, and other network components have logging features. These logging features are essential for network administrators to review and monitor. Many types of logs can be used. The following sections review some of the most common log file types.

On a Windows Server system, as with the other operating systems, events and occurrences are logged to files for later review. Windows Server and desktop systems use Event Viewer to view many of the key log files. The logs in Event Viewer can be used to find information on, for example, an error on the system or a security incident. Information is recorded into key log files; however, you will also see additional log files under certain conditions, such as if the system is a domain controller or is running a DHCP server application.

Event logs refer generically to all log files used to track events on a system. Event logs are crucial for finding intrusions and diagnosing current system problems. In a Windows environment, for example, three primary event logs are used: Security, Application, and System.

> **Note**
>
> Be sure that you know the types of information included in the types of log files.

Security Logs

A system's Security log contains events related to security incidents, such as successful and unsuccessful logon attempts and failed resource access. Security logs can be customized, meaning that administrators can fine-tune exactly what they want to monitor. Some administrators choose to track nearly every security event on the system. Although this might be prudent, it can often create huge log files that take up too much space. Figure 9.6 shows a Security log from a Windows system.

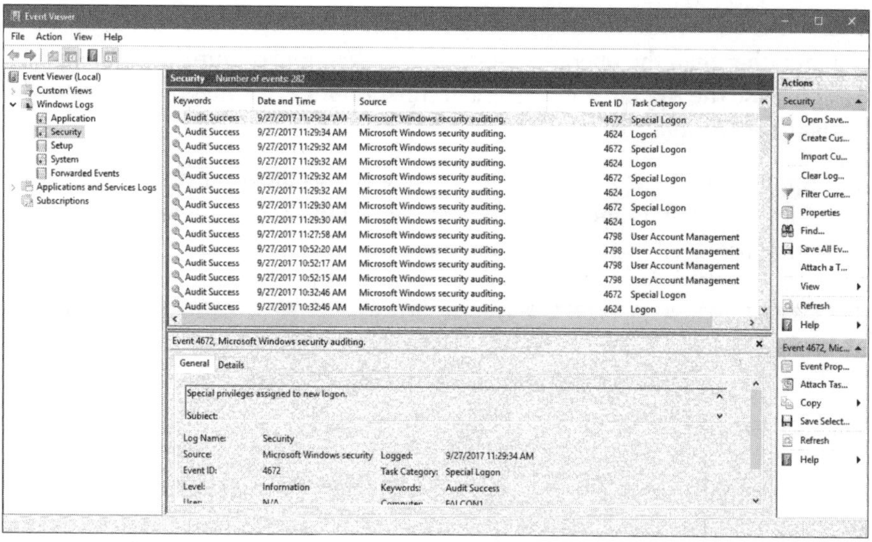

FIGURE 9.6   **A Windows Security log from Windows 10**

Figure 9.6 shows that some successful logons and account changes have occurred. A potential security breach would show some audit failures for logon or logoff attempts. To save space and prevent the log files from growing too big, administrators might choose to audit only failed logon attempts and not successful ones.

Each event in a Security log contains additional information to make it easy to get the details on the event:

▶ **Date:** The exact date the security event occurred.

▶ **Time:** The time the event occurred.

▶ **User:** The name of the user account that was tracked during the event.

▶ **Computer:** The name of the computer used when the event occurred.

▶ **Event ID:** The event ID tells you what event has occurred. You can use this ID to obtain additional information about the particular event. For example, you can take the ID number, enter it at the Microsoft support website, and gather information about the event. Without the ID, it would be difficult to find this information.

To be effective, Security logs should be regularly reviewed.

Application Log

This log contains information logged by applications that run on a particular system rather than the operating system itself. Vendors of third-party applications can use the Application log as a destination for error messages generated by their applications.

The Application log works in much the same way as the Security log. It tracks both successful events and failed events within applications. Figure 9.7 shows the details provided in an Application log.

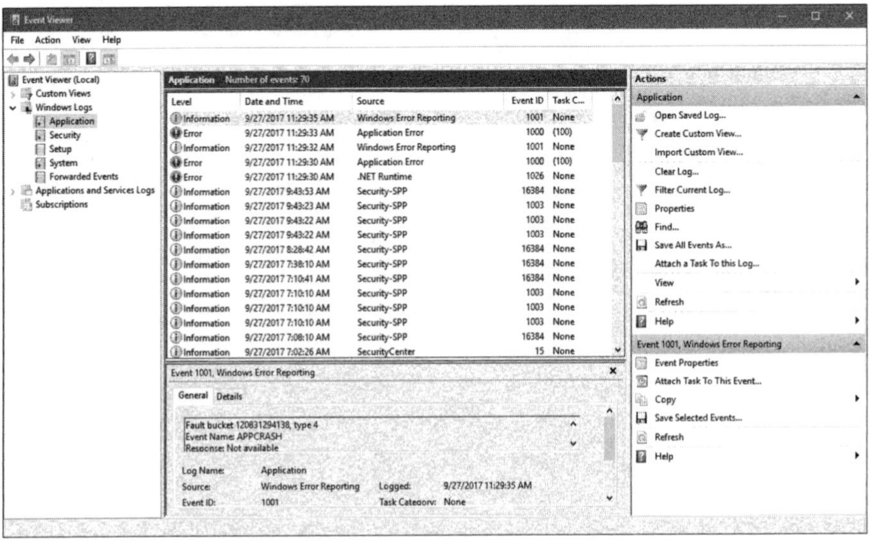

FIGURE 9.7 **An Application log in Windows 10**

Figure 9.7 shows that three types of events occurred: general application information events, a warning event, and error events. Vigilant administrators would likely want to check the event ID of both the event and warning failures to isolate the cause.

System Logs

System logs record information about components or drivers in the system, as shown in Figure 9.8. This is the place to look when you are troubleshooting a problem with a hardware device on your system or a problem with network connectivity. For example, messages related to the client element of *Dynamic Host Configuration Protocol (DHCP)* appear in this log. The System log is also the place to look for hardware device errors, time synchronization issues, or service startup problems.

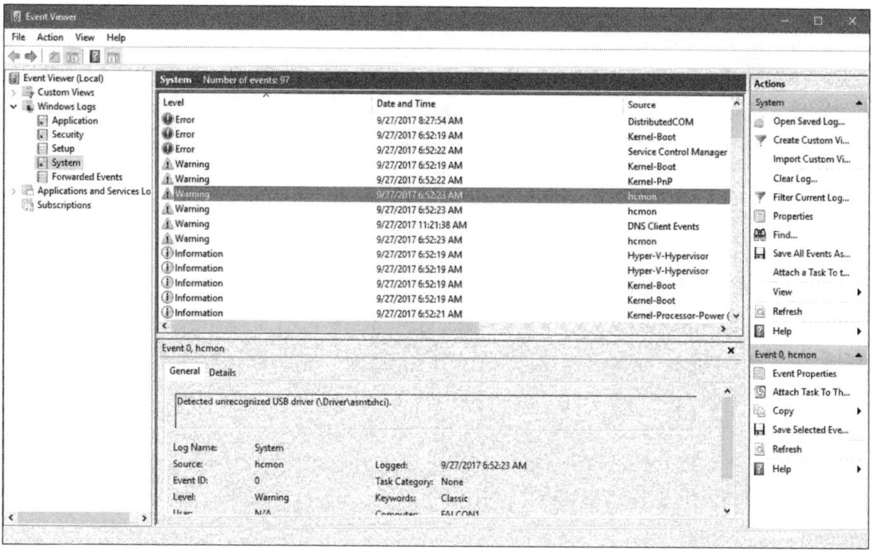

FIGURE 9.8   **A System log in Windows 10**

Syslog

In addition to the specific logs mentioned previously, most UNIX/Linux-based systems include the capability to write messages (either directly or through applications) to log files via *syslog*. This can be done for security or management reasons and provides a central means by which devices that otherwise could not write to a central repository can easily do so (often by using the logger utility).

History Logs

History logs are most often associated with the tracking of Internet surfing habits. They maintain a record of all sites that a user visits. Network administrators might review these for potential security or policy breaches, but generally these are not commonly reviewed.

Another form of history log is a compilation of events from other log files. For instance, one History log might contain all significant events over the past year from the Security log on a server. History logs are critical because they provide a detailed account of alarm events that can be used to track trends and locate problem areas in the network. This information can help you revise maintenance schedules, determine equipment replacement plans, and anticipate and prevent future problems.

> **Note**
>
> Application logs and system logs can often be viewed by any user. Security logs can be viewed only by users who use accounts with administrative privileges.

Log Management

While discussing these logs, it becomes clear that monitoring them can be a huge issue. That is where *log management (LM)* comes in. LM describes the process of managing large volumes of system-generated computer log files. LM includes the collection, retention, and disposal of all system logs. Although LM can be a huge task, it is essential to ensure the proper functioning of the network and its applications. It also helps you keep an eye on network and system security.

Configuring systems to log all sorts of events is the easy part. Trying to find the time to review the logs is an entirely different matter. To assist with this process, third-party software packages are available to help with the organization and reviewing of log files. To find this type of software, enter log management into a web browser, and you will have many options to choose from. Some have trial versions of their software that may give you a better idea of how LM works.

Patch Management

All applications, including productivity software, virus checkers, and especially the operating system, release patches and updates often designed to address potential security weaknesses. Administrators must keep an eye out for these patches and install them when they are released.

> **Note**
>
> The various types of updates discussed in this section apply to all systems and devices, including mobile devices and laptops, as well as servers and routers. Special server systems (and services) are typically used to deploy mass updates to clients in a large enterprise network.

Discussion items related to this topic include the following:

▶ **OS updates:** Most operating system updates relate to either functionality or security issues. For this reason, it is important to keep your systems up to date. Most current operating systems include the capability to automatically find updates and install them. By default, the automatic updates feature is usually turned on; you can change the settings if you do not want this enabled.

> **Note**
>
> Always test updates on a lab machine before rolling out on production machines.

▶ **Firmware updates:** Firmware updates keep the hardware interfaces working properly. Router manufacturers, for example, often issue patches when problems are discovered. Those patches need to be applied to the router to remove any security gaps that may exist.

> **ExamAlert**
>
> Just as security holes can exist with operating systems and applications (and get closed through patches), they can also exist in firmware and be closed through updates.

▶ **Driver updates:** The main reason for updating drivers is when you have a piece of hardware that is not operating correctly. The failure to operate can be caused by the hardware interacting with software it was not intended to prior to shipping (such as OS updates). Because the problem can be from the vendor or the OS provider, updates can be automatically included (such as with Windows Update) or found on the vendor's site.

▶ **Feature changes/updates:** Not considered as critical as security or functionality updates, feature updates and changes can extend what you could previously do and extend your time using the hardware/software combination you have.

▶ **Major versus minor updates:** Most updates are classified as major (must be done) or minor (can be done). Depending on the vendor, the difference in the two may be telegraphed in the numbering: An update of 4.0.0 would be a major update, whereas one of 4.10.357 would be considered a minor one.

ExamAlert

As a general rule, the smaller the number of the update, the less significant it is.

▶ **Vulnerability patches:** Vulnerabilities are weaknesses, and patches related to them should be installed correctly with all expediency. After a vulnerability in an OS, a driver, or a piece of hardware has been identified, the fact that it can be exploited is often spread quickly: a *zero-day exploit* is any attack that begins the very day the vulnerability is discovered.

Note

If attackers learn of the weakness the same day as the developer, they have the ability to exploit it until a patch is released. Often, the only thing that you as a security administrator can do between the discovery of the exploit and the release of the patch is to turn off the system. Although this can be a costly undertaking in terms of productivity, it can be the only way to keep the network safe.

▶ **Upgrading versus downgrading:** Not all changing needs to be upgrading. If, for example, a new patch is applied that changes the functionality of a hardware component to where it will no longer operate as you need it to, you can consider reverting back to a previous state. This is known as *downgrading* and is often necessary when dealing with legacy systems and implementations.

ExamAlert

For the exam, know that removing patches and updates is considered downgrading.

Before installing or removing patches, it is important to do a *configuration backup*. Many vendors offer products that perform configuration backups across the network on a regular basis and allow you to roll back changes if needed. Free tools are often limited in the number of devices they can work with, and some of the more expensive ones include the capability to automatically analyze and identify the changes that could be causing any problems.

Cram Quiz

1. Which of the following involves pushing the network beyond its limits, often taking down the network to test its limits and recovery procedures?

   - ○ **A.** Crash and burn
   - ○ **B.** Stress test
   - ○ **C.** Recovery test
   - ○ **D.** Load test

2. You suspect that an intruder has gained access to your network. You want to see how many failed logon attempts there were in one day to help determine how the person got in. Which of the following might you do?

   - ○ **A.** Review the History logs.
   - ○ **B.** Review the Security logs.
   - ○ **C.** Review the Logon logs.
   - ○ **D.** Review the Performance logs.

3. Which utility can be used to write syslog entries on a Linux-based operating system?

   - ○ **A.** memo
   - ○ **B.** record
   - ○ **C.** logger
   - ○ **D.** trace

4. Which of the following is not a standard component of an entry in a Windows-based Security log?

   - ○ **A.** Event ID
   - ○ **B.** Date
   - ○ **C.** Computer
   - ○ **D.** Domain
   - ○ **E.** User

5. You have just used a port scanner for the first time. On one port, it reports that there is not a process listening and access to this port will likely be denied. Which state is the port most likely to be considered to be in?

   ○ **A.** Listening

   ○ **B.** Closed

   ○ **C.** Filtered

   ○ **D.** Blocked

6. You are required to monitor discards, packet drops, resets, and problems with speed/duplex. Which of the following monitoring tools would assist you?

   ○ **A.** Interface

   ○ **B.** Power

   ○ **C.** Environmental

   ○ **D.** Application

7. By default, the automatic update feature on most modern operating systems is

   ○ **A.** Disabled

   ○ **B.** Turned on

   ○ **C.** Set to manual

   ○ **D.** Ineffective

8. What should you do if a weakness is discovered that affects network security, and no patch has yet been released?

   ○ **A.** Post information about the weakness on the vendor's site.

   ○ **B.** Call the press to put pressure on the vendor.

   ○ **C.** Ignore the problem and wait for the patch.

   ○ **D.** Take the at-risk system offline.

Cram Quiz Answers

1. **B.** Whereas load tests do not try to break the system under intense pressure, stress tests sometimes do. Stress testing has two goals. The first is to see exactly what the network can handle. It is useful to know the network's breaking point in case the network ever needs to be expanded. Second, stress testing allows administrators to test their backup and recovery procedures.

2. **B.** The Security logs can be configured to show failed or successful logon attempts as well as object access attempts. In this case, the administrator can review the Security logs and failed logon attempts to get the desired information. The failed logs will show the date and time when the failed attempts occurred.

3. **C.** The syslog feature exists in most UNIX/Linux-based distributions, and entries can be written using logger. The other options are not possibilities for writing syslog entries.

4. **D.** The standard components of an entry in a Windows-based Security log include the date, time, user, computer, and event ID. The domain is not a standard component of a log entry.

5. **B.** When a port is closed, no process is listening on that port and access to this port will likely be denied. When the port is open/listening, the host sends a reply indicating that a service is listening on the port. When the port is filtered or blocked, there is no reply from the host, meaning that the port is not listening or the port is secured and filtered.

6. **A.** An interface monitoring tool is invaluable for troubleshooting problems and errors that include utilization problems, discards, packet drops, resets, and problems with speed/duplex.

7. **B.** By default, the automatic update feature is usually turned on.

8. **D.** Often, the only thing that you as a security administrator can do, between the discovery of the exploit and the release of the patch, is to turn off the service. Although this can be a costly undertaking in terms of productivity, it can be the only way to keep the network safe.

Remote Access

▶ **Given a scenario, use remote access methods.**

CramSaver

If you can correctly answer these questions before going through this section, save time by skimming the Exam Alerts in this section and then completing the Cram Quiz at the end of the section.

1. True or false: VPNs require a secure protocol to safely transfer data over the Internet.

2. What port does SSH for connections?

3. What port does Telnet use for connections?

Answers

1. True. VPNs require a secure protocol, such as IPsec or SSL, to safely transfer data over the Internet.

2. SSH uses port 22 and TCP for connections.

3. Telnet uses port 23 for connections.

ExamAlert

Remember that this objective begins with "Given a scenario." That means that you may receive a drag and drop, matching, or "live OS" scenario where you have to click through to complete a specific objective-based task.

Several protocols are associated with remote-control access that you should be aware of: Remote Desktop Protocol (RDP), Secure Shell (SSH), Virtual Network Computing (VNC), and Telnet. RDP is used in a Windows environment and is now called *Remote Desktop Services (RDS)*. It provides a way for a client system to connect to a server, such as Windows Server, and, by using RDP, operate on the server as if they were local client applications. Such a configuration is known as *thin client computing*, whereby client systems use the resources of the server instead of their local processing power.

Windows products (server as well as client) have built-in support for Remote Desktop Connections. The underlying protocol used to manage the connection is RDP. RDP is a low-bandwidth protocol used to send mouse movements, keystrokes, and bitmap images of the screen on the server to the client computer. RDP does not actually send data over the connection—only screenshots and client keystrokes. RDP uses TCP and UDP port 3389.

SSH is a tunneling protocol originally created for UNIX/Linux systems. It uses encryption to establish a secure connection between two systems and provides alternative, security-equivalent applications for such utilities as Telnet, File Transfer Protocol (FTP), Trivial File Transfer Protocol (TFTP), and other communications-oriented applications. Although it is available with Windows and other operating systems, it is the preferred method of security for Telnet and other clear-text-oriented programs in the UNIX/Linux environment. SSH uses port 22 and TCP for connections.

Virtual Network Computing (VNC) enables remote login, in which clients can access their own desktops while being physically away from their computers. By default, it uses port 5900 and it is not considered overly secure.

Telnet enables sessions to be opened on a remote host and is one of the oldest TCP/IP protocols still in use today. On most systems, Telnet is blocked because of problems with security (it truly does not have any), and SSH is considered a secure alternative to Telnet that enables secure sessions to be opened on the remote host.

ExamAlert

Be sure that you know the ports associated with RDP (3389), Telnet (23), FTP (20, 21), VNC (5900), and SSH (22).

ExamAlert

The protocols described in this chapter enable access to remote systems and enable users to run applications on the system, using that system's resources. Only the user interface, keystrokes, and mouse movements transfer between the client system and the remote computer.

Remote File Access

File Transfer Protocol (FTP) is an application that allows connections to FTP servers for file uploads and downloads. FTP is a common application that uses ports 20 and 21 by default. It is used to transfer files between hosts on the Internet but is inherently insecure. A number of options have been released to try to create a more secure protocol, including *FTP over SSL (FTPS)*, which adds support for SSL cryptography, and *SSH File Transfer Protocol (SFTP)*, which is also known as Secure FTP.

An alternative utility for copying files is Secure Copy (SCP), which uses port 22 by default and combines an old remote copy program (RCP) from the first days of TCP/IP with SSH.

On the opposite end of the spectrum from a security standpoint is the *Trivial File Transfer Protocol (TFTP)*, which can be configured to transfer files between hosts without any user interaction (unattended mode). It should be avoided anywhere there are more secure alternatives.

VPNs

A *virtual private network (VPN)* encapsulates encrypted data inside another datagram that contains routing information. The connection between two computers establishes a switched connection dedicated to the two computers. The encrypted data is encapsulated inside *Point-to-Point Protocol (PPP)*, and that connection is used to deliver the data.

A VPN enables users with an Internet connection to use the infrastructure of the public network to connect to the main network and access resources as if they were logged on to the network locally. It also enables two networks to be connected to each other securely.

To put it more simply, a VPN extends a LAN by establishing a remote connection using a public network such as the Internet. A VPN provides a point-to-point dedicated link between two points over a public IP network. For many companies, the VPN link provides the perfect method to expand their networking capabilities and reduce their costs. By using the public network (Internet), a company does not need to rely on expensive private leased lines to provide corporate network access to its remote users. Using the Internet to facilitate the remote connection, the VPN enables network connectivity over a possibly long physical distance. In this respect, a VPN is a form of wide-area network (WAN).

> **Note**
>
> Many companies use a VPN to provide a cost-effective method to establish a connection between remote clients and a private network. There are other times a VPN link is handy. You can also use a VPN to connect one private LAN to another, known as LAN-to-LAN internetworking. For security reasons, you can use a VPN to provide controlled access within an intranet. As an exercise, try drawing what the VPN would look like in these two scenarios.

Components of the VPN Connection

A VPN enables anyone with an Internet connection to use the infrastructure of the public network to dial in to the main network and access resources as if the user were locally logged on to the network. It also enables two networks to securely connect to each other.

Many elements are involved in establishing a VPN connection, including the following:

▶ **VPN client:** The computer that initiates the connection to the VPN server.

▶ **VPN server:** Authenticates connections from VPN clients.

▶ **Access method:** As mentioned, a VPN is most often established over a public network such as the Internet; however, some VPN implementations use a private intranet. The network used must be IP based.

▶ **VPN protocols:** Required to establish, manage, and secure the data over the VPN connection. Point-to-Point Tunneling Protocol (PPTP) and Layer 2 Tunneling Protocol (L2TP) are commonly associated with VPN connections. These protocols enable authentication and encryption in VPNs. Authentication enables VPN clients and servers to correctly establish the identity of people on the network. Encryption enables potentially sensitive data to be guarded from the general public.

VPNs have become popular because they enable the public Internet to be safely used as a WAN connectivity solution.

> **ExamAlert**
>
> VPNs support analog modems, Integrated Services Digital Network (ISDN) wireless connections, and dedicated broadband connections, such as cable and digital subscriber line (DSL). Remember this for the exam.

VPN Pros and Cons

As with any technology, VPN has both pros and cons. Fortunately with VPN technology, these are clear cut, and even the cons typically do not prevent an organization from using VPNs in its networks. Using a VPN offers two primary benefits:

▶ **Cost:** If you use the infrastructure of the Internet, you do not need to spend money on dedicated private connections to link remote clients to the private network. Furthermore, when you use the public network, you do not need to hire support personnel to support those private links.

▶ **Easy scalability:** VPNs make it easy to expand the network. Employees who have a laptop with wireless capability can simply log on to the Internet and establish the connection to the private network.

Table 9.4 outlines some of the advantages and potential disadvantages of using a VPN.

TABLE 9.4 **Pros and Cons of Using a VPN**

Advantage	Description
Reduced cost	When you use the Internet, you do not need to rent dedicated lines between remote clients and a private network. In addition, a VPN can replace remote-access servers and long-distance dial-up network connections that were commonly used in the past by business travelers who needed access to their company intranet. This eliminates long-distance phone charges.
Network scalability	The cost to an organization to build a dedicated private network may be reasonable at first, but it increases exponentially as the organization grows. The Internet enables an organization to grow its remote client base without having to increase or modify an internal network infrastructure.
Reduced support	Using the Internet, organizations do not need to employ support personnel to manage a VPN infrastructure.
Simplified	With a VPN, a network administrator can easily add remote clients. All authentication work is managed from the VPN authentication server, and client systems can be easily configured for automatic VPN access.
Disadvantage	**Description**
Security	Using a VPN, data is sent over a public network, so data security is a concern. VPNs use security protocols to address this shortcoming, but VPN administrators must understand data security over public networks to ensure that data is not tampered with or stolen.
Reliability	The reliability of the VPN communication depends on the public network and is not under an organization's direct control. Instead, the solution relies on an Internet service provider (ISP) and its quality of service (QoS).

IPsec

The *IP Security (IPsec)* protocol is designed to provide secure communications between systems. This includes system-to-system communication in the same network, as well as communication to systems on external networks. IPsec is an IP layer security protocol that can both encrypt and authenticate network transmissions. In a nutshell, IPsec is composed of two separate protocols: *Authentication Header (AH)* and *Encapsulating Security Payload (ESP)*. AH provides the authentication and integrity checking for data packets, and ESP provides encryption services.

ExamAlert

IPsec relies on two underlying protocols: AH and ESP. AH provides authentication services, and ESP provides encryption services.

Using both AH and ESP, data traveling between systems can be secured, ensuring that transmissions cannot be viewed, accessed, or modified by those who should not have access to them. It might seem that protection on an internal network is less necessary than on an external network; however, much of the data you send across networks has little or no protection, allowing unwanted eyes to see it.

Note

The Internet Engineering Task Force (IETF) created IPsec, which you can use on both IPv4 and IPv6 networks.

IPsec provides three key security services:

▶ **Data verification:** Verifies that the data received is from the intended source

▶ **Protection from data tampering:** Ensures that the data has not been tampered with or changed between the sending and receiving devices

▶ **Private transactions:** Ensures that the data sent between the sending and receiving devices is unreadable by any other devices

IPsec operates at the network layer of the Open Systems Interconnect (OSI) reference model and provides security for protocols that operate at the higher layers. Thus, by using IPsec, you can secure practically all TCP/IP-related communications.

SSL/TLS/DTLS

Security is often provided by working with the Secure Sockets Layer (SSL) protocol and the Transport Layer Security (TLS) protocol. SSL VPN, also marketed as WebVPN and OpenVPN, can be used to connect locations that would run into trouble with firewalls and NAT when used with IPsec. It is known as an SSL VPN whether the encryption is done with SSL or TLS.

> **Note**
>
> SSL was first created for use with the Netscape web browser and is used with a limited number of TCP/IP protocols (such as HTTP and FTP). TLS is not only an enhancement to SSL, but also a replacement for it, working with almost every TCP/IP protocol. Because of this, TLS is popular with VPNs and VoIP applications. Just as the term *Kleenex* is often used to represent any paper tissue, whether or not it is made by Kimberly-Clark, *SSL* is often the term used to signify the confidentiality function, whether it is actually SSL in use or TLS (the latest version of which is 1.2).

The Datagram Transport Layer Security (DTLS) protocol is a derivation of SSL/TLS by the OpenSSL project that provides the same security services but strives to increase reliability.

The National Institute of Standards and Technology (NIST) publishes the *Guide to SSL VPNs*, which you can access at http://nvlpubs.nist.gov/nistpubs/Legacy/SP/nistspecialpublication800-113.pdf.

Site-to-Site and Client-to-Site

The scope of a VPN tunnel can vary, with the two most common variations being *site-to-site* and *client-to-site* (also known as *host-to-site*). A third variation is *host-to-host*, but it is really a special implementation of site-to-site. In a site-to-site implementation, as the name implies, whole networks are connected together. An example of this would be divisions of a large company. Because the networks are supporting the VPN, each gateway does the work, and the individual clients do not need to have any VPN.

In a client-to-site scenario, individual clients (such as telecommuters or travelers) connect to the network remotely. Because the individual client makes a direct connection to the network, each client doing so must have VPN client software installed.

> **ExamAlert**
>
> Be sure that you understand that site-to-site and client-to-site are the two most common types of VPNs.

HTTPS/Management URL

HTTP Secure (HTTPS) is the protocol used for "secure" web pages that users should see when they must enter personal information such as credit card numbers, passwords, and other identifiers. It combines HTTP with SSL/TLS to provide encrypted communication. The default port is 443, and the URL begins with https:// instead of http://.

This is the common protocol used for management URLs to perform tasks such as checking server status, changing router settings, and so on.

Out-of-Band Management

When a dedicated channel is established for managing network devices, it is known as *out-of-band management*. A connection can be established via a console router, or modem, and this can be used to ensure management connectivity independent of the status of in-band network connectivity (which would include serial port connections, VNC, and SSH). Out-of-band management lets the administrator monitor, access, and manage network infrastructure devices remotely and securely, even when everything else is down.

Cram Quiz

1. Which of the following protocols is used in thin-client computing?

   ○ **A.** RDP

   ○ **B.** PPP

   ○ **C.** PPTP

   ○ **D.** RAS

2. Your company wants to create a secure tunnel between two networks over the Internet. Which of the following protocols would you use to do this?

   ○ **A.** PAP

   ○ **B.** CHAP

   ○ **C.** PPTP

   ○ **D.** SLAP

3. Because of a recent security breach, you have been asked to design a security strategy that will allow data to travel encrypted through both the Internet and intranet. Which of the following protocols would you use?

- ○ **A.** IPsec
- ○ **B.** SST
- ○ **C.** CHAP
- ○ **D.** FTP

Cram Quiz Answers

1. **A.** RDP is used in thin-client networking, where only screen, keyboard, and mouse input is sent across the line. PPP is a dialup protocol used over serial links. PPTP is a technology used in VPNs. RAS is a remote-access service.

2. **C.** To establish the VPN connection between the two networks, you can use PPTP. PAP and CHAP are not used to create a point-to-point tunnel; they are authentication protocols. SLAP is not a valid secure protocol.

3. **A.** IPsec is a nonproprietary security standard used to secure transmissions both on the internal network and when data is sent outside the local LAN. IPsec provides encryption and authentication services for data communications. Answer B is not a valid protocol. Answer C, Challenge Handshake Authentication Protocol (CHAP), is a remote-access authentication protocol. Answer D is incorrect because FTP is a protocol used for large data transfers, typically from the Internet.

What's Next?

The primary goals of today's network administrators are to design, implement, and maintain secure networks. This is not always easy, and is the topic of Chapter 10, "Network Security." No network can ever be labeled "secure." Security is an ongoing process involving a myriad of protocols, procedures, and practices.

CHAPTER 10

Network Security

This chapter covers the following official Network+ objectives:

▶ Summarize the purposes of physical security devices.

▶ Explain authentication and access controls.

▶ Given a scenario, secure a basic wireless network.

▶ Summarize common networking attacks.

▶ Given a scenario, implement network device hardening.

▶ Explain common mitigation techniques and their purposes.

This chapter covers CompTIA Network+ objectives 4.1, 4.2, 4.3, 4.4, 4.5, and 4.6. For more information on the official Network+ exam topics, see the "About the Network+ Exam" section in the Introduction.

Network security is one of the toughest areas of IT to be responsible for. It seems as if a new threat surfaces on a regular basis and that you are constantly needing to learn new things just a half a step ahead of potential problems. This chapter focuses on some of the elements administrators use to keep their networks as secure as possible.

Physical Security and Device Hardening

▶ **Summarize the purposes of physical security devices.**

▶ **Given a scenario, implement network device hardening.**

CramSaver

If you can correctly answer these questions before going through this section, save time by skimming the Exam Alerts in this section and then completing the Cram Quiz at the end of the section.

1. True or false: All unnecessary services on a server should be disabled.

2. A system that uses any two items, such as smart cards and passwords, for authentication is referred to as a _____ system.

3. True or false: Common passwords should be used on similar system devices within the same geographic confines.

Answers

1. True. Unnecessary services serve no purpose and take up overhead. They also represent extra possibilities for an attacker to exploit and use to gain access to your system(s).

2. Two-factor authentication system.

3. False. Common passwords should be avoided at all cost because they serve to weaken the security of the system.

ExamAlert

Remember that this objective begins with "Given a scenario." That means that you may receive a drag and drop, matching, or "live OS" scenario where you have to click through to complete a specific objective-based task.

It does little good to have great network security if everything can be compromised by someone walking in your office, picking up your server, and walking out the front door with it. Physical security of the premises is equally important to an overall security implementation.

Ideally, your systems should have a minimum of three physical barriers:

▶ The external entrance to the building, referred to as a *perimeter*, which is protected by motion detection, burglar alarms, external walls, fencing, surveillance, and so on. This should be used with an access list, which should exist to specifically identify who can enter a facility and can be verified by a security guard or someone in authority. A mantrap can be used to limit access to only one or two people going into the facility at a time. A properly developed mantrap includes bulletproof glass, high-strength doors, and locks. In high-security and military environments, an armed guard, as well as video surveillance (IP cameras and CCTVs), should be used at the mantrap. After a person is inside the facility, additional security and authentication may be required for further entrance.

▶ A locked door with door access controls protecting the computer center and network closets; you should also rely on such items as ID badges, proximity readers/key fobs, or keys to gain access. Biometrics, such as fingerprint or retinal scans, can be used for authentication.

▶ The entrance to the computer room itself. This should be another locked door that is carefully monitored and protected by keypads and cipher locks. Although you try to keep as many intruders out with the other two barriers, many who enter the building could be posing as someone they are not—heating and air technicians, representatives of the landlord, and so on. Although these pretenses can get them past the first two barriers, they should still be stopped by the locked computer room door.

▶ Assets should have asset tracking tags attached to them that have unique identifiers for each client device in your environment (usually just incrementing numbers corresponding to values in a database) to help you identify and manage your IT assets. Additionally, tamper detection devices should be installed to protect against unauthorized chassis cover and component removal.

The objective of any physical barrier is to prevent access to computers and network systems. The most effective physical barrier implementations require that more than one physical barrier be crossed to gain access. This type of approach is called a multiple barrier system.

ExamAlert

Physical security is a recent addition to the Network+ exam. Be sure that you are familiar with the topics discussed here.

Adding Physical Security to the Mix

Physical security is a combination of good sense and procedure. The purpose of physical security is to restrict access to network equipment only to people who need it.

The extent to which physical security measures can be implemented to protect network devices and data depends largely on their location. For instance, if a server is installed in a cabinet located in a general office area, the only practical physical protection is to make sure that the cabinet door is locked and that access to keys for the cabinet is controlled. It might be practical to use other antitheft devices, but that depends on the location of the cabinet.

However, if your server equipment is located in a cupboard or dedicated room, access restrictions for the room are easier to implement and can be more effective. Again, access should be limited only to those who need it. Depending on the size of the room, this factor might introduce a number of other factors.

Servers and other key networking components are those to which you need to apply the greatest level of physical security. Nowadays, most organizations choose to locate servers in a cupboard or a specific room.

Access to the server room should be tightly controlled, and all access doors must be secured by some method, whether it is a lock and key or a retinal scanning system. Each method of server room access control has certain characteristics. Whatever the method of server room access, it should follow one common principle: control. Some access control methods provide more control than others.

Lock and Key

If access is controlled by lock and key, the number of people with a key should be restricted to only those people who need access. Spare keys should be stored in a safe location, and access to them should be controlled.

Following are some of the features of lock-and-key security:

▶ **Inexpensive:** Even a good lock system costs only a few hundred dollars.

▶ **Easy to maintain:** With no back-end systems and no configuration, using a lock and key is the easiest access control method.

▶ **Less control than other methods:** Keys can be lost, copied, and loaned to other people. There is no record of access to the server room and no way to prove that the key holder is entitled to enter.

> **Tip**
>
> If you use a lock and key for security, make sure that all copies of the original key are stamped DO NOT COPY. That way, it is more difficult for someone to get a copy because reputable key cutters will not make copies of such keys.

Swipe Card and PIN Access

If budgets and policies permit, swipe card and PIN entry systems are good choices for managing physical access to a server room. Swipe card systems use a credit card-sized plastic card read by a reader on the outside of the door. To enter the server room, you must swipe the card (run it through the reader), at which point it is read by the reader, which validates it. Usually, the swipe card's use to enter the room is logged by the card system, making it possible for the logs to be checked. In higher-security installations, it is common to have a swipe card reader on the inside of the room as well so that a person's exit can be recorded.

Although swipe card systems have relatively few disadvantages, they do need specialized equipment so that they can be coded with users' information. They also have the same drawbacks as keys in that they can be lost or loaned to other people. However, the advantage that swipe cards have over key systems is that swipe cards are hard to copy.

PIN pads can be used alone or with a swipe card system. PIN pads have the advantage of not needing any kind of card or key that can be lost. For the budget conscious, PIN pad systems that do not have any logging or monitoring capability and can be purchased for a reasonable price. Following are some of the characteristics of swipe card and PIN pad systems:

▶ **Moderately expensive:** Some systems, particularly those with management capabilities, are quite expensive.

▶ **Enhanced controls and logging:** Each time people enter the server room, they must key in a number or use a swipe card. This process enables systems to log who enters and when.

▶ **Some additional knowledge required:** Swipe card systems need special software and hardware that can configure the cards. Someone has to learn how to do this.

Biometrics

Although they might still seem like the realm of James Bond, biometric security systems are becoming far more common: Biometric systems work by using some unique characteristic of a person's identity—such as a fingerprint, a palm print, or a retina scan—to validate that person's identity.

Although the price of biometric systems has been falling over recent years, they are not widely deployed in small to midsized networks. Not only are the systems themselves expensive, but also their installation, configuration, and maintenance must be considered. Following are some of the characteristics of biometric access control systems:

▶ **Very effective:** Because each person entering the room must supply proof-of-person evidence, verification of the person entering the server area is as close to 100% reliable as you can get.

▶ **Nothing to lose:** Because there are no cards or keys, nothing can be lost.

▶ **Expensive:** Biometric security systems and their attendant scanners and software are still relatively expensive and can be afforded only by organizations that have a larger budget; however, prices are sure to drop as more people turn to this method of access control.

Two-Factor and Multifactor Authentication

When two or more access methods are included as part of the authentication process, you're implementing a *multifactor system*. A system that uses any two items—such as smart cards and passwords—is referred to as a *two-factor authentication* system. A multifactor system can consist of a two-factor system, a three-factor system, and so on. As long as more than one factor is involved in the authentication process, it is considered a multifactor system.

For obvious reasons, the two or more factors employed should not be from the same category. Although you do increase difficulty in gaining system access by requiring the user to enter two sets of username/password combinations, it is preferred to pair a single username/password combination with a biometric identifier or other check.

> **Note**
>
> Be sure that you understand that two-factor authentication is a subset of multifactor authentication.

Secured Versus Unsecured Protocols

As you know, any network needs a number of protocols to function. This includes both LAN and WAN protocols. Not all protocols are created the same. Some are designed for secure transfer, and others are not. Table 10.1 lists several protocols and describes their use.

TABLE 10.1 **Protocol Summary**

Protocol	Name	Description
FTP	File Transfer Protocol	A protocol for uploading and downloading files to and from a remote host. Also accommodates basic file management tasks. FTP uses ports 20 and 21.
SFTP	Secure File Transfer Protocol	A protocol for securely uploading and downloading files to and from a remote host. Based on SSH security. SFTP uses port 22.
HTTP	Hypertext Transfer Protocol	A protocol for retrieving files from a web server. Data is sent in clear text. HTTP uses port 80.
HTTPS	Hypertext Transfer Protocol Secure	A secure protocol for retrieving files from a web server. HTTPS uses SSL to encrypt data between the client and host. HTTPS uses port 443.
Telnet	Telnet	Enables sessions to be opened on a remote host. Telnet is not considered secure. Telnet uses port 23.
SSH	Secure Shell	A secure alternative to Telnet that enables secure sessions to be opened on a remote host. SSH uses port 22.
TLS	Transport Layer Security	A cryptographic protocol whose purpose is to verify that secure communications between a server and a client remain secure. TLS is an enhancement/ replacement for SSL.
ISAKMP	Internet Security Association and Key Management Protocol	Provides an independent framework for authentication and key exchange. The actual implementation is usually done by IPsec but could be handled by any implementation capable of negotiating, modifying, and deleting security associations.
RSH	A UNIX utility used to run command on a remote machine	Replaced by SSH because RSH sends all data in clear text.
SCP	Secure Copy Protocol	Enables files to be securely copied between two systems. Uses SSH technology to provide encryption services.

Protocol	Name	Description
RCP	Remote Copy Protocol	Copies files between systems, but transport is not secured.
SNMPv1/2	Simple Network Management Protocol versions 1 and 2	A network monitoring system used to monitor the network's condition. Both SNMPv1 and v2 are not secured.
SNMPv3	Simple Network Management Protocol version 3	An enhanced SNMP service offering both encryption and authentication services.
IPsec	IP security	Encrypts data during communication between two computers.
SLIP	Serial Line Interface Protocol	Provides basic encapsulation of the IP protocol over serial and modem connections.

ExamAlert

You will most certainly be asked questions on secure protocols and when they might be used. Review Table 10.1 before taking the Network+ exam.

Additional Device Hardening

In addition to physically securing network devices and opting to run secure protocols in favor of unsecured ones, some steps an administrator should take to further hardening include the following:

▶ **Change default credentials:** The easiest way for any unauthorized individual to access a device is by using the default credentials. Many routers, for example, come configured with an "admin" account and a simple value for the password ("admin," "password," and so on). Anyone owning one of those routers knows those values and could use them to access any other of the same make if the values have not been changed. To make it more difficult for unauthorized users to access your devices, change those default usernames and passwords as soon as you start using them.

▶ **Avoid common passwords:** It is a good thing to preach password security to users, but often administrators are guilty of using too-simplistic passwords on network devices such as routers, switches, and the like. Given the large number of devices in question, sometimes the same passwords are also used on multiple devices. Common sense tells every administrator that this is wrong, but often it is done anyway with the hope that no miscreant will try to gain unauthorized access. Don't be that administrator: use complex passwords and use a different password for each device, increasing the overall security of your network.

▶ **Upgrade firmware:** There is a reason why each firmware update is written. Sometimes, it is to optimize the device or make it more compatible with other devices. Other times, it is to fix security issues and/or head off identified problems. Keep firmware on your production machines current after first testing the upgrades on lab machines and verifying that you're not introducing any unwanted problems by installing.

▶ **Apply patches and updates:** Just as firmware upgrades are intended to strengthen or solve problems, patches and updates do the same with software (including operating systems). Test each release on a lab machine(s) to make sure you are not adding to network woes, and then keep your software current to harden it.

▶ **Verify file hashes:** File hashing is used to verify that the contents of files are unaltered. A hash is often created on a file before it is downloaded and then hashed after the download so the two values can be compared to make sure the contents are the same. When downloading files— particularly upgrades, patches, and updates—check hash values and use this one test to keep from installing those entities that have had Trojan horses attached to them.

▶ **Disable unnecessary services:** Every unnecessary service that is running on a server is akin to another door on a warehouse that someone unauthorized may choose to sneak in. Just as an effective way to secure a warehouse is to reduce the number of doors to only those needed, so too is it recommended that a server be secured by removing (disabling) services not in use.

▶ **Generate new keys:** Keys are used as a part of the encryption process, particularly with public key encryption (PKI), to encrypt and decrypt messages. The longer you use the same key, the longer the opportunity becomes for someone to crack that key. To increase security, generate new keys on a regular basis: The commands to do so will differ based on the utility that you are creating the keys for.

▶ **Disable unused ports:** Disabling unnecessary services (mentioned previously) increases security by removing doors that someone could use to enter the server. Similarly, IP ports that are not needed for devices also represent doors that could be used to sneak in. It is highly recommended that unused ports be disabled to increase security along with device ports (both physical and virtual ports).

> **ExamAlert**
>
> The items appearing in the bulleted list are the topics beneath objective 4.5; make sure you know them for the exam.

Cram Quiz

1. Which of the following is used to verify that the contents of files are unaltered?

   - ○ **A.** Key generation
   - ○ **B.** File hashing
   - ○ **C.** Biometrics
   - ○ **D.** Asset tracking

2. Which of the following is a secure alternative to Telnet that enables secure sessions to be opened on a remote host?

   - ○ **A.** SSH
   - ○ **B.** RSH
   - ○ **C.** IPsec
   - ○ **D.** RDP

3. Which of the following can be used to limit access to only one or two people going into the facility at a time?

   - ○ **A.** Mantrap
   - ○ **B.** Min cage
   - ○ **C.** Tholian web
   - ○ **D.** Cloud minder

4. Which of the following systems use a credit card-sized plastic card that is read by a reader on the outside of the door?

   ○ **A.** Contiguity reader

   ○ **B.** Key fob

   ○ **C.** Swipe card

   ○ **D.** Cipher lock

Cram Quiz Answers

1. **B.** File hashing is used to verify that the contents of files are unaltered.

2. **A.** SSH is a secure alternative to Telnet that enables secure sessions to be opened on a remote host.

3. **A.** A mantrap can be used to limit access to only one or two people going into the facility at a time.

4. **C.** Swipe card systems use a credit card-sized plastic card read by a reader on the outside of the door. To enter the server room, you must swipe the card (run it through the reader), at which point it is read by the reader, which validates it.

Authentication and Access Controls

▶ **Explain authentication and access controls.**

CramSaver

If you can correctly answer these questions before going through this section, save time by skimming the Exam Alerts in this section and then completing the Cram Quiz at the end of the section.

1. True or false: Filtering network traffic using a system's MAC address typically is done using an ACL.

2. True or false: LDAP is a protocol that provides a mechanism to access and query directory services systems.

3. Which access control model uses an access control list (ACL) to determine access?

Answers

1. True. Filtering network traffic using a system's MAC address typically is done using an ACL.

2. True. LDAP (Lightweight Directory Access Protocol) is a protocol that provides a mechanism to access and query directory services systems.

3. Discretionary access control (DAC) uses an access control list (ACL) to determine access. The ACL is a table that informs the operating system of the rights each user has to a particular system object, such as a file, a folder, or a printer.

Access control describes the mechanisms used to filter network traffic to determine who is and who is not allowed to access the network and network resources. Firewalls, proxy servers, routers, and individual computers all can maintain access control to some degree by protecting the *edges* of the network. By limiting who can and cannot access the network and its resources, it is easy to understand why access control plays a critical role in security strategy. Several types of access control strategies exist, as discussed in the following sections.

Be sure that you can identify the purpose and types of access control.

Mandatory Access Control

Mandatory access control (MAC) is the most secure form of access control. In systems configured to use mandatory access control, administrators dictate who can access and modify data, systems, and resources. MAC systems are commonly used in military installations, financial institutions, and, because of new privacy laws, medical institutions.

MAC secures information and resources by assigning sensitivity labels or attributes to objects and users. When users request access to an object, their sensitivity level is compared to the object's. A label is a feature applied to files, directories, and other resources in the system. It is similar to a confidentiality stamp. When a label is placed on a file, it describes the level of security for that specific file. It permits access by files, users, programs, and so on that have a similar or higher security setting.

Discretionary Access Control

Unlike mandatory access control, discretionary access control (DAC) is not enforced from the administrator or operating system. Instead, access is controlled by an object's owner. For example, if a secretary creates a folder, he decides who will have access to that folder. This access is configured using permissions and an access control list (ACL).

DAC uses an ACL to determine access. The ACL is a table that informs the operating system of the rights each user has to a particular system object, such as a file, a folder, or a printer. Each object has a security attribute that identifies its ACL. The list has an entry for each system user with access privileges. The most common privileges include the ability to read a file (or all the files in a folder), to write to the file or files, and to execute the file (if it is an executable file or program).

Microsoft Windows servers/clients, Linux, UNIX, and Mac OS are among the operating systems that use ACLs. The list is implemented differently by each operating system.

In Windows Server products, an ACL is associated with each system object. Each ACL has one or more *access control entries (ACEs)* consisting of the name of a user or group of users. The user can also be a role name, such as "secretary" or "research." For each of these users, groups, or roles, the access privileges are stated in a string of bits called an access mask. Generally, the system administrator or the object owner creates the ACL for an object.

> **Note**
>
> A server on a network that has the responsibility of being a repository for accounts (user/computer) is often referred to as a *network controller*. A good example of this is a domain controller on a Microsoft Active Directory–based network.

Rule-Based Access Control

Rule-based access control (RBAC) controls access to objects according to established rules. The configuration and security settings established on a router or firewall are a good example.

When a firewall is configured, rules are set up that control access to the network. Requests are reviewed to see if the requestor meets the criteria to be allowed access through the firewall. For instance, if a firewall is configured to reject all addresses in the 192.166.x.x IP address range, and the requestor's IP is in that range, the request would be denied.

In a practical application, RBAC is a variation on MAC. Administrators typically configure the firewall or other device to allow or deny access. The owner or another user does not specify the conditions of acceptance, and safeguards ensure that an average user cannot change settings on the devices.

Role-Based Access Control

> **Note**
>
> Note that both *rule-based* and *role-based* access control use the acronym RBAC.

In role-based access control (RBAC), access decisions are determined by the roles that individual users have within the organization. Role-based access requires the administrator to have a thorough understanding of how a particular organization operates, the number of users, and each user's exact function in that organization.

Because access rights are grouped by role name, the use of resources is restricted to individuals who are authorized to assume the associated role. For example, within a school system, the role of teacher can include access to certain data, including test banks, research material, and memos. School administrators might have access to employee records, financial data, planning projects, and more.

The use of roles to control access can be an effective means of developing and enforcing enterprise-specific security policies and for streamlining the security management process.

Roles should receive only the privilege level necessary to do the job associated with that role. This general security principle is known as the *least privilege concept*. When people are hired in an organization, their roles are clearly defined. A network administrator creates a user account for a new employee and places that user account in a group with people who have the same role in the organization.

Least privilege is often too restrictive to be practical in business. For instance, using teachers as an example, some more experienced teachers might have more responsibility than others and might require increased access to a particular network object. Customizing access to each individual is a time-consuming process.

> **ExamAlert**
>
> Although a Security+ objective and concept, you might be asked about the concept of least privilege. This refers to assigning network users the privilege level necessary to do the job associated with their role—nothing more and nothing less.

RADIUS and TACACS+

Among the potential issues network administrators face when implementing remote access are utilization and the load on the remote-access server. As a network's remote-access implementation grows, reliance on a single remote-access server might be impossible, and additional servers might be required. RADIUS can help in this scenario.

> **ExamAlert**
>
> RADIUS is a protocol that enables a single server to become responsible for all remote-access authentication, authorization, and auditing (or accounting) services.

RADIUS functions as a client/server system. The remote user dials in to the remote-access server, which acts as a RADIUS client, or *network access server (NAS)*, and connects to a RADIUS server. The RADIUS server performs authentication, authorization, and auditing (or accounting) functions and returns the information to the RADIUS client (which is a remote-access server running RADIUS client software); the connection is either established or rejected based on the information received.

Terminal Access Controller Access Control System (TACACS) is a security protocol designed to provide centralized validation of users who are attempting to gain access to a router or NAS. Like RADIUS, TACACS is a set of security protocols designed to provide AAA of remote users. TACACS+ is a proprietary version of TACACS from Cisco and is the implementation commonly in use in networks today. TACACS+ uses TCP port 49 by default.

Although both RADIUS and TACACS+ offer AAA services for remote users, some noticeable differences exist:

▶ TACACS+ relies on TCP for connection-oriented delivery. RADIUS uses connectionless UDP for data delivery.

▶ RADIUS combines authentication and authorization, whereas TACACS+ can separate their functions.

ExamAlert

Both RADIUS and TACACS+ provide authentication, authorization, and accounting services. One notable difference between TACACS+ and RADIUS is that TACACS+ relies on the connection-oriented TCP, whereas RADIUS uses the connectionless UDP.

Kerberos Authentication

Kerberos is an *Internet Engineering Task Force (IETF)* standard for providing authentication. It is an integral part of network security. Networks, including the Internet, can connect people from all over the world. When data travels from one point to another across a network, it can be lost, stolen, corrupted, or misused. Much of the data sent over networks is sensitive, whether it is medical, financial, or otherwise. A key consideration for those responsible for the network is maintaining the confidentiality of the data. In the networking world, Kerberos plays a significant role in data confidentiality.

In a traditional authentication strategy, a username and password are used to access network resources. In a secure environment, it might be necessary to provide a username and password combination to access each network service or resource. For example, a user might be prompted to type in her username and password when accessing a database, and again for the printer, and again for Internet access. This is a time-consuming process, and it can also present a security risk. Each time the password is entered, there is a chance that someone will see it being entered. If the password is sent over the network without encryption, it might be viewed by malicious eavesdroppers.

Kerberos was designed to fix such problems by using a method requiring only a *single sign-on*. This single sign-on enables a user to log in to a system and access multiple systems or resources without the need to repeatedly reenter the username and password. Additionally, Kerberos is designed to have entities authenticate themselves by demonstrating possession of secret information.

Kerberos is one part of a strategic security solution that provides secure authentication services to users, applications, and network devices by eliminating the insecurities caused by passwords stored or transmitted across the network. Kerberos is used primarily to eliminate the possibility of a network "eavesdropper" tapping into data over the network—particularly usernames and passwords. Kerberos ensures data integrity and blocks tampering on the network. It employs message privacy (encryption) to ensure that messages are not visible to eavesdroppers on the network.

For the network user, Kerberos eliminates the need to repeatedly demonstrate possession of private or secret information.

ExamAlert

Kerberos is a nonproprietary protocol and is used for cross-platform authentication. It's the main authentication protocol used with Windows servers.

Kerberos is designed to provide strong authentication for client/server applications by using secret key cryptography. Cryptography is used to ensure that a client can prove its identity to a server (and vice versa) across an unsecure network connection. After a client and server have used Kerberos to prove their identity, they can also encrypt all their communications to ensure privacy and data integrity.

ExamAlert

Kerberos enables secure authentication over an unsecure network such as the Internet.

The key to understanding Kerberos is to understand its secret key cryptography. Kerberos uses *symmetric key cryptography*, in which both client and server use the same encryption key to cipher and decipher data.

In secret key cryptography, a plain-text message can be converted into cipher text (encrypted data) and then converted back into plain text using one key. Thus, two devices share a secret key to encrypt and decrypt their communications. Figure 10.1 shows the symmetric key process.

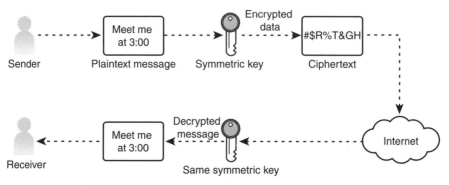

FIGURE 10.1 **The symmetric key process**

Kerberos authentication works by assigning a unique key, called a *ticket*, to each client that successfully authenticates to a server. The ticket is encrypted and contains the user's password, which is used to verify the user's identity when a particular network service is requested. Each ticket is time stamped. It expires after a period of time, and a new one is issued. Kerberos works in the same way that you go to a movie. First, you go to the ticket counter, tell the person what movie you want to see, and get your ticket. After that, you go to a turnstile and hand the ticket to someone else, and then you're "in." In simplistic terms, that's Kerberos.

Local Authentication

Most of the time, the goal is to authenticate the user using a centralized authentication server or service of some type. When that cannot be done—such as when there is no Internet connectivity available—then authentication is done locally by the operating system using values stored within it. In Windows, for example, the Local Authentication Subsystem (LASS) performs this function and allows users access to the system after their stored username and password variables match.

Lightweight Directory Access Protocol

Lightweight Directory Access Protocol (LDAP) is a protocol that provides a mechanism to access and query directory services systems. In the context of the Network+ exam, these directory services systems are most likely to be UNIX based or Microsoft Active Directory based. Although LDAP supports command-line queries executed directly against the directory database, most LDAP interactions are via utilities such as an authentication program (network logon) or locating a resource in the directory through a search utility.

Using Certificates

A *public key infrastructure (PKI)* is a collection of software, standards, and policies combined to enable users from the Internet or other unsecured public networks to securely exchange data. PKI uses a public and private cryptographic key pair obtained and shared through a trusted authority. Services and components work together to develop the PKI. Some of the key components of a PKI include the following:

▶ **Certificates:** A form of electronic credentials that validates users, computers, or devices on the network. A certificate is a digitally signed statement that associates the credentials of a public key to the identity of the person, device, or service that holds the corresponding private key.

▶ **Certificate authorities (CAs):** CAs issue and manage certificates. They validate the identity of a network device or user requesting data. CAs can be either independent third parties, known as public CAs, or they can be organizations running their own certificate-issuing server software, known as private CAs.

▶ **Certificate templates:** Templates used to customize certificates issued by a certificate server. This customization includes a set of rules and settings created on the CA and used for incoming certificate requests.

▶ **Certificate revocation list (CRL):** A list of certificates that were revoked before they reached the certificate expiration date. Certificates are often revoked because of security concerns, such as a compromised certificate.

Auditing and Logging

Auditing is the process of monitoring occurrences and keeping a log of what has occurred on a system. A system administrator determines which events should be audited. Tracking events and attempts to access the system helps prevent unauthorized access and provides a record that administrators can analyze to make security changes as necessary. It also provides administrators with solid evidence if they need to look into improper user conduct.

> **Caution**
>
> Be sure that you can identify the purpose of authentication, authorization, and accounting.

The first step in auditing is to identify what system events to monitor. After the system events are identified, in a Windows environment, the administrator can choose to monitor the success or failure of a system event. For instance, if "logon" is the event being audited, the administrator might choose to log all unsuccessful logon attempts, which might indicate that someone is attempting to gain unauthorized access. Conversely, the administrator can choose to audit all successful attempts to monitor when a particular user or user group is logging on. Some administrators prefer to log both events. However, overly ambitious audit policies can reduce overall system performance.

Multifactor Authentication Factors

Previously in this chapter, multifactor authentication was defined as having two or more access methods included as part of the authentication process; the examples given were using smart cards and passwords. The factors used in authentication systems or methods are based on one or more of these five factors:

- ▶ **Something you know**, such as a password or PIN

- ▶ **Something you have**, such as a smart card, token, or identification device

- ▶ **Something you are**, such as your fingerprints or retinal pattern (often called biometrics)

- ▶ **Somewhere you are** (based on geolocation)

- ▶ **Something you do**, such as an action you must take to complete authentication

> **ExamAlert**
>
> Be able to identify the five types of factors used in multifactor authentication.

Access Control

Today, there are many ways to establish access into networks. You could fill an entire tome with a discussion of the possibilities. CompTIA has reduced the topics associated with this subject to six: 802.1x, NAC, port security, MAC filtering, captive portal, and access control lists. The last item was discussed with discretionary access control at the beginning of this section; what follows discusses each of the remaining five topics in order.

802.1X

The IEEE standard 802.1X defines port-based security for wireless network access control. As such, it offers a means of authentication and defines the Extensible Authentication Protocol (EAP) over IEEE 802, which is often known as EAP over LAN (EAPOL). The biggest benefit of using 802.1X is that the access points and the switches do not need to do the authentication but instead rely on the authentication server to do the work.

Network Access Control (NAC)

Network access control (NAC) is a method to restrict access to the network based on identity or posture (discussed later in this chapter). This was created by Cisco to enforce privileges and make decisions on a client device based on information gathered from it (such as the vendor and version of the antivirus software running). If the wanted information is not found (such as that the anti-virus definitions are a year old), the client can be placed in a *quarantine network* area to keep it from infecting the rest of the network. It can also be placed in a *guest network* and/or allowed to run *nonpersistent* (versus persistent) *agents*.

A *posture assessment* is any evaluation of a system's security based on settings and applications found. In addition to looking at such values as settings in the Registry or dates of files, NACs can also check *802.1X* values—the group of networking protocols associated with authentication of devices attempting to connect to the network. 802.1X works with EAP (discussed later in this chapter).

> **ExamAlert**
>
> As you prepare for the exam, be sure that you can identify posture assessment as any evaluation of a system's security based on settings and applications found.

Port Security

Port security works at level 2 of the OSI model and allows an administrator to configure switch ports so that only certain MAC addresses can use the port. This is a common feature on both Cisco's Catalyst as well as Juniper's EX Series switches and essentially differentiates so-called dumb switches from managed (or intelligent) switches. Similarly, Dynamic ARP Inspection (DAI) works with these and other smart switches to protect ports from ARP spoofing.

MAC Filtering

Another name for a network card or network adapter is a *network controller*. Every controller has a unique MAC address associated with it. Filtering network traffic using a system's MAC address typically is done using an ACL. This list keeps track of all MAC addresses and is configured to allow or deny access to certain systems based on the list. As an example, look at the MAC ACL from a router. Figure 10.2 shows the MAC ACL screen. Specific MAC addresses can be either denied or accepted, depending on the configuration. It would be possible, for example, to configure it so that only the system with the MAC address of 02-00-54-55-4E-01 can authenticate to the router.

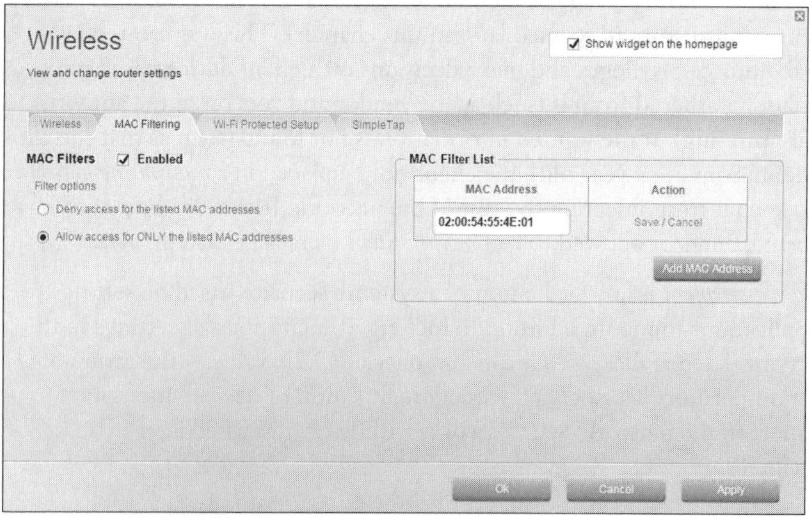

FIGURE 10.2 **A MAC ACL**

> **Note**
>
> When configuring security for wireless networks, filtering by MAC address is a common practice. Typically, in MAC filtering security, MAC addresses can be added to an "allow" ACL or "deny" ACL.

Captive Portal

Most public networks, including Wi-Fi hotspots, use a *captive portal*, which requires users to agree to some condition before they use the network or Internet. The condition could be to agree to the acceptable use policy, payment charges for the time they are using the network, and so forth.

One of the most popular implementations of captive portals is a Cisco application in its Identity Services Engine. However, there have been vulnerabilities identified with it, which allow attackers to intercept clear-text values.

Cram Quiz

1. Which of the following ports is used by TACACS+ by default?

   ○ **A.** 49
   ○ **B.** 51
   ○ **C.** 53
   ○ **D.** 59

2. Which of the following is the main authentication protocol used with Windows servers?

   ○ **A.** LDAP
   ○ **B.** Kerberos
   ○ **C.** L2TP
   ○ **D.** TFTP

3. What are the security tokens used with Kerberos known as?

   ○ **A.** Coins
   ○ **B.** Vouchers
   ○ **C.** Tickets
   ○ **D.** Gestures

4. Which of the following is NOT one of the factors associated with multifactor authentication?

- ○ **A.** Something you like
- ○ **B.** Something you are
- ○ **C.** Something you do
- ○ **D.** Something you have

Cram Quiz Answers

1. **A.** TACACS+ uses TCP port 49 by default.

2. **B.** Kerberos is the main authentication protocol used with Windows servers.

3. **C.** The tokens used for security in Kerberos are known as tickets.

4. **A.** Something you like is not one of the five factors used in multifactor authentica-tion. The five legitimate possibilities are the following: something you know, some-thing you have, something you are, somewhere you are, and something you do.

Securing Wireless Networks

▶ **Given a scenario, secure a basic wireless network.**

CramSaver

If you can correctly answer these questions before going through this section, save time by skimming the Exam Alerts in this section and then completing the Cram Quiz at the end of the section.

1. What can be used to secure an EAP tunnel by using a certificate on the server side?

2. What does WPA mandate the use of?

3. What type of key does WPA2 Personal utilize?

Answers

1. PEAP can be used to secure an EAP tunnel by using a certificate on the server side.

2. WPA mandates the use of TKIP.

3. WPA2 Personal uses a preshared key.

ExamAlert

Remember that this objective begins with "Given a scenario." That means that you may receive a drag and drop, matching, or "live OS" scenario where you have to click through to complete a specific objective-based task.

Wireless systems transmit data through the air and can be much more difficult to secure than those dependent on wires that can be physically protected. The growth of wireless systems in every workplace and home creates many opportunities for attackers looking for signals that can be easily intercepted. This section discusses various types of wireless systems that you'll likely encounter and some of the security issues associated with this technology.

WPA, WPA2, TKIP-RC4, and CCMP-AES

The Wi-Fi Protected Access (WPA) and Wi-Fi Protected Access 2 (WPA2) technologies were designed to address the core, easy-to-crack problems of earlier technologies, such as Wired Equivalent Privacy (WEP). These technologies were created to implement the 802.11i standard. The difference between WPA and WPA2 is that the former implements most, but not all, of 802.11i in order to be able to communicate with older wireless devices that might still need an update through their firmware to be compliant. WPA uses the RC4 encryption algorithm with TKIP, whereas WPA2 implements the full standard and is not compatible with older devices.

Although WPA mandates the use of TKIP, WPA2 requires Counter Mode with Cipher Block Chaining Message Authentication Code Protocol (CCMP). CCMP uses 128-bit AES encryption with a 48-bit initialization vector. With the larger initialization vector, it increases the difficulty in cracking and minimizes the risk of a replay attack. WPA (with TKIP) was used as an intermediate solution, implementing a portion of the 802.11i standard. The ultimate solution, a full implementation of the 802.11i standard, is WPA2 (with CCMP).

Wireless Authentication and Authorization

Choosing the correct authentication protocol for remote clients is an important part of designing a secure remote-access strategy. After they are authenticated, users have access to the network and servers. Extensible Authentication Protocol (EAP) provides a framework for authentication that is often used with wireless networks. Among the EAP types adopted by the WPA/WPA2 standard are PEAP, EAP-FAST, and EAP-TLS. EAP was developed in response to an increasing demand for authentication methods that use other types of security devices, such as token cards, smart cards, and digital certificates.

To simplify network setup, a number of small office and home office (SOHO) routers use a series of EAP messages to allow new hosts to join the network and use WPA/WPA2. Known as Wi-Fi Protected Setup (WPS), this often requires the user to do something to complete the enrollment process: press a button on the router within a short time period, enter a PIN, or bring the new device close by (so that near field communication can take place).

Cisco, RSA, and Microsoft worked together to create Protected Extensible Authentication Protocol (PEAP). There is now native support for it in Windows (which previously favored EAP-TLS). Although many consider PEAP and EAP-TLS to be similar, PEAP is more secure because it establishes an encrypted channel between the server and the client.

EAP-FAST (Flexible Authentication via Secure Tunneling) was designed by Cisco to allow for the use of certificates to establish a TLS tunnel in which client credentials are verified.

To put EAP implementations in a chronological order, think EAP-TLS, EAP-FAST, and then PEAP. In between came EAP-TTLS, a form of EAP-TLS that adds tunneling (Extensible Authentication Protocol—Tunneled Transport Layer Security). Of all the choices, PEAP is the one with more vendors than just Cisco and thus is currently favored for use today.

Shared, Preshared, and Open Keys

During the authentication process, keyed security measures are applied before communication can take place. On many APs, authentication can be set to either *shared* key authentication or *open* authentication. The default setting for older APs typically is open authentication. Open authentication enables access with only the SSID and/or the correct WEP key for the AP. The problem with open authentication is that if you do not have other protection or authentication mechanisms in place, your wireless network is totally open to intruders. When set to shared key mode, the client must meet security requirements before communication with the AP can occur.

Shared requires that a WEP key be configured on both the client system and the AP. This makes authentication with WEP-Shared mandatory, so it is more secure for wireless transmission. WPA-PSK, the acronym for Wi-Fi Protected Access with *Preshared* Key, is a stronger form of encryption in which keys are automatically changed and authenticated between devices after a specified period of time or after a specified number of packets have been transmitted.

> **Note**
>
> One implementation of WPA is known as WPA2 Personal. This implementation uses a preshared key, whereas WPA2 Enterprise needs an authentication server.

MAC Filtering

To increase wireless security, some APs enable you to configure MAC address filtering and guest access. MAC address filtering enables you to limit access to only those specified hosts. Guest access uses a different password and network name and enables visitors to use the Internet without having access to the rest of the network (thus avoiding your data and computers).

Geofencing

Any wireless technology, but usually GPS and sometimes RFID, can be used to create a virtual geographic boundary. This boundary is called a *geofence*. After that boundary is defined, software can be used to trigger a response when a device enters or leaves that area. A section of a supermarket, for example, can be configured to text a coupon code to iPhones for a percentage off milk purchases to any phone coming within 10 feet of the dairy section.

Similar technology can be used to take attendance in a classroom, at a meeting location, and so on. Because events can be triggered for not only entering a zone, but also leaving it, it could be used to send a message to parents if a child leaves the virtually defined neighborhood, and so on. Still in its infancy, geofencing technology is expected to grow in acceptance and application over the next few years.

Cram Quiz

1. Both WPA and WPA2 were created to implement which 802.11 standard?

   ○ **A.** x

   ○ **B.** d

   ○ **C.** i

   ○ **D.** g

2. WPA uses which encryption algorithm?

   ○ **A.** MD5

   ○ **B.** RC4

   ○ **C.** CCMP

   ○ **D.** AES

3. Which of the following technologies can be used to create a virtual perimeter for mobile devices?

    ○ **A.** Polygon sites

    ○ **B.** RADIUS zones

    ○ **C.** Geofencing

    ○ **D.** DMZ

Cram Quiz Answers

1. **C.** The WPA and WPA2 technologies were created to implement the 802.11i standard.

2. **B.** WPA uses the RC4 encryption algorithm with TKIP.

3. **C.** Geofencing can be used to create a virtual perimeter for mobile devices.

Common Networking Attacks

▶ **Summarize common networking attacks.**

Malicious software, or malware, is a serious problem in today's computing environments. It is often assumed that malware is composed of viruses. Although this typically is true, many other forms of malware by definition are not viruses, but are equally undesirable. Although we commonly associate them with coming from the outside, do not overlook the possibility for them to come from *inside threats* as well (particularly malicious employees who feel slighted because they did not get a raise or recognition they feel they deserve and have now become an insider threat).

Malware encompasses many types of malicious software and all were intended by their developer to have an adverse effect on the network. The following sections look at some of the more malevolent types.

Denial-of-Service and Distributed Denial-of-Service Attacks

Denial-of-service (DoS) attacks are designed to tie up network bandwidth and resources and eventually bring the entire network to a halt. This type of attack is done simply by flooding a network with more traffic than it can handle. When more than one computer is used in the attack, it is technically known as a *distributed DoS (DDoS)* attack. These typically use a *botnet* to launch a *coordinated attack* through a *traffic spike*. Almost every attack of this type today is DDoS, and we will use DoS to mean both.

A DoS attack is not designed to steal data but rather to cripple a network and, in doing so, cost a company huge amounts of money. It is possible, in fact, for the attack to be an *unintentional*, or *friendly*, *DoS attack* coming from the inside. Just as with friendly fire in combat, it matters not that it was unintentional, it does just as much damage.

The effects of DoS attacks include the following:

▶ Saturating network resources, which then renders those services unusable

▶ Flooding the network media, preventing communication between computers on the network

▶ Causing user downtime because of an inability to access required services

▶ Causing potentially huge financial losses for an organization because of network and service downtime.

Types of DoS Attacks

Several types of DoS attacks exist, and each seems to target a different area. For instance, they might target bandwidth, network service, memory, CPU, or hard drive space. When a server or other system is overrun by malicious requests, one or more of these core resources breaks down, causing the system to crash or stop responding. A *permanent DoS attack* continues for more than a short period of time and requires you to change your routing, IP addresses, or other configurations to get around it.

Fraggle

In a *Fraggle attack*, spoofed UDP packets are sent to a network's broadcast address. These packets are directed to specific ports, such as port 7 or port 19, and, after they are connected, can flood the system.

Smurfing

The *Smurf attack* is similar to a Fraggle attack. However, a ping request is sent to a broadcast network address, with the sending address spoofed so that many ping replies overload the victim and prevent it from processing the replies.

Ping of Death

In a *ping of death attack*, an oversized *Internet Control Message Protocol (ICMP)* datagram is used to crash IP devices that were manufactured before 1996.

SYN Flood

In a typical TCP session, communication between two computers is initially established by a three-way handshake, referred to as a SYN, SYN/ACK, ACK. At the start of a session, the client sends a SYN message to the server. The server acknowledges the request by sending a SYN/ACK message back to the client. The connection is established when the client responds with an ACK message.

In a *SYN attack*, the victim is overwhelmed with a flood of SYN packets. Every SYN packet forces the targeted server to produce a SYN/ACK response and then wait for the ACK acknowledgment. However, the attacker doesn't respond with an ACK, or spoofs its destination IP address with a nonexistent address so that no ACK response occurs. The result is that the server begins filling up with half-open connections. When all the server's available resources are tied up on half-open connections, it stops acknowledging new incoming SYN requests, including legitimate ones.

Buffer Overflow

A *buffer overflow* is a type of DoS attack that occurs when more data is put into a buffer (typically a memory buffer) than it can hold, thereby overflowing it (as the name implies).

Distributed Reflective DoS

This type of attack is also called an *amplification attack*, and it targets public UDP servers. Two of the most common protocols/servers that a *distributed reflective DoS (DRDoS) attack* usually goes after are Domain Name Service (DNS) and Network Time Protocol (NTP) servers, but Simple Network Management Protocol (SNMP), NetBIOS, and other User Datagram Protocol (UDP) protocols are also susceptible.

> **ExamAlert**
>
> As you study for the exam, be sure to know that reflective, amplified, and distributed are varieties/characteristics of Denial of Service (DoS) attacks.

ICMP Flood

An *ICMP flood*, also known as a ping flood, is a DoS attack in which large numbers of ICMP messages are sent to a computer system to overwhelm it. The result is a failure of the TCP/IP protocol stack, which cannot tend to other TCP/IP requests.

Other Common Attacks

This section details some of the more common attacks used today.

Social Engineering

Social engineering is a common form of cracking. It can be used by both out-siders and people within an organization. *Social engineering* is a hacker term for tricking people into revealing their password or some form of security information. It might include trying to get users to send passwords or other information over email, shoulder surfing, or any other method that tricks users into divulging information. Social engineering is an attack that attempts to take advantage of human behavior.

Logic Bomb

Software programs or code snippets that execute when a certain predefined event occurs are known as *logic bombs*. Such a bomb may send a note to an attacker when a user is logged on to the Internet and is accessing a certain application, for example. This message could inform the attacker that the user is ready for an attack and open a backdoor. Similarly, a programmer could create a program that always makes sure his/her name appears on the payroll roster; if it doesn't, then key files begin to be erased. Any code that is hidden within an application and causes something unexpected to happen constitutes a logic bomb.

Rogue Access Points and Evil Twins

A *rogue access point* describes a situation in which a wireless access point has been placed on a network without the administrator's knowledge. The result is that it is possible to remotely access the rogue access point because it likely does not adhere to company security policies. So, all security can be compro-mised by a cheap wireless router placed on the corporate network. An *evil twin attack* is one in which a rogue wireless access point poses as a legitimate wireless service provider to intercept information users transmit.

Advertising Wireless Weaknesses

These attacks start with *war driving*—driving around with a mobile device looking for open wireless access points with which to communicate and look-ing for weak implementations that can be cracked (called *WEP cracking* or *WPA cracking*). They then lead to *war chalking*—those who discover a way in to the network leave signals (often written in chalk) on, or outside, the premise to notify others that the vulnerability is there. The marks can be on the sidewalk, the side of the building, a nearby signpost, and so on.

Phishing

Often users receive a variety of emails offering products, services, information, or opportunities. Unsolicited email of this type is called *phishing* (pronounced "fishing"). This technique involves a bogus offer sent to hundreds of thousands or even millions of email addresses. The strategy plays the odds. For every 1,000 emails sent, perhaps one person replies. Phishing can be dangerous because users can be tricked into divulging personal information such as credit card numbers or bank account information. Today, phishing is performed in several ways. Phishing websites and phone calls are also designed to steal money or personal information.

Ransomware

With *ransomware*, software—often delivered through a Trojan horse—takes control of a system and demands that a third party be paid. The "control" can be accomplished by encrypting the hard drive, by changing user password information, or via any of a number of other creative ways. Users are usually assured that by paying the extortion amount (the ransom), they will be given the code needed to revert their systems to normal operations.

DNS Poisoning

With *DNS poisoning*, the DNS server is given information about a name server that it thinks is legitimate when it isn't. This can send users to a website other than the one to which they wanted to go, reroute mail, or do any other type of redirection wherein data from a DNS server is used to determine a destination. Another name for this is *DNS spoofing*, and fast flux is one of the most popular techniques. It is used by botnets to hide the delivery sites behind a changing network of compromised hosts that act as proxies.

ARP Cache Poisoning

Address Resolution Protocol (ARP) poisoning tries to convince the network that the attacker's MAC address is the one associated with an IP address so that traffic sent to that IP address is wrongly sent to the attacker's machine.

Spoofing

Spoofing is a technique in which the real source of a transmission, file, or email is concealed or replaced with a fake source. This technique enables an attacker, for example, to misrepresent the original source of a file available for download. Then he can trick users into accepting a file from an untrusted source, believing it is coming from a trusted source.

Deauthentication

Deauthentication is also known as a disassociation attack. With this type of attack, the intruder sends a frame to the AP with a spoofed address to make it look like it came from the victim that disconnects the user from the network. Because the victim is unable to keep a connection with the AP, it increases their chances of choosing to use another AP—a rogue one or one in a hotel or other venue that they have to pay extra to use. A number of hotels had suits filed against them by the Federal Trade Commission for launching attacks of this type and generating revenue by requiring their guests to pay for "premium" services rather than being able to use the free Wi-Fi.

Brute Force

There are a number of ways to ascertain a password, but one of the most common is a *brute force attack* in which one value after another is guessed until the right value is found. Although that could take forever if done manually, software programs can take lots of values in a remarkably short period of time. WPS attacks, for example, have become much more common since the technology (Wi-Fi Protected Setup) is susceptible to brute force attacks used to guess the user's PIN. When an attacker gains access, the attacker is then on the Wi-Fi network.

VLAN Hopping

VLAN hopping, as the name implies, is an exploit of resources on a Virtual LAN that is made possible because the resources exist on said Virtual LAN. There is more than one method by which this occurs, but in all of them the result is the same: An attacking host on a VLAN gains access to resources on other VLANs that are not supposed to be accessible to them (becoming a compromised system). Again, regardless of the method employed, the solution is to properly configure the switches to keep this from happening.

Man-in-the-Middle Attacks

In a *man-in-the-middle attack*, the intruder places himself between the sending and receiving devices and captures the communication as it passes by. The interception of the data is invisible to those sending and receiving the data. The intruder can capture the network data and manipulate it, change it, examine it, and then send it on. Wireless communications are particularly susceptible to this type of attack. A rogue access point, a wireless AP that has been installed without permission, is an example of a man-in-the-middle attack. If the attack is done with FTP (using the port command), it is known as an *FTP bounce* attack.

Exploits and Zero-Day Attacks

When a hole is found in a web browser or other software, and miscreants begin exploiting it the very day it is discovered by the developer (bypassing the 1- to 2-day response time many software providers need to put out a patch after the hole has been found), it is known as an *exploit attack* or *zero-day attack*. Zero-day attacks are incredibly difficult to respond to. If attackers learn of the weakness the same day as the developer, they have the ability to exploit it until a patch is released. Often, the only thing you as a security administrator can do between the discovery of the exploit and the release of the patch is to turn off the service. Although this can be a costly undertaking in terms of productivity, it is the only way to keep the network safe.

Vulnerabilities and Prevention

The threat from malicious code is a real concern. You need to take precautions to protect your systems. Although you might not eliminate the threat, you can significantly reduce it.

One of the primary tools used in the fight against malicious software is antivirus/antimalware software. Antimalware software (which includes antivirus software and more) is available from a number of companies, and each offers similar features and capabilities. You can find solutions that are host based, cloud/server based, or network based. The following is a list of the common features and characteristics of antivirus software:

▶ **Real-time protection:** An installed antivirus program should continuously monitor the system looking for viruses. If a program is downloaded, an application opened, or a suspicious email received, the real-time virus monitor detects and removes the threat. The virus application sits in the background, largely unnoticed by the user.

▶ **Virus scanning:** An antivirus program must scan selected drives and disks, either locally or remotely. You can manually run scanning or schedule it to run at a particular time.

▶ **Scheduling:** It is a best practice to schedule virus scanning to occur automatically at a predetermined time. In a network environment, this typically is off hours, when the overhead of the scanning process won't impact users.

▶ **Live updates:** New viruses and malicious software are released with alarming frequency. It is recommended that the antivirus software be configured to regularly receive virus updates.

▶ **Email vetting:** Emails represent one of the primary sources of virus delivery. It is essential to use antivirus software that provides email scanning for both inbound and outbound email.

▶ **Centralized management:** If used in a network environment, it is a good idea to use software that supports managing the virus program from the server. Virus updates and configurations need to be made only on the server, not on each client station.

Managing the threat from viruses is considered a proactive measure, with antivirus software only part of the solution. A complete security protection strategy requires many aspects to help limit the risk of malware, viruses, and other threats:

▶ **Develop in-house policies and rules:** In a corporate environment or even a small office, you need to establish what information can be placed on a system. For example, should users download programs from the Internet? Can users bring in their own storage media, such as USB flash drives? Is there a corporate BYOD policy restricting the use of personal smartphones and other mobile devices?

▶ **Monitoring virus threats:** With new viruses coming out all the time, you need to check whether new viruses have been released and what they are designed to do.

▶ **Educate users:** One of the keys to a complete antivirus solution is to train users in virus prevention and recognition techniques. If users know what to look for, they can prevent a virus from entering the system or network. Back up copies of important documents. It should be mentioned that no solution is absolute, so care should be taken to ensure that the data is backed up. In the event of a malicious attack, redundant information is available in a secure location.

▶ **Automate virus scanning and updates:** You can configure today's antivirus software to automatically scan and update itself. Because such tasks can be forgotten and overlooked, it is recommended that you have these processes scheduled to run at predetermined times.

▶ **Don't run unnecessary services:** Know every service that is running on your network and the reason for it. If you can avoid running the service, equate it with putting another lock on the door and do so.

▶ **Keep track of open ports:** Just as you don't want unnecessary services running, you don't want unnecessary ports left open. Every one of them is an unguarded door through which a miscreant can enter.

▶ **Avoid unencrypted channels and clear-text credentials:** The days when these were acceptable have passed. Continuing to use them is tantamount to inviting an attack.

▶ **Shun unsecure protocols:** Once upon a time, clear-text passwords were okay to use because risks of anyone getting on your network who should not were minimal. During those days, it was okay to use unsecure protocols as well because the priority was on ease of use as opposed to data protection. All of this went out of acceptance decades ago and you must—in the interest of security—be careful with the following unsecure protocols: Telnet, HTTP, SLIP, FTP, TFTP, and SNMP (v1 and v2). Secure alternatives—offering the same functionality, but adding acceptable levels of security—are available for each. Where possible, opt instead for SSH, SNMPv3, TLS/SSL, SFTP, HTTPS, and IPsec.

▶ **Patches and updates:** All applications, including productivity software, virus checkers, and especially the operating system, release patches and updates often, designed to address potential security weaknesses.

Administrators must keep an eye out for these patches and install them when they are released. Pay particular attention to unpatched/legacy systems and keep them as secure as possible.

One of the best tools to use when dealing with problems is knowledge. In several locations, CompTIA stresses that user education is important, but even more important is that administrators know what is going on and keep learning from what is going on now and what has gone on in the past. As an example, *TEMPEST* is the name of a project commenced by the U.S. government in the late 1950s that all administrators should be familiar with. TEMPEST was concerned with reducing electronic noise from devices that would divulge intelligence about systems and information. This program has become a standard for computer systems certification. *TEMPEST shielding protection* means that a computer system doesn't emit any significant amounts of electromagnetic interference (EMI) or radio frequency interference (RFI) (*RF emanation*). For a device to be approved as a TEMPEST, it must undergo extensive testing, done to exacting standards that the U.S. government dictates. Today, control zones and white noise are used to accomplish the shielding. TEMPEST-certified equipment often costs twice as much as non-TEMPEST equipment.

> **ExamAlert**
>
> Know some of the ways to prevent networking attacks and mitigate vulnerabilities.

Cram Quiz

1. Which of the following is an attack in which a rogue wireless access point poses as a legitimate wireless service provider to intercept information users transmit?

   ○ **A.** Zero day

   ○ **B.** Phishing

   ○ **C.** Evil twin

   ○ **D.** Social engineering

2. Which of the following is a type of DoS attack that occurs when more data is put into a buffer than it can hold?

   ○ **A.** Dictionary attack

   ○ **B.** Buffer overflow

   ○ **C.** Worm

   ○ **D.** Trojan horse

3. Which of the following is an attack in which something that appears as a helpful or harmless program carries and delivers a malicious payload?

○ **A.** Worm

○ **B.** Phish

○ **C.** Evil twin

○ **D.** Trojan horse

4. Which of the following is an attack in which users are tricked into revealing their passwords or some form of security information?

○ **A.** Bluesnarfing

○ **B.** Phishing

○ **C.** Evil twin

○ **D.** Social engineering

Cram Quiz Answers

1. **C.** An evil twin attack is one in which a rogue wireless access point poses as a legitimate wireless service provider to intercept information users transmit.

2. **B.** A buffer overflow is a type of DoS attack that occurs when more data is put into a buffer than it can hold.

3. **D.** Trojan horses appear as helpful or harmless programs but, when installed, carry and deliver a malicious payload.

4. **D.** Social engineering is a term for tricking people (users) into revealing their passwords or some form of security information.

Mitigation Techniques

▶ **Explain common mitigation techniques and their purposes.**

CramSaver

If you can correctly answer these questions before going through this section, save time by skimming the Exam Alerts in this section and then completing the Cram Quiz at the end of the section.

1. True or false: A honeypot is a trap that allows the intruder in but does not allow access to sensitive data.

2. True or false: A root guard is used to prevent misuse of BPDU packets on a switch.

Answers

1. True. A honeypot is a trap that allows the intruder in but does not allow access to sensitive data.

2. True. A root guard is used to prevent misuse of BPDU packets on a switch.

The previous section looked at some of the more common types of networking attacks and concluded with a discussion of vulnerability prevention. This section continues that discussion by focusing on mitigation techniques. Mitigation is defined as the action of reducing the severity, seriousness, or painfulness of something. When it comes to network security, mitigation is the actions, techniques, and ways of reducing the possibility of an attack and the severity of one that may occur. The focus of this section is on issues related to that topic.

Signature Management

Digital signatures are the electronic equivalent of a sealed envelope and are intended to ensure that a file has not been altered in transit. Any file with a digital signature is used to verify not only the publishers of the content or file, but also to verify the content integrity at the time of download. On the network, PKI enables you to issue certificates to internal developers/contractors and enables any employee to verify the origin and integrity of downloaded applications.

Device Hardening

The first section of this chapter looked at network device hardening. Know that it is important to change default passwords, keep firmware current, and disable unused elements (ports, services, and the like).

Change Native VLAN

On switches, the native VLAN is the only VLAN that is not tagged in a trunk. This means that native VLAN frames are transmitted unchanged. By default, the native VLAN is port 1, and that default represents a weakness in that it is something known about your network that an attacker could use. To strengthen security, albeit a small amount, you can change the native VLAN to another port. The command(s) used to do so are dependent on the vendor and model of your port but can be easily found online.

Switch and Port Protection

Switches and ports have been mentioned already, but it is worth bringing them up again because they can represent quite a weakness. Be sure to secure switches, disable unused ports, and be on the lookout or aware of the issues discussed in the following sections.

> **ExamAlert**
>
> As you study for the exam, know that securing switches, disabling unused ports, and using common-sense solutions can go far in improving network security.

Spanning Tree

The *Spanning Tree Protocol (STP)* is defined as IEEE 802.1d and the more recent Rapid Spanning Tree 802.1w. This protocol can be a godsend when it comes to solving certain problems with switches. Loops, for example, can occur when more than one bridge or switch is implemented on the network. In this scenario, the devices can confuse each other by leading one another to believe that a host is located on a certain segment when it is not. To combat the loop problem, STP enables bridge/switch interfaces to be assigned a value that is then used to control the learning process.

Flood Guards, BPDU Guards, and Root Guards

Because switches can be subject to DoS attacks, *flood guards* are used to look for and prevent malicious traffic from bringing the switch to a halt. Whether it is DoS in question, or DDoS, a flood guard is used as protection for a switch and can be purchased as a standalone device or with another.

Similarly, a *bridge protocol data unit (BPDU) guard* prevents looping on a switch. It protects the spanning tree domain from external influence by moving a nontrunking port into an error state when a BPDU is received on that port. BPDUs are data messages that are exchanged across the switches via spanning tree protocol topology. These data packets contain information on ports, addresses, priorities, and costs and ensure that the data ends up where it was intended to go; the guard shuts down interfaces that receive BPDUs instead of putting them into the spanning tree blocking state where they could cause looping.

Root guards are similar to BPDU guards in that they are used to prevent malicious exploitation of BPDU packets. The difference is that a root guard is used to prevent another switch from becoming the BPDU superior. Root guard is needed when you connect a network that you manage to one that you do not.

DHCP Snooping

Although it sounds like a bad thing, *DHCP snooping* is just the opposite. It is the capability for a switch to look at packets and drop DHCP traffic that it determines to be unacceptable based on the defined rules. The purpose of this is to prevent rogue DHCP servers from offering IP addresses to DHCP clients.

Demilitarized Zones (Perimeter Network)

An important firewall-related concept is the *demilitarized zone (DMZ)*, sometimes called a *perimeter network*. A DMZ is part of a network where you place servers that must be accessible by sources both outside and inside your network. However, the DMZ is not connected directly to either network, and it must always be accessed through the firewall. The military term DMZ is used because it describes an area that has little or no enforcement or policing.

Using DMZs gives your firewall configuration an extra level of flexibility, protection, and complexity. Figure 10.3 shows a DMZ configuration.

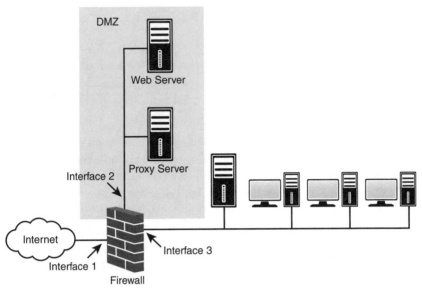

FIGURE 10.3 **A DMZ configuration**

By using a DMZ, you can create an additional step that makes it more difficult for an intruder to gain access to the internal network. In Figure 10.3, for example, an intruder who tried to come in through Interface 1 would have to spoof a request from either the web server or proxy server into Interface 2 before it could be forwarded to the internal network. Although it is not impossible for an intruder to gain access to the internal network through a DMZ, it is difficult.

ExamAlert

Be prepared to identify the purpose of a DMZ.

VLAN Network Segmentation

By dividing one network into smaller subnetworks, it is possible to optimize it in a number of ways. The segmentation is accomplished with switches and VLANs, and the separation can be done to isolate such things as heavy load systems or certain protocols. By moving those to their own subnetwork, the result should be performance increases for other parts of the network.

> **Note**
>
> Popular today is using *virtual machines (VMs)* to segment or separate systems (software) from the main OS (host versus guest) and the rest of the network through virtual switches.

Privileged User Account

Enforcing user privileges can be fairly taxing. If the user does not have least privileges (discussed earlier in this chapter), the user's escalated privileges could allow them to access data to which they would not otherwise have access and cause harm to it—intentional or not. Be cognizant of the fact that you won't have the same control over user accounts in the cloud as you do locally, and when someone locks his account by entering the wrong password too many times in a row, you or they could be at the mercy of the hours that the technical staff is available at the provider.

You want to carefully monitor all privileged users accounts (admin, root, and so on) and apply more protection to them than to any other accounts because of the power they have. Give privileges to users only as needed, and try to limit elevated permissions to being used only when needed (and then returning to regular user permissions until elevated ones are needed again).

File Integrity Monitoring

File hashing was discussed earlier in terms of verifying that the files downloaded are what you expect them to be. The same concept for files you may download should be applied to files residing on your system. Use checksums and file integrity systems to monitor your files and make certain the ones you are backing up are unchanged and complete.

Role Separation

Separation of duties policies are designed to reduce the risk of fraud and to prevent other losses in an organization. A good policy will require more than one person to accomplish key processes. This may mean that the person who processes an order from a customer isn't the same person who generates the invoice or deals with the billing.

Separation of duties helps prevent various problems, such as an individual embezzling money from a company. To embezzle funds successfully, an individual would need to recruit others to commit an act of collusion—that is, an agreement between two or more parties established for the purpose of committing deception or fraud. Collusion, when part of a crime, is also a criminal act in and of itself.

In addition, separation-of-duties policies can help prevent accidents from occurring in an organization. Suppose that you're managing a software development project. You want someone to perform a quality assurance test on a new piece of code before it's put into production. Establishing a clear separation of duties prevents development code from entering production status until quality testing is accomplished.

Many banks and financial institutions require multiple steps and approvals to transfer money. This helps reduce errors and minimizes the likelihood of fraud.

Using ACLs to Restrict Access

Earlier in this chapter, the section "Authentication and Access Controls" discussed access control lists. The main item to take away is that an ACL defines who can access resources, and there must be an inherent understanding by the system that unless permission has been explicitly granted, it is denied.

Honeypots and Honeynets

When talking about network security, honeypots and honeynets are often mentioned. Honeypots are a rather clever approach to network security but perhaps a bit expensive. A *honeypot* is a system set up as a decoy to attract and deflect attacks from hackers. The server decoy appears to have everything a regular server does—OS, applications, and network services. The attacker thinks he is accessing a real network server, but he is in a network trap.

The honeypot has two key purposes. It can give administrators valuable information on the types of attacks being carried out. In turn, the honeypot can secure the real production servers according to what it learns. Also, the honeypot deflects attention from working servers, allowing them to function without being attacked.

A honeypot can do the following:

▶ Deflect the attention of attackers from production servers

▶ Deter attackers if they suspect their actions may be monitored with a honeypot

▶ Allow administrators to learn from the attacks to protect the real servers

▶ Identify the source of attacks, whether from inside the network or outside

One step up from the honeypot is the honeynet. The *honeynet* is an entire network set up to monitor attacks from outsiders. All traffic into and out of the network is carefully tracked and documented. This information is shared with network professionals to help isolate the types of attacks launched against networks and to proactively manage those security risks. Honeynets function as a production network, using network services, applications, and more. Attackers don't know that they are actually accessing a monitored network.

Penetration Testing

It is becoming more common for companies to hire penetration testers to test their system's defenses. Essentially, a penetration tester will use the same techniques that a hacker would use to find any flaws in a system's security. These flaws may be discovered by means other than directly accessing the system, such as collecting information from public databases, talking to employees/partners, dumpster diving, and social engineering. This is known as *passive reconnaissance*. In contrast to this, *active reconnaissance* directly focuses on the system (port scans, traceroute information, network mapping, and so forth) to identify weaknesses that could be used to launch an attack.

When doing penetration testing, it is important to have a scope document outlining the extent of the testing that is to be done. It is equally important to have permission from an administrator who can authorize such testing—in writing—authorizing the testing to be conducted.

One weakness a good penetration test looks for is escalation of privilege; that is, a hole created when code is executed with higher privileges than those of the user running it. By breaking out of the executing code, the users are left with higher privileges than they should have.

Three types of penetration testing are Black Box (the tester has absolutely no knowledge of the system and is functioning in the same manner as an outside attacker), White Box (the tester has significant knowledge of the system, which simulates an attack from an insider—a rogue employee), and Gray Box (a middle ground between the first two types of testing. In gray box testing, the tester has some limited knowledge of the target system).

> **Note**
>
> With so many security-related topics now appearing on the Network+ exam, you have a good head start on Security+ certification study after you successfully finish taking this exam.

Cram Quiz

1. Which of the following is NOT one of the types of penetration testing?

   - ○ **A.** Black Box
   - ○ **B.** White Box
   - ○ **C.** Red Box
   - ○ **D.** Gray Box

2. Which of the following enables bridge/switch interfaces to be assigned a value that is then used to control the learning process?

   - ○ **A.** LGH
   - ○ **B.** STP
   - ○ **C.** eDiscovery
   - ○ **D.** DTP

3. Which of the following is one step up from the honeypot?

   - ○ **A.** Geofence
   - ○ **B.** VLAN
   - ○ **C.** DMZ
   - ○ **D.** Honeynet

Cram Quiz Answers

1. **C.** The three types of penetration testing are Black Box, White Box, and Gray Box. The differences among them are based on how much knowledge of the target system is provided to the tester.

2. **B.** STP enables bridge/switch interfaces to be assigned a value that is then used to control the learning process.

3. **D.** One step up from the honeypot is the honeynet.

What's Next?

The final chapter of this book focuses on all areas of network troubleshooting, including troubleshooting best practices and some of the tools and utilities you use to assist in the troubleshooting process.

No matter how well a network is designed and how many preventive maintenance schedules are in place, troubleshooting is always necessary. Because of this, network administrators must develop those troubleshooting skills.

CHAPTER 11

Network Troubleshooting

This chapter covers the following official Network+ objectives:

▶ Explain the network troubleshooting methodology.

▶ Given a scenario, use the appropriate tool.

▶ Given a scenario, troubleshoot common network service issues.

This chapter covers CompTIA Network+ objectives 5.1, 5.2, and 5.5. For more information on the official Network+ exam topics, see the "About the Network+ Exam" section in the Introduction.

Many duties and responsibilities fall under the umbrella of network administration. Of these, one of the most practiced is that of troubleshooting. No matter how well a network is designed and how many preventive maintenance schedules are in place, troubleshooting is always necessary. Because of this, network administrators must develop those troubleshooting skills.

This chapter focuses on all areas of troubleshooting, including troubleshooting best practices and some of the tools and utilities you can use to assist in the troubleshooting process.

Troubleshooting Steps and Procedures

▶ **Explain the network troubleshooting methodology.**

CramSaver

If you can correctly answer these questions before going through this section, save time by skimming the Exam Alerts in this section and then completing the Cram Quiz at the end of the section.

1. What are the key sources from which you can gain information about a computer problem?

2. What is the final step in the network troubleshooting methodology CompTIA expects test takers to follow?

Answers

1. It is important to get as much information as possible about the problem. You can glean information from three key sources: the computer (in the form of logs and error messages), the computer user experiencing the problem, and your own observation.

2. Document the findings, the actions, and the outcomes.

Regardless of the problem, effective network troubleshooting follows some specific steps. These steps provide a framework in which to perform the troubleshooting process. When you follow them, they can reduce the time it takes to isolate and fix a problem. The following sections discuss the common troubleshooting steps and procedures as identified by the CompTIA Network+ objectives:

1. Identify the problem.

   ▶ Gather information.

   ▶ Duplicate the problem, if possible.

   ▶ Question users.

   ▶ Identify symptoms.

   ▶ Determine if anything has changed.

   ▶ Approach multiple problems individually.

2. Establish a theory of probable cause.

   ▶ Question the obvious.

   ▶ Consider multiple approaches:

▶ Top-to-bottom/bottom-to-top OSI model.

▶ Divide and conquer.

3. Test the theory to determine the cause:

   ▶ After the theory is confirmed, determine the next steps to resolve the problem.

   ▶ If the theory is not confirmed, reestablish a new theory or escalate.

4. Establish a plan of action to resolve the problem and identify potential effects.

   1. Implement the solution or escalate as necessary.

   2. Verify full system functionality and, if applicable, implement preventive measures.

   3. Document findings, actions, and outcomes.

ExamAlert

You should expect questions asking you to identify the troubleshooting steps in exact order.

Identify the Problem

The first step in the troubleshooting process is to establish exactly what the problem is. This stage of the troubleshooting process is all about information gathering, identifying symptoms, questioning users, and determining if anything has changed. To get this information, you need knowledge of the operating system used, good communication skills, and a little patience. You need to get as much information as possible about the problem. You can glean information from three key sources: the computer (in the form of logs and error messages), the computer user experiencing the problem, and your own observation.

After you have listed the symptoms, you can begin to identify some of the potential causes of those symptoms.

ExamAlert

You do not need to know where error messages are stored on an operating system. You need to know only that the troubleshooting process requires you to read system-generated log errors.

Identify Symptoms

Some computer problems are isolated to a single user in a single location; others affect several thousand users spanning multiple locations. Establishing the affected area is an important part of the troubleshooting process, and it often dictates the strategies you use to resolve the problem.

ExamAlert

You might be provided with either a description of a scenario or a description augmented by a network diagram. In either case, you should carefully read the description of the problem, step by step. In most cases, the correct answer is fairly logical, and the wrong answers can be easily identified.

Problems that affect many users are often connectivity issues that disable access for many users. Such problems often can be isolated to wiring closets, network devices, and server rooms. The troubleshooting process for problems that are isolated to a single user often begins and ends at that user's workstation. The trail might indeed lead you to the wiring closet or server, but that is probably not where the troubleshooting process began. Understanding who is affected by a problem can give you the first clues about where the problem exists. For example, a change in Dynamic Host Configuration Protocol (DHCP) scope by a new administrator might affect several users, whereas a user playing with the TCP/IP settings of a single computer can affect only that person.

Determine Whether Anything Has Changed

Whether there is a problem with a workstation's access to a database or an entire network, they were working at some point. Although many people claim that their computer "just stopped working," that is unlikely. Far more likely is that changes to the system or network have caused the problem. Look for newly installed applications, applied patches or updates, new hardware, a physical move of the computer, or a new username and password. Establishing any recent changes to a system can often lead you in the right direction to isolate and troubleshoot a problem.

Establish a Theory of Probable Cause

> **ExamAlert**
>
> When approaching a problem, start by questioning the obvious. If that fails, consider ways to tackle the issue from multiple approaches. Consider using a top-to-bottom or bottom-to-top model approach (such as working through the OSI model stack) and assigning any co-workers you have to divide and conquer the problem.

A single problem on a network can have many causes, but with appropriate information gathering, you can eliminate many of them. When you look for a probable cause, it is often best to look at the easiest solution first and then work from there. Even in the most complex of network designs, the easiest solution is often the right one. For instance, if a single user cannot log on to a network, it is best to confirm network settings before replacing the network interface card (NIC). Remember, though, that at this point you need to determine only the most probable cause, and your first guess might be incorrect. It might take a few tries to determine the correct cause of the problem.

> **ExamAlert**
>
> Avoid discounting a possible answer because it seems too easy. Many of the troubleshooting questions are based on possible real-world scenarios, some of which do have easy or obvious solutions.

Test the Theory to Determine Cause

After questioning the obvious, you need to establish a theory. After you formulate a theory, you should attempt to confirm it. An example might be a theory that users can no longer print because they downloaded new software that changed the print drivers, or that they can no longer run the legacy application they used to run after the latest service pack was installed.

If the theory can be confirmed, you must plot a course of action—a list of the next steps to take to resolve the problem. If the theory cannot be confirmed (in the example given, no new software was downloaded and no service pack was applied), you must establish a new theory or consider escalating the problem.

Establish a Plan of Action

After identifying a cause, but before implementing a solution, you should establish a plan for the solution. This is particularly a concern for server systems
in which taking the server offline is a difficult and undesirable prospect. After
identifying the cause of a problem on the server, it is absolutely necessary to
plan for the solution. The plan must include the details of when the server or
network should be taken offline and for how long, what support services are in
place, and who will be involved in correcting the problem.

Planning is an important part of the whole troubleshooting process and can
involve formal or informal written procedures. Those who do not have experience troubleshooting servers might wonder about all the formality, but this
attention to detail ensures the least amount of network or server downtime and
the maximum data availability.

> **Tip**
>
> If part of an action plan includes shutting down a server or another similar event that
> can impact many users, it is a best practice to let users know when they will be shut
> out of the network. This allows them to properly shut off any affected applications
> and not be frustrated by not being able to access the network or other services.

With the plan in place, you should be ready to implement a solution—that is,
apply the patch, replace the hardware, plug in a cable, or implement some other
solution. In an ideal world, your first solution would fix the problem; however,
unfortunately this is not always the case. If your first solution does not fix the
problem, you need to retrace your steps and start again.

You must attempt only one solution at a time. Trying several solutions at once
can make it unclear which one corrected the problem.

Implement the Solution or Escalate

After the corrective change has been made to the server, network, or workstation, you must test the results—never assume. This is when you find out if you
were right and the remedy you applied worked. Don't forget that first impres-
sions can deceive, and a fix that seems to work on first inspection might not
have corrected the problem.

The testing process is not always as easy as it sounds. If you are testing a connectivity problem, it is not difficult to ascertain whether your solution was
successful. However, changes made to an application or to databases you are

unfamiliar with are much more difficult to test. It might be necessary to have people who are familiar with the database or application run the tests with you in attendance.

Determine Whether Escalation Is Necessary

Sometimes the problems you encounter fall outside the scope of your knowledge. Few organizations expect their administrators to know everything, but organizations do expect administrators to fix any problem. To do this, you often need additional help.

> **Note**
>
> System administration is often as much about knowing whom and what to refer to in order to get information about a problem as it is about actually fixing the problem.

Technical escalation procedures do not follow a specific set of rules; rather, the procedures to follow vary from organization to organization and situation to situation. Your organization might have an informal arrangement or a formal one requiring documented steps and procedures to be carried out. Whatever the approach, general practices should be followed for appropriate escalation.

Unless otherwise specified by the organization, the general rule is to start with the closest help and work out from there. If you work in an organization that has an IT team, talk with others on your team; every IT professional has had different experiences, and someone else may know about the issue at hand. If you are still struggling with the problem, it is common practice to notify a supervisor or head administrator, especially if the problem is a threat to the server's data or can bring down the server.

Suppose that, as a server administrator, you notice a problem with a hard disk in a RAID 1 array on a Linux server. You know how to replace drives in a failed RAID 1 configuration, but you have no experience working with software RAID on a Linux server. This situation would most certainly require an escalation of the problem. The job of server administrator in this situation is to notice the failed RAID 1 drive and to recruit the appropriate help to repair the RAID failure within Linux.

> **Note**
>
> When you are confronted with a problem, it is yours until it has been solved or passed to someone else. Of course, the passing on of an issue requires that both parties know that it has been passed on.

Verify Full System Functionality

At times, you might apply a fix that corrects one problem but creates another. Many such circumstances are hard to predict—but not always. For instance, you might add a new network application, but the application requires more bandwidth than your current network infrastructure can support. The result would be that overall network performance would be compromised.

Everything done to a network can have a ripple effect and negatively affect another area of the network. Actions such as adding clients, replacing hubs or switches, and adding applications can all have unforeseen results. It is difficult to always know how the changes you make to a network might affect the network's functioning. The safest thing to do is assume that the changes you make will affect the network in some way and realize that you have to figure out how. This is when you might need to think outside the box and try to predict possible outcomes.

It is imperative that you verify full system functionality before you are satisfied with the solution. After you obtain that level of satisfaction, you should look at the problem and ascertain if any preventive measures should be implemented to keep the same problem from occurring again.

Document the Findings, Actions, and Outcomes

Although it is often neglected in the troubleshooting process, documentation is as important as any of the other troubleshooting procedures. Documenting a solution involves keeping a record of all the steps taken during the fix—not necessarily just the solution.

For the documentation to be of use to other network administrators in the future, it must include several key pieces of information. When documenting a procedure, you should include the following information:

▶ **When:** When was the solution implemented? You must know the date, because if problems occur after your changes, knowing the date of your fix makes it easier to determine whether your changes caused the problems.

▶ **Why:** Although it is obvious when a problem is being fixed why it is being done, a few weeks later, it might become less clear why that solution was needed. Documenting why the fix was made is important because if the same problem appears on another system, you can use this information to reduce the time needed to find the solution.

▶ **What:** The successful fix should be detailed, along with information about any changes to the configuration of the system or network that were made to achieve the fix. Additional information should include version numbers for software patches or firmware, as appropriate.

▶ **Results:** Many administrators choose to include information on both successes and failures. The documentation of failures might prevent you from going down the same road twice, and the documentation of successful solutions can reduce the time it takes to get a system or network up and running.

▶ **Who:** It might be that information is left out of the documentation or someone simply wants to ask a few questions about a solution. In both cases, if the name of the person who made a fix is in the documentation, he or she can easily be tracked down. Of course, this is more of a concern in environments that have a large IT staff or if system repairs are performed by contractors instead of company employees.

Cram Quiz

1. A user reports that she can no longer access a legacy database. What should be one of the first questions you ask?

   ○ **A.** What has changed since the last time you accessed that database?

   ○ **B.** How many help calls have you placed in the past few months?

   ○ **C.** Who originally installed or created that database?

   ○ **D.** How long have you worked here?

2. You've spent 2 hours trying to fix a problem and then realize that it falls outside of your area of expertise and ability to fix. What should you do in most organizations?

   ○ **A.** Let the user immediately know that she needs to call someone else; then exit the scene so another person can help.

   ○ **B.** Formulate a workaround; then document the problem and bring it up at the next meeting.

   ○ **C.** Escalate the issue with a supervisor or manager.

   ○ **D.** Continue working on the problem, trying as many solutions as you can find, until you solve the problem.

3. You get numerous calls from users who cannot access an application. Upon investigation, you find that the application crashed. You restart the application, and it appears to run okay. What is the next step in the troubleshooting process?

   ○ **A.** Email the users to let them know that they can use the application again.

   ○ **B.** Test the application to ensure that it operates correctly.

   ○ **C.** Document the problem and the solution.

   ○ **D.** Reload the application executables from the CD, and restart it.

4. A user tells you that she is having a problem accessing her email. What is the first step in the troubleshooting process?

   ○ **A.** Document the problem.

   ○ **B.** Make sure that the user's email address is valid.

   ○ **C.** Discuss the problem with the user.

   ○ **D.** Visit the user's desk to reload the email client software.

5. You have successfully fixed a problem with a server and have tested the application and let the users back on to the system. What is the next step in the troubleshooting process?

   ○ **A.** Document the problem.

   ○ **B.** Restart the server.

   ○ **C.** Document the problem and the solution.

   ○ **D.** Clear the error logs of any reference to the problem.

Cram Quiz Answers

1. **A.** Establishing any recent changes to a system can often lead you in the right direction to isolate and troubleshoot a problem.

2. **C.** When a problem is outside of your ability to fix, you must escalate the issue. Unless otherwise specified by the organization, the general rule is to start with the closest help and work out from there. None of the other options are acceptable choices.

3. **B.** After you fix a problem, you should test it fully to ensure that the network operates correctly before you allow users to log back on. The steps described in answers A and C are valid but only after the application has been tested. Answer D is incorrect because you would reload the executable only as part of a systematic troubleshooting process. Because the application loads, it is unlikely that the executable has become corrupted.

4. **C.** Not enough information is provided for you to come up with a solution. In this case, the next troubleshooting step would be to talk to the user and gather more information about exactly what the problem is. All the other answers are valid troubleshooting steps but only after the information gathering has been completed.

5. **C.** After you have fixed a problem, tested the fix, and let users back on to the system, you should create detailed documentation that describes the problem and the solution. Answer A is incorrect because you must document both the problem and the solution. You do not need to restart the server, so Answer B is incorrect. Answer D would be performed only after the system's documentation has been created.

Hardware and Software Troubleshooting Tools

▶ **Given a scenario, use the appropriate tool.**

CramSaver

If you can correctly answer these questions before going through this section, save time by skimming the Exam Alerts in this section and then completing the Cram Quiz at the end of the section.

1. What tools are used to attach twisted-pair network cable to connectors within a patch panel?

2. What are the two parts of a toner probe?

Answers

1. Punchdown tools are used to attach twisted-pair network cable to connectors within a patch panel.

2. A toner probe has two parts: the tone generator, or toner, and the tone locator, or probe.

ExamAlert

Remember that this objective begins with "Given a scenario." That means that you may receive a drag and drop, matching, or "live OS" scenario where you have to click through to complete a specific objective-based task.

A large part of network administration involves having the right tools for the job and knowing when and how to use them. Selecting the correct tool for a networking job sounds like an easy task, but network administrators can choose from a mind-boggling number of tools and utilities.

Given the diverse range of tools and utilities available, it is unlikely that you will encounter all the tools available—or even all those discussed in this chapter. For the Network+ exam, you are required to have general knowledge of the tools available and what they are designed to do.

Until networks become completely wireless, network administrators can expect to spend some of their time using a variety of media-related troubleshooting and installation tools. Some of these tools (such as the tone generator and locator) may be used to troubleshoot media connections, and others (such as wire crimpers and punchdown tools) are used to create network cables and connections.

The Basic Tools

Although many costly, specialized networking tools and devices are available to network administrators, the most widely used tools cost only a few dollars: the standard screwdrivers we use on almost a daily basis. As a network administrator, you can expect with amazing regularity to take the case off a system to replace a network interface card (NIC) or perhaps remove the cover from a hub or switch to replace a fan. Advanced cable testers and other specialized tools will not help you when a screwdriver is needed.

Wire Crimpers, Strippers, and Snips

Wire crimpers are tools you might regularly use. Like many things, making your own cables can be fun at first, but the novelty soon wears off. Basically, a wire crimper is a tool that you use to attach media connectors to the ends of cables. For instance, you use one type of wire crimper to attach RJ-45 connectors on unshielded twisted-pair (UTP) cable. You use a different type of wire crimper to attach British Naval Connectors/Bayonet Neill-Concelman (BNCs) to coaxial cabling.

> **Tip**
>
> When making cables, always order more connectors than you need; a few mishaps will probably occur along the way.

In a sense, you can think of a wire crimper as a pair of special pliers. You insert the cable and connector separately into the crimper, making sure that the wires in the cable align with the appropriate connectors. Then, by squeezing the crimper's handles, you force metal connectors through the cable's wires, making the connection between the wire and the connector.

When you crimp your own cables, you need to be sure to test them before putting them on the network. It takes only a momentary lapse to make a mistake when creating a cable, and you can waste time later trying to isolate a problem in a faulty cable.

Two other commonly used wiring tools are strippers and snips. Wire strippers come in a variety of shapes and sizes. Some are specifically designed to strip the outer sheathing from coaxial cable, and others are designed to work best with UTP cable. All strippers are designed to cleanly remove the sheathing from wire to make sure a clean contact can be made.

Many administrators do not have specialized wire strippers unless they do a lot of work with copper-based wiring. However, standard wire strippers are good things to have on hand.

Wire snips are tools designed to cleanly cut the cable. Sometimes network administrators buy cable in bulk and use wire snips to cut the cable into desired lengths. The wire strippers are then used to prepare the cable for the attachment of the connectors.

> **Note**
>
> Punchdown tools are used to attach twisted-pair network cable to connectors within a patch panel. Specifically, they connect twisted-pair wires to the insulation displacement connector (IDC).

Tone Generator and Probes

A *toner probe* is a device that can save a network installer many hours of frustration. This device has two parts: the *tone generator*, or toner, and the *tone locator*, or probe. The toner sends the tone, and at the other end of the cable, the probe receives the toner's signal. This tool makes it easier to find the beginning and end of a cable. You might hear the tone generator and tone locator referred to as the *fox and hound*.

As you might expect, the purpose of the tone probe is to generate a signal that is transmitted on the wire you are attempting to locate. At the other end, you press the probe against individual wires. When it makes contact with the wire that has the signal on it, the locator emits an audible signal or tone.

The tone locator probe is a useful device, but it does have some drawbacks. First, it often takes two people to operate one at each end of the cable. Of course, one person could just keep running back and forth, but if the cable is run over great distances, this can be a problem. Second, using the toner probe is time consuming because it must be attached to each cable independently.

> **Note**
>
> Many problems that can be discovered with a tone generator are easy to prevent by taking the time to properly label cables. If the cables are labeled at both ends, you will not need to use such a tool to locate them.

> **Note**
>
> Toner probes are specifically used to locate cables hidden in floors, ceilings, or walls and to track cables from the patch panels to their destinations.

Loopback Adapter

A number of items fall under the loopback umbrella, and all of them serve the same purpose—they allow you to test a device/configuration/connectivity component using a dummy. The most popular loopback is the address used with ping (discussed later in this chapter), but Windows also includes a *loopback adapter*, which is a dummy network card (no hardware) used for testing a virtual network environment.

Various loopback adapters—actual hardware—can be purchased and used to test Ethernet jacks, fiber jacks, and so on.

Protocol Analyzer

Protocol analyzers are used to do just that—analyze network protocols such as TCP, UDP, HTTP, and FTP. Protocol analyzers can be hardware or software based. In use, protocol analyzers help diagnose computer networking problems, alert you to unused protocols, identify unwanted or malicious network traffic, and help isolate network traffic-related problems.

Like packet sniffers, protocol analyzers capture the communication stream between systems. But unlike the sniffer, the protocol analyzer captures more than network traffic; it reads and decodes the traffic. Decoding allows the administrator to view the network communication in English. From this, administrators can get a better idea of the traffic that is flowing on the network. As soon as unwanted or damaged traffic is spotted, analyzers make it easy to isolate and repair. For example, if there is a problem with specific TCP/IP communication, such as a broadcast storm, the analyzer can find the source of the TCP/IP problem and isolate the system causing the storm. Protocol analyzers also provide many real-time trend statistics that help you justify to management the purchase of new hardware.

You can use protocol analyzers for two key reasons:

▶ **Identify protocol patterns:** By creating a historical baseline of analysis, administrators can spot trends in protocol errors. That way, when a protocol error occurs, it can be researched in the documentation to see if that error has occurred before and what was done to fix it.

▶ **Decoding information:** Capturing and decoding network traffic allows administrators to see what exactly is going on with the network at a protocol level. This helps find protocol errors as well as potential intruders.

Caution

Protocol analyzers enable administrators to examine the bandwidth that a particular protocol is using.

Media/Cable Testers

A media tester, also called a *cable tester*, defines a range of tools designed to test whether a cable properly works. Any tool that facilitates the testing of a cable can be deemed a cable tester. However, a specific tool called a *media tester* enables administrators to test a segment of cable, looking for shorts, improperly attached connectors, or other cable faults. All media testers tell you whether the cable works correctly and where the problem in the cable might be.

Generically, the phrase *line tester* can be used for any device that tests a media line. Although products are available that are Ethernet line testers, fiber line testers, and so on, most often a "line tester" is used to check telephone wiring and usually includes RJ-11 plugs as well as alligator clips.

A *cable certifier* is a type of tester that enables you to certify cabling by testing it for speed and performance to see that the implementation will live up to the ratings. Most stress and test the system based on noise and error testing. You need to know that the gigabit cable you think you have run is actually providing that speed to the network.

TDR and OTDR

A *time domain reflectometer (TDR)* is a device used to send a signal through a particular medium to check the cable's continuity. Good-quality TDRs can locate many types of cabling faults, such as a severed sheath, damaged conductors, faulty crimps, shorts, loose connectors, and more. Although network administrators will not need to use a tool such as this every day, it could significantly help in the troubleshooting process. TDRs help ensure that data sent across the network is not interrupted by poor cabling that may cause faults in data delivery.

> **Note**
>
> TDRs work at the physical layer of the OSI model, sending a signal through a length of cable, looking for cable faults.

Because the majority of network cabling is copper based, most tools designed to test cabling are designed for copper-based cabling. However, when you test fiber-optic cable, you need an optical tester.

An optical cable tester performs the same basic function as a wire media tester, but on optical media. The most common problem with an optical cable is a break in the cable that prevents the signal from reaching the other end. Due to the extended distances that can be covered with fiber-optic cables, degradation is rarely an issue in a fiber-optic LAN environment.

Ascertaining whether a signal reaches the other end of a fiber-optic cable is relatively easy, but when you determine that there is a break, the problem becomes locating the break. That's when you need a tool called an *optical time domain reflectometer (OTDR)*. By using an OTDR, you can locate how far along in the cable the break occurs. The connection on the other end of the cable might be the source of the problem, or perhaps there is a break halfway along the cable. Either way, an OTDR can pinpoint the problem.

Unless you work extensively with fiber-optic cable, you are unlikely to have an OTDR or even a fiber-optic cable tester in your toolbox. Specialized cabling contractors will have them, though, so knowing they exist is important.

You can use a *light meter* to certify and troubleshoot fiber. A light source is placed on one end and the light meter is used at the opposite end to measure loss.

Multimeter

One of the simplest cable-testing devices is a *multimeter*. By using the continuity setting, you can test for shorts in a length of coaxial cable. Or if you know the correct cable pinouts and have needlepoint probes, you can test twisted-pair cable.

A basic multimeter combines several electrical meters into a single unit that can measure voltage, current, and resistance. Advanced models can also measure temperature.

A multimeter has a display, terminals, probes, and a dial to select various measurement ranges. A digital multimeter has a numeric digital display, and an analog has a dial display. Inside a multimeter, the terminals are connected to different resistors, depending on the range selected.

Network multimeters can do much more than test electrical current:

▶ **Ping specific network devices:** A multimeter can ping and test response times of key networking equipment, such as routers, DNS servers, DHCP servers, and more.

▶ **Verify network cabling:** You can use a network multimeter to isolate cable shorts, split pairs, and other faults.

▶ **Locate and identify cable:** Quality network multimeters enable administrators to locate cables at patch panels and wall jacks using digital tones.

▶ **Documentation ability:** Multimeter results can be downloaded to a PC for inspection. Most network multimeters provide a means such as USB ports to link to a PC.

Spectrum Analyzer

A *spectrum analyzer* measures the magnitude of an input signal versus frequency within the full frequency range of the instrument and can be used for a wide range of signals. Today, they are commonly used with Wi-Fi to reveal Wi-Fi hotspots and detect wireless network access with LED visual feedback. Such devices can be configured to scan specific frequencies. When working with 802.11b/g/n/ac networks, you will most certainly require scanning for 2.4 GHz or 5 GHz RF signals.

Such devices can be used in the troubleshooting process to see where and how powerful RF signals are. Given the increase in wireless technologies, RF detectors are sure to continue to increase in popularity.

Packet Sniffers

Packet sniffers, also referred to as *packet/network analyzers*, are commonly used on networks. They are either a hardware device or software that basically eavesdrops on transmissions traveling throughout the network and can be helpful in performing *packet flow monitoring*. The packet sniffer quietly captures data and saves it to be reviewed later. Packet sniffers can also be used on the Internet to capture data traveling between computers. Internet packets often have long distances to travel, going through various servers, routers, and gateways. Anywhere along this path, packet sniffers can quietly sit and collect data. Given the capability of packet sniffers to sit and silently collect data packets, it is easy to see how they could be exploited.

> **Note**
>
> As the name implies, a packet sniffer is a program that targets packets of data transmitted over the Internet and looks for data within them. One of the dangers that disgruntled employees pose is that they are already allowed on your network and thus they have the ability to use a packet sniffer on the network. Through packet sniffing, they can intercept data far beyond what they would or should have access to.

You should use two key defenses against packet sniffers to protect your network:

▶ Use a switched network, which most today are. In a switched network, data is sent from one computer system and is directed from the switch only to intended targeted destinations. In an older network using traditional hubs, the hub does not switch the traffic to isolated users but to all users connected to the hub's ports. This shotgun approach to network transmission makes it easier to place a packet sniffer on the network to obtain data.

▶ Ensure that all sensitive data is encrypted as it travels. Ordinarily, encryption is used when data is sent over a public network such as the Internet, but it may also be necessary to encrypt sensitive data on a LAN. Encryption can be implemented in a number of ways. For example, connections to web servers can be protected using the Secure Sockets Layer (SSL) protocol and HTTPS. Communications to mail servers can also be encrypted using SSL. For public networks, the IPsec protocol can provide end-to-end encryption services.

Port Scanner

Port scanners are software-based security utilities designed to search a network host for open ports on a TCP/IP-based network. As a refresher, in a TCP/IP-based network, a system can be accessed through one of 65,535 available port numbers. Each network service is associated with a particular port.

> **Note**
>
> Chapter 3, "Addressing, Routing, and Switching," includes a list of some of the most common TCP/IP suite protocols and their port assignments.

Many of the thousands of ports are closed by default; however, many others, depending on the OS, are open by default. These are the ports that can cause trouble. Like packet sniffers, port scanners can be used by both administrators and hackers. Hackers use port scanners to try to find an open port that they can use to access a system. Port scanners are easily obtained on the Internet either for free or for a modest cost. After it is installed, the scanner probes a computer system running TCP/IP, looking for a UDP or TCP port that is open and listening.

When a port scanner is used, several port states may be reported:

► **Open/listening:** The host sent a reply indicating that a service is listening on the port. There was a response from the port.

► **Closed or denied or not listening:** No process is listening on that port. Access to this port will likely be denied.

► **Filtered or blocked:** There was no reply from the host, meaning that the port is not listening or the port is secured and filtered.

> **Note**
>
> Sometimes, an Internet service provider (ISP) takes the initiative and blocks specific traffic entering its network before the traffic reaches the ISP's customers, or after the traffic leaves the customers and before it exits the network. This is done to protect customers from well-known attacks.

Because others can potentially review the status of our ports, it is critical that administrators know which ports are open and potentially vulnerable. As mentioned, many tools and utilities are available for this. The quickest way to get an overview of the ports used by the system and their status is to issue the netstat -a command from the command line. The following is a sample of the output from the netstat -a command and active connections for a computer system:

Proto	Local Address	Foreign Address	State
TCP	0.0.0.0:135	mike-PC:0	LISTENING
TCP	0.0.0.0:10114	mike-PC:0	LISTENING
TCP	0.0.0.0:10115	mike-PC:0	LISTENING
TCP	0.0.0.0:20523	mike-PC:0	LISTENING
TCP	0.0.0.0:20943	mike-PC:0	LISTENING
TCP	0.0.0.0:49152	mike-PC:0	LISTENING
TCP	0.0.0.0:49153	mike-PC:0	LISTENING
TCP	0.0.0.0:49154	mike-PC:0	LISTENING
TCP	0.0.0.0:49155	mike-PC:0	LISTENING
TCP	0.0.0.0:49156	mike-PC:0	LISTENING
TCP	0.0.0.0:49157	mike-PC:0	LISTENING
TCP	127.0.0.1:5354	mike-PC:0	LISTENING
TCP	127.0.0.1:27015	mike-PC:0	LISTENING

```
TCP    127.0.0.1:27015           mike-PC:49187           ESTABLISHED
TCP    127.0.0.1:49187           mike-PC:27015           ESTABLISHED
TCP    192.168.0.100:49190       206.18.166.15:http      CLOSED
TCP    192.168.1.66:139          mike-PC:0               LISTENING
TCP    [::]:135                  mike-PC:0               LISTENING
TCP    [::]:445                  mike-PC:0               LISTENING
TCP    [::]:2869                 mike-PC:0               LISTENING
TCP    [::]:5357                 mike-PC:0               LISTENING
TCP    [::]:10115                mike-PC:0               LISTENING
TCP    [::]:20523                mike-PC:0               LISTENING
TCP    [::]:49152                mike-PC:0               LISTENING
TCP    [::]:49153                mike-PC:0               LISTENING
TCP    [::]:49154                mike-PC:0               LISTENING
TCP    [::]:49155                mike-PC:0               LISTENING
TCP    [::]:49156                mike-PC:0               LISTENING
TCP    [::]:49157                mike-PC:0               LISTENING
UDP    0.0.0.0:123               *:*
UDP    0.0.0.0:500               *:*
UDP    0.0.0.0:3702              *:*
UDP    0.0.0.0:3702              *:*
```

As you can see from the output, the system has many listening ports. Not all these suggest that a risk exists, but the output does let you know that there are many listening ports and that they might be vulnerable. To test for actual vulnerability, you use a port scanner. For example, you can use a free online scanner to probe the system. Many free online scanning services are available. Although a network administrator might use these free online tools out of curiosity, for better security testing, you should use a quality scanner.

Caution

Administrators use the detailed information revealed from a port scan to ensure network security. Port scans identify closed, open, and listening ports. However, port scanners also can be used by people who want to compromise security by finding open and unguarded ports.

Wi-Fi Analyzer

As more networks go wireless, you need to pay special attention to issues associated with them. *Wireless survey tools* can be used to create heat maps showing the quantity and quality of wireless network coverage in areas. They can also allow you to see access points (including rogues) and security settings. These can be used to help you design and deploy an efficient network, and they can also be used (by you or others) to find weaknesses in your existing network (often marketed for this purpose as *Wi-Fi analyzers*).

Bandwidth Speed Tester and Looking Glasses

Two types of websites that can be invaluable when it comes to networking are *speed test sites* and *looking-glass sites*. Speed test sites, as the name implies, are *bandwidth speed testers* that report the speed of the connection that you have to them and can be helpful in determining if you are getting the rate your ISP has promised.

Looking-glass sites are servers running *looking-glass (LG)* software that allow you to see routing information. The servers act as a read-only portal giving information about the backbone connection. Most of these servers will show ping information, trace (tracert/traceroute) information, and Border Gateway Protocol (BGP) information.

> ## ExamAlert
>
> Think of a looking-glass site as a graphical interface to routing-related information.

Environmental Monitors

When discussing environmental monitoring, you often refer to the temperature of the server and network equipment rooms. In general, the heat tolerance range for computer equipment is surprisingly wide. For example, consider a typical server system, which can happily operate in a range between 50°F and 93°F (10° and 33.8° Celsius). That is a spread of 43°F (23.8°C), plenty of room in a normal heated environment. But the problem is that if you maintain a computer room at either the upper or lower end of these levels, the equipment will run, but for how long, no one knows.

Although no specific figures relate to the recommended temperature of server rooms, the accepted optimum is around 70° to 72°F (21° to 22°C). At this temperature, the equipment in the room should be able to operate, and those working in the room should not get too cold. Human beings generally require a higher temperature than computer equipment, which is why placing servers in an office space with staff is not ideal.

Many people assume that the biggest problem with servers and network equipment is overheating. To some extent, this is true; servers in particular generate a great deal of heat and can overheat to the point where components fail. But this is only one heat-related issue. A more significant, and more gradual, problem is that of temperature consistency.

Heat causes components to expand, and cooling causes them to contract. Even the slightest temperature shift causes the printed circuit boards and chips to shift, and if they shift too much or too often, the chance of their becoming separated from their connections is greatly increased. This is known as *chip creep*. Keeping the heat at a moderate and constant level reduces the expansion and contraction of the boards and increases the components' reliability.

> **ExamAlert**
>
> Never wedge open a door to an environmentally controlled room, no matter how cold you get. An open door not only defeats the purpose of the controlled environment, it can damage air conditioning units.

Environmental monitors are part of how administrators keep their equipment rooms at the right temperature. The environmental monitor sits in the equipment room and constantly documents changes in room temperature and humidity. If radical changes in temperature are detected, an alert is sent to the administrator. This can sometimes occur if someone leaves a door to the server room open, the air conditioning breaks, or some piece of network hardware is producing a lot of heat. Although network environmental monitors might not often be needed, just having them installed gives administrators peace of mind.

Keeping It Cool

Fortunately, the solution to the heat problem is relatively simple. You use an air conditioning unit. The only problem is, you cannot use just any old A/C unit. Having a late-1960s window unit might be better than nothing, but you need high-quality protection.

High-quality air conditioning systems fall under the domain of industrial *heating, ventilation, and air conditioning (HVAC)* equipment. Server environment-specific air conditioning units are designed to maintain a constant temperature. High-quality units guarantee an accuracy of plus or minus 1°F. Most units have an audible alarm, but some also can communicate with management systems so that the server room temperature can be monitored remotely. Although the icy blast of a server room air conditioning system might not be welcomed by those who have to work in it for an extended period of time, the discomfort is far outweighed by the benefit to the server equipment.

Calculating the correct size and type of air conditioning unit can be a tricky proposition. Air conditioning systems are rated on how many cubic feet they can cool. Using this figure, and estimating the increase in temperature caused by the hardware in the room, you will have the basic information you need to choose an A/C unit. However, the calculation should take into account potential future growth. In some cases, a standby A/C unit is also installed. Whether such a system is required depends on how much fault tolerance you need and are willing to pay for.

Cram Quiz

1. While you were away, an air conditioning unit malfunctioned in a server room, and some equipment overheated. Which of the following would have alerted you to the problem?

   ○ **A.** Multimeter

   ○ **B.** Environmental monitor

   ○ **C.** TDR

   ○ **D.** OTDR

2. What tool would you use when working with an IDC?

   ○ **A.** Wire crimper

   ○ **B.** Media tester

   ○ **C.** OTDR

   ○ **D.** Punchdown tool

3. As a network administrator, you work in a wiring closet where none of the cables have been labeled. Which of the following tools are you most likely to use to locate the physical ends of the cable?

   ○ **A.** Toner probe

   ○ **B.** Wire crimper

   ○ **C.** Punchdown tool

   ○ **D.** `ping`

4. You are installing a new system into an existing star network, and you need a cable that is 45 feet long. Your local vendor does not stock cables of this length, so you are forced to make your own. Which of the following tools do you need to complete the task?

   ○ **A.** Optical tester

   ○ **B.** Punchdown tool

   ○ **C.** Crimper

   ○ **D.** UTP splicer

Cram Quiz Answers

1. **B.** Environmental monitors are used in server and network equipment rooms to ensure that the temperature does not fluctuate too greatly. In the case of a failed air conditioner, the administrator is alerted to the drastic changes in temperature. Multimeters, TDRs, and OTDRs are used to work with copper-based media.

2. **D.** You use a punchdown tool when working with an IDC. All the other tools are associated with making and troubleshooting cables; they are not associated with IDCs.

3. **A.** The toner probe tool, along with the tone locator, can be used to trace cables. Crimpers and punchdown tools are not used to locate a cable. The ping utility would be of no help in this situation.

4. **C.** When attaching RJ-45 connectors to UTP cables, the wire crimper is the tool you use. None of the other tools listed are used in the construction of UTP cable.

Command-Line Troubleshooting Tools

▶ Given a scenario, use the appropriate tool.

CramSaver

If you can correctly answer these questions before going through this section, save time by skimming the Exam Alerts in this section and then completing the Cram Quiz at the end of the section.

1. What TCP/IP command can be used to troubleshoot DNS problems?

2. What is the Linux, Mac OS, and UNIX equivalent of the `ipconfig` command?

3. What utility is the part of the TCP/IP suite and has the function of resolving IP addresses to MAC addresses?

Answers

1. The `nslookup` command is a TCP/IP diagnostic tool used to troubleshoot DNS problems. On Linux, UNIX, and Mac OS systems, you can also use the `dig` command for the same purpose.

2. The `ifconfig` command is the Linux, Mac OS, and UNIX equivalent of the `ipconfig` command.

3. The function of `arp` is to resolve IP addresses to MAC addresses.

ExamAlert

Remember that this objective begins with "Given a scenario." That means that you may receive a drag and drop, matching, or "live OS" scenario where you have to click through to complete a specific objective-based task.

For anyone working with TCP/IP networks, troubleshooting connectivity is something that must be done. This section describes the tools used in the troubleshooting process and identifies scenarios in which they can be used.

You can use many utilities when troubleshooting TCP/IP. Although the utilities available vary from platform to platform, the functionality between platforms is quite similar. Table 11.1 lists the TCP/IP troubleshooting tools covered on the Network+ exam, along with their purpose.

TABLE 11.1 **Common TCP/IP Troubleshooting Tools and Their Purposes**

Tool	Description
`tracert/traceroute`	Used to track the path a packet takes as it travels across a network. `tracert` is used on Windows systems; `traceroute` is used on UNIX, Linux, and Mac OS systems.
`tracert -6` `traceroute6` `traceroute -6`	Performs the same function as `tracert/traceroute`, but using the IPv6 protocol in place of IPv4.
`ping`	Used to test connectivity between two devices on a network with IPv4.
`ping6/ping -6`	Used to test connectivity between two devices on a network using the IPv6 protocol in place of IPv4.
`pathping`	A Windows-based utility that combines the functionality of `ping` and `tracert` to test connectivity between two devices on a network.
`arp`	Used to view and work with the IP address to MAC address resolution cache.
`arp ping`	Uses ARP to test connectivity between systems rather than using Internet Control Message Protocol (ICMP), as done with a regular `ping`.
`netstat`	Used to view the current TCP/IP connections on a system.
`iptables`	Used to configure Linux kernel firewall.
`ipconfig`	Used to view and renew TCP/IP configuration on a Windows system.
`ifconfig`	Used to view TCP/IP configuration on a UNIX, Linux, or Mac OS system.
`nslookup/dig`	Used to perform manual DNS lookups. `nslookup` can be used on Windows, UNIX, Mac OS, and Linux systems. `dig` can be used on UNIX, Linux, and Mac OS systems.
`tcpdump`	A Linux-based packet analyzer.
`route`	Used to view and configure the routes in the routing table.
`nmap`	A popular vulnerability scanner.

The following sections look in more detail at these utilities and the output they produce.

> **Note**
>
> Many of the utilities discussed in this chapter have a help facility that you can access by typing the command followed by /? or -?. On a Windows system, for example, you can get help on the `netstat` utility by typing `netstat /?`. Sometimes, using a utility with an invalid switch also brings up the help screen.

> **ExamAlert**
>
> Be prepared to identify what tool to use in a given scenario. Remember, there might be more than one tool that could be used. You will be expected to pick the best one for the situation described.

You will be asked to identify the output from a command, and you should be able to interpret the information provided by the command. In a performance-based question, you may be asked to enter the appropriate command for a given scenario.

The Trace Route Utility (`tracert/traceroute`)

The trace route utility does exactly what its name implies—it traces the route between two hosts. It does this by using ICMP echo packets to report information at every step in the journey. Each of the common network operating systems provides a trace route utility, but the name of the command and the output vary slightly on each. However, for the purposes of the Network+ exam, you should not concern yourself with the minor differences in the output format. Table 11.2 shows the `traceroute` command syntax used in various operating systems.

> **Note**
>
> The phrase *trace route utility* is used in this section to refer generically to the various route-tracing applications available on common operating systems. In a live environment, you should become familiar with the version of the tool used on the operating systems you are working with.

TABLE 11.2 **Trace Route Utility Commands**

Operating System	Trace Route Command Syntax
Windows systems	`tracert IP address`
	`tracert -6 IP address`
Linux/UNIX/Mac OS	`traceroute IP address`
	`traceroute6 IP address`
	`traceroute -6 IP address`

ExamAlert

Be prepared to identify the IP tracing command syntax used with various operating systems for the exam. Review Table 11.2 for this information.

`traceroute` provides a lot of useful information, including the IP address of every router connection it passes through and, in many cases, the name of the router (although this depends on the router's configuration). `traceroute` also reports the length, in milliseconds, of the round-trip the packet made from the source location to the router and back. This information can help identify where network bottlenecks or breakdowns might be. The following is an example of a successful `tracert` command on a Windows system:

```
C:\> tracert 24.7.70.37

Tracing route to c1-p4.sttlwal.home.net [24.7.70.37]
 over a maximum of 30 hops:
 1 30 ms 20 ms 20 ms 24.67.184.1
 2 20 ms 20 ms 30 ms rd1ht-ge3-0.ok.shawcable.net
 [24.67.224.7]
 3 50 ms 30 ms 30 ms rc1wh-atm0-2-1.vc.shawcable.net
 [204.209.214.193]
 4 50 ms 30 ms 30 ms rc2wh-pos15-0.vc.shawcable.net
 [204.209.214.90]
 5 30 ms 40 ms 30 ms rc2wt-pos2-0.wa.shawcable.net
 [66.163.76.37]
 6 30 ms 40 ms 30 ms c1-pos6-3.sttlwal.home.net [24.7.70.37]
Trace complete.
```

Similar to the other common operating systems covered on the Network+ exam, the `tracert` display on a Windows-based system includes several columns of information. The first column represents the hop number. You may recall that *hop* is the term used to describe a step in the path a packet takes as it crosses the network. The next three columns indicate the round-trip time, in milliseconds, that a packet takes in its attempts to reach the destination. The last column is the hostname and the IP address of the responding device.

However, not all trace route attempts are successful. The following is the output from a `tracert` command on a Windows system that does not manage to get to the remote host:

```
C:\> tracert comptia.org

Tracing route to comptia.org [216.119.103.72]
over a maximum of 30 hops:
 1 27 ms 28 ms 14 ms 24.67.179.1
 2 55 ms 13 ms 14 ms rd1ht-ge3-0.ok.shawcable.net
[24.67.224.7]
 3 27 ms 27 ms 28 ms rc1wh-atm0-2-1.shawcable.net
[204.209.214.19]
 4 28 ms 41 ms 27 ms rc1wt-pos2-0.wa.shawcable.net
[66.163.76.65]
 5 28 ms 41 ms 27 ms rc2wt-pos1-0.wa.shawcable.net
[66.163.68.2]
 6 41 ms 55 ms 41 ms c1-pos6-3.sttlwa1.home.net
[24.7.70.37]
 7 54 ms 42 ms 27 ms home-gw.st6wa.ip.att.net
[192.205.32.249]
 8 * * * Request timed out.
 9 * * * Request timed out.
10 * * * Request timed out.
11 * * * Request timed out.
12 * * * Request timed out.
13 * * * Request timed out.
14 * * * Request timed out.
15 * * * Request timed out.
```

In this example, the trace route request gets to only the seventh hop, at which point it fails. This failure indicates that the problem lies on the far side of the device in step 7 or on the near side of the device in step 8. In other words, the device at step 7 is functioning but might not make the next hop. The cause of the problem could be a range of things, such as an error in the routing table or a faulty connection. Alternatively, the seventh device might be operating at 100%, but device 8 might not be functioning at all. In any case, you can isolate the problem to just one or two devices.

> **Note**
>
> In some cases, the owner of a router might configure it to not return ICMP traffic like that generated by `ping` or `traceroute`. If this is the case, the `ping` or `traceroute` will fail just as if the router did not exist or was not operating.

The trace route utility can also help you isolate a heavily congested network. In the following example, the trace route packets fail in the midst of the `tracert` from a Windows system, but subsequently they continue. This behavior can be an indicator of network congestion:

```
C:\> tracert comptia.org

Tracing route to comptia.org [216.119.103.72]over a maximum of 30
hops:
 1 96 ms 96 ms 55 ms 24.67.179.1
 2 14 ms 13 ms 28 ms rd1ht-ge3-0.ok.shawcable.net
[24.67.224.7]
 3 28 ms 27 ms 41 ms rc1wh-atm0-2-1.shawcable.net
[204.209.214.19]
 4 28 ms 41 ms 27 ms rc1wt-pos2-0.wa.shawcable.net
[66.163.76.65]
 5 41 ms 27 ms 27 ms rc2wt-pos1-0.wa.shawcable.net
[66.163.68.2]
 6 55 ms 41 ms 27 ms c1-pos6-3.sttlwa1.home.net [24.7.70.37]
 7 54 ms 42 ms 27 ms home-gw.st6wa.ip.att.net
[192.205.32.249]
 8 55 ms 41 ms 28 ms gbr3-p40.st6wa.ip.att.net
[12.123.44.130]
 9 * * * Request timed out.
10 * * * Request timed out.
11 * * * Request timed out.
12 * * * Request timed out.
13 69 ms 68 ms 69 ms gbr2-p20.sd2ca.ip.att.net
[12.122.11.254]
14 55 ms 68 ms 69 ms gbr1-p60.sd2ca.ip.att.net
[12.122.1.109]
15 82 ms 69 ms 82 ms gbr1-p30.phmaz.ip.att.net
[12.122.2.142]
16 68 ms 69 ms 82 ms gar2-p360.phmaz.ip.att.net
[12.123.142.45]
17 110 ms 96 ms 96 ms 12.125.99.70
18 124 ms 96 ms 96 ms light.crystaltech.com [216.119.107.1]
19 82 ms 96 ms 96 ms 216.119.103.72
Trace complete.
```

Generally speaking, trace route utilities enable you to identify the location of a problem in the connectivity between two devices. After you determine this location, you might need to use a utility such as ping to continue trouble-shooting. In many cases, as in the examples provided in this chapter, the routers might be on a network such as the Internet and therefore not within your control. In that case, you can do little except inform your ISP of the problem.

When dealing with IPv6, the same tools exist, but are followed with -6; so, tracert becomes tracert -6, and traceroute becomes traceroute -6.

ping

Most network administrators are familiar with the ping utility and are likely to use it on an almost daily basis. The basic function of the ping command is to test the connectivity between the two devices on a network. All the command is designed to do is determine whether the two computers can see each other and to notify you of how long the round-trip takes to complete.

Although ping is most often used on its own, a number of switches can be used to assist in the troubleshooting process. Table 11.3 shows some of the commonly used switches with ping on a Windows system.

TABLE 11.3 **ping Command Switches**

Option	Description
ping -t	Pings a device on the network until stopped
ping -a	Resolves addresses to hostnames
ping -n count	Specifies the number of echo requests to send
ping -r count	Records the route for count hops
ping -s count	Time stamp for count hops
ping -w timeout	Timeout in milliseconds to wait for each reply
ping -6 or ping6	Pings a device on the network using IPv6 instead of IPv4

ExamAlert

You will likely be asked about ping, its switches used, and how ping can be used in a troubleshooting scenario.

---

ping works by sending ICMP echo request messages to another device on the network. If the other device on the network hears the ping request, it automatically responds with an ICMP echo reply. By default, the ping command on a

Windows-based system sends four data packets; however, using the -t switch, a continuous stream of ping requests can be sent.

ping is perhaps the most widely used of all network tools; it is primarily used to verify connectivity between two network devices. On a good day, the results from the ping command are successful, and the sending device receives a reply from the remote device. Not all ping results are that successful. To use ping effectively, you must interpret the results of a failed ping command.

The Destination Host Unreachable Message

The "Destination Host Unreachable" error message means that a route to the destination computer system cannot be found. To remedy this problem, you might need to examine the routing information on the local host to confirm that the local host is correctly configured, or you might need to make sure that the default gateway information is correct. The following is an example of a ping failure that gives the "Destination Host Unreachable" message:

```
Pinging 24.67.54.233 with 32 bytes of data:
Destination host unreachable.
Destination host unreachable.
Destination host unreachable.
Destination host unreachable.
Ping statistics for 24.67.54.233:
  Packets: Sent = 4, Received = 0, Lost = 4 (100% loss),
Approximate round trip times in milli-seconds:
  Minimum = 0ms, Maximum = 0ms, Average = 0ms
```

The Request Timed Out Message

The "Request Timed Out" error message is common when you use the ping command. Essentially, this error message indicates that your host did not receive the ping message back from the destination device within the designated time period. Assuming that the network connectivity is okay on your system, this typically indicates that the destination device is not connected to the network, is powered off, or is not correctly configured. It could also mean that some intermediate device is not operating correctly. In some rare cases, it can also indicate that the network has so much congestion that timely delivery of the ping message could not be completed. It might also mean that the ping is being sent to an invalid IP address or that the system is not on the same network as the remote host, and an intermediary device is not correctly configured. In any of these cases, the failed ping should initiate a troubleshooting process that might involve other tools, manual inspection, and possibly reconfiguration. The following example shows the output from a ping to an invalid IP address:

```
C:\> ping 169.76.54.3

Pinging 169.76.54.3 with 32 bytes of data:

Request timed out.
Request timed out.
Request timed out.
Request timed out.

Ping statistics for 169.76.54.3:
 Packets: Sent = 4, Received = 0, Lost = 4 (100%
Approximate round trip times in milli-seconds:
 Minimum = 0ms, Maximum = 0ms, Average = 0ms
```

During the ping request, you might receive some replies from the remote host that are intermixed with "Request Timed Out" errors. This is often the result of a congested network. An example follows; notice that this example, which was run on a Windows system, uses the -t switch to generate continuous pings:

```
C:\> ping -t 24.67.184.65

Pinging 24.67.184.65 with 32 bytes of data:

Reply from 24.67.184.65: bytes=32 time=55ms TTL=127
Reply from 24.67.184.65: bytes=32 time=54ms TTL=127
Reply from 24.67.184.65: bytes=32 time=27ms TTL=127
Request timed out.
Request timed out.
Request timed out.
Reply from 24.67.184.65: bytes=32 time=69ms TTL=127
Reply from 24.67.184.65: bytes=32 time=28ms TTL=127
Reply from 24.67.184.65: bytes=32 time=28ms TTL=127
Reply from 24.67.184.65: bytes=32 time=68ms TTL=127
Reply from 24.67.184.65: bytes=32 time=41ms TTL=127

Ping statistics for 24.67.184.65:
 Packets: Sent = 11, Received = 8, Lost = 3 (27% loss),
Approximate round trip times in milli-seconds:
 Minimum = 27ms, Maximum = 69ms, Average = 33ms
```

In this example, three packets were lost. If this continued on your network, you would need to troubleshoot to find out why packets were dropped.

The Unknown Host Message

The "Unknown Host" error message is generated when the hostname of the destination computer cannot be resolved. This error usually occurs when you `ping` an incorrect hostname, as shown in the following example, or try to use `ping` with a hostname when hostname resolution (via DNS or a HOSTS text file) is not configured:

```
C:\> ping www.comptia.ca

Unknown host www.comptia.ca
```

If the ping fails, you need to verify that the ping is sent to the correct remote host. If it is, and if name resolution is configured, you have to dig a little more to find the problem. This error might indicate a problem with the name resolution process, and you might need to verify that the DNS or WINS server is available. Other commands, such as `nslookup` or `dig`, can help in this process.

The Expired TTL Message

The Time To Live (TTL) is a key consideration in understanding the `ping` command. The function of the TTL is to prevent circular routing, which occurs when a ping request keeps looping through a series of hosts. The TTL counts each hop along the way toward its destination device. Each time it counts one hop, the hop is subtracted from the TTL. If the TTL reaches 0, it has expired, and you get a message like the following:

```
Reply from 24.67.180.1: TTL expired in transit
```

If the TTL is exceeded with `ping`, you might have a routing problem on the network. You can modify the TTL for `ping` on a Windows system by using the `ping -i` command.

Troubleshooting with `ping`

Although `ping` does not completely isolate problems, you can use it to help identify where a problem lies. When troubleshooting with `ping`, follow these steps:

1. Ping the IP address of your local loopback using the command `ping 127.0.0.1`. If this command is successful, you know that the TCP/IP protocol suite is installed correctly on your system and is functioning. If you cannot ping the local loopback adapter, TCP/IP might need to be reloaded or reconfigured on the machine you are using.

> **ExamAlert**
>
> The loopback is a special function within the TCP/IP protocol stack that is supplied for troubleshooting purposes. The Class A IP address 127.*x.x.x* is reserved for the IPv4 loopback. Although convention dictates that you use 127.0.0.1, you can use any address in the 127.*x.x.x* range, except for the network number itself (127.0.0.0) and the broadcast address (127.255.255.255). You can also ping by using the default hostname for the local system, which is called localhost (for example, `ping localhost`). The same function can be performed in IPv6 by using the address ::1.

2. Ping the assigned IP address of your local network interface card (NIC). If the ping is successful, you know that your NIC is functioning on the network and has TCP/IP correctly installed. If you cannot ping the local NIC, TCP/IP might not be correctly bound to the NIC, or the NIC drivers might be improperly installed.

3. Ping the IP address of another known good system on your local network. By doing so, you can determine whether the computer you are using can see other computers on the network. If you can ping other devices on your local network, you have network connectivity.

   If you cannot ping other devices on your local network, but you could ping the IP address of your system, you might not be connected to the network correctly.

4. After you confirm that you have network connectivity for the local network, you can verify connectivity to a remote network by sending a ping to the IP address of the default gateway.

5. If you can ping the default gateway, you can verify remote connectivity by sending a ping to the IP address of a system on a remote network.

> **ExamAlert**
>
> You might be asked to relate the correct procedure for using `ping` for a connectivity problem. A performance-based question may ask you to implement the `ping` command to test for connectivity.

Using just the `ping` command in these steps, you can confirm network connectivity on not only the local network, but also on a remote network. The whole process requires as much time as it takes to enter the command, and you can do it all from a single location.

If you are an optimistic person, you can perform step 5 first. If that works, all the other steps will also work, saving you the need to test them. If your step 5 trial fails, you can go to step 1 and start the troubleshooting process from the beginning.

> **Note**
>
> All but one of the `ping` examples used in this section show the `ping` command using the IP address of the remote host. It is also possible to `ping` the Domain Name Service (DNS) name of the remote host (for example, `ping www.comptia.org`, `ping server1`). However, you can do this only if your network uses a DNS server. On a Windows-based network, you can also `ping` by using the Network Basic Input/ Output System (NetBIOS) computer name.

When dealing with IPv6, the same tools exist, but are followed with 6 or -6; so, `ping` becomes `ping6` or `ping -6`.

`pathping`

As great as `ping` is, at times you might wish for the additional information and functionality provided by `tracert`. To address that need on a Windows system, you can use `pathping`. It combines the features of the other two tools into one.

ARP

Address Resolution Protocol (ARP) is used to resolve IP addresses to MAC addresses. This is significant because on a network, devices find each other using the IP address, but communication between devices requires the MAC address.

> **ExamAlert**
>
> Remember that the function of ARP is to resolve IP addresses to Layer 2 or MAC addresses.

When a computer wants to send data to another computer on the network, it must know the MAC address (physical address) of the destination system. To discover this information, ARP sends out a discovery packet to obtain the MAC address. When the destination computer is found, it sends its MAC address to the sending computer. The ARP-resolved MAC addresses are stored temporarily on a computer system in the ARP cache. Inside this ARP cache is a list of matching MAC and IP addresses. This ARP cache is checked before a discovery packet is sent to the network to determine whether there is an existing entry.

Entries in the ARP cache are periodically flushed so that the cache does not fill up with unused entries. The following code shows an example of the arp command with the output from a Windows system:

```
C:\> arp -a

Interface: 24.67.179.22 on Interface 0x3
 Internet Address Physical Address Type
 24.67.179.1 00-00-77-93-d8-3d dynamic
```

As you might notice, the type is listed as dynamic. Entries in the ARP cache can be added statically or dynamically. Static entries are added manually and do not expire. The dynamic entries are added automatically when the system accesses another on the network.

As with other command-line utilities, several switches are available for the arp command. Table 11.4 shows the available switches for Windows-based systems.

TABLE 11.4 **arp Switches**

Switch	Description
-a or -g	Displays both the IP and MAC addresses and whether they are dynamic or static entries
inet_addr	Specifies a specific Internet address
-N if_addr	Displays the ARP entries for a specified network interface
eth_addr	Specifies a MAC address
if_addr	Specifies an Internet address
-d	Deletes an entry from the ARP cache
-s	Adds a static permanent address to the ARP cache

arp ping

Earlier in this chapter we talked about the ping command and how it is used to test connectivity between devices on a network. Using the ping command is often an administrator's first step to test connectivity between network devices. If the ping fails, it is assumed that the device you are pinging is offline. But this may not always be the case.

Most companies now use firewalls or other security measures that may block Internet Control Message Protocol (ICMP) requests. This means that a ping request will not work. Blocking ICMP is a security measure; if a would-be hacker cannot hit the target, he may not attack the host.

If ICMP is blocked, you have still another option to test connectivity with a device on the network: the `arp ping`. As mentioned, the ARP utility is used to resolve IP addresses to MAC addresses. The `arp ping` utility does not use the ICMP protocol to test connectivity like `ping` does; rather, it uses the ARP protocol. However, ARP is not routable, and the `arp ping` cannot be routed to work over separate networks. The `arp ping` works only on the local subnet.

Just like with a regular `ping`, an `arp ping` specifies an IP address; however, instead of returning regular ping results, the `arp ping` responds with the MAC address and name of the computer system. So, when a regular `ping` using ICMP fails to locate a system, the `arp ping` uses a different method to find the system. With `arp ping`, you can directly ping a MAC address. From this, you can determine whether duplicate IP addresses are used and, as mentioned, determine whether a system is responding.

`arp ping` is not built in to Windows, but you can download a number of programs that allow you to ping using ARP. Linux, however, has an `arp ping` utility ready to use.

The `netstat` Command

The `netstat` command displays the protocol statistics and current TCP/IP connections on the local system. Used without any switches, the `netstat` command shows the active connections for all outbound TCP/IP connections. In addition, several switches are available that change the type of information `netstat` displays. Table 11.5 shows the various switches available for the `netstat` utility.

TABLE 11.5 `netstat` **Switches**

Switch	Description
-a	Displays the current connections and listening ports
-e	Displays Ethernet statistics
-n	Lists addresses and port numbers in numeric form
-p	Shows connections for the specified protocol
-r	Shows the routing table
-s	Lists per-protocol statistics
interval	Specifies how long to wait before redisplaying statistics

ExamAlert

You can use the `netstat` and `route print` commands to show the routing table on a local or remote system.

The `netstat` utility is used to show the port activity for both TCP and UDP connections, showing the inbound and outbound connections. When used without switches, the `netstat` utility has four information headings.

▶ **Proto:** Lists the protocol being used, either UDP or TCP

▶ **Local address:** Specifies the local address and port being used

▶ **Foreign address:** Identifies the destination address and port being used

▶ **State:** Specifies whether the connection is established

In its default use, the `netstat` command shows outbound connections that have been established by TCP. The following shows sample output from a `netstat` command without using any switches:

```
C:\> netstat

Active Connections
 Proto Local Address Foreign Address State
 TCP laptop:2848 MEDIASERVICES1:1755 ESTABLISHED
 TCP laptop:1833 www.dollarhost.com:80 ESTABLISHED
 TCP laptop:2858 194.70.58.241:80 ESTABLISHED
 TCP laptop:2860 194.70.58.241:80 ESTABLISHED
 TCP laptop:2354 www.dollarhost.com:80 ESTABLISHED
 TCP laptop:2361 www.dollarhost.com:80 ESTABLISHED
 TCP laptop:1114 www.dollarhost.com:80 ESTABLISHED
 TCP laptop:1959 www.dollarhost.com:80 ESTABLISHED
 TCP laptop:1960 www.dollarhost.com:80 ESTABLISHED
```

```
TCP laptop:1963 www.dollarhost.com:80 ESTABLISHED
TCP laptop:2870 localhost:8431 TIME_WAIT
TCP laptop:8431 localhost:2862 TIME_WAIT
TCP laptop:8431 localhost:2863 TIME_WAIT
TCP laptop:8431 localhost:2867 TIME_WAIT
TCP laptop:8431 localhost:2872 TIME_WAIT
```

As with any other command-line utility, the `netstat` utility has a number of switches. The following sections briefly explain the switches and give sample output from each.

netstat -e

The `netstat -e` command shows the activity for the NIC and displays the number of packets that have been both sent and received. Here's an example:

```
C:\WINDOWS\Desktop> netstat -e

Interface Statistics

  Received Sent

Bytes 17412385 40237510
Unicast packets 79129 85055
Non-unicast packets 693 254
Discards 0 0
Errors 0 0
Unknown protocols 306
```

As you can see, the `netstat -e` command shows more than just the packets that have been sent and received:

▶ **Bytes:** The number of bytes that the NIC has sent or received since the computer was turned on.

▶ **Unicast packets:** Packets sent and received directly by this interface.

▶ **Nonunicast packets:** Broadcast or multicast packets that the NIC picked up.

▶ **Discards:** The number of packets rejected by the NIC, perhaps because they were damaged.

▶ **Errors:** The errors that occurred during either the sending or receiving process. As you would expect, this column should be a low number. If it is not, this could indicate a problem with the NIC.

▶ **Unknown protocols:** The number of packets that the system could not recognize.

netstat -a

The netstat -a command displays statistics for both Transport Control
Protocol (TCP) and User Datagram Protocol (UDP). Here is an example of
the netstat -a command:

```
C:\WINDOWS\Desktop> netstat -a

Active Connections

Proto Local Address Foreign Address State
TCP laptop:1027 LAPTOP:0 LISTENING
TCP laptop:1030 LAPTOP:0 LISTENING
TCP laptop:1035 LAPTOP:0 LISTENING
TCP laptop:50000 LAPTOP:0 LISTENING
TCP laptop:5000 LAPTOP:0 LISTENING
TCP laptop:1035 msgr-ns41.msgr.hotmail.com:1863 ESTABLISHED
TCP laptop:nbsession LAPTOP:0 LISTENING
TCP laptop:1027 localhost:50000 ESTABLISHED
TCP laptop:50000 localhost:1027 ESTABLISHED
UDP laptop:1900 *:*
UDP laptop:nbname *:*
UDP laptop:nbdatagram *:*
UDP laptop:1547 *:*
UDP laptop:1038 *:*
UDP laptop:1828 *:*
UDP laptop:3366 *:*
```

As you can see, the output includes four columns, which show the protocol, the
local address, the foreign address, and the port's state. The TCP connections
show the local and foreign destination addresses and the connection's current
state. UDP, however, is a little different. It does not list a state status because, as
mentioned throughout this book, UDP is a connectionless protocol and does
not establish connections. The following list further explains the information
provided by the netstat -a command:

▶ **Proto:** The protocol used by the connection.

▶ **Local address:** The IP address of the local computer system and the port
number it is using. If the entry in the local address field is an asterisk (*),
the port has not yet been established.

▶ **Foreign address:** The IP address of a remote computer system and the
associated port. When a port has not been established, as with the UDP
connections, *:* appears in the column.

▶ **State:** The current state of the TCP connection. Possible states include
established, listening, closed, and waiting.

netstat -r

The netstat -r command is often used to view a system's routing table.
A system uses a routing table to determine routing information for TCP/IP
traffic. The following is an example of the netstat -r command from a
Windows system:

```
C:\WINDOWS\Desktop> netstat -r

Route table

==========================================================================
==========================================================================
Active Routes:
Network Destination Netmask Gateway Interface Metric
 0.0.0.0 0.0.0.0 24.67.179.1 24.67.179.22 1
 24.67.179.0 255.255.255.0 24.67.179.22 24.67.179.22 1
 24.67.179.22 255.255.255.255 127.0.0.1 127.0.0.1 1
 24.255.255.255 255.255.255.255 24.67.179.22 24.67.179.22 1
 127.0.0.0 255.0.0.0 127.0.0.1 127.0.0.1 1
 224.0.0.0 224.0.0.0 24.67.179.22 24.67.179.22 1
255.255.255.255 255.255.255.255 24.67.179.22 2 1
Default Gateway: 24.67.179.1
==========================================================================
Persistent Routes:
 None
```

Caution

The netstat -r command output shows the same information as the output from
the route print command.

netstat -s

The netstat -s command displays a number of statistics related to the TCP/IP
protocol suite. Understanding the purpose of every field in the output is
beyond the scope of the Network+ exam, but for your reference, sample output
from the netstat -s command is shown here:

```
C:\> netstat -s

IP Statistics

 Packets Received = 389938
 Received Header Errors = 0
 Received Address Errors = 1876
 Datagrams Forwarded = 498
 Unknown Protocols Received = 0
```

```
Received Packets Discarded = 0
Received Packets Delivered = 387566
Output Requests = 397334
Routing Discards = 0
Discarded Output Packets = 0
Output Packet No Route = 916
Reassembly Required = 0
Reassembly Successful = 0
Reassembly Failures = 0
Datagrams Successfully Fragmented = 0
Datagrams Failing Fragmentation = 0
Fragments Created = 0
```

```
ICMP Statistics

  Received Sent
  Messages 40641 41111
  Errors 0 0
  Destination Unreachable 223 680
  Time Exceeded 24 0
  Parameter Problems 0 0
  Source Quenches 0 0
  Redirects 0 38
  Echos 20245 20148
  Echo Replies 20149 20245
  Timestamps 0 0
  Timestamp Replies 0 0
  Address Masks 0 0
  Address Mask Replies 0 0
```

```
TCP Statistics

  Active Opens = 13538
  Passive Opens = 23132
  Failed Connection Attempts = 9259
  Reset Connections = 254
  Current Connections = 15
  Segments Received = 330242
  Segments Sent = 326935
  Segments Retransmitted = 18851
```

```
UDP Statistics

  Datagrams Received = 20402
  No Ports = 20594
  Receive Errors = 0
  Datagrams Sent = 10217
```

iptables

The iptables utility is used to configure the firewall in Linux. It requires elevated/administrative/root privileges to run, and the executable itself is installed in /usr/sbin/iptables.

ipconfig

The ipconfig command is a technician's best friend when it comes to viewing the TCP/IP configuration of a Windows system. Used on its own, the ipconfig command shows basic information, such as the name of the local network interface, the IP address, the subnet mask, and the default gateway. Combined with the /all switch, it shows a detailed set of information, as shown in the following example:

```
C:\> ipconfig /all

Windows IP Configuration
  Host Name . . . . . . . . . . . . : server
  Primary Dns Suffix . . . . . . . :
  Node Type . . . . . . . . . . . . : Hybrid
  IP Routing Enabled. . . . . . . . : No
  WINS Proxy Enabled. . . . . . . . : No
  DNS Suffix Search List. . . . . . : tampabay.rr.com
Ethernet adapter Local Area Connection:
  Connection-specific DNS Suffix  . : tampabay.rr.com
  Description . . . . . . . . . . . : Broadcom NetLink (TM) Gigabit
Ethernet
  Physical Address. . . . . . . . . : 00-25-64-8C-9E-BF
  DHCP Enabled. . . . . . . . . . . : Yes
  Autoconfiguration Enabled . . . . : Yes
  Link-local IPv6 Address . . . . . : fe80::51b9:996e:9fac:7715%10
(Preferred)
  IPv4 Address. . . . . . . . . . . : 192.168.1.119(Preferred)
  Subnet Mask . . . . . . . . . . . : 255.255.255.0
  Lease Obtained. . . . . . . . . . : Wednesday, January 28, 2018
6:00:54 AM
  Lease Expires . . . . . . . . . . : Thursday, January 29, 2018
6:00:54 AM
  Default Gateway . . . . . . . . . : 192.168.1.1
  DHCP Server . . . . . . . . . . . : 192.168.1.1
  DHCPv6 IAID . . . . . . . . . . . : 234890596
  DHCPv6 Client DUID. . . . . . . . :
00-01-00-01-13-2A-5B-37-00-25-64-8C-9E-BF
  DNS Servers . . . . . . . . . . . : 192.168.1.1
  NetBIOS over Tcpip. . . . . . . . : Enabled
  Connection-specific DNS Suffix Search List :
  tampabay.rr.com
```

As you can imagine, you can use the output from the `ipconfig /all` command in a massive range of troubleshooting scenarios. Table 11.6 lists some of the most common troubleshooting symptoms, along with where to look for clues about solving them in the `ipconfig /all` output.

> **Note**
>
> When looking at `ipconfig` information, you should be sure that all information is present and correct. For example, a missing or incorrect default gateway parameter limits communication to the local segment.

TABLE 11.6 **Common Troubleshooting Symptoms that** `ipconfig` **Can Help Solve**

Symptom	Field to Check in the Output
The user cannot connect to any other system.	Ensure that the TCP/IP address and subnet mask are correct. If the network uses DHCP, ensure that DHCP is enabled.
The user can connect to another on the same subnet but cannot connect to a remote system.	Ensure the default gateway is configured correctly.
The user is unable to browse the Internet.	Ensure the DNS server parameters are correctly configured.
The user cannot browse across remote subnets.	Ensure the WINS or DNS server parameters are correctly configured, if applicable.

> **ExamAlert**
>
> You should be prepared to identify the output from an `ipconfig` command in relationship to a troubleshooting scenario.

Using the `/all` switch might be the most popular, but there are a few others. These include the switches listed in Table 11.7.

> **ExamAlert**
>
> `ipconfig` and its associated switches are widely used by network administrators and therefore should be expected to make an appearance on the exam.

TABLE 11.7 `ipconfig` **Switches**

Switch	Description
?	Displays the `ipconfig` help screen
/all	Displays additional IP configuration information
/release	Releases the IPv4 address of the specified adapter
/release6	Releases the IPv6 address of the specified adapter
/renew	Renews the IPv4 address of a specified adapter
/renew6	Renews the IPv6 address of a specified adapter
/flushdns	Purges the DNS cache
/registerdns	Refreshes the DHCP lease and reregisters the DNS names
/displaydns	Used to display the information in the DNS cache

> **Tip**
>
> The `ipconfig /release` and `ipconfig /renew` commands work only when your system is using DHCP.

> **ExamAlert**
>
> The `ipconfig` command on the Windows client and Windows Server operating systems provides additional switches and functionality geared toward Active Directory and Dynamic DNS. You do not need to be concerned with these switches for the exam, but you can view information on them by using the `ipconfig /?` command.

ifconfig

ifconfig performs the same function as `ipconfig`, but on a Linux, UNIX, or Mac OS system. Because Linux relies more heavily on command-line utilities than Windows, the Linux and UNIX version of `ifconfig` provides much more functionality than `ipconfig`. On a Linux or UNIX system, you can get information about the usage of the `ifconfig` command by using `ifconfig -help`. The following output provides an example of the basic `ifconfig` command run on a Linux system:

```
eth0 Link encap:Ethernet HWaddr 00:60:08:17:63:A0
 inet addr:192.168.1.101 Bcast:192.168.1.255 Mask:255.255.255.0
 UP BROADCAST RUNNING MTU:1500 Metric:1
 RX packets:911 errors:0 dropped:0 overruns:0 frame:0
```

```
TX packets:804 errors:0 dropped:0 overruns:0 carrier:0
collisions:0 txqueuelen:100
Interrupt:5 Base address:0xe400

lo Link encap:Local Loopback
   inet addr:127.0.0.1 Mask:255.0.0.0
   UP LOOPBACK RUNNING MTU:3924 Metric:1
   RX packets:18 errors:0 dropped:0 overruns:0 frame:0
   TX packets:18 errors:0 dropped:0 overruns:0 carrier:0
   collisions:0 txqueuelen:0
```

Although the `ifconfig` command displays the IP address, subnet mask, and default gateway information for both the installed network adapter and the local loopback adapter, it does not report DHCP lease information. Instead, you can use the `pump -s` command to view detailed information on the DHCP lease, including the assigned IP address, the address of the DHCP server, and the time remaining on the lease. You can also use the `pump` command to release and renew IP addresses assigned via DHCP and to view DNS server information.

nslookup

`nslookup` is a utility used to troubleshoot DNS-related problems. Using `nslookup`, you can, for example, run manual name resolution queries against DNS servers, get information about your system's DNS configuration, or specify what kind of DNS record should be resolved.

When `nslookup` is started, it displays the current hostname and the IP address of the locally configured DNS server. You then see a command prompt that allows you to specify further queries. This is known as *interactive* mode. Table 11.8 lists the commands you can enter in interactive mode.

TABLE 11.8 `nslookup` **Switches**

Switch	Description
All	Prints options, as well as current server and host information
[no] debug	Prints debugging information
[no] d2	Prints exhaustive debugging information
[no] defname	Appends the domain name to each query
[no] recurse	Asks for a recursive answer to the query
[no] search	Uses the domain search list
[no] vc	Always uses a virtual circuit

Switch	Description
domain=NAME	Sets the default domain name to NAME
srchlist=N1 [/N2/.../N6]	Sets the domain to N1 and the search list to N1, N2, and so on
root=NAME	Sets the root server to NAME
Retry=X	Sets the number of retries to X
timeout=X	Sets the initial timeout interval to X seconds
Type=X	Sets the query type (for example, A, ANY, CNAME, MX, NS, PTR, SOA, or SRV)
querytype=X	Same as type
Class=X	Sets the query class (for example, IN [Internet], ANY)
[no]msxfr	Uses Microsoft fast zone transfer
ixfrver=X	The current version to use in an IXFR transfer request
server NAME	Sets the default server to NAME, using the current default server
Exit	Exits the program

Instead of using interactive mode, you can execute nslookup requests directly at the command prompt. The following listing shows the output from the nslookup command when a domain name is specified to be resolved:

```
C:\> nslookup comptia.org

Server: nsc1.ht.ok.shawcable.net
Address: 64.59.168.13

Non-authoritative answer:
Name: comptia.org
Address: 208.252.144.4
```

As you can see from the output, nslookup shows the hostname and IP address of the DNS server against which the resolution was performed, along with the hostname and IP address of the resolved host.

dig

dig is used on a Linux, UNIX, or Mac OS system to perform manual DNS lookups. dig performs the same basic task as nslookup, but with one major distinction: The dig command does not have an interactive mode and instead uses only command-line switches to customize results.

dig generally is considered a more powerful tool than nslookup, but in the course of a typical network administrator's day, the minor limitations of nslookup are unlikely to be too much of a factor. Instead, dig is often the tool of choice for DNS information and troubleshooting on UNIX, Linux, or Mac OS systems. Like nslookup, dig can be used to perform simple name resolution requests. The output from this process is shown in the following listing:

```
; <<>> DiG 8.2 <<>> examcram.com
;; res options: init recurs defnam dnsrch
;; got answer:
;; ->>HEADER<<- opcode: QUERY, status: NOERROR, id: 4
;; flags: qr rd ra; QUERY: 1, ANSWER: 1, AUTHORITY: 2, ADDITIONAL: 0
;; QUERY SECTION:
;; examcram.com, type = A, class = IN

;; ANSWER SECTION:
examcram.com.  7h33m IN A 63.240.93.157

;; AUTHORITY SECTION:
examcram.com.  7h33m IN NS usrxdns1.pearsontc.com.
examcram.com.  7h33m IN NS oldtxdns2.pearsontc.com.

;; Total query time: 78 msec
;; FROM: localhost.localdomain to SERVER: default - 209.53.4.130
;; WHEN: Sat Oct 16 20:21:24 2018
;; MSG SIZE sent: 30 rcvd: 103
```

As you can see, dig provides a number of pieces of information in the basic output—more so than nslookup. Network administrators can gain information from three key areas of the output: ANSWER SECTION, AUTHORITY SECTION, and the last four lines of the output.

The ANSWER SECTION of the output provides the name of the domain or host being resolved, along with its IP address. The *A* in the results line indicates the record type that is being resolved.

The AUTHORITY SECTION provides information on the authoritative DNS servers for the domain against which the resolution request was performed. This information can be useful in determining whether the correct DNS servers are considered authoritative for a domain.

The last four lines of the output show how long the name resolution request took to process and the IP address of the DNS server that performed the resolution. It also shows the date and time of the request, as well as the size of the packets sent and received.

The `tcpdump` Command

The `tcpdump` command is used on Linux/UNIX systems to print the contents of network packets. It can read packets from a network interface card or from a previously created saved packet file and write packets to either standard output or a file.

The `route` Utility

The `route` utility is an often-used and very handy tool. With the `route` command, you display and modify the routing table on your Windows and Linux systems. Figure 11.1 shows the output from a `route print` command on a Windows system.

```
C:\>route print
===========================================================================
Interface List
 10...00 25 64 8c 9e bf ......Broadcom NetLink (TM) Gigabit Ethernet
  1...........................Software Loopback Interface 1
 14...00 00 00 00 00 00 00 e0 Teredo Tunneling Pseudo-Interface
 15...00 00 00 00 00 00 00 e0 Microsoft ISATAP Adapter #2
===========================================================================

IPv4 Route Table
===========================================================================
Active Routes:
Network Destination        Netmask          Gateway       Interface  Metric
          0.0.0.0          0.0.0.0      192.168.1.1   192.168.1.119     10
        127.0.0.0        255.0.0.0         On-link         127.0.0.1    306
        127.0.0.1  255.255.255.255         On-link         127.0.0.1    306
  127.255.255.255  255.255.255.255         On-link         127.0.0.1    306
      192.168.1.0    255.255.255.0         On-link     192.168.1.119    266
    192.168.1.119  255.255.255.255         On-link     192.168.1.119    266
    192.168.1.255  255.255.255.255         On-link     192.168.1.119    266
        224.0.0.0        240.0.0.0         On-link         127.0.0.1    306
        224.0.0.0        240.0.0.0         On-link     192.168.1.119    266
  255.255.255.255  255.255.255.255         On-link         127.0.0.1    306
  255.255.255.255  255.255.255.255         On-link     192.168.1.119    266
===========================================================================
Persistent Routes:
  None

IPv6 Route Table
===========================================================================
Active Routes:
 If Metric Network Destination      Gateway
 14     58 ::/0                     On-link
  1    306 ::1/128                  On-link
 14     58 2001::/32               On-link
 14    306 2001:0:9d38:6ab8:2001:1013:3f57:fe88/128
                                    On-link
 10    266 fe80::/64                On-link
 14    306 fe80::/64                On-link
 14    306 fe80::2001:1013:3f57:fe88/128
                                    On-link
 10    266 fe80::51b9:996e:9fac:7715/128
                                    On-link
  1    306 ff00::/8                 On-link
 14    306 ff00::/8                 On-link
 10    266 ff00::/8                 On-link
===========================================================================
Persistent Routes:
  None
```

FIGURE 11.1   **The output from a** `route` `print` **command on a Windows system**

> **Note**
>
> The discussion here focuses on the Windows `route` command, but other operating systems have equivalent commands. On a Linux system, for example, the command is also `route`, but the usage and switches are different.

In addition to displaying the routing table, the Windows version of the route command has a number of other switches, as detailed in Table 11.9. For complete information about all the switches available with the route command on a Windows system, type route at the command line. To see a list of the route command switches on a Linux system, use the command route -help.

TABLE 11.9 **Switches for the route Command in Windows**

Switch	Description
add	Enables you to add a static route to the routing table.
delete	Enables you to remove a route from the routing table.
change	Enables you to modify an existing route.
-p	When used with the add command, makes the route permanent. If the -p switch is not used when a route is added, the route is lost upon reboot.
print	Enables you to view the system's routing table.
-f	Removes all gateway entries from the routing table.

nmap

nmap is a free download for Windows or Linux used to scan ports on machines. Those scans can show what services are running as well as information about the target machine's operating system. The utility can be used to scan a range of IP addresses or just a single IP address.

Cram Quiz

1. What command can you issue from the command line to view the status of the system's ports?

   ○ **A.** netstat -p

   ○ **B.** netstat -o

   ○ **C.** netstat -a

   ○ **D.** netstat -y

2. Which of the following tools can you use to perform manual DNS lookups on a Linux system? (Choose two.)

   ○ **A.** dig

   ○ **B.** nslookup

   ○ **C.** tracert

   ○ **D.** dnslookup

3. Which of the following commands generates a "Request Timed Out" error message?

   ○ **A.** `ping`

   ○ **B.** `netstat`

   ○ **C.** `ipconfig`

   ○ **D.** `nbtstat`

4. Which of the following commands would you use to add a static entry to the ARP table of a Windows system?

   ○ **A.** `arp -a IP Address MAC Address`

   ○ **B.** `arp -s MAC Address IP Address`

   ○ **C.** `arp -s IP Address MAC Address`

   ○ **D.** `arp -i IP Address MAC Address`

5. Which command created the following output?

   ```
   Server: nen.bx.ttfc.net
   Address: 209.55.4.155

   Name: examcram.com
   Address: 63.240.93.157
   ```

   ○ **A.** `nbtstat`

   ○ **B.** `ipconfig`

   ○ **C.** `tracert`

   ○ **D.** `nslookup`

Cram Quiz Answers

1. **C.** Administrators can quickly determine the status of common ports by issuing the `netstat -a` command from the command line. This command output lists the ports used by the system and whether they are open and listening.

2. **A, B.** Both the `dig` and `nslookup` commands can be used to perform manual DNS lookups on a Linux system. You cannot perform a manual lookup with the `tracert` command. There is no such command as `dnslookup`.

3. **A.** The `ping` command generates a "Request Timed Out" error when it cannot receive a reply from the destination system. None of the other commands listed produce this output.

4. **C.** The command `arp -s` IP Address MAC Address would correctly add a static entry to the ARP table. None of the other answers are valid ARP switches.

5. **D.** The output was produced by the `nslookup` command. The other commands listed produce different output.

Troubleshooting Common Network Service Issues

▶ **Given a scenario, troubleshoot common network service issues.**

CramSaver

If you can correctly answer these questions before going through this section, save time by skimming the Exam Alerts in this section and then completing the Cram Quiz at the end of the section.

1. What one, hardcoded address must be unique on a network for networking to function properly?

2. What can you try to do to handle DHCP exhaustion if you cannot increase the scope?

3. A client has an incorrect gateway configured. What is the most likely manifestation of this error?

Answers

1. The MAC address must be unique for each network interface card and there can be no duplicates.

2. You can shorten the lease period for each client and, hopefully, recover addresses sooner for issue to other clients.

3. With an incorrect gateway, the client will not be able to access networking services beyond the local network.

ExamAlert

Remember that this objective begins with "Given a scenario." That means that you may receive a drag and drop, matching, or "live OS" scenario where you have to click through to complete a specific objective-based task.

You will no doubt find yourself troubleshooting networking problems much more often than you would like to. When you troubleshoot these problems, a methodical approach is likely to pay off.

> **ExamAlert**
>
> Wiring problems are related to the cable used in a network. For the purposes of the exam, infrastructure problems are classified as those related to network devices, such as hubs, switches, and routers.

Common Problems to Be Aware Of

In the eyes of CompTIA and the Network+ exam, you should be aware of some problems more than others. Although subsequent sections look at problems in particular areas, pay special attention to those that fall within this section as you study for the exam.

Names Not Resolving

When the wrong Domain Name Service (DNS) values (typically primary and secondary) are entered during router configuration, users cannot take advantage of the DNS service. Depending on where the wrong values are given, name resolution may not occur (if all values are incorrect), or resolution could take a long time (if only the primary value is incorrect), thus giving the appearance that the web is taking a long time to load.

Make sure the correct values appear for DNS entries in the router configuration to avoid name resolution problems.

Incorrect Gateway

The default gateway configured on the router is where the data goes after it leaves the local network. Although many routes can be built dynamically, it is often necessary to add the first routes when installing/replacing a router. You can use the `ip route` command on most Cisco routers to do this from the command line, or most routers include a graphical interface for simplifying the process.

When you have the gateways configured, use the `ping` and `tracert/ traceroute` utilities to verify connectivity and proper configuration.

> **ExamAlert**
>
> Know the tools to use to test connectivity.

Incorrect Netmask

When the subnet mask is incorrect, the router thinks the network is divided into segments other than how it is actually configured. Because the purpose of the router is to route traffic, a wrong value here can cause it to try to route traffic to subnets that do not exist. The value of the subnet mask on the router must match the true configuration of the network.

Duplicate IP Address

Every IP address on a network must be unique. This is true not only for every host, but for the router as well, and every network card in general. The scope of the network depends on the size of the network that the card is connected to; if it is connected to the LAN, the IP address must be unique on that LAN, whereas if it is connected to the Internet, it must be unique on it.

If there is a duplicate address, in the best scenario you will receive messages indicating duplicate IP addresses, and in the worst scenario, network traffic will become unreliable. In all cases, you must correct the problem and make certain duplicate addresses exist nowhere on your network, including the routers.

Duplicate MAC Addresses

The MAC address is hardcoded into the NIC and cannot be changed. It consists of two components—one identifying the vendor and the other a serial number so that it will be unique. Of all things on the network, this is the one value that must stay constant for ARP, RARP, and other protocols to be able to translate IP addresses to machines and have communication across the network.

Given that, the only way for a MAC address to not be unique is for someone to be trying to add a rogue device impersonating another (typically a server). If this is the case, there will be serious problems on the network, and you must find—and disable—the unauthorized device immediately.

Expired IP Address

DHCP leases IP addresses to clients and—when functioning properly—continues to renew those leases as long at the client needs them. An expired address can mean that the DHCP server is down or unavailable, and the client will typically lose its address, rendering it unable to continue communicating on the network.

Each system must be assigned a unique IP address so that it can communicate on the network. Clients on a LAN have a private IP address and matching subnet mask. Table 11.10 shows the private IP ranges. If a system has the wrong IP or subnet mask, it cannot communicate on the network. If the client system has *misconfigured DHCP settings*, such as an IP address in the 169.254.0.0 APIPA range, the system is not connected to a DHCP server and is not able to communicate beyond the network.

TABLE 11.10 **Private Address Ranges**

Class	Address Range	Default Subnet Mask
A	10.0.0.0 to 10.255.255.255	255.0.0.0
B	172.16.0.0 to 172.31.255.255	255.255.0.0
C	192.168.0.0 to 192.168.255.255	255.255.255.0

> **ExamAlert**
>
> You need to know the private address ranges in Table 11.10.

Rogue DHCP Server

A *rogue DHCP server* is any DHCP server on the network that was added by an unauthorized party and is not under the administrative control of the network administrators. It can be used to give false values or to set clients up for network attacks, such as man in the middle.

Untrusted SSL Certificate

An *untrusted SSL certificate* is usually one that is not signed or that has expired. Sometimes, this issue can be caused by a client using an older browser or one that is not widely supported. As a general rule, though, users should be instructed to stop attempting to visit a site if they see this error.

Incorrect Time

Incorrect time on a network can be more than just an annoyance, because timestamps are important in the event of trying to document an attack. Most network devices use Network Time Protocol (NTP) to keep the system time as defined by a designated server. Make sure that server has the correct time on it and is updated, patched, and secured just as you would any other network critical server.

Exhausted DHCP Scope

The DHCP scope is the pool of possible IP addresses a DHCP server can issue. If that pool becomes exhausted and not enough addresses are available for the devices needing to connect, devices will not be given the values they need (many will then resort to using APIPA addresses in the 169.254 range, as discussed earlier.

The only solution is to increase the scope and/or decrease the lease time. If you reduce the lease time from days to hours, more addresses should become available as hosts leave the network at the end of their shifts, and those values become available for use by others.

Blocked TCP/UDP Ports

As a security rule, only needed ports should be enabled and allowed on a network. Unfortunately, you don't always have a perfect idea of which ports you need, and it is possible to inadvertently have some blocked TCP/UDP ports that you need to use.

If you find your firewall is blocking a needed port, open that port (make an exception) and allow it to be used.

Incorrect Firewall Settings

Incorrect firewall settings typically fall under the category of blocking ports that you need open (previously addressed) or allowing ports that you don't need. From a security perspective, the latter situation is the worse because every open port represents a door that an intruder could use to access the system or at least a vulnerability. Be sure to know which ports are open, and close any that are not needed.

Incorrect ACL Settings

The purpose of an Access Control List (ACL) is to define who/what can access your system. Incorrect ACL settings could keep too many off, but typically the error is allowing too many on. Used properly, an ACL can enable devices in your network to ignore requests from specified users or systems or to grant them certain network privileges. You may find that a certain IP address is constantly scanning your network, and you can block this IP address. If you block it at the router, the IP address will automatically be rejected anytime it attempts to use your network.

Unresponsive Service

When a service does not respond, it could be due to overload, being down, or bad configuration. The first order of business is to ascertain which of these three the situation is and then decide what you need to do to fix it. If the server/service is overloaded, look for a way to increase the capacity or balance the load. If the server/service is down, investigate why and what needs to be done to bring it back up again. If the server/service is misconfigured, make the necessary changes to configure it properly.

Hardware Failure

If you are looking for a challenge, troubleshooting hardware infrastructure problems is for you. It is often not an easy task and usually involves many processes, including baselining and performance monitoring. One of the keys to identifying the hardware failure is to know what devices are used on a particular network and what each device is designed to do. Table 11.11 lists some of the common hardware components used in a network infrastructure, as well as some common problem symptoms and troubleshooting methods.

TABLE 11.11 **Common Network Hardware Components, Their Functions, and Troubleshooting Strategies**

Networking Device	Function	Troubleshooting and Failure Signs
Hub	Hubs are used with a star network topology and UTP cable to connect multiple nodes.	Because hubs connect multiple network devices, if many devices are unable to access the network, the hub may have failed. When a hub fails, all devices connected to it cannot access the network. In addition, hubs use broadcasts and forward data to all the connected ports, increasing network traffic. When network traffic is high and the network is operating slowly, it may be necessary to replace slow hubs with switches.
Switch	Like hubs, switches are used with a star topology to create a central connectivity device.	The inability of several network devices to access the network may indicate a failed switch. If the switch fails, all devices connected to the switch cannot access the network. Switches forward data only to the intended recipient, allowing them to manage data better than hubs.

Networking Device	Function	Troubleshooting and Failure Signs
Router	Routers are used to separate broadcast domains and to connect different networks.	If a router fails, network clients are unable to access remote networks connected by the router. For example, if clients access a remote office through a network router, and the router fails, the remote office is unavailable. You can test router connectivity using utilities such as `ping` and `tracert`.
Wireless access point	Wireless access points provide the bridge between the wired and wireless network.	If wireless clients cannot access the wired network, the AP may have failed. However, you should check many configuration settings first.

ExamAlert

Be familiar with the devices listed in Table 11.11 and their failure signs.

For more information on network hardware devices and their functions, refer to Chapter 4, "Network Components and Devices."

Cram Quiz

1. Although many routes can be built dynamically, it is often necessary to add the first routes when installing/replacing a router. Which of the following commands can you use on most Cisco routers to do this from the command line?

   ○ **A.** `ip route`

   ○ **B.** `add route`

   ○ **C.** `first route`

   ○ **D.** `route change`

2. Which of the following best describes the function of the default gateway?

   ○ **A.** It converts hostnames to IP addresses.

   ○ **B.** It converts IP addresses to hostnames.

   ○ **C.** It enables systems to communicate with systems on a remote network.

   ○ **D.** It enables systems to communicate with routers.

3. Consider the following figure. Which of the following statements is true?

Internet Protocol Version 4 (TCP/IPv4) Properties

General

You can get IP settings assigned automatically if your network supports this capability. Otherwise, you need to ask your network administrator for the appropriate IP settings.

- ○ Obtain an IP address automatically
- ◉ Use the following IP address:

IP address:	192 . 168 . 2 . 3
Subnet mask:	255 . 255 . 255 . 0
Default gateway:	192 . 168 . 2 . 3

- ○ Obtain DNS server address automatically
- ◉ Use the following DNS server addresses:

| Preferred DNS server: | 192 . 168 . 2 . 45 |
| Alternate DNS server: | 192 . 168 . 2 . 46 |

☐ Validate settings upon exit   Advanced...

OK   Cancel

- ○ **A.** The system cannot access the local network.
- ○ **B.** The system cannot access remote networks.
- ○ **C.** The system cannot have hostname resolution.
- ○ **D.** The system has the wrong subnet mask.

4. Which of the following bits of IP information are mandatory to join the network? (Choose two.)

- ○ **A.** Subnet mask
- ○ **B.** IP address
- ○ **C.** DNS address
- ○ **D.** Default gateway

Cram Quiz Answers

1. A. Although many routes can be built dynamically, it is often necessary to add the first routes when installing/replacing a router. You can use the `ip route` command on most Cisco routers to do this from the command line.

2. C. The default gateway enables the system to communicate with systems on a remote network, without the need for explicit routes to be defined. The default gateway can be assigned automatically using a DHCP server or can be input manually.

3. **B.** The IP addresses of the client system and the default gateway are the same. This error probably occurred when the IP address information was input. In this configuration, the client system would likely access the local network and resources but not remote networks because the gateway address to remote networks is wrong. The DNS, IP, and subnet mask settings are correct.

4. **A, B.** Configuring a client requires at least the IP address and a subnet mask. The default gateway, DNS server, and WINS server are all optional, but network functionality is limited without them.

What's Next?

Congratulations! You finished the reading and are now familiar with all the objectives on the Network+ exam. You are now ready for the practice exams. There are two 100 multiple-choice question exams to help you determine how prepared you are for the actual exam and which topics you need to review further.

Glossary

Numbers and Symbols

10GBaseT A 2006 standard to provide 10 Gbps connections over unshielded or shielded twisted pair cables, over distances up to 100 meters using category 6a (category 6 can reach 55 meters).

100BaseT The IEEE 802.3 specification for running Ethernet at 100 Mbps over twisted-pair cabling. The maximum length of a 100BASET segment is 100 meters (328 feet).

1000BaseLX A standard for Gigabit Ethernet intended for use with long-wavelength (LX) transmissions over long cable runs of fiber optic cabling.

1000BaseSX A fiber optic Gigabit Ethernet standard for operation over multimode fiber.

1000BaseT An IEEE 802.3ab standard that specifies Gigabit Ethernet over Category 5 or better UTP cable. The standard allows for full-duplex transmission using four pairs of twisted cable up to 100 meters.

568A/568B standards Telecommunications standards from the Telecommunications Industry Association (TIA) and the Electronics Industry Association (EIA). These 568 standards specify the pin arrangements for the RJ-45 connectors on UTP or STP cables. The number 568 refers to the order in which the wires within the UTP cable are terminated and attached to the connector.

A

A   An address record. This refers to one of three machines typically: the host sending data, the host receiving data, or an intermediary between the two (the next hop).

AAA   Authentication, authorization, and accounting. Authentication is the process to determine whether someone is authorized to use the network—if the person can log on to the network. Authorization refers to identifying the resources a user can access after the user is authenticated. Accounting refers to the tracking methods used to identify who uses the network and what they do on the network.

AAAA   Authentication, authorization, accounting, and auditing. Authentication is the process to determine whether someone is authorized to use the network—if the person can log on to the network. Authorization refers to identifying the resources a user can access after the user is authenticated. Accounting refers to the tracking methods used to identify who uses the network and what they do on the network. Auditing refers to the ability to associate actions with the machine/user in question.

AAAA record   The DNS record that maps a hostname to a 128-bit

IPv6 address. This is also known as the IPv6 address record.

access point (AP)   A transmitter and receiver (transceiver) device commonly used to facilitate communication between a wireless client and a wired network. Wireless APs are used with the wireless infrastructure network topology to provide a connection point between WLANs and a wired Ethernet LAN.

ACK   The acknowledgment message sent between two hosts during a TCP session.

ACL (access control list)   The list of trustees assigned to a file or directory. A trustee can be any object available to the security subsystem. The term ACL is also used with routers and firewall systems to refer to the list of permitted computers or users.

Active Directory   Used in Windows network environments, this is a directory services system that enables network objects to be stored in a database. This database can then be divided and distributed among different servers on the network.

active hub   A hub that has power supplied to it for the purposes of regenerating the signals that pass through it.

ad hoc topology   Defines a wireless network layout whereby devices communicate directly among themselves without using an access point. Sometimes called an unmanaged or peer-to-peer wireless topology.

address   A set of numbers used to identify and locate a resource or device on a network. An example is an IP address such as 192.168.2.1.

administrator   A person responsible for the control and security of the user accounts, resources, and data on a network.

Administrator account   On a Windows system, the default account that has rights to access everything and to assign rights to other users on the network. Unlike other user accounts, the Administrator account cannot be deleted.

ADSL (asymmetric digital subscriber line)   A service that transmits digital voice and data over existing (analog) phone lines.

AES (Advanced Encryption Standard)   An encryption algorithm for securing sensitive networks used by U.S. government agencies. Has become the encryption standard for corporate networks.

AH (Authentication Header)   One of the two separate protocols IPsec consists of (the other being ESP). AH provides the authentication and integrity checking for data packets.

antivirus software   A software application that detects and removes viruses.

AP (wireless access point)   A network device that offers connectivity between wireless clients and (usually) a wired portion of the network.

APC (angle polished connector)   A connector commonly used with fiber cables—usually single mode—to

keep the signal from bouncing back down the line.

APIPA (Automatic Private IP Addressing)   A technology implemented on certain Windows platforms through which a system assigns itself an IP address in the absence of a DHCP server. Addresses are assigned from the 169.254.*x.x* address range.

application layer   Layer 7 of the OSI model, which provides support for end users and for application programs using network resources.

application-level firewall Application-layer firewalls operate at the application layer of the OSI model. Application layer firewalls can inspect data packets traveling to or from an application.

application log   A log file on a Windows system that provides information on events that occur within an application.

APT (Advanced Persistent Tool) Although CompTIA uses *Tool*, most use *Threat* as the last word of the acronym. In either case, it is an unauthorized person in a network, undetected, for an exceedingly long period of time.

archive bit   A flag that is set on a file after it has been created or altered. Some backup methods reset the flag to indicate that it has been backed up.

ARIN (American Registry for Internet Numbers)   The regional Internet registry responsible for managing both IPv4 and IPv6 IP number distribution.

ARP (Address Resolution Protocol)
A protocol in the TCP/IP suite used to resolve IP addresses to MAC addresses. Specifically, the ARP command returns a Layer 2 address for a Layer 3 address.

ARP ping   The ARP utility that resolves IP addresses to MAC addresses. The ARP ping utility tests connectivity by pinging a MAC address directly.

ARP table   A table of entries used by ARP to store resolved ARP requests. Entries can also be manually stored.

array   A group of devices arranged in a fault-tolerant configuration. *See also* RAID.

AS (autonomous system)   A collection of connected IP routing prefixes under the control of a network administrator or entity that offers a common and defined routing policy to the Internet.

ASIC (application-specific integrated circuit)   An integrated circuit designed for a particular use instead of for general-purpose uses.

ASP (application service provider)   A vendor who provides computer-based services over the network.

attenuation   The loss of signal experienced as data transmits over distance and across the network medium.

ATM (Asynchronous Transfer Mode)
A packet-switching technology that provides transfer speeds ranging from 1.544 Mbps to 622 Mbps.

AUP (acceptable use policy)   A policy created by an organization defining what is acceptable on their resources (network, computers, and so on).

authentication   The process by which a user's identity is validated on a network. The most common authentication method is a username and password combination.

B

B (bearer) channel   In ISDN, a 64 Kbps channel that carries data. *See also* D (delta) channel.

backbone   A network segment that acts as a trunk between other network segments. Backbones typically are high-bandwidth implementations, such as fiber-optic cable.

backup schedule   A document or plan that defines what type of backups are made, when, and what data is backed up.

bandwidth   The width of the range of electrical frequencies, or how many channels the medium can support. Bandwidth correlates to the amount of data that can traverse the medium at one time, but other factors determine the maximum speed supported by a cable.

baseband   A term applied to any medium that can carry only a single data signal at a time. Compare with broadband.

baseline   A measurement of performance of a device or system for the purposes of future comparison. Baselining is a common server administration task.

baud rate   The speed or rate of signal transfer. Baud rate bandwidth is measured in cycles per second, or hertz (Hz). The word *baud* is derived from the name of French telegraphy expert J. M. Baudot.

BCP (business continuity plan) The strategy for addressing potential threats to a company and creation of systems to aid in the prevention of threats and recovery from problems.

beaconing   In a wireless network, beaconing refers to the continuous transmission of small packets (beacons) that advertise the presence of a base station (access point).

BERT (bit-error rate test)   A test to see the number of received bits of a data stream that has changed due to noise, interference, or other distortion.

BGP (Border Gateway Protocol) Used between gateway hosts on the Internet. BGP examines the routing table, which contains a list of known routers, the addresses they can reach, and a cost metric associated with the path to each router so that the best available route is chosen. BGP communicates between the routers using TCP.

binary   A base 2 numbering system used in digital signaling. It uses only the numbers 1 and 0.

binding   The process of associating a protocol with a NIC.

biometrics   The science and technology of measuring and analyzing biological data. Biometrics are used for security purposes to analyze and compare characteristics such as voice patterns, retina patterns, and hand measurements.

BIOS (Basic Input/Output System) A basic set of instructions that a device needs to operate.

bit   An electronic digit used in the binary numbering system. Bit is a contraction of the terms *binary* and *digit*.

blackout   A total loss of electrical power.

BLE (Bluetooth Low Energy)   A form of Bluetooth networking technology that uses very little energy.

Bluetooth   A low-cost, short-range RF technology designed to replace many of the cords used to connect devices. Bluetooth uses 2.4 GHz RF and provides transmission speeds up to 24 Mbps.

BNC (British Naval Connector/ Bayonet Neill-Concelman) connector   A family of connectors typically associated with thin coaxial cabling and 10BASE2 networks. BNC connectors use a twist-and-lock mechanism to connect devices to the network.

BOOTP (Bootstrap Protocol)   A TCP/IP protocol used by a network device to obtain an IP address and other network information, such as server address and default gateway from a configuration server.

bound medium   Describes any medium that has physical constraints, such as coaxial, fiber-optic, and twisted pair. Compare with unbound medium.

boundless medium *See* unbound medium.

BPDU (bridge protocol data unit) Identifies the status of ports and bridges across the network. BPDUs are simple data messages exchanged between switches. They contain information on ports and provide the status of those ports to other switches.

BRI (Basic Rate Interface) An ISDN digital communications line that consists of three independent channels: two B channels each at 64 Kbps and one D channel at 16 Kbps. ISDN BRI is often referred to as 2B+D. *See also* ISDN and PRI.

bridge A device that connects and passes packets between two network segments that use the same communications protocol. Bridges operate at the data link layer of the OSI model. A bridge filters, forwards, or floods an incoming frame based on the packet's MAC address.

bridging address table A list of MAC addresses that a bridge keeps and uses when it receives packets. The bridge uses the bridging address table to determine which segment the destination address is on before it sends the packet to the next interface or drops the packet (if it is on the same segment as the sending node).

broadband A communications strategy that uses analog or digital signaling over multiple communications channels.

broadcast A packet-delivery system in which a copy of a packet is transmitted to all hosts attached to the network.

broadcast storm An undesirable condition in which broadcasts become so numerous that they bog down the flow of data across the network.

brownout A short-term decrease in the voltage level, usually caused by the startup demands of other electrical devices.

BSSID (basic service set identifier) The BSSID is the MAC address of the wireless access point (AP).

buffer An area of memory in a device used to temporarily store data before it is forwarded to another device or location.

bus topology A linear LAN architecture in which all devices connect to a common cable, called a bus or backbone.

butt set The butt set is typically associated with telephony systems. It is used to test and access the phone line using clip wires that attach to the phone cable.

BYOD (bring your own device) A policy governing employees bringing personally owned devices (laptops, smartphones, and the like) to the workplace and the use of those devices to access company data.

byte A set of bits (usually 8) that operate as a unit to signify a character.

C

CaaS (Communication as a Service) A cloud computing model for providing ubiquitous access to shared pools of configurable resources.

cable modem A device that provides Internet access over cable television lines.

cable stripper A tool used to strip the sheathing from copper cabling.

cable tester A device used to check for electrical continuity along a length of cable. *Cable tester* is a generic term that can be applied to devices such as volt/ohm meters and TDRs.

caching-only server A type of DNS server that operates the same way as secondary servers except that a zone transfer does not take place when the caching-only server is started.

CAM (content addressable memory) A type of computer memory used in high-speed searching applications.

CAN (campus-area network) A wide-area network (WAN) created to service a campus area.

CARP (Common Address Redundancy Protocol) A protocol that enables multiple hosts on the same network to share a set of IP addresses and thus provides failover redundancy. It is commonly used with routers and firewalls and can provide load balancing.

carrier A signal that carries data. The carrier signal is modulated to create peaks and troughs, which represent binary bits.

CASB (cloud access security broker) Software that sits between cloud service users and cloud applications to monitor all activity and enforce security policies.

CAT (Computer and Telephone) A designation of resources, usually wiring, used to provide service to computers or telephones.

CAT3 Data-grade cable that can transmit data up to 10 Mbps with a possible bandwidth of 16 MHz.

CAT5 Data-grade cable that typically was used with Fast Ethernet operating at 100 Mbps with a transmission range of 100 meters.

CAT5e Data-grade cable used on networks that run at 10/100 Mbps and even up to 1000 Mbps. Category 5e cabling can be used up to 100 meters, depending on the implementation and standard used. Category 5e cable provides a minimum of 100 MHz of bandwidth.

CAT6 High-performance UTP cable that can transmit data up to 10 Gbps.

CAT6a Also called augmented 6. Offers improvements over Category 6 by offering a minimum of 500 MHz of bandwidth. It specifies transmission distances up to 100 meters with 10 Gbps networking speeds.

CAT7 Offers improvements over Category 6a by offering 600 MHz of bandwidth and improved crosstalk suppression. It specifies transmission distances up to 100 meters with 10 Gbps networking speeds.

CCTV (closed-circuit TV) An acronym for video cameras used to watch a particular place and send (transmit) to a particular location.

CDMA (code division multiple access) A multiple-access channel method used to provide bandwidth sharing.

change control A process in which a detailed record of every change made to the network is documented.

channel A communications path used for data transmission.

CHAP (Challenge Handshake Authentication Protocol) A protocol that challenges a system to verify identity. CHAP is an improvement over Password Authentication Protocol (PAP) in which one-way hashing is incorporated into a three-way handshake. RFC 1334 applies to both PAP and CHAP.

checksum A basic method of error checking that involves calculating the sum of bytes in a section of data and then embedding the result in the packet. When the packet reaches the destination, the calculation is performed again to make sure that the value is still the same.

CIDR (classless interdomain routing) An IP addressing scheme that enables a single IP address to designate many unique IP addresses. CIDR addressing uses an IP address followed by a / and the IP network prefix. An example of a CIDR address is 192.168.100.0/16. CIDR is sometimes called supernetting.

circuit-level firewall A type of network security system whereby network traffic is filtered based on specified session rules and may be restricted to recognized computers only.

circuit switching A method of sending data between two parties in which a dedicated circuit is created at the beginning of the conversation and is broken at the end. All data transported during the session travels over the same path, or circuit.

Class A network A TCP/IP network that uses addresses from 1 to 126 and supports up to 126 subnets with 16,777,214 unique hosts each.

Class B network A TCP/IP network that uses addresses from 128 to 191 and supports up to 16,384 subnets with 65,534 unique hosts each.

Class C network A TCP/IP network that uses addresses from 192 to 223 and supports up to 2,097,152 subnets with 254 unique hosts each.

Class D network Class D network addresses within the range of 224.0.0.0 to 239.255.255.255 are used for multicasting data to multicast-capable hosts on a network.

client A node that uses the services from another node on a network.

client/server networking A networking architecture in which front-end, or client, nodes request and process data stored by the back-end, or server, node.

cloud computing   The hosting, storage, and delivery of computing as a service rather than a product. The end user accesses remotely stored programs and other resources through the Internet without the need for expensive local networking devices, services, and support. Various industry cloud computing concepts include public, private, hybrid, and community cloud.

clustering   A technology that enables two or more computers to act as a single system to provide improved fault tolerance, load balancing, and failover capability.

CNAME (canonical name)   Specifies an alias or nickname for a canonical hostname record in a Domain Name System (DNS) database. CNAME records are used to give a single computer multiple names (aliases).

coaxial cable   A data cable, commonly referred to as coax, that is made of a solid copper core insulated and surrounded by braided metal and covered with a thick plastic or rubber covering. Coax is the standard cable used in cable television and in older bus topology networks.

cold site   A disaster recovery site that provides office space, but the customer provides and installs all the equipment needed to continue operations.

cold spare   A redundant piece of hardware stored in case a component should fail. Typically used for server systems.

collision   The result of two frames simultaneously transmitting on an Ethernet network and colliding, thereby destroying both frames.

collision domain   A segment of an Ethernet network between managing nodes, where only one packet can be transmitted at a time. Switches, bridges, and routers can be used to segment a network into separate collision domains.

communication   The transfer of information between nodes on a network.

concentrator   A device that combines several communications channels into one. It is often used to combine multiple terminals into one line.

connectionless communication   Packet transfer in which delivery is not guaranteed.

connection-oriented communication   Packet transfer in which delivery is guaranteed.

connectivity   The linking of nodes on a network for communication to take place.

convergence   When a change in the network routing is made, it takes some time for the routers to detect and accommodate this change; this is known as convergence.

copy backup   Normally, a backup of the entire hard drive. A copy backup is similar to a full backup, except that the copy backup does not alter the state of the archive bits on files.

CoS (class of service) A parameter used in data and voice to differentiate the types of payloads being transmitted.

cost A value used to encourage or discourage the use of a certain route through a network. Routes that are to be discouraged are assigned a higher cost, and those that are to be encouraged are assigned a lower cost. *See also* metric.

CPU (central processing unit) The main processor in a computing device.

cracker A person who attempts to break software code or gain access to a system to which he or she is not authorized. *See also* hacker.

cracking The process of attempting to break software code, normally to defeat copyright protection or alter the software's functioning. Also the process of attempting to gain unauthorized access to a computer system. *See also* hacker.

CRAM-MD5 A challenge-response authentication mechanism.

CRC (cyclical redundancy check) A method used to check for errors in packets that have been transferred across a network. A computation bit is added to the packet and recalculated at the destination to determine whether the entire content of the packet has been correctly transferred.

crimper A tool used to join connectors to the ends of network cables.

crossover cable A cable that can be used to directly connect two devices—such as two computer systems—or as a means to expand networks that use devices such as hubs or switches. A traditional crossover cable is a UTP cable in which the wires are crossed for the purposes of placing the transmit line of one device on the receive line of the other. A T1 crossover is used to connect two T1 CSU/DSU devices in a back-to-back configuration.

crosstalk Electronic interference caused when two wires are too close to each other, and the adjacent cable creates interference.

CSMA/CA (carrier sense multiple access with collision avoidance) A contention media access method that uses collision-avoidance techniques.

CSMA/CD (carrier sense multiple access with collision detection) A contention media access method that uses collision-detection and retransmission techniques.

CSU/DSU (channel service unit/data service unit) Acts as a translator between the LAN data format and the WAN data format. Such a conversion is necessary because the technologies used on WAN links are different from those used on LANs.

cut-through packet switching A switching method that does not copy the entire packet into the switch buffers. Instead, the destination address is captured into the switch, the route to the destination node is determined, and the packet is quickly sent out the corresponding port. Cut-through packet switching maintains a low latency.

CVW (collaborative virtual workspace)   An environment, often called a CVE, used for collaboration and interaction of participants that may be spread over large distances.

CWDM (course wave-division multiplexing)   Contrary to the CompTIA acronym, most in the industry use *coarse* for the *C* portion and it is a method of multiplexing in which different signals operate at different speeds. The best example of this is cable modems, allowing for different speeds of uploading and downloading.

D

DaaS (Desktop as a Service)   Software that separates the desktop environment and associated application software from the physical client device that is used to access it.

data field   In a frame, the field or section that contains the data.

data link layer   Layer 2 of the OSI model, which is above the physical layer. Data comes off the cable, goes through the physical layer, and goes into the data link layer. The data link layer has two distinct sublayers: MAC and LLC.

datagram   An information grouping transmitted as a unit at the network layer. *See also* packet.

dB   Decibels. A measurement.

DB-25   A 25-pin connector used for serial port or parallel port connection between PCs and peripheral devices.

DB-9   A nine-pin connector used for serial port or parallel port connection between PCs and peripheral devices.

D (delta) channel   The channel used on ISDN to communicate signaling and other related information. Use of the D channel leaves the B channels free for data communication. *See also* B (bearer) channel.

DCS (distributed computer system)   A system in which the whole is divided into many parts. The best example of this is using multiple computers to work together and appear to the user as a single entity.

DDNS (Dynamic Domain Name Service)   A form of DNS that enables systems to be registered and deregistered with DNS dynamically. DDNS is facilitated by DHCP, which passes IP address assignments to the DNS server for entry into the DNS server records. This is in contrast with the conventional DNS system, in which entries must be manually made.

DDoS (distributed denial of service) attack   A DoS attack that utilizes more than one computer in the attack. *See* DoS (denial of service) attack.

dedicated line   A dedicated circuit used in WANs to provide a constant connection between two points.

default gateway Normally a router or a multihomed computer to which packets are sent when they are destined for a host on a different network.

demarcation point The point at which communication lines enter a customer's premises. Sometimes shortened to simply *demarc*.

destination address The network address to which data is sent.

DHCP (Dynamic Host Configuration Protocol) A protocol that provides dynamic IP addressing to DHCP-enabled workstations on the network.

dial-up networking Refers to the connection of a remote node to a network using POTS.

differential backup A backup of only the data that has been created or changed since the previous full backup. In a differential backup, the state of the archive bits is not altered.

dig On a Linux, UNIX, or Mac OS system, you can use the dig command to perform manual DNS lookups.

directory services A system that enables network resources to be viewed as objects stored in a database. This database can then be divided and distributed among different servers on the network. An example of directory services includes LDAP or Microsoft Active Directory.

disaster recovery plan A plan for implementing duplicate computer services if a natural disaster, a

human-made disaster, or another catastrophe occurs. A disaster recovery plan includes offsite backups and procedures to activate information systems in alternative locations.

distance-vector routing A type of routing in which a router uses broadcasts to inform neighboring routers on the network of the routes it knows about. Compare with link-state routing.

DLC (data link control) The service provided by the data link layer of the OSI model.

DLP (data leak prevention) Also commonly expressed as data loss prevention, it is a system designed to detect and respond to potential breaches.

DLR (device level ring) A protocol that provides a means of detecting, managing, and recovering from faults in a ring-based topology network.

DMZ (demilitarized zone) An area for placing web and other servers that serve the general public outside the firewall, thereby isolating them from internal network access.

DNAT (Destination Network Address Translation) A technique for transparently changing the destination of an end route and performing the inverse function for any replies.

DNS (Domain Name Service) A service/system/server used to translate domain names, such as www.quepublishing.com, into IP addresses, such as 165.193.123.44.

DNS uses a hierarchical namespace that enables the database of hostname-to-IP address mappings to be distributed across multiple servers.

DOCSIS (Data-Over-Cable Service Interface Specification) A telecommunications standard for transmitting high-speed data over existing cable TV systems.

domain A logical boundary of an Active Directory structure on Windows servers. Also, a section of the DNS namespace.

domain name server A server that runs application software that enables the server to perform a role associated with the DNS service.

DoS (denial of service) attack A type of hacking attack in which the target system is overwhelmed with requests for service, which keeps it from servicing any requests— legitimate or otherwise.

downtime A period of time during which a computer system or network is unavailable. This may be due to scheduled maintenance or hardware or software failure.

DR (designated router) An OSPF router intended to reduce network traffic by maintaining the complete routing database and then sending updates to the other routers on the shared network segment.

DSCP (differentiated services code point) An architecture that specifies a simple and coarse-grained mechanism for classifying and managing network traffic and providing QoS on modern networks.

DSL (digital subscriber line) A public network technology that delivers high bandwidth over conventional copper wiring over limited distances.

DSSS (direct sequence spread spectrum) A modulation technique in which the transmitted signal takes up more than the information signal that modulates the carrier or broadcast frequency.

DSU (data service unit) A network communications device that formats and controls data for transmission over digital lines. A DSU is used with a CSU.

DTE (data terminal equipment) A device used at the user end of a user network interface that serves as a data source, a destination, or both. DTE devices include computers, protocol translators, and multiplexers.

DWDM (dense wavelength-division multiplexing) A form of multiplexing optical signals that replaces SONET/SDH regenerators with erbium doped fiber amplifiers (EDFAs) and can also amplify the signal and allow it to travel a greater distance. The main components of a DWDM system include a terminal multiplexer, line repeaters, and a terminal demultiplexer.

dynamic routing A routing system that enables routing information to be communicated between devices automatically and that can recognize changes in the network topology and update routing tables accordingly. Compare with static routing.

dynamic window   A flow control mechanism that prevents the sender of data from overwhelming the receiver. The amount of data that can be buffered in a dynamic window varies in size, hence its name.

E

E1 (E-Carrier Level 1)   An E1 link operates over two separate sets of wires, typically twisted-pair cable, and carries data at a rate of 2.048 million bits per second. E1 is the European equivalent of T1 used in the United States.

E3 (E-Carrier Level 3)   An E3 link carries 16 E1 signals with a data rate of 34.368 million bits per second. E3 is the European equivalent of T3 used in the United States.

EAP (Extensible Authentication Protocol)   An extension of PPP that supports authentication methods more secure than a standard username and password combination. EAP is commonly used as an authentication protocol for token cards, smart cards, and digital certificates.

EDNS (Extension Mechanisms for DNS)   As specified by the Internet Engineering Task Force as RFC 2671, EDNS increases the size of the flags fields, return codes, and label types available in basic DNS.

EGP (exterior gateway protocol)   The exterior gateway protocol defines distance-vector protocols commonly used between hosts on the Internet to exchange routing table information. BGP is an example of an EGP. *See* BGP.

EIA/TIA   The Electronic Industries Alliance/Telecommunications Industry Association is a trade organization responsible for a number of communications standards.

EIGRP (Enhanced Interior Gateway Routing Protocol)   A protocol that enables routers to exchange information more efficiently than earlier network protocols. Routers configured to use EIGRP keep copies of their neighbors' routing information and query these tables to help find the best possible route for transmissions to follow.

EMI (electromagnetic interference)   External interference of electromagnetic signals that causes a reduction in data integrity and increased error rates in a transmission medium.

encapsulation   A technique used by protocols in which header and trailer information is added to the protocol data unit as it is passed down through the protocol stack on a sending system. The reverse process, decapsulation, is performed at the receiving system as the packet travels up through the protocol suite.

encryption   Modifying data for security purposes prior to transmission so that the data cannot be read without the decryption method.

ESD (electrostatic discharge)   A condition created when two objects of dissimilar electrical charge come into contact with each other. The result is that a charge from the object with the higher electrical charge discharges itself into the object with the lower-level charge. This discharge can be harmful to computer components and circuit boards.

ESP (Encapsulated Security Packets)   One of the two separate protocols IPsec consists of (the other being AH). ESP provides encryption services.

ESS (extended service set)   The ESS refers to two or more basic service sets (BSS) connected, therefore using multiple APs. The ESS is used to create WLANs or larger wireless networks and is a collection of APs and clients.

ESSID (extended service set identifier)   The terms *ESSID* and *SSID* are used interchangeably, but they are different. The SSID is the name used with basic service set (BSS) networks, and the ESSID is the network name used with an ESS wireless network design. With an ESS, not all APs necessarily use the same name.

Ethernet   The most common LAN technology. Ethernet can be implemented using coaxial, twisted-pair, or fiber-optic cable. Ethernet typically uses the CSMA/CD media access method and has various implementation standards.

EUI (extended unique identifier)   A naming convention for MAC addresses.

Event Viewer   A utility available on Windows server systems and client systems. It is commonly used to gather systems information and also is used in the troubleshooting process.

F

failover   The automatic switching from one device or system to another. Servers can be configured in a failover configuration so that if the primary server fails, the secondary server automatically takes over.

Fast Ethernet   The IEEE 802.3u specification for data transfers of up to 100 Mbps over twisted-pair cable. *See also* 100BASE-FX, 100BASE-T, and 100BASE-TX.

fault tolerance   The capability of a component, system, or network to endure a failure.

FC (Fibre Channel)   *See* Fibre Channel.

FCoE (Fibre Channel over Ethernet)   A technology that encapsulates Fibre Channel frames over Ethernet networks allowing FC to use 10 Gigabit Ethernet networks (or higher) while preserving the Fibre Channel protocol.

FCS (frame check sequence)   A method of error detection added to a frame in a communications protocol.

FDDI (Fiber Distributed Data Interface)   A high-speed data transfer technology designed to extend the capabilities of existing LANs by using a dual-ring topology and a token-passing access method.

FDM (frequency-division multiplexing) A technology that divides the output channel into multiple smaller-bandwidth channels, each of which uses a different frequency range.

FHSS (frequency hopping spread spectrum) A multiple access method of transferring radio signals in the frequency-hopping code division multiple access (FH-CDMA) scheme.

fiber-optic cable Also known as fiber optics or optical fiber, a physical medium that can conduct modulated light transmissions. Compared with other transmission media, fiber-optic cable is more expensive, but it is not susceptible to EMI or crosstalk, and it is capable of high data rates and increased distances.

Fibre Channel A technology that defines full gigabit-per-second (commonly runs at 2-, 4-, 8-, and 16-gigabit per second data rates) data transfer over fiber-optic cable. Commonly used with storage-area network (SAN) implementations.

firewall A program, system, device, or group of devices that acts as a barrier between one network and another. Firewalls are configured to enable certain types of traffic to pass while blocking others.

flow control A method of controlling the amount of data transmitted within a given period of time. Different types of flow control exist. *See also* dynamic window and static window.

FM (frequency modulation) One form of radio modulation, this communication technique transmits information over a radio wave.

FQDN (fully qualified domain name) The entire domain name. It specifies the name of the computer, the domain in which it resides, and the top-level DNS domain (for example, www.marketing.quepublishing.com).

fragment-free switching A switching method that uses the first 64 bytes of a frame to determine whether the frame is corrupted. If this first part is intact, the frame is forwarded.

frame A grouping of information transmitted as a unit across the network at the data link layer of the OSI model.

Frame Length field In a data frame, the field that specifies the length of a frame.

Frame Type field In a data frame, the field that names the protocol being sent in the frame.

frequency The number of cycles of an alternating current signal over a unit of time. Frequency is expressed in hertz (Hz).

FTP (File Transfer Protocol) A protocol that provides for the transfer of files between two systems. FTP users authenticate using clear-text sign-in procedures, making FTP an unsecure protocol. FTP is part of the TCP/IP suite and operates at Layer 7 of the OSI model.

FTPS (File Transfer Protocol Security) A file transfer protocol that uses SSL/TLS to add security.

F-type connecter A screw-type connector used with coaxial cable. In computing environments, it is most commonly used to connect cable modems to ISP equipment or incoming cable feeds.

full backup A backup in which files, regardless of whether they have been changed, are copied to the backup medium. In a full backup, the files' archive bits are reset.

full duplex A system in which data simultaneously transmits in two directions. Compare with half duplex.

G

gateway A hardware or software solution that enables communications between two dissimilar networking systems or protocols. A gateway can operate at any layer of the OSI model but is commonly associated with the application layer.

Gb (gigabit) 1 billion bits, or 1000 Mb.

GBIC (gigabit interface converter) A Gigabit Ethernet and Fibre Channel transceiver standard.

Gbps (gigabits per second) The throughput of a given network medium in terms of 1 billion bps.

Gigabit Ethernet An IEEE 802.3 specification that defines standards for data transmissions of 1 Gbps. *See also* 1000BASE-T.

GLBP (Gateway Load Balancing Protocol) A proprietary Cisco protocol that adds basic load-balancing functionality in an attempt to overcome the limitations of existing redundant router protocols.

GPG (GNU Privacy Guard) An IETF RFC 4880-compliant alternative to the PGP suite of cryptographic software.

GRE (generic routing encapsulation) A routing encapsulation method that comes in a plain wrapper.

GSM (Global System for Mobile Communications) A standard created by the European Telecommunications Standards Institute (ETSI) used to describe communication protocols for second-generation (2G) cellular networks and devices. It has now become the default global standard for mobile communications in more than 219 countries and territories.

guaranteed flow control A method of flow control in which the sending and receiving hosts agree on a rate of data transmission. After the rate is determined, the communication takes place at the guaranteed rate until the sender is finished. No buffering takes place at the receiver.

H

HA (high availability) A system goal/attribute aimed at ensuring operational uptime higher than normal.

hacker A person who carries out attacks on a computer software program. *See also* cracker.

half duplex   A connection in which data is transmitted in both directions but not simultaneously. Compare with full duplex.

handshake   The initial communication between two data communication devices, during which they agree on protocol and transfer rules for the session.

hardware address   The hardware-encoded MAC address burned into every NIC.

hardware loopback   A device plugged into an interface for the purposes of simulating a network connection. This enables the interface to be tested as if it is operating while connected.

HDLC (High-Level Data Link Control)   An ISO developed bit-oriented synchronous data link layer protocol used for point-to-point or point-to-multipoint connections.

HDMI (High-Definition Multimedia Interface)   An audio/video interface for transferring data and compressed or uncompressed data to a monitor, projector, television, or digital audio device.

HIDS (host intrusion detection system)   A intrusion detection system that is based at the host (rather than the network). It monitors and analyzes data coming to and from the host.

HIPS (host intrusion prevention system)   A intrusion prevention system that is based at the host (rather than the network). It responds and reacts to threats coming to and from the host.

hop   The means by which routing protocols determine the shortest way to reach a given destination. Each router constitutes one hop. If a router is four hops away from another router, for example, three routers, or hops, exist between the first router and the destination. In some cases, the final step is also counted as a hop.

horizontal cross-connect   Ties the telecommunication room to the end user. Specifically, the horizontal cabling extends from the telecommunications outlet, or network outlet with RJ-45 connectors, at the client end. It includes all cable from that outlet to the telecommunication room to the horizontal cross-connect. The term *horizontal cross-connect* refers to the distribution point for the horizontal cable.

host   Typically refers to any device on the network that has been assigned an IP address.

host firewall   A firewall system installed and configured on and used for an individual host. Contrast to a network firewall that provides firewall services for all network nodes.

host ID   An identifier used to uniquely identify a client or resource on a network.

hostname   A name assigned to a system for the purposes of identifying it on the network in a more user-friendly manner than by the network address.

HOSTS file   A text file that contains hostname-to-IP address mappings.

All commonly used platforms accommodate static name resolution using the HOSTS file.

hot site A disaster recovery term used to describe an alternative network site that can be immediately functional in the event of a disaster at the primary site.

hot spare In a RAID configuration, a drive that sits idle until another drive in the RAID array fails, at which point the hot spare takes over the role of the failed drive.

hotspot An area in which an access point provides public wireless broadband network services to mobile visitors through a WLAN. Hotspots are often located in heavily populated places such as airports, hotels, and coffee shops.

hot swap The removal and replacement of a component in a system while the power is still on and the system is functioning.

HSPA (High-Speed Packet Access) A telephony protocol designed to increase speeds over previous protocols by combining features from others.

HSRP (Hot Standby Router Protocol) A Cisco proprietary protocol used for establishing redundant gateways.

HT (High Throughput) A feature of 802.11n for increased throughput on the network. The newer Very High Throughput (VHT) 802.11ac standard further increases network throughput.

HTTP (Hypertext Transfer Protocol) A protocol used by web browsers to transfer pages, links, and graphics from the remote node to the user's computer.

HTTPS (Hypertext Transfer Protocol Secure) A protocol that performs the same function as HTTP but does so over an encrypted link, ensuring the confidentiality of any data that is uploaded or downloaded. Also referred to as S-HTTP.

hub A largely obsolete hardware device that acts as a connection point on a network that uses twisted-pair cable. It operates at the physical layer of the OSI model and forwards signals to all ports. Also known as a concentrator or a multiport repeater.

HVAC (heating, ventilation, and air conditioning) A self-defining acronym.

Hz (hertz) Equivalent to cycles per second, hertz is the unit of frequency defined as the number of cycles per second of a periodic phenomenon.

I

IaaS (Infrastructure as a Service) The most basic method of cloud service computing; the users install everything from the operating system up.

IANA (Internet Assigned Numbers Authority) An organization responsible for IP addresses, domain names, and protocol parameters. Some functions of IANA, such as domain name assignment, have been devolved into other organizations.

ICA (Independent Computer Architecture) Contrary to the CompTIA acronym, the *C* is more correctly *Computing*, and this is a Cisco proprietary protocol for application servers.

ICANN (Internet Corporation for Assigned Names and Numbers) The nonprofit organization responsible for coordinating domain names and addresses.

ICMP (Internet Control Message Protocol) A network layer Internet protocol documented in RFC 792 that reports errors and provides other information relevant to IP packet processing. Utilities such as ping and tracert use functionality provided by ICMP.

ICS (Internet connection sharing) The use of one device with access to the Internet as an access point for other devices to connect.

ICS (industrial control system) A general term used to describe industrial control systems such as supervisory control and data acquisition (SCADA) systems.

IDF Some networks use multiple wiring closets. When this is the case, the wiring closet, known as the main distribution frame (MDF), connects to secondary wiring closets, or intermediate distribution frames (IDFs). *See also* MDF.

IDS (intrusion detection system) A software application or hardware device that monitors a network

or system for malicious or non-policy-related activity and reports to a centralized management system.

IEEE (Institute of Electrical and Electronics Engineers) A professional organization that, among other things, develops standards for networking and communications.

IEEE 1394 A standard that defines a system for connecting up to 63 devices on an external bus. IEEE 1394 is used with consumer electronic devices such as video cameras and MP3 players. IEEE 1394 is based on a technology developed by Apple called FireWire. FireWire was subsequently replaced by Thunderbolt.

IEEE 802.1 A standard that defines the OSI model's physical and data link layers. This standard allows two IEEE LAN stations to communicate over a LAN or WAN and is often called the internetworking standard.

IEEE 802.1X An IEEE security standard designed for authenticating wireless devices. This standard uses Extensible Authentication Protocol (EAP) to provide a central authentication server to authenticate each user on the network.

IEEE 802.3 A standard that specifies physical layer attributes, such as signaling types, data rates, and topologies, as well as the media access method used. It also defines specifications for the implementation of the physical layer and the MAC sublayer of the data link layer, using CSMA/CD. This standard also includes the original specifications for Fast Ethernet.

IEEE 802.11 The original IEEE wireless standard, which defines standards for wireless LAN communication.

IEEE 802.11a A wireless networking standard operating in the 5 GHz band. 802.11a supports a maximum theoretical data rate of 54 Mbps. Depending on interference, 802.11a could have a range of 150 feet at the lowest speed setting. Higher-speed transmissions would see a lower range. 802.11a uses the CSMA/CA media access method and is incompatible with 802.11b and 802.11g.

IEEE 802.11ac The 802.11ac wireless standard provides even higher throughput for WLANs on the 5 GHz frequency range. The specifications goal is at least 1 gigabit per second throughput for multistation WLANs and a single station link throughput of at least 500 Mbps. It supports MIMO spatial streams as well as the newer MU-MIMO technology. 802.11ac is backward compatible with 802.11b, g, and n.

IEEE 802.11b A commonly deployed IEEE wireless standard that uses the 2.4 GHz RF range and offers speeds up to 11 Mbps. Under ideal conditions, the transmission range can be as far as 75 meters.

IEEE 802.11g An IEEE wireless standard that is backward compatible with 802.11b. 802.11g offers a data rate of 54 Mbps. Like 802.11b, 802.11g uses the 2.4 GHz RF range.

IEEE 802.11n The 802.11n wireless standard significantly increased throughput in both the 2.4 GHz and 5 GHz frequency range. The baseline goal of the standard reaches speeds of 100 Mbps, but given the right conditions, 802.11n speeds can reach 600 Mbps. 802.11n is backward compatible with 802.11b and g.

IETF (Internet Engineering Task Force) A group of research volunteers responsible for specifying the protocols used on the Internet and the architecture of the Internet.

ifconfig A command used on Linux- and UNIX-based systems to obtain configuration for and configure network interfaces.

IGMP (Internet Group Management Protocol) A protocol used for communication between devices within the same multicast group. IGMP provides a mechanism for systems to detect and make themselves aware of other systems in the same group.

IGP The interior gateway protocol (IGP) identifies the protocols used to exchange routing information between routers within a LAN or interconnected LANs. *See* EGP.

IGRP (Interior Gateway Routing Protocol) A distance vector interior gateway protocol (IGP) developed by Cisco.

IKE (Internet Key Exchange) An IPsec protocol that uses X.509 certificates for authentication.

IMAP4 (Internet Message Access Protocol version 4) A protocol that enables email to be retrieved from a remote server. It is part of the TCP/IP suite, and it is similar in operation to POP3 but offers more functionality.

incremental backup   A backup of only files that have been created or changed since the last backup. In an incremental backup, the archive bit is cleared to indicate that a file has been backed up.

infrared   A wireless data communication method that uses light pulses in the infrared range as a carrier signal.

infrastructure topology   A wireless topology that defines a wireless network composed of an access point connected to a wired LAN. Wireless devices communicate with the wired LAN through the access point (AP).

inherited rights   The file system or directory access rights valid at a given point as a result of those rights being assigned at a higher level in the directory structure.

intelligent hub/switch   A hub or switch that contains some management or monitoring capability.

intelligent UPS   A UPS that has associated software for monitoring and managing the power provided to the system. For information to be passed between the UPS and the system, the UPS and system must be connected, which normally is achieved through a serial or USB connection.

interface   A device, such as a card or plug, that connects pieces of

hardware with a computer so that information can be moved from place to place (for example, between computers and printers, hard drives, and other devices, or between two or more nodes on a network). Also, the part of an application or operating system that the user sees.

interference   Anything that can compromise a signal's quality. On bound media, crosstalk and EMI are examples of interference. In wireless environments, atmospheric conditions that degrade a signal's quality would be considered interference.

internal loopback address Functionality built in to the TCP/IP stack that enables you to verify the correct functioning of the stack. You can ping any IPv4 address in the 127.x.x.x range, except the network address (127.0.0.0) or the broadcast address (127.255.255.255). The address 127.0.0.1 is most commonly used. In IPv6, the localhost (loopback) address is 0:0:0:0:0:0:0:1 or can also be expressed as ::1.

Internet domain name   The name of an area of the DNS namespace. The Internet domain name normally is expressed along with the top-level domain to which it belongs (for example, comptia.org).

Internet layer   In the TCP/IP architectural model, the layer responsible for addressing, packaging, and routing functions. Protocols that operate at this layer are responsible for encapsulating packets into Internet datagrams. All necessary routing algorithms are run here.

internetwork   A group of networks connected by routers or other connectivity devices so that the networks function as one network.

InterNIC (Internet Network Information Center)   Now known just as NIC (Network Information Center), this is the organization that was primarily responsible for domain name allocation.

intrusion detection   The process or procedures that warn you about successful or failed unauthorized access to a system.

IoT (Internet of Things)   A network of physical devices embedded with software, sensors, actuators, and network connectivity that enable these objects to collect and exchange data.

IP (Internet Protocol)   A network layer protocol, documented in RFC 791, that offers a connectionless internetwork service. IP provides features for addressing, packet fragmentation and reassembly, type-of-service specification, and security.

IP address   The unique address used to identify the network number and node address of a device connected to a TCP/IP network. IPv4 addresses typically are expressed in dotted-decimal format, such as 192.168.1.1. A typical IPv6 address looks like 2001:0:4137:9e76:18d1:2094:b980:a30.

IPS (intrusion prevention system)   A network device that continually scans the network, looking for inappropriate activity.

ipconfig   A Windows command that provides information about the configuration of the TCP/IP parameters, including the IP address.

IPsec (IP Security)   A protocol used to provide strong security standards for encryption and authentication on virtual private networks.

IPv4 (Internet Protocol version 4)   A suite of protocols used for communication on a local area network and for accessing the Internet.

IPv6 (Internet Protocol version 6)   The newer version of IP, which has a larger range of usable addresses than IPv4, and enhanced security.

IrDA   A wireless networking technology that uses infrared beams to send data transmissions between devices.

ISAKMP (Internet Security Association and Key Management Protocol)   Defined by RFC 2408, ISAKMP is a protocol typically used by IKE for key exchange.

iSCSI (Internet Small Computer System Interface)   An IP-based networking storage standard for linking and managing data storage facilities. iSCSI allows SCSI commands to be sent over IP networks, including LANs, WANs, and the Internet.

ISDN (Integrated Services Digital Network)   An internationally adopted standard for providing end-to-end digital communications between two points. ISDN is a dialup technology allowing data, voice, and other source traffic to be transmitted over a dedicated link.

ISDN terminal adapter A device that enables communication over an ISDN link.

IS-IS (Intermediate System-to-Intermediate System) A link-state protocol that discovers the shortest path for data to travel using the shortest path first (SPF) algorithm. IS-IS routers distribute topology information to other routers, allowing them to make the best path decisions.

ISO (International Organization for Standardization) A voluntary organization founded in 1946 that is responsible for creating international standards in many areas, including communications and computers. This also includes the development of the OSI model.

ISP (Internet service provider) A company or organization that provides facilities for clients to access the Internet.

IT (information technology) A fascinating field of study and career choice.

ITS (intelligent transportation system) A traffic management system intended for use in creating smart transportation networks.

IV (initialization vector) A fixed-size input used in cryptography. The larger initialization vector, the more it increases the difficulty in cracking and minimizes the risk of replay.

K

Kb (kilobit) 1000 bits.

Kbps (Kilobits per second) A measurement of the number of kilobits transmitted, or capable of being transmitted, in a second.

KB (kilobyte) 1000 bytes.

Kerberos A network authentication protocol designed to ensure that the data sent across networks is encrypted and safe from attack. Its primary purpose is to provide authentication for client/server applications.

KVM (keyboard video mouse) A device that allows one keyboard, one mouse, and one monitor to be used with multiple devices.

L

L2TP (Layer 2 Tunneling Protocol) A VPN protocol that defines its own tunneling protocol and works with the advanced security methods of IPsec. L2TP enables PPP sessions to be tunneled across an arbitrary medium to a home gateway at an ISP or corporation.

LACP (Link Aggregation Control Protocol) An IEEE specification that provides a control method of bundling several physical ports into one single channel.

LAN (local-area network) A group of connected computers located in a single geographic area—usually a building or office—that shares data and services.

latency The delay induced by a piece of equipment or device used to transfer data.

LC (local connector) A media connector used with fiber-optic cabling.

LDAP (Lightweight Directory Access Protocol) A protocol used to access and query compliant directory services systems, such as Microsoft Active Directory.

learning bridge A bridge that builds its own bridging address table instead of requiring someone to manually enter information. Most modern bridges are learning bridges. Also called a smart bridge.

LEC (local exchange carrier) A regulatory term used in telephony to represent the local telephone provider.

LED (light-emitting diode) A type of semiconductor that emits light and is commonly used in displays.

legacy An older computer system or technology.

line conditioner A device used to stabilize the flow of power to the connected component. Also known as a power conditioner or voltage regulator.

link light An LED on a networking device, such as a hub, switch, or NIC. The illumination of the link light indicates that, at a hardware level, the connection is complete and functioning.

link-state routing A dynamic routing method in which routers tell neighboring routers of their

existence through packets called link-state advertisements (LSAs). By interpreting the information in these packets, routers can create maps of the entire network. Compare with distance-vector routing.

Linux A UNIX-like operating system kernel created by Linus Torvalds. Linux is distributed under an open-source license agreement, as are many of the applications and services that run on it.

LLC (logical link control) layer A sublayer of the data link layer of the OSI model. The LLC layer provides an interface for network layer protocols and the MAC sublayer.

LLDP (Link Layer Discovery Protocol) A protocol used by network devices for advertising on an IEEE 802 local area network.

logical addressing scheme The addressing method used in providing manually assigned node addressing.

logical topology The appearance of the network to the devices that use it, even if in physical terms the layout of the network is different. *See also* physical topology.

loop A continuous circle that a packet takes through a series of nodes in a network until it eventually times out.

loopback plug A device used for loopback testing.

loopback testing A troubleshooting method in which the output and input wires are crossed or shorted in a manner that enables all outgoing data to be routed back into the card.

LSA (link state advertisements) A method of OSPF communication in which the router sends the local routing topology to all other local routers in the same OSPF area.

LTE (Long-Term Evolution) A wireless communication standard more commonly referred to as 4G LTE.

LWAPP (Lightweight Access Point Protocol) More commonly known as Lightweight, this is a protocol simplifying communication with multiple access points at the same time.

M

MaaS (Mobility as a Service) Also known as Transportation as a Service, this is a shift toward mobility solutions that are consumed as a service as opposed to personal vehicles.

MAC (Media Access Control) address A six-octet number, described in hexadecimal, that uniquely identifies a host on a network. It is a unique number burned into the network interface.

MAC layer In the OSI model, the lower of the two sublayers of the data link layer. It is defined by the IEEE as being responsible for interaction with the physical layer.

MAN (metropolitan-area network) A network that spans a defined geographic location, such as a city or suburb.

master name server The supplying name server that has authority in a DNS zone.

Mb (megabit) 1 million bits. Used to rate transmission transfer speeds.

Mbps (megabits per second) A measurement of the number of megabits sent, or capable of being sent, in a second.

MB (megabyte) 1 million bytes. Usually refers to file size.

MBps (megabytes per second) A measurement of the number of megabytes sent in a second.

MDF The main distribution frame is a type of wiring closet. The primary wiring closet for a network typically holds the majority of the network gear, including routers, switches, wiring, servers, and more. This is also typically the wiring closet where outside lines run into the network. This main wiring closet is known as the MDF. One of the key components in the MDF is a primary patch panel. The network connector jacks attached to this patch panel lead out to the building for network connections. *See also* IDF.

MDI (medium-dependent interface) A type of port found on Ethernet networking devices, such as hubs and switches, in which the wiring is straight through. MDI ports are sometimes called uplink ports. They are intended for use as connectivity points to other hubs and switches.

MDIX (media dependent interface crossover) A type of port found on Ethernet networking devices in which the wiring is crossed so that the transmit line of one device becomes the receive line of the other. MDI-X is used to connect hubs and switches to client computers.

media converter   Network media converters are used to interconnect different types of cables within an existing network. For example, the media converter can be used to connect newer Gigabit Ethernet technologies with older 100BASE-T networks.

media tester   Defines a range of software or hardware tools designed to test a particular media type.

mesh   A type of network topology in which each node connects to every other node. The mesh network provides a high level of redundancy because it provides alternative routes for data to travel should a single route become unavailable.

metric   A value that can be assigned to a route to encourage or discourage the use of the route. *See also* cost.

MGCP (Media Gateway Control Protocol)   A protocol for controlling IP-based media gateways through the public switched telephone networks (PSTNs).

MIB (Management Information Base)   A data set that defines the criteria that can be retrieved and set on a device using SNMP.

microsegmentation   The process of using switches to divide a network into smaller segments.

microwaves   A wireless technology sometimes used to transmit data between buildings and across vast distances.

MIMO (multiple input, multiple output)   The use of multiple antennas—often at both the transmitter and receiver—to improve communications in IEEE 802.11n and 802.11ac Wi-Fi networks.

MLA (master license agreement)   The main contract defining services to be offered by a provider.

MMF (multimode fiber)   A type of fiber in which many beams of light travel through the cable, bouncing off the cable walls. This strategy actually weakens the signal, reducing the length and speed at which the data signal can travel. *See also* SMF.

modem (modulator-demodulator)   A device used to modulate and demodulate the signals that pass through it. It converts the direct current pulses of the serial digital code from the controller into the analog signals compatible with the telephone network.

MOA (memorandum of agreement)   An agreement expressing a convergence of will between the parties and indicating an intended common line of action.

MOU (memorandum of understanding)   An agreement (bilateral or multilateral) between parties defining terms and conditions of an agreement.

MPLS (multiprotocol label switching) A technology designed to speed up network traffic flow by moving away from the use of traditional routing tables. Instead of routing tables, MPLS uses short labels to direct packets and forward them through the network.

MS-CHAP (Microsoft Challenge Handshake Authentication Protocol) An implementation of CHAP specific to Microsoft operating systems and commonly offered in both server and desktop operating systems.

MSA (master service agreement) A contract between parties, in which the parties agree to most of the terms that will govern future transactions or future agreements.

MSDS (material safety data sheet) A document defining the hazards of working with a chemical or compound, safety precautions, and guidelines for dealing with spills or accidents.

MT-RJ connector A media connector used with fiber-optic cabling.

MTBF (mean time between failures) The predicted time between inherent failures of a system.

MTTR (mean time to recovery) The average time that a device will take to recover from a failure.

MTU (maximum transmission unit) The largest data size that a protocol/layer can transmit.

multicast A single-packet transmission from one sender to a specific group of destination nodes.

multihomed A term used to refer to a device that has more than one network interface.

multimeter A tool used to measure voltage, current, and resistance.

multiplatform A term used to refer to a programming language, technology, or protocol that runs on different types of CPUs or operating systems.

multiplexing A technique of combining multiple channels over a transmission path and then recovering or demultiplexing the separate channels at the receiving end. Examples include FDM, TDM, CDM, and WDM.

MU-MIMO (multiuser multiple input, multiple output) A set of advanced MIMO technologies included with IEEE 802.11ac that dramatically enhances wireless throughput.

MX (Mail Exchanger) A DNS record entry used to identify the mail server.

N

NAC (Network Access Control) A computer networking security solution that uses a set of network protocols with the goal to unify endpoint security solutions such as antivirus, vulnerability assessment, and authentication.

name server A server that contains a database of name resolution information used to resolve network names to network addresses.

NAS (network-attached storage) An array of disks providing network storage capacity to the users on the network. It is a specialized file-level computer storage device connected to a network.

NAT (Network Address Translation) A standard that enables the translation of IP addresses used on one network to a different IP address that is acceptable for use on another network. This translation enables multiple systems to access an external network, such as the Internet, through a single IP address.

NCP (Network Control Protocol) A protocol used to define control between network protocols or layers.

NDR (non-delivery receipt) A message informing the sender that a previous message has not been delivered because a delivery problem occurred.

NetBEUI (NetBIOS Extended User Interface) A nonroutable, Microsoft proprietary networking protocol designed for use in small networks.

NetBIOS (Network Basic Input/ Output System) A software application that enables different applications to communicate between computers on a LAN.

netstat A Windows operating system command-line utility that displays protocol statistics and current TCP/IP network connections.

network card *See* NIC.

network ID The part of a TCP/IP address that specifies the network portion of the IP address. The

network ID is determined by the class of the address, which in turn is determined by the subnet mask used.

network interface layer The bottom layer of the TCP/IP architectural model, which is responsible for sending and receiving frames.

network layer Layer 3 of the OSI model, which is where routing based on node addresses (IP addresses) occurs.

network operating system An operating system that runs on the servers on a network. Network operating systems include Windows Server, UNIX, and Linux.

NFC (near field communication) Any protocol that enables two electronic devices to establish communication by bringing them within 1.6 inches of each other. This is gaining in popularity for use with a smartphone and electronic payment systems.

NFS (Network File System) A file sharing and access protocol most commonly associated with UNIX and Linux systems.

NGFW (Next Generation Firewall) Combining a traditional firewall with any other network device (such as an intrusion prevention system) to get additional functionalities.

NIC (network interface card) A hardware component that serves as the interface, or connecting component, between a network and the node. It has a transceiver, a MAC address, and a physical connector for the network cable. Also called a network adapter or network card.

NIDS (network intrusion detection system) An intrusion detection system that analyzes and monitors at the network level rather than the host level.

NIPS (network intrusion prevention system) A network security system that monitors, blocks, and reports malicious network activity.

NIU (network interface unit) A generic term for a network interface device (NID) or point of demarcation.

nm (nanometer) A measurement equal to one billionth of a meter.

NMS (network management system) An application that acts as a central management point for network management. Most NMS systems use SNMP to communicate with network devices. *See also* SNMP.

NNTP (Network News Transfer Protocol) An Internet protocol that controls how news articles are to be queried, distributed, and posted. NNTP uses port 119.

noise Another name for EMI. *See also* EMI.

nslookup Windows and Linux/ UNIX command-line utility used to query Domain Name System (DNS) servers and clients to obtain DNS information.

NTP (Network Time Protocol) A protocol used to communicate time synchronization information between devices on the network. NTP is part of the TCP/IP suite. NTP uses port 123.

O

OCSP (online certificate status protocol) A protocol used for obtaining the revocation status of an X.509 digital certificate.

OCx (Optical Carrier) A set of standards used for digital signals with SONET fiber networks.

OS (operating system) The main computer program that manages and integrates all the applications running on a computer. The OS handles all interactions with the processor.

OSI (Open Systems Interconnect) reference model A seven-layer model created by the ISO to standardize and explain the interactions of networking protocols.

OSPF (Open Shortest Path First) A link-state routing protocol used on TCP/IP networks. Compare with distance-vector routing.

OTDR (optical time-domain reflectometer) A tool used to locate problems with optical media, such as cable breaks.

OUI (Organizationally Unique Identifier) A 24-bit number that uniquely identifies a vendor, a manufacturer, or other organization globally or worldwide.

P

PaaS (Platform as a Service) A cloud computing service model in which the provider supplies the operating system and the user is responsible for the stack above it.

packet A packet refers to a unit of data that travels in communication networks.

packet filtering A firewall method in which each packet that attempts to pass through the firewall is examined to determine its contents. The packet is then allowed to pass, or it is blocked, as appropriate.

packet sniffer A device or application that enables data to be copied from the network and analyzed. In legitimate applications, it is a useful network troubleshooting tool.

PAN (personal-area network) A network layout whereby devices work together in close proximity to share information and services, commonly using technologies such as Bluetooth or infrared.

PAP (Password Authentication Protocol) A simple authentication protocol in which the username and password are sent to the remote-access server in clear text, making it possible for anyone listening to network traffic to steal both. PAP typically is used only when connecting to older UNIX-based remote-access servers that do not support any additional authentication protocols.

passive hub A hub that has no power and therefore does not regenerate the signals it receives. Compare with active hub.

password A set of characters used with a username to authenticate a user on a network and to provide the user with rights and permissions to files and resources.

PAT (Port Address Translation) A variation on NAT (Network Address Translation). With PAT, all systems on the LAN are translated into the same IP address, but with a different port number assignment. *See also* NAT.

patch A fix for a bug in a software application. Patches can be downloaded from the Internet to correct errors or security problems in software applications.

patch cable A cable, normally twisted pair, used to connect two devices. Strictly speaking, a patch cable is the cable that connects a port on a hub or switch to the patch panel, but today people commonly use the term to refer to any cable connection.

patch panel A device in which the cables used in coaxial or twisted-pair networks converge and are connected. The patch panel is usually in a central location.

PC (personal computer) A general-purpose computer intended for use by individual users.

PCM (phase change memory) A type of nonvolatile random-access memory (RAM).

PDoS (permanent denial of service) A Denial of Service type attack that damages a system so badly that it requires replacement or reinstallation of hardware.

PDU (protocol data unit)   Data that contains control information, such as address information and user information.

peer-to-peer networking   A network environment that does not have dedicated servers, where communication occurs between similarly capable network nodes that act as both clients and servers.

permissions   Authorization provided to users that allows them to access objects on a network. Network administrators generally assign permissions. Permissions are slightly different from but are often used with rights.

PGP (Pretty Good Privacy) A popular encryption/decryption program used for cryptography.

physical address   The MAC address on every NIC. The physical address is applied to a NIC by the manufacturer. Except for rare occurrences, it is never changed.

physical layer   Layer 1 of the OSI model, where all physical connectivity is defined.

physical network diagram   A diagram that displays the physical layout of a network, including placement of systems and all network cabling.

physical topology   The actual physical layout of the network. Common physical topologies include star, bus, mesh, and ring. Compare with logical topology.

ping   A TCP/IP stack utility that works with ICMP and that uses echo requests and replies to test connectivity to other systems.

PKI (public key infrastructure)   A collection of software, standards, and policies combined to enable users from the Internet or other unsecured public networks to securely exchange data. PKI uses a public and private cryptographic key pair obtained and shared through a trusted authority.

plenum   The space between the structural ceiling and a drop-down ceiling. It is commonly used for heating, ventilation, and air conditioning systems and to run network cables.

plug and play   An architecture designed to enable the operating system to detect hardware devices and for the driver to be automatically loaded and configured.

PoE (Power over Ethernet)   A technology that enables electrical power to be transmitted over twisted-pair Ethernet cable. The power is transferred, along with data, to provide power to remote devices.

policies and procedures Policies refer to an organization's documented rules regarding what is to be done, or not done, and why. Network procedures differ from policies in that they identify the way in which tasks are to be performed.

polling   The media access method for transmitting data in which a controlling device is used to contact each node to determine whether it has data to send.

POP3 (Post Office Protocol version 3)   A protocol that is part of the TCP/IP suite used to retrieve mail stored on a remote server. The most commonly used version of POP is POP3. POP3 is an application layer protocol.

port   In physical networking terms, a pathway on a networking device that enables other devices to be connected. In software terms, a port is the entry point into an application, a system, or a protocol stack.

port mirroring   A process by which two ports on a device, such as a switch, are configured to receive the same information. Port mirroring is useful in troubleshooting scenarios.

POTS (plain old telephone system)   The current analog public telephone system. *See also* PSTN.

PPP (Point-to-Point Protocol)   A common dial-up networking protocol that includes provisions for security and protocol negotiation. Provides host-to-network and switch-to-switch connections for one or more user sessions.

PPPoE (Point-to-Point Protocol over Ethernet)   An Internet connection authentication protocol that uses two separate technologies, Ethernet and PPP, to provide a method for multiple users to share a common digital subscriber line (DSL), cable modem, or wireless connection to the Internet.

PPTP (Point-to-Point Tunneling Protocol)   A protocol that encapsulates private network data in IP packets. These packets are transmitted over synchronous and asynchronous circuits to hide the Internet's underlying routing and switching infrastructure from both senders and receivers.

presentation layer   Layer 6 of the OSI model, which prepares information to be used by the application layer.

PRI (Primary Rate Interface)   A high-level network interface standard for use with ISDN. PRI is defined as having a rate of 1.544 Mbps, and it consists of a single 64 Kbps D channel plus 23 T1 B channels for voice or data. *See also* BRI and ISDN.

primary name server   The DNS server that offers zone data from files stored locally on the machine.

private network   A network to which access is limited, restricted, or controlled. Most corporate networks are private networks. Compare with public network.

proprietary   A standard or specification created by a single manufacturer, vendor, or other private enterprise.

protocol   A set of rules or standards that control data transmission and other interactions between networks, computers, peripheral devices, and operating systems.

protocol analyzer   Protocol analyzers can be hardware- or software-based, with their primary function being to analyze network protocols such as TCP, UDP, HTTP, FTP, and more.

proxy A device, application, or service that acts as an intermediary between two hosts on a network, eliminating the capability for direct communication.

proxy server A server that acts as a go-between for a workstation and the Internet. A proxy server typically provides an increased level of security, caching, NAT, and administrative control.

PSK (pre-shared key) A value (key) shared with another party so that they can encrypt messages to then be securely sent.

PSTN (public switched telephone network) A term that refers to all the telephone networks and services in the world. The same as POTS, PSTN refers to the world's collection of interconnected public telephone networks that are both commercial and government owned. All the PSTN is digital, except the connection between local exchanges and customers (which is called the local loop or last mile), which remains analog.

PTP (Point-to-Point) More commonly referenced as PPP, this protocol is used to establish a direct connection between two nodes.

PTR (pointer) A DNS record used to map an IP address to a hostname.

PUA (privileged user agreement) Established, and agreed upon, rules of behavior that define what privileged users can and cannot do with their elevated permissions.

public network A network, such as the Internet, to which anyone can connect with the most minimal of restrictions. Compare with private network.

punchdown block A device used to connect network cables from equipment closets or rooms to other parts of a building. Connections to networking equipment such as hubs or switches are established from the punchdown block. Also used in telecommunications wiring to distribute phone cables to their respective locations throughout the building.

punchdown tool A hand tool that enables the connection of twisted-pair wires to wiring equipment such as a patch panel.

PVC (permanent virtual circuit) A permanent dedicated virtual link shared in a Frame Relay network, replacing a hardwired dedicated end-to-end line.

Q–R

QoS (quality of service) Describes the strategies used to manage and increase the flow of network traffic. QoS features enable administrators to predict bandwidth use, monitor that use, and control it to ensure that bandwidth is available to the applications that need it.

QSFP (quad small factor pluggable) A compact, hot-pluggable transceiver used for data communications.

RADIUS (Remote Authentication Dial-In User Service) A security standard that employs a client/server model to authenticate remote network users. Remote users are authenticated using a challenge-and-response mechanism between the remote-access server and the RADIUS server.

RARP (Reverse Address Resolution Protocol) A protocol, part of the TCP/IP suite, that resolves MAC addresses to IP addresses. Its relative ARP resolves IP addresses to MAC addresses. RARP resides on the network layer of the OSI model.

RAS (Remote Access Service) A Windows service that enables access to the network through remote connections.

RDP (Remote Desktop Protocol) A presentation layer protocol that supports a Remote Desktop Connection between an RDP client (formerly known as "Windows Terminal Client") and a server.

regulations Regulations are actual legal restrictions with legal consequences.

remote control In networking, having physical control of a remote computer through software.

remote node A node or computer connected to a network through a remote connection. Dialing in to the Internet from home is an example of the remote node concept.

repeater A device that regenerates and retransmits signals on a network. Repeaters usually are used to strengthen signals going long distances.

resolver A system that requests the resolution of a name to an IP address. This term can be applied to both DNS and WINS clients.

restore To transfer data from backup media to a server. The opposite of backup.

RF (radio frequency) A rate of oscillation used by radio waves and radio signals.

RFC (Request For Comments) The process by which standards relating to the Internet, the TCP/IP suite, and associated technologies are created, commented on, and approved.

RFI (radio frequency interference) Interference that affects radio frequency communication.

RFP (request for proposal) A document that solicits proposals, often through a bidding process.

RG (Radio Guide) More frequently used as *Radio Grade*, this is a specification commonly used with connection types.

RG-6/59 Designations for the coaxial cable used in thin coaxial networks that operate on the Ethernet standard.

rights An authorization provided to users that allows them to perform certain tasks. The network administrator generally assigns rights. Slightly different from but often used with the term *permissions*.

RIP (Routing Information Protocol) A protocol that uses hop count as a routing metric to control the direction and flow of packets between routers on an internetwork.

RJ (Registered Jack) A specification for a family of cable connectors.

RJ-11 connector A connector used with telephone systems. Can have up to six conductors.

RJ-45 connector A connector used with twisted-pair cable. Can support eight conductors for four pairs of wires.

route The entire path between two nodes on a network.

router A device that works at the network layer of the OSI model to control the flow of data between two or more network segments.

RPO (recovery point objective) The maximum acceptable period in which data might be lost from a major incident.

RSA An algorithm for public-key cryptography. Can be used for encryption purposes. RSA is used as a secure solution for e-commerce.

RSH (Remote Shell) A protocol, and corresponding application, used to remotely run a shell across an IP-based network.

RSTP (Rapid Spanning Tree Protocol) The default protocol for preventing loops on Ethernet networks.

RTO (recovery time objective) The acceptable duration of time within which a business process must

be restored after a disaster to avoid unacceptable consequences associated with a break in business continuity.

RTP (Real-Time Transport Protocol) The Internet-standard protocol for the transport of real-time data, including audio and video.

RTSP (Real-Time Streaming Protocol) A protocol used for establishing and maintaining communications with a media server.

RTT (Round Trip Time or Real Transfer Time) A measurement of the length of time it takes for data to be sent and returned.

S

SA (security association) The establishment of shared security attributes between two entities on a network to support secure communications between them.

SaaS (Software as a Service) A cloud computing service model in which a user runs everything supplied by the provider.

sag A momentary drop in the voltage provided by a power source.

SC (Standard Connector) A type of connector used with fiber cabling.

SCADA (supervisory control and data acquisition) A system operating with coded signals to remotely control a device or equipment.

SCP (Secure Copy Protocol)   A basic file-copying protocol that uses Secure Shell (SSH) technology to provide security to the transfer.

SDLC (software development life cycle)   The life cycle of software development.

SDN (software defined network)   An approach to networking that allows network administrators to programmatically manage network behavior dynamically via open interfaces and provide abstraction of lower-level functionality.

SDP (Session Description Protocol)   A format of streaming media initialization parameters.

SDSL (symmetrical digital subscriber line)   A DSL implementation that offers the same speeds for uploads and downloads. It is not widely implemented in the home/small business environment and cannot share a phone line.

secondary name server   A type of DNS server that gets its zone data from another DNS name server that has authority in that zone.

Security log   A log located in the Windows Event Viewer that provides information on audit events that the administrator has determined to be security-related. These events include logons, attempts to log on, attempts to access areas that are denied, and attempts to log on outside normal hours.

segment   A physical section of a network.

server   A network node that fulfills service requests for clients. Usually referred to by the type of service it performs, such as file server, communications server, or print server.

server-based application   An application run from a network share rather than from a copy installed on a local computer.

server-based networking   A network operating system dedicated to providing services to workstations, or clients. *See also* client/server networking.

service pack   A software update that fixes multiple known problems and in some cases provides additional functionality to an application or operating system.

session   How long the dialog remains open between two nodes.

session layer   Layer 5 of the OSI model, which establishes, manages, and terminates sessions between applications on different nodes.

SFP (small form-factor pluggable)   A line of small optical transceivers that have recently become available.

SFTP (Secure File Transfer Protocol)   An implementation of File Transfer Protocol (FTP) that uses Secure Shell (SSH) technology to provide additional authentication and encryption services for file transfers.

SGCP (Simple Gateway Control Protocol)   A communication protocol used with VoIP.

SHA (Secure Hash Algorithm) A cryptographic hash algorithm used in security and defined by the United States National Security Agency.

shared system The infrastructure component routed directly into an internetwork's backbone for optimal systems access. It provides connectivity to servers and other shared systems.

SIEM (Security Information and Event Management) Any of a family of products that combine security information management and event management to achieve a more holistic approach to security.

SIP (Session Initiation Protocol) An application layer protocol designed to establish and maintain multimedia sessions such as Internet telephony calls.

SLA (service level agreement) An agreement between a customer and provider detailing the level of service to be provided on a regular basis and in the event of problems.

SLIP (Serial Line Internet Protocol) An antiquated IP-based protocol for modem connections and serial ports.

SMB (server message block) An application-layer network protocol used primarily for providing shared access to files, printers, and ports as well as miscellaneous communications between nodes.

SMF (single-mode fiber) A type of fiber that uses a single direct beam of light, thus allowing for greater distances and increased transfer speeds. *See also* MMF.

SMS (Short Message Service) A text-based communication service for phones, web, and other devices.

SMTP (Simple Mail Transfer Protocol) An Internet protocol used for the transfer of email messages and attachments.

SNAT (Static NAT) A simple form of NAT. SNAT maps a private IP address directly to a static unchanging public IP address. *See also* NAT.

SNMP (Simple Network Management Protocol) Provides network devices with a method to monitor and control network devices; manage configurations, statistics collection, performance, and security; and report network management information to a management console. SNMP is part of the TCP/IP suite.

SNMP agent A software component that enables a device to communicate with, and be contacted by, an SNMP management system.

SNMP trap An SNMP utility that sends an alarm to notify the administrator that something within the network activity differs from the established threshold, as defined by the administrator.

SNTP (Simple Network Time Protocol) An IP-based protocol used to coordinate time among devices across the network.

SOA (start of authority) A record of information containing data on DNS zones and other DNS records.

A DNS zone is the part of a domain for which an individual DNS server is responsible. Each zone contains a single SOA record.

SOHO (small office/home office) A small network typically serving 1 to 10 users.

SONET (Synchronous Optical Network) A U.S. standard for data transmission that operates at speeds up to 2.4 Gbps over optical networks referred to as OC-x, where x is the level. The international equivalent of SONET is Synchronous Digital Hierarchy (SDH).

SOP (standard operating procedure) The normal, accepted way that business is conducted.

source address The address of the host that sent the frame. The source address is contained in the frame so that the destination node knows who sent the data.

source-route bridge A bridge used in source-route bridging to send a packet to the destination node through the route specified by the sending node.

SOW (statement of work) A formal document that defines work activities to be performed for a client.

SPB (Shortest Path Bridging) Defined in IEEE 802.1aq, this is a standard defining a routing (Layer 2) protocol.

SPI (stateful packet inspection) A type of firewall that works at the network layer and keeps track of the state of active connections.

spike An instantaneous, dramatic increase in the voltage input to a device. Spikes are responsible for much of the damage done to network hardware components.

SPS (standby power supply) A type of power supply in which the SPS monitors the power line and switches to battery power as soon as it detects a problem. During the time it takes to switch to battery power, the computer does not receive any power and may power down. This is in contrast to an online UPS, which constantly provides battery power.

SSH (Secure Shell) An application, such as Telnet, that enables a session to be opened on a remote host. SSH differs from Telnet in that it provides additional authentication methods and encryption for data as it traverses the network. SSH uses TCP/IP port 22.

SSID (service set identifier) A unique client identifier sent over the WLAN that acts as a simple password used for authentication between a wireless client and an access point. The SSID is used to differentiate between networks. Therefore, the client system and the AP must use the same SSID.

SSL (Secure Sockets Layer) A method of securely transmitting information to and receiving information from a remote website. SSL is implemented through HTTPS. SSL operates at the presentation layer of the OSI model and uses TCP/IP port 443.

ST (Straight Tip or Snap Twist) A type of connector used with cabling.

STA (Spanning Tree Algorithm) A standard defined by IEEE 802.1 as part of STP to eliminate loops in an internetwork with multiple paths.

star A type of physical network design in which all nodes connect to a centralized device—in most cases a network switch.

static IP address An IP address manually assigned to a network device, as opposed to dynamically via DHCP.

static routing A routing method in which all routes must be entered into a device manually and in which no route information is exchanged between routing devices on the network. Compare with dynamic routing.

static window A mechanism used in flow control that prevents the sender of data from overwhelming the receiver. The amount of data that can be buffered in a static window is configured dynamically by the protocol.

ST connector ST refers to a type of fiber connector.

storage-area network (SAN) A subnetwork of storage devices, usually found on high-speed networks and shared by all servers on a network.

store-and-forward A fast-packet-switching method that produces higher latency than other switching methods because the entire contents of the packet are copied into the switch's onboard buffers. CRC calculations are performed before the packet can be passed on to the destination address.

STP (shielded twisted-pair) Twisted-pair network cable that has shielding to insulate the cable from EMI.

STP (Spanning Tree Protocol) A protocol developed to eliminate the loops caused by the multiple paths in an internetwork. STP is defined in IEEE 802.1.

subdomain A privately controlled segment of the DNS namespace that exists under other segments of the namespace as a division of the main domain. Sometimes also called a child domain.

subnet A logical division of a network, based on the address to which all the devices on the network are assigned.

subnet mask A 32-bit address used to mask, or screen, a portion of an IP address to differentiate the part of the address that designates the network and the part that designates the host.

subnetting The process of using parts of the node portion of an assigned IP address to create more network IDs. Although subnetting increases the number of network IDs, it decreases the number of node addresses available for each network ID.

supernetting The process of aggregating IP network addresses and using them as a single network address range.

surge A voltage increase that is less dramatic than that of a spike but can last much longer. Sometimes called a swell. The opposite of a brownout.

surge protector An inexpensive and simple device placed between a power outlet and a network component to protect the component from spikes and surges. Also known as a surge suppressor.

SVC (switched virtual circuit) A virtual circuit dynamically established on demand to form a dedicated link. It is broken when transmission is complete.

switch A Layer 2 networking device that forwards frames based on destination addresses.

SYN A message sent to initiate a TCP session between two devices. The full term is *synchronization packet*.

synchronous transmission A digital signal transmission method that uses a precise clocking method and a predefined number of bits sent at a constant rate.

syslog (system log) A log, accessed through Event Viewer on Windows Server platforms, that provides information and warnings on events logged by operating system components and hardware devices. These events include driver failures, device conflicts, read/write errors, timeouts, and bad block errors.

T

T1/E1 T1 lines are a form of T-Carrier lines that offer transmission speeds of 1.544 Mbps. E1 refers to the European equivalent of T1. *See also* T-carrier.

T1 crossover *See* crossover cable.

T3/E3 T3 carrier lines offer transmission speeds of up to 44.736 Mbps, using 672 64 Kbps B channels. E3 refers to the European equivalent of T3. *See also* T-carrier.

TA (terminal adaptor) Also known as *adapter*, this is a device that connects a node to an ISDN network.

TACACS (Terminal Access Controller Access-Control System) A family of related protocols handling remote authentication and related services for networked access control through a centralized server.

TACACS+ (Terminal Access Controller Access Control System Plus) A security protocol designed to provide centralized validation of users who are attempting to gain access to a router or network access server (NAS). TACACS+ is a set of security protocols designed to provide authentication, authorization, and accounting (AAA) of remote users. TACACS+ uses TCP port 49 by default.

T-carrier (terrestrial carrier) T-carrier lines are high-speed dedicated digital lines that can be leased from telephone companies. T-carrier lines can support both voice and data transmissions and are often used to create point-to-point private networks.

TCP (Transmission Control Protocol) A connection-oriented, reliable data transmission communication service that operates at the transport layer of the OSI model. TCP is part of the TCP/IP suite.

TCP/IP (Transmission Control Protocol/Internet Protocol) A suite of protocols that includes TCP and IP. TCP/IP was originally designed for use on large internetworks but has now become the de facto protocol for networks of all sizes.

TCP/IP socket A socket, or connection to an endpoint, used in TCP/IP communication transmissions.

TDM (time-division multiplexing) Divides a single communication channel into multiple channels, enabling data signals to be transferred simultaneously as subchannels in one communication channel. Despite being only a single channel, data signals take turns sending data.

TDR (time-domain reflectometer) A device used to test copper cables to determine whether and where a break is on the cable. For optical cables, an optical TDR is used.

Telco (telephone company) A slang term for the telephone provider in question.

Telnet A standard terminal emulation protocol in the TCP/IP

stack. Telnet is used to perform terminal emulation over TCP/IP via remote terminal connections, enabling users to log in to remote systems and use resources as if they were connected to a local system. Telnet has been replaced in most instances by the more secure SSH.

temperature monitor A device used to monitor temperature typically in a server room or wiring closet.

Terminal Services A service on Windows Server platforms that enables clients to connect to the server as if it were a multiuser operating system. All the processing for the client session is performed on the server. Only screen updates and user input are transmitted across the network connection. Window Server 2008 R2 and later versions have replaced Terminal Services with Remote Desktop Services (RDS).

TFTP (Trivial File Transfer Protocol) A simplified version of FTP that enables file transfers but does not offer any security or file management capabilities. TFTP uses TCP/IP port 69.

throughput tester A device used to test the actual data throughput of a network cable.

TIA (Telecommunications Industry Association) An organization that, along with the Electronic Industries Association (EIA), develops standards for telecommunications technologies.

TKIP (Temporal Key Integrity Protocol) Designed to address the shortcomings of the WEP security protocol. TKIP is an encryption protocol defined in IEEE 802.11i.

T-line A digital communication line used in WANs. Commonly used T designations are T1 (Trunk Level 1) and T3 (Trunk Level 3). It is also possible to use only part of a T1 line, which is known as fractional T1. T1 lines support a data transmission rate of up to 1.544 Mbps.

TLS (Transport Layer Security) A security protocol designed to ensure privacy between communicating client/server applications. When a server and client communicate, TLS ensures that no one can eavesdrop and intercept or otherwise tamper with the data message. TLS is the successor to SSL.

TMS (transportation management system) A software module that sits between warehouse management and an ERP system.

token A frame that provides controlling information. In a token ring network, the node that possesses the token is the one that is allowed to transmit next.

tone generator A device used with a tone locator to locate and diagnose problems with twisted-pair cabling. Commonly referred to as fox and hound.

toner probe A network tool used to locate the ends of a run of network cable.

topology The shape or layout of a physical network and the flow of data through the network. *See also*

logical topology and physical topology.

ToS (Type of Service) A field in an IPv4 header that defines such things as the priority of the packet.

TPM (trusted platform module) A secure cryptoprocessor standard that employs a dedicated microcontroller to secure hardware by integrating cryptographic keys into the device.

trace route A function of the TCP/IP suite, implemented in utilities such as traceroute and tracert, which enables the entire path of a packet to be tracked between source and destination hosts. It is used as a troubleshooting tool.

tracert A Windows command-line utility used to track the route a data packet takes to get to its destination.

transmit To send data using light, electronic, or electric signals. In networking, this is usually done in the form of digital signals composed of bits.

transparent bridging A situation in which the bridges on a network tell each other which ports on the bridge should be opened and closed, which ports should be forwarding packets, and which ports should be blocking packets—all without the assistance of any other device.

transport layer Layer 4 of the OSI model. Protocols at this layer perform functions such as segmenting data so that it can be sent over the network and then reassembling the segmented data on the receiving end. The transport layer also deals with some of the errors that can occur in a stream of data, such as dropped and duplicated packets.

transport protocol A communications protocol responsible for establishing a connection and ensuring that all data has arrived safely. It is defined in Layer 4 of the OSI model.

Trojan A type of program that appears legitimate but performs some illicit activity when it is run.

TTL (Time To Live) A value assigned to a packet of data to prevent it from moving around the network indefinitely. The TTL value is decremented each time the packet crosses a router, until it reaches 0, at which point it is removed from the network.

TTLS (Tunneled Transport Layer Security) An extension of TLS that adds tunneling and is often combined with EAP.

twisted pair A type of cable that uses multiple twisted pairs of copper wire.

U

UC (unified communications) A combination of real-time (instant messaging, VoIP, and so on) with non-real-time (email, SMS, and so on) communications on the same platform.

UDP (User Datagram Protocol) A communications protocol that provides connectionless, unreliable communication services and operates at the transport layer of the OSI model. It requires a network layer protocol such as IP to guide it to the destination host.

unbound medium (or boundless medium) Any medium that does not have physical constraints. Examples of unbound media are infrared, wireless, and microwave. Compare with bound medium.

UNC (Universal Naming Convention) An industry-naming standard for computers and resources that provides a common syntax that should work in most systems, including Windows and UNIX. An example of a UNC name is \\servername\sharename.

unicast Communication that takes place over a network between a single sender and a single receiver.

UPC (Ultra Polished Connector) A type of connector used with fiber networks.

UPS (uninterruptible power supply) A system that provides protection against power surges and power outages. During blackouts, a UPS gives you time to shut down systems or devices on the network before the temporary power interruption becomes permanent. A UPS is also called battery backup.

uptime How long a device has been on and operating.

URL (uniform resource locator) A name used to identify a website and subsequently a page on the Internet. An example of a URL is www.quepublishing.com/products.

USB (universal serial bus) A type of interface between a computer system and peripheral devices. The USB interface enables you to add or remove devices without shutting down the computer. USB supports up to 127 devices. USB also supports autodetection and plug and play.

UTM (unified threat management) An approach to threat management that combines multiple security-related products (antivirus software, IPS, and so on) into a single management console.

UTP (unshielded twisted-pair) A type of cable that uses multiple twisted pairs of copper wire in a casing that does not provide much protection from EMI. The most common network cable in Ethernet networks, UTP is rated in categories including Category 1 through Category 7, as well as Category 5e and Category 6a.

V

VDSL (variable digital subscriber line) An asymmetric version of DSL that supports high-bandwidth applications such as VoIP and HDTV. It is the fastest available form of DSL and uses fiber-optic cabling.

vertical cross-connect The main or vertical cross-connect is the location where outside cables enter the building for distribution. This may include Internet and phone cabling.

virus A software program designed specifically to adversely affect a system or network. A virus is usually designed to be passed on to other systems with which it comes in contact.

VLAN (virtual LAN) A group of devices located on one or more LAN segments, whose configuration is based on logical instead of physical connections. This enables the devices to operate as if they were connected to the same physical switch, regardless of whether they are connected to the same switch.

VNC (virtual network connection) Enables remote login, in which clients can access their own desktops while being physically away from their computers.

VoIP (Voice over IP) Any of a number of technologies that enable voice communication across the Internet Protocol.

volume set Multiple disks or partitions of disks that have been configured to read as one drive.

VPN (virtual private network) A network that uses a public network such as the Internet as a backbone to connect two or more private networks. A VPN provides users with the equivalent of a private network in terms of security. VPNs can also be used as a means of establishing secure remote connectivity between a remote system and another network.

VRF (virtual routing and forwarding) A technology that allows multiple instances of a routing table to coexist within the same router at the same time.

VRRP (Virtual Router Redundancy Protocol)   An IP-based routing protocol that automatically assigns available routers to participating hosts.

VTC (video teleconference)   Any combination of audio and video real-time technologies.

VTP (VLAN Trunking Protocol) A Cisco proprietary protocol that manages the addition, deletion, and renaming of VLANs for the entire network. Information about changes to a VLAN or the addition of a new VLAN to a network is distributed to all switches on the network simultaneously and does not need to be done one at a time.

W

WAF (web application firewall)   A firewall that filters, monitors, and blocks HTTP traffic to and from a web application; this differs from a regular firewall in that the WAF is able to filter the content of specific web applications.

WAN (wide-area network)   A data communications network that serves users across a broad geographic area. WANs often use transmission devices such as modems or CSUs/DSUs to carry signals over leased lines or common carrier lines.

WAP (Wireless Application Protocol / Wireless Access Point)   A protocol for wireless mobile access (now outdated) and the devices that make it possible for hosts to connect (widely used).

warm site   A disaster recovery site offering most equipment and applications. Compare to a cold site that refers to a disaster recovery site with limited hardware and typically only a reserved location. A hot site is one with duplicate hardware and software and can be operational within minutes of a disaster.

web server   A server that runs an application and makes the contents of certain directories on that server, or other servers, available to clients for download, via a protocol such as HTTP.

WEP (Wired Equivalent Privacy) A data encryption method used to protect the transmission between 802.11 wireless clients and access points. WEP security has come under scrutiny because it uses an insufficient key length and provides no automated method for distributing the keys.

Wi-Fi   A voluntary standard that manufacturers can adhere to, which aims to create compatibility between wireless devices. Wi-Fi is an abbreviation for wireless fidelity.

WINS (Windows Internet Name Service)   A NetBIOS name-to-IP address resolution service that runs on Windows Server platforms.

WINS database   A dynamically built database of NetBIOS names and IP addresses used by WINS.

wire crimper   A tool used to create networking cables. The type of wire crimping tool used depends on the cable being made.

wireless channel   The band of frequency used for wireless communications. Each IEEE wireless standard specifies the channels that can be used.

wireless networking   Networking that uses any unbound media, such as infrared, microwave, or radio waves.

wiring schematics   Network documentation designed to show the physical wiring of a network. The wiring schematic can often be used in the troubleshooting process.

WLAN (wireless LAN)   A local-area network created using wireless transmission methods, such as radio or infrared, rather than traditional wired solutions.

WMS (warehouse management system)   A software module that is used to provide management tools for warehouse operations.

workstation   A client computer on a network that does not offer any services of its own but that uses the services of the servers on the network.

worm   A self-replicating program that can perform destructive acts to a single computer or across a network, both wired and wireless.

WPA (Wi-Fi Protected Access)   A data encryption method used on 802.11 wireless LANs. WPA is an industry-supported standard designed to address WEP's security shortcomings.

WPA2 (Wi-Fi Protected Access v2) A secure wireless data encryption method based on 802.11i that replaces WPA.

WPS (Wi-Fi Protected Setup)   A security standard created by the Wi-Fi Alliance to increase security features of networks. The most visible manifestation of this is the button on some home routers that must be pressed to allow a new device to connect to the network within a short time period. Currently, WPS is not considered secure because flaws in the WPS PIN feature have been identified.

WWN (World Wide Name)   A unique identifier assigned to a manufacturer by the Institute of Electrical and Electronic Engineers (IEEE). It is hard-coded into a Fibre Channel (FC) device.

WWW (World Wide Web)   A service running on the Internet that has become so successful that it is often mistaken for the Internet itself.

X–Z

XDSL (extended digital subscriber line)   All the variations of DSL available are lumped together under the label XDSL.

XML (Extensible Markup Language)   A set of rules for the encoding of documents in a machine-readable format.

Zeroconf (zero configuration)   A set of tools and tricks/techniques that exist within TCP/IP with the goal of allowing devices to connect and configure without an administrator needing to manually configure anything.

zone transfer   The passing of DNS information from one name server to a secondary name server.

Index

Symbols

A

M

PRI (Primary Rate Interface) ISDN, 161–162

private clouds, 270

private networks, 84–86

private ranges, 85

privileged user accounts, 393

probable cause, 403

problem identification, 401–402

procedures, 299–300

propagation time, 186

Protected Extensible Authentication Protocol (PEAP), 374

protocol analyzers, 413–414

protocol-based VLANs (virtual LANs), 121

protocols. *See individual protocol names*

proximity readers, 23

proxy servers, 151–153

PSTN (Public Switched Telephone Network), 110, 184–185

PTR (pointer) records, 69, 70

public clouds, 270

public key cryptography, 366

public key infrastructure (PKI), 367

public networks, 84–85

punchdown tools, 219

PVC cables, 203

PVCs (permanent virtual circuits), 167

Q

QoS (Quality of Service), 129–130, 271

QSFP (Quad Small Form-factor Pluggable), 210

quarantine networks, 369

R

Radio Frequency Identification. *See* RFID (Radio Frequency Identification)

radio frequency (RF), 16, 238–241, 260

RADIUS, 154, 363–364

RADSL (rate-adaptive DSL), 177

rain fade, 186

ransomware, 382

RARP (Reverse Address Resolution Protocol), 35, 62

rate-adaptive DSL (RADSL), 177

RDP (Remote Desktop Protocol), 58, 60, 340

RDS (Remote Desktop Services), 58, 340

Real-time Transport Protocol (RTP), 36–37

re-association, 247

receiver port (RX), 210

records (DNS), 70–71

redundancy, 6, 312

reflection, 260–261

refraction, 260–261

regulations, 301–302

relays (DHCP), 75

reliability of wireless mesh topology, 10

remote access, 340–342

    HTTPS (Hypertext Transfer Protocol Secure), 347

    out-of-band management, 347

    VPNs (virtual private networks), 342–346

Remote Desktop Protocol. *See* RDP (Remote Desktop Protocol)

Remote Desktop Services (RDS), 58, 340

Remote Switched Port Analyzer (RSPAN), 125

Request For Comments (RFCs), 43

"Request Timed Out" error message, 431–432

reservations (DHCP), 73

resolution process

    DNS (Domain Name System), 65–67

    NetBIOS (Network Basic Input/Output System), 72

To receive your 10% off
Exam Voucher, register
your product at:

www.pearsonitcertification.com/register

and follow the instructions.